Managing Software Supply Chains

Ying Wang • Shing-Chi Cheung • Hai Yu •
Zhiliang Zhu

Managing Software Supply Chains

Theory and Practice

Springer

Ying Wang
Software College
Northeastern University
Shenyang, Liaoning, China

Hai Yu
Software College
Northeastern University
Shenyang, Liaoning, China

Shing-Chi Cheung
Department of Computer Science
and Engineering
The Hong Kong University of Science
and Technology
Hong Kong, China

Zhiliang Zhu
Software College
Northeastern University
Shenyang, Liaoning, China

ISBN 978-981-96-1796-8 ISBN 978-981-96-1797-5 (eBook)
https://doi.org/10.1007/978-981-96-1797-5

This Springer imprint is published by the registered company Springer Nature Singapore Pte Ltd.
The registered company address is: 152 Beach Road, #21-01/04 Gateway East, Singapore 189721, Singapore

Foreword

It is with immense pleasure I introduce "Managing Software Supply Chains: Theory and Practice," a timely and important contribution by Ying Wang, Shing-Chi Cheung, Hai Yu, and Zhiliang Zhu, experienced and highly regarded authors in software engineering. This book serves as a vital resource, shedding light on the complex realm of software supply chain management with clarity and innovation.

In the fast-paced landscape of contemporary software development, effective management of software supply chains has become a pivotal cornerstone supporting industry growth and evolution. Through their systematic and in-depth exploration, the authors navigate the complexities of open-source software supply chains, a critical and emerging domain capturing the attention of industry practitioners, researchers, and policymakers alike.

The challenges posed by dependencies in software development are complex and formidable. This book is dedicated to unraveling these challenges. It eloquently addresses the phenomenon of "dependency hell," a state often characterized by incompatibilities, version conflicts, bloated dependencies, and security vulnerabilities. By providing a holistic view and offering ecosystem-level strategies, this book equips readers with the necessary methods and tools to navigate and mitigate these challenges effectively.

"Managing Software Supply Chains" is a testament to the authors' deep understanding of the subject matter. Drawing from a rich wealth of research and practical experience, the book outlines fundamental concepts and delves into the nuances of modeling software supply chains and analyzing their evolutionary trajectories. The insights shared in this book have already found real-world applications, with techniques endorsed and adopted by industry leaders such as `Microsoft Corporation` and `Huawei Technologies Co. Ltd.`

This book is a valuable resource for a diverse audience, including software engineering researchers, students, and industry professionals. Providing a comprehensive overview of software supply chain fundamentals and practical guidance on their implementation, it offers a new and essential guide for understanding and managing dependencies in software development.

I commend the authors' dedication and expertise in crafting this much-needed seminal book, and hope it can serve as both a roadmap and an inspiration as you navigate the exciting and challenging world of software product management. May it stimulate a new wave of research, innovation, and collaboration in software engineering research and practice.

Happy reading and warm regards.

Department of Computer Science, ETH Zurich Zhendong Su
October 28, 2024

Preface

Open-source software supply chains wield significant influence in the software industry, drawing substantial interest from enterprises, researchers, and policymakers. Leveraging third-party libraries to build software applications is a common practice aimed at cost savings and software quality enhancement. However, heavy reliance on external libraries often leads to a state of "dependency hell," marked by issues like incompatibilities, conflicting versions, bloated dependencies, and the inclusion of vulnerable library versions. Despite extensive research on software dependency management and the evolution of software supply chains, questions linger regarding the variances in dependency challenges across programming language ecosystems and how best to address the dependency hell phenomenon from an ecosystem-wide perspective.

The aim of this book is to offer: (1) a comprehensive literature review on software supply chains, (2) discussions on modeling software supply chains and analyzing their evolutionary behaviors, (3) ecosystem-level strategies for diagnosing various dependency issues and automating problem resolution with cost-benefit analysis, and (4) provision of a toolkit and datasets to support future research and assist practitioners in addressing the challenges of dependency management. The methodologies outlined in this book have been previously presented in top-tier conferences and journals, with some techniques officially integrated into products by `Microsoft Corporation` and `Huawei Technologies Co Ltd.`. This book is designed to provide readers with a solid understanding of software supply chain fundamentals and practical guidance on implementing theory and techniques in real-world industrial settings.

The main audience of this book is software engineering researchers and students with an academic background interested in learning about dependency management of third-party libraries, quality assurance of software supply chains, and evolution of open-source software ecosystems. It will also be of interest to industrialists including software engineers, quality professionals, and software managers, as well as motivated general readers. They will benefit from our systematic studies on the dependency hell phenomenon in various programming language communities (Java, Python, Golang, .NET, Node.js, etc.) and the valuable associated artifacts (a toolkit and datasets). This book enables faster advances in the software engineering research area, a better selection of research targets, and a timely adoption of promising results.

The book is divided into five parts. Part I (Chap. 1) presents several main concepts used throughout this book, and a survey of research literature to discuss two decades of progress in the software supply chain area. Part II (Chap. 2) focuses on how to model the software supply chains and analyze the ecosystem evolution behaviors. Part III (Chap. 3) discusses the dependency issues in software supply chains, including compatibility issues, dependency conflicts, bloated dependencies, and vulnerable dependencies. Part IV (Chaps. 4–8) presents ecosystem-level techniques that can help practitioners to combat dependency issues. This book has associated artefacts, mostly described in Part V (Chap. 9), which make it unique. We provide tools and datasets of library dependency metadata and vulnerability metadata to facilitate future research.

Chapter 1, entitled "***Introducing Software Supply Chain***," defines software supply chain and presents several main concepts in this area, including dependency manager, library central repository, software building mechanisms, and semantic versioning rules. Moreover, this chapter presents a systematic review of software supply chain related research. We collect 383 papers published in the past two decades to discuss the publication trends, distribution of publications, main contribution types, and research focuses in this area.

Chapter 2, entitled "***Modeling Software Supply Chains and Analyzing Their Evolutionary Behaviors***," introduces an ecological network model to depict the open source software supply chain. Based on the model, we compare different resolving rules across various programming ecosystems. Besides, it presents three types of evolution behaviors including library ecosystem scale growth, library version updates (i.e., frequencies of version updates, lags of version updates and library migrations), and complexity increases. We further discuss the causal relationship between evolution behaviors and dependency issues and elaborate the dependency issue types in Chap. 3.

Chapter 3 discusses five common dependency issues: compatibility problems arising from API breaking changes, violations of open-source license agreements, conflicts due to multiple library versions, bloated dependencies with excessive or redundant components, and the propagation of vulnerable dependencies through outdated dependencies. Extensive research has been conducted to understand and address these issues, emphasizing the importance of careful dependency management, resolving conflicts, and actively updating dependencies to ensure software functionality, compliance, performance, and security.

Chapters 4–8 present ecosystem level approaches to combat dependency issues. In Chap. 4, we conduct an empirical study on compatibility issues of machine learning (ML) libraries and present a technique to diagnose these problems. An ML pipeline's performance can vary significantly across different configurations of ML library versions. ML library compatibility (MLC) issues result in inferior performance, such as inefficient executions, numeric errors, and crashes. This chapter can inspire a symbiotic ecosystem where researchers, tool builders, and library vendors work together to assist developers in combating MLC issues.

In Chap. 5, we empirically studied a set of real dependency conflict (DC) issues, learning their common fixing strategies and developers' preferences in adopting these strategies. Based on these findings, we proposed an automated technique to repair DC issues, which formulates the repair task as a binary integer linear optimization problem to effectively derive an optimal fix in line with the learnt developers' preferences.

In Chap. 6, we present a technique to assist developers in reliably removing bloated dependencies from software projects, which is enhanced by practical static reflection analyses and drives debloating solutions by weighing the benefits against the costs of dependency management. Based on this technique, we conducted a large-scale study on Java projects to unveil the landscapes of bloated dependencies in the Maven ecosystem.

In Chap. 7, we conduct the first empirical study to explore the vulnerability impacts across different programming ecosystems. It is found that 82,951 projects in PyPI and Maven ecosystems are directly or indirectly dependent on vulnerable C libraries. Our study arouses the awareness of CLV issues (cross-language invocations of vulnerable libraries) in popular ecosystems and presents related analysis results.

In Chap. 8, we conducted an empirical study to learn the scale of packages that block the propagation of vulnerability fixes in the ecosystem and investigate their evolution characteristics. Furthermore, we distilled the remediation strategies that have demonstrated effects on mitigating the fix propagation lags. Leveraging our empirical findings, we propose an ecosystem-level technique, for deriving feasible remediation strategies to boost the propagation of vulnerability fixes.

In Chap. 9, we provide a toolkit named "***League of Legends***" including five available tools to combat dependency issues in multiple ecosystems: *Piecer* (for machine learning pipelines/libraries), *NuFix* (for .NET), *Slimming* (for Java), *Insight* (across Java/Python to C/C++ ecosystems), and *Plumber* (for Node.js). We also provide datasets of library dependency metadata and vulnerability metadata to facilitate future research.

Finally, we reflect on insights gleaned from current studies, explore the changing landscape of software supply chains in the age of large language models, and offer recommendations for future research in the **Epilogue** of this book.

Shenyang, China — Ying Wang
Hong Kong, China — Shing-Chi Cheung
Shenyang, China — Hai Yu
Shenyang, China — Zhiliang Zhu
October, 2023

Contents

Part I An Overview of Software Supply Chain Research

1 Introducing Software Supply Chain ... 3
1.1 Definitions ... 3
1.2 A Survey of Research Literature ... 6
1.2.1 Literature Collection ... 6
1.2.2 Research Review: Two Decades of Progress ... 9
1.2.3 Publication Trends ... 9
1.2.4 Distribution of Publications ... 10
1.2.5 Main Contribution Types and Research Focuses ... 11
1.3 Conclusion ... 13
References ... 13

Part II Modeling and Analyzing Software Supply Chain

2 Modeling Software Supply Chains and Analyzing Their Evolutionary Behaviors ... 17
2.1 Model Definition ... 17
2.2 Comparisons of Dependency Resolving Rules Across Different Ecosystems ... 18
2.3 Evolutionary Behaviors of Open-Source Supply Chain ... 22
2.3.1 Library Ecosystem Scale Growth ... 22
2.3.2 Library Version Updates ... 23
2.3.3 Complexity Increases ... 24
2.4 Conclusion ... 26
References ... 26

Part III Dependency Issues in Software Supply Chain

3 Common Types of Dependency Issues ... 35
3.1 Compatibility Issues ... 35
3.1.1 Issue Impacts ... 36

3.1.2 Issue Types ... 37
3.2 Open-Source License Violation ... 38
3.2.1 Issue Impacts ... 39
3.2.2 Issue Types ... 39
3.3 Dependency Conflicts ... 40
3.3.1 Issue Impacts ... 41
3.3.2 Issue Types ... 41
3.4 Bloated Dependencies ... 42
3.4.1 Issue Impacts ... 43
3.4.2 Issue Types ... 43
3.5 Propagation of Vulnerable Dependencies ... 44
3.5.1 Issue Impacts ... 45
3.5.2 Issue Types ... 46
3.6 Conclusion ... 46
References ... 47

Part IV Ecosystem-Level Techniques Combating Dependency Issues

4 Detecting Compatibility Issues for Machine Learning Libraries ... 55
4.1 Introduction ... 55
4.2 Preliminaries ... 57
4.2.1 Background ... 57
4.2.2 Motivation ... 58
4.2.3 Piecer ... 59
4.3 Empirical Study ... 59
4.3.1 Data Collection ... 61
4.3.2 RQ1: Common ML Library Combinations ... 63
4.3.3 RQ2: Impacts of Different ML Library Version Combinations ... 65
4.3.4 RQ3: Root Causes of Performance Inconsistencies ... 71
4.4 Application of Empirical Findings ... 75
4.5 Implications ... 79
4.6 Threats to Validity ... 80
4.7 Related Work ... 80
4.8 Conclusion and Future Work ... 81
References ... 81

5 Diagnosing NuGet Dependency Conflicts ... 87
5.1 Introduction ... 87
5.2 Background ... 90
5.2.1 Fragmentation of .NET Ecosystem ... 90
5.2.2 NuGet Dependency Maze ... 91
5.3 Empirical Study ... 93
5.3.1 Data Collection ... 93
5.3.2 RQ1: Fixing Strategies ... 95

5.3.3 RQ2: Configuration Preferences ... 97
5.4 Methodology ... 98
5.4.1 Overall Architecture ... 99
5.4.2 Dependency Maze Graph ... 100
5.4.3 Seeking Safe Fixes ... 101
5.4.4 Seeking Risky Fixes ... 103
5.4.5 Tuning Hyperparameters ... 104
5.5 Evaluation ... 104
5.5.1 Benchmark Construction ... 105
5.5.2 RQ3: Effectiveness of *NuFix* ... 106
5.5.3 RQ4: Usefulness of *NuFix* ... 111
5.6 Threats to Validity ... 113
5.7 Related Work ... 113
5.8 Conclusion and Future Work ... 114
References ... 115

6 Streamlining Software Bloated Dependencies ... 121
6.1 Introduction ... 121
6.2 Motivation and Challenges ... 124
6.2.1 Resolving Java Reflections ... 124
6.2.2 Removing Bloated Dependencies ... 125
6.3 Slimming Approach ... 127
6.3.1 Static Reflection Analysis ... 128
6.3.2 Bloated Dependency Analysis ... 132
6.4 Evaluation ... 133
6.4.1 Data Collection ... 134
6.4.2 RQ1: Effectiveness of Reflection Analysis ... 135
6.4.3 RQ2: Reliability of Debloating Solutions ... 137
6.5 Large-Scale Analysis ... 139
6.5.1 Landscapes of Bloated Dependencies ... 139
6.5.2 RQ3: Usefulness of *Slimming* ... 142
6.6 Discussions ... 144
6.7 Related Work ... 145
6.7.1 Java Reflection Analysis ... 145
6.7.2 Software Debloating ... 145
6.8 Conclusion and Future Work ... 146
References ... 146

7 Exploring Cross Ecosystem Vulnerability Impacts ... 149
7.1 Introduction ... 150
7.2 Background ... 152
7.2.1 C Library Releases and Their Naming Rules ... 152
7.2.2 A Motivating Example ... 153
7.3 Insight Approach ... 154
7.3.1 C Library Extraction ... 155
7.3.2 C Project Version Tracing ... 155

7.3.3 Vulnerable C-API Analysis 157
7.4 Empirical Study and Evaluation 158
7.4.1 Data Collection 160
7.4.2 RQ1: Effectiveness of *Insight* 161
7.4.3 RQ2: Pervasive Dependency on C Libraries 163
7.4.4 RQ3: Cross-Ecosystem Vulnerability Impacts 165
7.4.5 RQ4: Usefulness of *Insight* 167
7.4.6 RQ5: Fixing Strategies and Challenges 169
7.5 Threats to Validity 171
7.6 Related Work 171
7.7 Conclusion and Future Work 173
References 173

8 Boosting the Propagation of Vulnerability Fixes in the *npm* Ecosystem 179
8.1 Introduction 179
8.2 Background 183
8.2.1 Disclosed Vulnerabilities in the *npm* Ecosystem 183
8.2.2 npm Package Version Constraints 184
8.2.3 Terminology 185
8.3 Empirical Study 187
8.3.1 Vulnerability Propagation Model 188
8.3.2 RQ1: Scale of Blocking Packages 191
8.3.3 RQ2: Evolution of Blocking Chains 194
8.3.4 RQ3: Remediation Patterns 198
8.4 The Plumber Approach 203
8.4.1 Monitoring the Evolution of the npm Ecosystem 204
8.4.2 Identifying Pivotal Blocking Chains 206
8.4.3 Deriving Remediation Schemes 207
8.5 Evaluation and an Ecosystem-Level Study 209
8.5.1 RQ4: Effectiveness of *Plumber* 211
8.5.2 RQ5: Remediation Challenges 214
8.5.3 RQ6: Usefulness of *Plumber* 216
8.5.4 Discussions 222
8.6 Threats to Validity 225
8.7 Related Work 226
8.8 Conclusion and Future Work 228
References 229

Part V Tools and Datasets

9 "League of Legends" Toolkit 235
9.1 *Piecer*: Detecting Compatibility Issues for Machine Learning Libraries 235
9.1.1 Tool Description 235
9.1.2 How Does *Piecer* Work? 236

9.2 *NuFix*: Repairing Dependency Conflict Issues in the .NET Ecosystem ... 238
9.2.1 Tool Description ... 238
9.2.2 How Does *NuFix* Work? ... 238
9.3 *Slimming*: Streamlining Software Bloated Dependencies in the Java Ecosystem ... 240
9.3.1 Tool Description ... 240
9.3.2 How Does *Slimming* Work? ... 240
9.4 *Insight*: Exploring Cross Ecosystem Vulnerability Impacts ... 242
9.4.1 Tool Description ... 242
9.4.2 How Does *Insight* Work? ... 242
9.5 *Plumber*: Boosting the Propagation of Vulnerability Fixes in the *npm* Ecosystem ... 244
9.5.1 Tool Description ... 244
9.5.2 How Does *Plumber* Work? ... 244
9.6 Library Dependency Metadata ... 246
9.7 Vulnerability Metadata ... 247
References ... 249

10 Epilogue ... 251
10.1 Lessons Learned ... 251
10.2 Landscape of Software Supply Chains in the LLM Era ... 252
10.3 Future Research ... 255

Part I
An Overview of Software Supply Chain Research

Chapter 1
Introducing Software Supply Chain

Abstract The significance of researching the open-source software supply chain lies in gaining a deep understanding and effectively managing dependency relationships, evolution trends, security, and sustainability in software development. This ultimately enhances the success rate, quality, and security of software projects. This introductory chapter first introduces four fundamental concepts related to the management and maintenance of the open-source software supply chain. Next, we comprehensively collected authoritative journal papers and conference papers from the past two decades (2001–2024) in the field, covering empirical studies, case studies, metric methods and analysis frameworks, techniques, tools, and other aspects. We provide an overview of the research status and trends in the open-source software supply chain by analyzing fundamental information such as publication dates, publishing journals, and the types of major contributions found in each paper.

1.1 Definitions

To facilitate the representation of open-source software supply chain, its modeling, evolution, dependency issues, and corresponding governance techniques, this chapter introduces four fundamental concepts related to the management and maintenance of open-source software libraries: *Dependency Manager*, *Library Central Repository*, *Software Building Mechanisms*, and *Semantic Versioning Rules*.

Open-Source Software Supply Chain Open-source software supply chain refers to the interconnected network of entities, processes, and resources involved in modern software development and maintenance activities. It encompasses all upstream and downstream open-source software communities, source code repositories, binary software repositories, dependency managers, and software central repositories, as well as developers, maintainers, and foundation organizations. This supply chain network is formed based on dependency, composition, and other constraint relationships. It includes activities such as code development, integration, testing, version control, packaging, deployment, and updates. The structure of the

Y. Wang et al., *Managing Software Supply Chains*,
https://doi.org/10.1007/978-981-96-1797-5_1

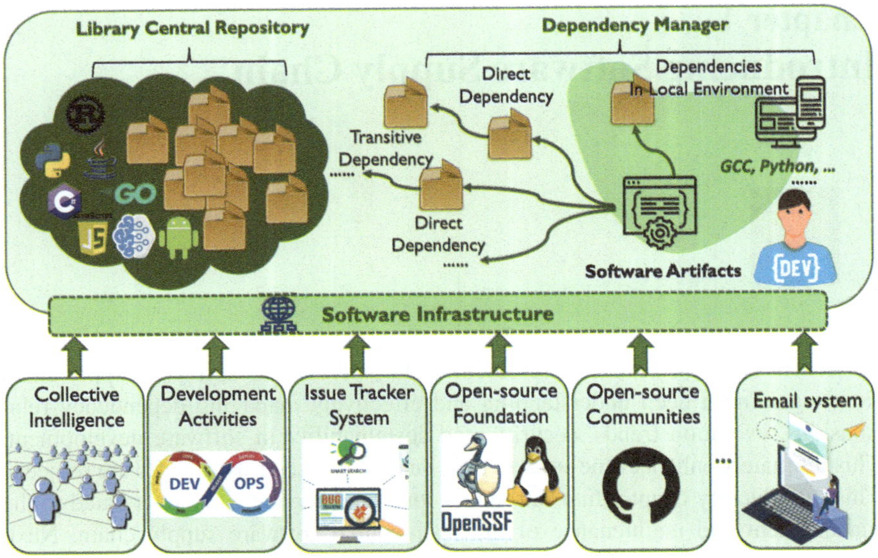

Fig. 1.1 Diagram of the open-source software supply chain

open-source software supply chain is depicted in Fig. 1.1. The software supply chain aims to ensure the reliable and secure delivery of software while managing dependencies, vulnerabilities, licensing, and quality assurance throughout the life cycle of the software product [1–4].

Dependency Manager A dependency manager is a collection of systems or tools used to resolve dependency configurations and automate the installation, upgrading, and usage of software libraries, in the software project development process. Dependency managers greatly facilitate the reuse of third-party software libraries and simplify the software project build and testing processes.

Dependency managers were first introduced in Unix distributions in the 1990s [5]. In Linux- and Unix-based environments, various dependency managers have been developed by the community to facilitate dependency management, such as Red Hat's *yum*, Debian's *apt*, and others. Subsequently, different programming language communities have also introduced dependency managers with distinct features. Examples include *Maven* and *Gradle* for Java and *npm* for JavaScript. Over the past two decades, the functionalities of many dependency managers are gradually expanding and improving. In addition to being able to manage third-party software libraries, they also encompass the entire software life cycle, including building, testing, deploying, and releasing [6].

Library Central Repository: The software central repository refers to a centralized storage and distribution platform created and managed by dependency manager teams. It functions as a comprehensive repository for software libraries that serve the needs of the broader open-source community. It primarily focuses on hosting commonly used software libraries within a specific programming language community.

The software central repository acts as a reliable and accessible source for developers to discover, download, and manage the dependencies required for their software projects. It provides a centralized location where developers can find a wide range of software libraries and packages that are compatible with their chosen programming language [7]. One notable example is the PyPI (Python Package Index) central repository, which serves as the software central repository for the Python programming language. PyPI stores a vast collection of Python software libraries, which are organized and made available for developers to utilize. As of May 2024, PyPI houses around 538,392 Python software libraries, encompassing a staggering total of 5.67 million versions [8].

Software Building Mechanisms Throughout the evolutionary history of software building mechanisms, the approach to dependency management has undergone significant transformations. It has evolved from a method of managing autonomous software libraries with static, closed, and controllable characteristics to a more dynamic, open, and challenging-to-control style centered on a software central repository. This approach emphasizes centralized management and automated configuration, enabling efficient handling of dependencies within software projects [9]. The dependency manager operates within the software project's build environment, enabling it to parse the dependency configuration file. It leverages remote retrieval to obtain software libraries, encompassing both direct and transitive dependencies, from the software central repository. Additionally, the dependency manager calculates dependency constraints, acquires resolution solutions, and meticulously installs software libraries in a user-specified order and adhering to a predefined set of rules.

Semantic Versioning Rules Semantic versioning rules define a standardized numbering system for software versions, utilizing three-digit version numbers: *major.minor.patch*. The major version number increases when there are API-incompatible modifications compared to previous versions, indicating significant changes. The minor version number increases when new features are added in a backward-compatible manner, signifying incremental improvements. Similarly, the patch version number increases when defects are fixed in a backward-compatible manner, ensuring stability. These rules are widely embraced by programming language communities to ensure the sustainable evolution of open-source software library ecosystems [10]. It is expected that developers of software libraries adhere to these conventions during the iteration of versions, promoting compatibility and effective dependency management.

To summarize, *library central repository* is the physical embodiment of the open-source software library ecosystem and serves as the foundation for modeling and analysis. *Dependency manager* plays a crucial role in determining the dependency configuration and installation rules for software projects. It interacts with modern *software building mechanisms* and represents a significant factor in the occurrence of dependency issues. During the evolution of a software library, strict adherence by library developers to *semantic versioning rules* becomes pivotal. This adherence directly impacts the compatibility of software library version updates, thus determining the sustainable evolution of the *open-source software supply chain*.

1.2 A Survey of Research Literature

This book employs the systematic literature review method proposed by Wohlin et al. [11] combining with the literature collection approach presented by Sobrinho et al. [12] to conduct a comprehensive overview of research on the open-source supply chain. In this chapter, we provide a detailed description of the research methodology.

1.2.1 Literature Collection

The process of literature collection mainly involves determining the scope of journals/conferences and the "snowballing" technique for selecting related papers. To ensure the relevance and authority of literature, we established selection criteria in Sect. 1.2.1.1. As shown in Fig. 1.2, to overcome the limitations of keyword-based search methods and ensure a comprehensive coverage of papers from authoritative journals/conferences in the field of open-source supply chain, this book underwent two rounds of selection and expansion to obtain the final paper collection. The specific steps are as follows:

- ***First-round literature selection:***
  - **(1-a)** *First round of journal/conference scope selection:* As shown in Table 1.1 (Step 1-a), we selected seven influential academic journals and conferences in the field of software engineering as the initial scope for our first round of screening.
  - **(1-b)** *First round of paper selection:* The journals/conferences obtained from Step (1-a) were further screened according to the four criteria outlined in Sect. 1.2.1.1 for all papers published between January 2001 and April 2023. This resulted in a total of **126** papers.
  - **(1-c)** *First round of related work selection:* According to the "snowballing" approach [11], we organized and collected the references cited in the papers obtained from Step (1-b). Following the criteria outlined in Sect. 1.2.1.1, we further screened the references and identified **136** papers. After merging and removing duplicates with the papers from Step (1-b), we obtained a preliminary set of **212** papers.
- ***Second-round literature selection:***
  - **(2-a)** *Second round of journal/conference scope selection:* We conducted a frequency analysis of the journals/conferences in the preliminary set of papers

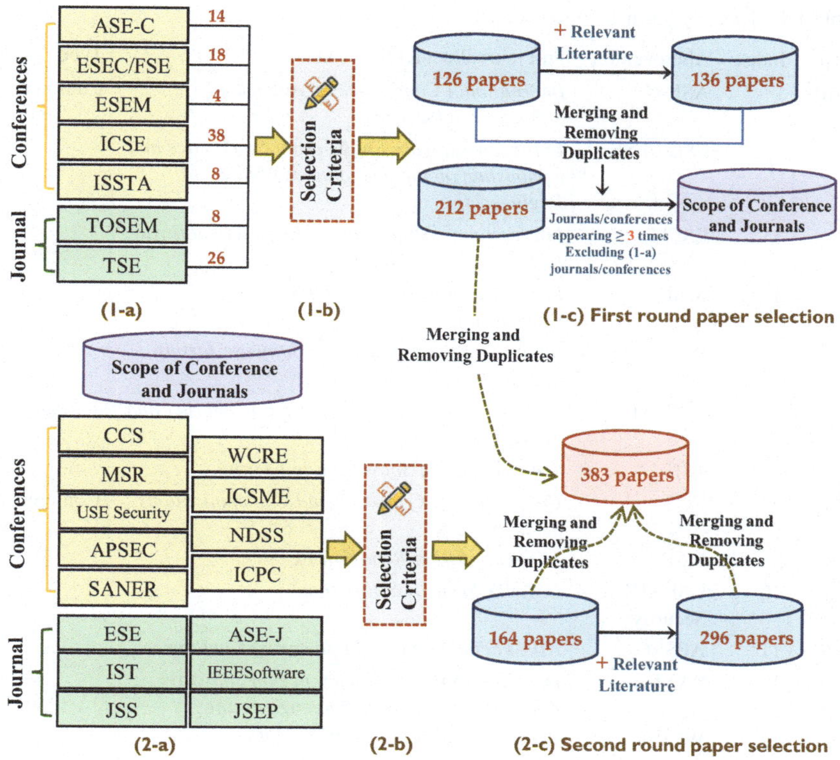

Fig. 1.2 Paper collection process

and selected those that appeared three times or more as the final scope of journals/conferences. As shown in Table 1.1, we identified a total of 19 conferences and 8 journals.

- **(2-b)** *Second round of paper selection:* Among the journals/conferences within the final scope, excluding those from Step (1-b), we applied the criteria outlined in Sect. 1.2.1.1 to screen all papers published between January 2001 and April 2023. This resulted in a total of **164** papers.
- **(2-c)** *Second round of related work selection:* Once again, using the "snowballing" approach [11], we applied the criteria outlined in Sect. 1.2.1.1 to screen the references cited in the papers obtained from Step (2-b). This resulted in a total of **296** references. After merging and removing duplicates from the papers from Step (2-b), we obtained the final set of papers, totaling **383**.

Table 1.1 Selecting journal/conference set

Steps	Index	Abbreviation	Full journal/conference name	Type
(1-a)	1	ASE-C	*International Conference on Automated Software Engineering*	Conference
	2	ESEC/FSE	*European Software Engineering Conference and Symposium on the Foundations of Software Engineering*	
	3	ESEM	*International Symposium on Empirical Software Engineering and Measurement*	
	4	ICSE	*International Conference on Software Engineering*	
	5	ISSTA	*International Symposium on Software Testing and Analysis*	
	6	TOSEM	*ACM Transactions on Software Engineering and Methodology*	Journal
	7	TSE	*Transactions on Software Engineering*	
(2-a)	8	CCS	*Conference on Computer and Communications Security*	Conference
	9	MSR	*Mining Software Repositories*	
	10	USENIX Security	*USENIX Security Symposium*	
	11	APSEC	*Asia-Pacific Software Engineering Conference*	
	12	SANER	*IEEE International Conference on Software Analysis, Evolution, and Reengineering*	
	13	WCRE	*Working Conference on Reverse Engineering*	
	14	ICSME	*IEEE International Conference on Software Maintenance and Evolution*	
	15	NDSS	*Network and Distributed System Security Symposium*	
	16	ICPC	*International Conference on Program Comprehension*	
	17	ESE	*Empirical Software Engineering*	Journal
	18	IST	*Journal of Information Security and Applications*	
	19	JSS	*Journal of Systems and Software*	
	20	ASE-J	*Automated Software Engineering*	
	21	IEEE Software	*IEEE Software*	
	22	JSEP	*Journal of Software: Evolution and Process*	
(2-c)	23	ECOOP	*European Conference on Object-Oriented Programming*	Conference
	24	OOPSLA	*ACM SIGPLAN International Conference on Object-Oriented Programming Systems, Languages, and Applications*	
	25	ICSR	*International Conference on Software Reuse*	
	26	OSS	*International Conference on Open-Source Systems*	
	27	WISEC	*Wireless Network Security*	

1.2.1.1 Literature Selection Criteria

To ensure the relevance and authority of the collected papers, we have established the following literature selection criteria:

(1) **Relevance of the papers:** This book focuses on research work related to modeling and analysis, evolution and maintenance, quality assurance, and management of open-source software library ecosystems. We used the search keywords "software ecosystem," "software supply chain," "software dependencies," and "third-party libraries" to collect research literature relevant to these topics. Specifically, we collected papers where the keywords "software ecosystem," "software supply chain," "software dependencies," or "third-party libraries" appeared in the paper title, keywords, or abstract. While the search results may include occasional papers that use these keywords coincidentally but are not relevant to the modeling and analysis, evolution and maintenance, quality assurance, and management aspects in this field, four graduate students in our research group carefully read and cross-validated the papers to exclude irrelevant literature.
(2) **Integrity of the papers:** We prioritize the most comprehensive and up-to-date versions of papers. If a conference paper has been expanded and further developed into a journal paper, we only retain the journal paper version and exclude the conference paper version.
(3) **Authority of the papers:** We exclude book chapters, master's theses, doctoral dissertations, and other forms of papers and only retain peer-reviewed and formally published papers.
(4) **Length of the papers:** We collect papers with a page count of eight or more pages (excluding the reference section).

1.2.2 Research Review: Two Decades of Progress

We provide an overview of the research status and trends in the open-source software supply chain by analyzing fundamental information such as publication dates, publishing journals, and the types of major contributions found in each paper.

1.2.3 Publication Trends

Although we attempted to collect research work in the field of open-source software supply chain from 2001 to 2023, supplemented by authoritative journal and conference papers until April 2024, the results indicate that relevant research work only began to emerge from 2005 onward. Figure 1.3a illustrates the distribution of the number of papers published each year, indicating a rapid growth in the number of

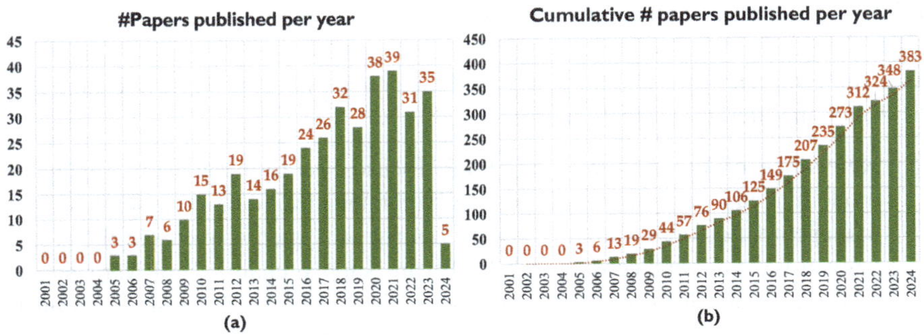

Fig. 1.3 Publication trends

publications from 2010 to 2023, spanning over a decade. The emergence of a large amount of research can be attributed to the rapid development and evolution of the open-source ecosystem in the past decade, as well as the widespread adoption of third-party software libraries in modern software projects, which has led to a series of quality issues in the open-source software supply chain, attracting the attention of practitioners and researchers.

We observed the publication trend in the field of open-source software supply chain research over the past two decades by fitting the cumulative number of papers published to a power function. As shown in Fig. 1.3b, the slope of the fitted curve significantly increased between 2010 and 2023, reaching a peak determination coefficient (R^2) of 0.99746. This indicates that, as the open-source ecosystem continues to thrive and become more complex, we can predict a substantial and continuous growth in research on software supply chain in the future.

1.2.4 Distribution of Publications

Figure 1.4 presents the distribution of publication outlets for the papers. Among the 383 papers we collected, 61.9% of the research was published in authoritative conferences in the field of software engineering, while 38.1% was published in journals. Among the 237 conference papers, six conferences, namely ICSE, MSR, SANER, ESEC/FSE, ICSM, and ASE, accounted for 33.0% of the published papers in the field of open-source software supply chain research. Among them, ICSE had the highest number of publications related to this research, with a total of 46 papers published from 2001 to 2024. MSR and SANER followed closely behind, with 25 and 18 papers published, respectively, and both showed a significant growth trend in the past 5 years. Among the 146 journal papers, the majority were published in the past decade. TSE, ESE, and JSS accounted for 27.5% of the publications, while TOSEM and IST accounted for only 11.2% of the publications.

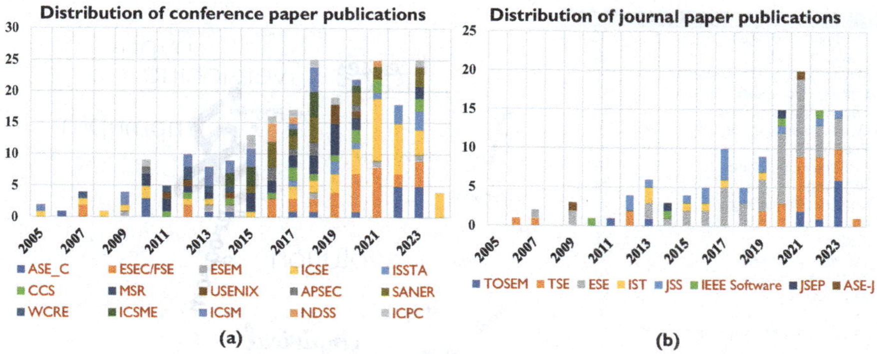

Fig. 1.4 Distribution of journal/conference paper publications

Table 1.2 The main contribution types of the collected papers

Main contribution	Description of contribution	#Papers
Empirical study	The papers explore valuable insights by collecting and analyzing evolutionary metadata of software repositories in the open-source community, i.e., dependency issues, dependence relationships, and the introduced vulnerabilities	162
	The papers explore valuable insights by conducting interviews or surveys with developers, users, and other individuals to gather their perspectives on real-world issues	9
	The papers explore valuable insights by analyzing data, such as issue reports and knowledge-based questions, in the open-source community. This analysis helps identify causes, symptoms, and solutions for defects, providing heuristic discoveries for developers	16
Metric method	The papers propose metric methods or analytical frameworks to investigate certain evolutionary behaviors or specific issues of the open-source software libraries	34
Technique	The papers propose technical solutions or frameworks to detect or address specific dependency issues in the open-source software ecosystem	83
Tool	The papers develop tools to address specific dependency issues in the open-source software ecosystem	100
Survey	The paper summarizes and analyzes the data, information, and key viewpoints from research papers related to the software supply chain	7

Note: Some papers develop techniques/tools based on the findings derived from empirical studies

1.2.5 Main Contribution Types and Research Focuses

As shown in Table 1.2, we categorized the research topics of collected papers into five categories: *empirical study*, *metric method*, *technique*, *tool*, and *survey*. Among the collected papers, **162** papers conducted empirical studies by collecting

Keywords	Frequency
Third-party Libraries	123
Empirical Study	102
Mining Software Repositories	91
Software Ecosystem Evolution	67
Security Vulnerabilities	65
Open-source Software Ecosystem	58
API Breaking Change	40
API usage	39
Semantic Versioning	37
npm	34
Android	31
Software Licenses	20
Software Reuse	19
API Evolution	19
PyPI	18
Dependency Management	17
Dependency Network	11
Software Maintenance	10
Program Analysis	10

Fig. 1.5 Top 20 keywords in terms of frequency the in collected papers

and analyzing the evolution metadata of software repositories in open-source communities (such as dependency relevant issue reports, introduced vulnerabilities, etc.) to explore valuable findings. Nine papers investigated valuable findings by conducting interviews or surveys with developers, users, and other individuals regarding dependency management practices. Sixteen papers provided heuristic implications for problem solutions by analyzing the causes, symptoms, and fixes of dependency defects. Thirty-four papers proposed metric methods or analysis frameworks to investigate certain evolutionary behaviors or specific issues in open-source software ecosystem. For addressing various software dependency issues, **83** papers proposed effective techniques, and **100** papers developed corresponding tools. Currently, only seven papers have reviewed research work related to open-source software supply chain.

We analyzed the keywords of each paper, counted their frequency of occurrence, and revealed the research hotspots of the papers. By sorting the keyword frequencies in descending order, we obtained the research hotspots as shown in Fig. 1.5. The top 20 keywords in terms of frequency are third-party libraries, empirical studies, mining software repositories, software ecosystem evolution, security vulnerabilities, open-source software ecosystem, API breaking changes, API usage, semantic versioning, *npm*, *Android*, software licenses, software reuse, API evolution, *PyPI*, dependency management, dependency network, software maintenance, and program analysis.

Based on the information extracted from the 383 collected papers (as presented in Table 1.2 and Fig. 1.5), empirical study and software repository mining have emerged as the most commonly utilized research approaches in the field of the open-source software supply chain. These approaches have been adopted in 187 papers, enabling investigations into various aspects such as evolutionary analysis of open-source ecosystems (60 papers, 32.1%), vulnerability assessments (51 papers, 27.3%), analysis of API breaking changes (36 papers, 19.3%), and examination of open-source licenses (22 papers, 11.8%). Researchers attempt to extract valuable knowledge from empirical investigations to enhance the sustainable evolution of the open-source software supply chain. Notably, *npm*, *PyPI*, and Android are highly focused open-source software ecosystems.

However, it is important to note that research on the open-source software supply chain is still in its early stages, and there is an urgent need for researchers to conduct in-depth exploration in areas such as quality assurance, tool support, and new paradigms in software ecosystems. These areas present opportunities for further research and have the potential to contribute to advancements in governing the open-source software supply chain.

1.3 Conclusion

In our comprehensive analysis of 383 collected papers, it is evident that the field of software supply chain heavily relies on empirical studies and software repository mining as key methodologies. These approaches have been widely adopted, with 154 papers utilizing them to investigate the evolutionary analysis of open-source software supply chains and address dependency issues. The aim has been to extract valuable knowledge that can significantly enhance the sustainable evolution of open-source software supply chain.

Notably, our findings indicate that the majority of research, accounting for 61.9%, was published in prestigious academic conferences renowned for their influence in the software engineering domain. Conferences such as ICSE, MSR, SANER, ESEC/FSE, ICSM, and ASE have served as platforms for researchers to share their insights and advancements. Additionally, 38.1% of the research was published in esteemed software engineering journals like TSE, TOSEM, JSS, and IST, further contributing to the body of knowledge in the field.

Of particular focus in this book is the exploration of dependency defects in open-source software supply chain, which are significantly influenced by the evolutionary behaviors of software libraries, software building mechanisms, and semantic versioning rules. In the subsequent chapters, we will delve deeper into these aspects, combining the insights from the collected 383 papers and our own research work.

References

1. Liang GY, Wu YJ, Wu JZ, Zhao C. Open source software supply chain for reliability assurance of operating systems. J Softw. 2020;31(10):3056–73.
2. Zhi J, Minghui Z, Yuxia Z. Open source software and its eco-systems: today and tomorrow. Sci Technol Rev. 2016;34(14):42–48.
3. Xu C, Qin Y, Yu P, et al. Theories and techniques for growing software: paradigm and beyond. Sci Sin Inform. 2020;50(11):1595–1611.

4. Ohm M, Plate H, Sykosch A, et al. Backstabber's knife collection: a review of open source software supply chain attacks. In: Detection of intrusions and malware, and vulnerability assessment: 17th international conference, DIMVA 2020, Lisbon, June 24–26, 2020, Proceedings 17. Springer International Publishing, Cham; 2020. p. 23–43.
5. Abate P, Di Cosmo R, Gousios G, et al. Dependency solving is still hard, but we are getting better at it. In: 2020 IEEE 27th international conference on software analysis, evolution and reengineering (SANER); 2020. p. 547-551.
6. Soto-Valero C, et al. A comprehensive study of bloated dependencies in the maven ecosystem. Empir Softw Eng 2021;26(3):45.
7. Wang Y, et al. Watchman: monitoring dependency conflicts for python library ecosystem. In: Proceedings of the ACM/IEEE 42nd international conference on software engineering; 2020.
8. PyPI, The Python Package Index (PyPI) is a repository of software for the Python programming language: https://pypi.org/
9. Peng Y, Hu R, Wang R, et al. Less is more? An empirical study on configuration issues in Python PyPI ecosystem. In: Proceedings of the IEEE/ACM 46th international conference on software engineering; 2024. p. 1–12.
10. Preston-Werner T. Semantic Versioning 2.0.0, Semantic Versioning. https://semver.org/
11. Wohlin C. Guidelines for snowballing in systematic literature studies and a replication in software engineering. In: Proceedings of the 18th international conference on evaluation and assessment in software engineering, London; 2014. p. 1–10.
12. de Paulo Sobrinho EV, De Lucia A, de Almeida Maia M, et al. A systematic literature review on bad smells-5 W's: which, when, what, who, where. IEEE Trans Softw Eng 2018;47:17–66.

Part II
Modeling and Analyzing Software Supply Chain

Chapter 2
Modeling Software Supply Chains and Analyzing Their Evolutionary Behaviors

Abstract The supply chain formed by tens of thousands of interdependent open-source software libraries has brought convenience to software development while also posing unprecedented challenges in dependency management. The exponential growth in the scale of software libraries and their intricate dependency relationships has led to a significant increase in the complexity of the supply chain. On the one hand, defects with any software library in the supply chain can potentially impact other libraries in the chain, amplifying the magnitude of losses. On the other hand, any software library can be affected by problems originating from other libraries in the supply chain, making issue identification and resolution difficult. In this backdrop, many researchers focused on characterizing, abstracting, and analyzing the dependency relationships among software libraries and exploring the evolutionary behaviors of open-source software ecosystems based on the library dependency models.

2.1 Model Definition

Modeling the dependency relationships among open-source software libraries is a primary approach for understanding and observing the evolution of software ecosystems. In research work, software libraries are typically represented as a directed graph $G = (V, E)$, where nodes V represent a collection of software library versions in the central repository (i.e., *Maven* and *PyPI*), and edges $E = \{(Lib_i \rightarrow Lib_j, Cons) | Lib_i, Lib_j \in V\}$ represent a set of dependency relationships between software library versions. For the dependency relationship $Lib_i \rightarrow Lib_j$, the version of the downstream software library, Lib_j, is determined by the version constraint $Cons$ imposed by the upstream software library, Lib_i, as well as the dependency resolution rules defined by dependency managers.

However, the dependency managers in different programming language communities customize distinct syntax rules for management and resolution of software libraries:

Y. Wang et al., *Managing Software Supply Chains*,
https://doi.org/10.1007/978-981-96-1797-5_2

- ***In terms of dependency management***, apart from allowing software to explicitly declare specific versions of upstream libraries they depend on, it also enables the declaration of version ranges (e.g., $<$2.1.0) to constrain the versions of third-party libraries. More importantly, language communities like Python and JavaScript have customized semantic versioning constraint rules, allowing developers to have flexible version control using operators like $\wedge$, $\sim$, and others. For example, a version constraint like 2.1. = $\sim$ 2.1.0 indicates that compatible library versions within the range [2.1.0, 2.2.0) can be installed.
- ***In terms of dependency resolution***, the dependency managers *pip* and *npm* for Python and JavaScript, respectively, will parse the dependency configuration script and resolve to the latest version that satisfies the version range constraint (e.g., resolving and installing version 2.1.9 of a software library within the range [2.1.0, 2.2.0)). On the other hand, the *NuGet* dependency manager for C# will choose the oldest version within the version constraint range (e.g., resolving and installing version 2.1.0 of a software library within the range [2.1.0, 2.2.0)).

2.2 Comparisons of Dependency Resolving Rules Across Different Ecosystems

Existing research [1–15] has aimed to model the dependency relationships among software libraries, encompassing ten programming language ecosystems. In studies [3, 4, 10], the acquisition of dependency metadata for the modeling process was sourced from ***libraries.io*** [16], an open data platform that monitors the evolution of libraries released in the central repository. Other research work obtained dependency configuration files by crawling software projects from different ecosystems and constructed library dependency models based on their distinct syntax rules of dependency resolution.

Drawing from the literature mentioned above, we present a comprehensive comparison of dependency management strategies across different programming language ecosystems, including Java, Python, Go, JavaScript, Rust, R, C#, PHP, Ruby, and C/C++. This comparison is outlined in Table 2.1. **Researchers and practitioners need an effective approach to precisely model the dependency relationships among software libraries in these ecosystems, taking into account both the differences and commonalities in their dependency management strategies.** In summary, the key findings are as follows:

- ***Java Ecosystem:*** The commonly used dependency managers in the Java ecosystem are *Apache Maven* [17] and *Gradle* [18]. *Maven* is an XML-based tool that uses a `pom.xml` file to define project dependencies and build configurations. *Gradle*, on the other hand, is a tool that provides a more flexible and extensible way of configuring builds. Java developers use the *Maven* as the library central repository, maintained by *Apache Maven*.

Table 2.1 Comparisons of dependency management strategies across different ecosystems

Ecosystem	Library central repository	Dependency manager	Dependency configuration file	Dependency resolution rules	Literature
Java	*Maven*	*Maven, Gradle*	`pom.xml`, `build.gradle`	*Specific version or SemVer (latest version available)*	[2, 7, 10, 14]
Python	*PyPI*	*pip*	`setup.py`, `setup.cfg`, `requirements.txt`, `pyproject.toml`	*PEP 440 specification (latest version available)*	[10]
Go	*proxy.golang.org*	*Go command-line tool*	`go.mod`	*SemVer (latest version available)*	[5]
JavaScript	*npm Registry*	*npm, Yarn*	`package.json`	*SemVer (latest version available)*	[3, 4, 6, 8, 10, 11, 13, 15]
Rust	*Crates.io*	Cargo	`cargo.toml`	*SemVer (latest version available)*	[3, 4, 6]
R	*CRAN*	*CRAN*	`Decription`	*latest version*	[3, 4, 7, 9]
C#	*NuGet*	*NuGet*	`PackageRefenrence`	*SemVer (oldest version available)*	[3, 4]
PHP	*Packagist*	*Composer*	`composer.json`	*SemVer (latest version available)*	[3, 4, 10]
Ruby	*RubyGems*	*Bundler*	`Gemfile`	*SemVer (latest version available)*	[3, 4, 6, 10]
C/C++	*RedHat, Debian, etc.*	*apt, yum*	Package metadata	*Specific version or SemVer (latest version available)*	[1, 5, 12]

Both *Maven* and *Gradle* employ a strict versioning scheme known as Semantic Versioning (*SemVer*) to manage dependencies. By default, Maven follows the *"nearest-wins."* It resolves conflicts by selecting the version closest to the root of the dependency tree. Maven supports version ranges specified using square brackets "[ ]" and parentheses "()" to define inclusive or exclusive version boundaries. It also allows the use of version qualifiers like *"snapshot"* or *"release"* to specify whether to include snapshot versions or only stable releases. In contrast, *Gradle* uses a *"conflict resolution strategy"* to resolve conflicts when multiple versions of a dependency are found. It allows users to define their preferred resolution strategy, such as *"latest version available," "oldest version available,"* or *"strict version matching"*.

- ***Python Ecosystem:*** The most commonly used dependency manager in the Python ecosystem is *pip* [19]. It allows installation, upgrading, and uninstallation of Python libraries from the command line and resolves project dependencies. Python uses *PyPI* [20] as the library central repository and defines the *PEP 440* specification for versioning and version constraints in dependency management. *PEP 440* specifies a format for version numbers, allowing pre-release and post-release versions, provides operators for version constraints, and ensures consistent version comparison and ordering. Dependency resolution in *pip* typically follows a *"latest version available"* strategy. *pip* not only tries to download and install the latest available dependency versions but also supports locking dependencies to specific versions by specifying them in the `requirements.txt` file.
- ***Go Ecosystem:*** The primary dependency manager in the Go language is the *Go command-line* tool itself. Go does not have a separate official library central repository but relies on the proxy and caching mechanisms of *Go Modules*. Developers can choose to use *proxy.golang.org*[21] or other proxy servers to speed up dependency downloads. *Go Modules* use *SemVer* rules for resolving and managing dependency versions. Developers can specify the desired dependency versions range in the `go.mod` file, such as specific version numbers, version ranges, or locking to specific major versions.
- ***JavaScript Ecosystem:*** *npm* and *Yarn* are the most widely used dependency managers for installing, managing, and publishing JavaScript libraries. JavaScript uses the *npm Registry* [22] as the library central repository. Dependency version resolution in JavaScript also follows the *SemVer* rules, which allows developers to specify the version range of dependencies in the `package.json` file, such as specific version numbers, version ranges, or locking to specific major versions.
- ***Rust Ecosystem:*** *Cargo* [23] is Rust's official build tool and dependency manager, providing powerful dependency resolution, building, and testing capabilities. Rust uses *Crates.io* [24] as the library central repository. Dependency version resolution in Rust follows *SemVer* rules and *"latest version available"* strategy. *Cargo* resolves and downloads appropriate dependency versions based on the dependency declarations in the project's `Cargo.toml` file.
- ***R Ecosystem:*** The commonly used dependency manager in the ***R*** ecosystem is CRAN [25]. ***R*** uses *CRAN* (Comprehensive R Archive Network) as the

library central repository. When installing ***R*** libraries, the dependency manager always attempts to download and install the latest available dependency versions configured in `Decription` file.

- ***C# Ecosystem:*** C# projects commonly use the *NuGet* [26] and *NuGet Gallery* [27] as the dependency manager and library central repository, respectively. Dependency resolution in C# ecosystem typically follows *NuGet*'s *SemVer* rules. Developers can specify the desired version range of dependencies in the configuration file `*.csproj`, and the resolution usually follows a *"oldest version available"* strategy.
- ***PHP Ecosystem:*** The commonly used dependency manager and library central repository in the PHP ecosystem are *Composer* [28] and *Packagist* [29], respectively. Dependency resolution in PHP typically combines *SemVer* rules with *"latest version available"* strategy, and it is handled by *Composer* in `composer.json` file.
- ***Ruby Ecosystem:*** The commonly used dependency manager in the Ruby language is *Bundler* [30], which resolves dependencies based on the project's `Gemfile` and automatically installs required dependencies from the library central repository *RubyGems.org* [31]. Dependency resolution in Ruby typically follows *SemVer* rules. Developers can specify the version range of dependencies in the project's `Gemfile` and use the *"latest version available"* strategy to install third-party libraries.
- ***C/C++ Ecosystem:*** There are multiple options for build tools in the C/C++ ecosystem, such as *GNU Make* [32], *CMake* [33], *Autotools* [34], etc. C/C++ does not have a unified official library central repository or build tool. In Linux distributions, *apt* (Advanced Package Tool) [35] and *yum* (Yellowdog Updater, Modified) [36] are the commonly used dependency managers. *apt* is primarily used in *Debian-based* distributions such as *Debian* and *Ubuntu*. It provides a command-line interface, including tools like *apt-get* and *apt-cache*, for searching, installing, updating, and removing software libraries. *yum* is primarily used in *Red Hat-based* distributions such as *Red Hat Enterprise Linux* and *CentOS*. It provides a command-line interface, including tools like *yum* and *dnf*, for managing software libraries.

  apt and *yum* rely on the library maintainers to specify version requirements in the package metadata. The version numbers in the package metadata are typically in a format that follows the conventions of *SemVer* rules. Both *apt* and *yum* follow a *"latest version available"* strategy by default. When resolving dependencies, they aim to install the latest version that satisfies the specified requirements and resolves any conflicts. However, it is important to note that this behavior can be influenced or customized through configuration options or package pinning.

Java, Python, JavaScript, Rust, Ruby, Go, and PHP languages have similar syntax rules for dependency resolution, and they follow the *SemVer* rules and install the latest library versions that satisfy the specified version constraints. In ***R*** ecosystem, software projects always use the latest version of third-party libraries. The dependency manager *NuGet* in C# ecosystem installs third-party libraries that satisfy their version constraints based on the *"oldest version available"* rule. C/C++ projects do not have a unified official library central repository or build tool. The commonly used dependency managers *apt* and *yum* in Linux distributions rely on the library maintainers to specify version requirements in the package metadata. They follow a *"latest version available"* strategy by default to resolve dependencies. ***The aforementioned dependency management strategies directly impact the dependency modeling and evolutionary analysis methodologies within their respective library ecosystems.***

2.3 Evolutionary Behaviors of Open-Source Supply Chain

Research has been conducted on the evolutionary behaviors of open-source software libraries based on the modeling of their dependency relationships. The asynchronous evolutionary of upstream and downstream libraries within open-source software supply chain serves as the underlying cause of dependency issues. Hence, comprehending the evolutionary behaviors of software libraries becomes a vital prerequisite for governing the open-source software supply chain. Out of the 383 papers collected in Chap. 1 within the field of open-source software supply chain, 95 papers specifically focus on the evolutionary behaviors of software libraries. These papers delve into the expansion of library ecosystem scale, library version updates, and the growing complexity observed in various programming language communities.

2.3.1 Library Ecosystem Scale Growth

Research indicates that the open-source software library ecosystems for different programming languages have experienced substantial growth. Both the quantity of libraries and the number of dependency relationships among libraries demonstrate a consistent upward trend. However, variations exist between different communities. This chapter will delve into the growth trends of open-source software library ecosystems from the aforementioned perspectives:

- ***Number of Libraries:*** Based on empirical research [2–4, 11, 13, 37–47], certain ecosystems show linear growth in library quantity, such as *Maven*, *Cargo*, *CPAN*, *NuGet*, and *Linux*. Conversely, ecosystems like *npm* and *Packagist* exhibit exponential growth in library quantity. Notably, the *RubyGems* ecosystem displays varying growth patterns in package quantity over different years. It experienced linear growth from 2007 to 2016 and shifted to exponential growth from 2012 to 2017.

- ***Number of Dependency Relationships Among Libraries:*** According to research from literature [2–4, 6, 11, 37, 38, 40–43], certain library ecosystems, including *RubyGems*, *Packagist*, *CRAN*, *Cargo*, and *Packgist*, exhibit linear growth in the number of dependency relationships. Conversely, ecosystems such as *Maven*, *npm*, *CPAN*, *NuGet*, and *Linux* demonstrate exponential growth in the number of dependency relationships. Analyzing the empirical study results from the literature reveals that the evolution trends of library dependencies may vary among different programming language ecosystems. Nonetheless, overall, these ecosystems demonstrate a growth trend in terms of scale.

2.3.2 Library Version Updates

The continuous growth and version updates of software libraries contribute to the sustainable evolution of open-source library ecosystems. Existing research examines the ongoing updating behaviors of libraries in various programming language communities, focusing on the following aspects:

- ***Number of Library Version Updates:*** Combining the empirical investigations carried out in various programming language communities, as documented in literature [3, 4, 11, 38, 40, 42, 48], it becomes evident that there is a general increase in the monthly number of version updates for software libraries. However, variations in community age, developer practices, and version release policies across different programming language communities contribute to differences in the quantity of version updates: **(a)** In 2015, approximately 60% of *npm* libraries, 48% of *CRAN* libraries, and 27% of *RubyGems* libraries had undergone at least one version update, indicating an overall level of activity. **(b)** Analyzing the statistical data from 1999 to 2018, it was discovered that the monthly number of version updates in the *CRAN* ecosystem followed an exponential growth pattern. This trend can be attributed to *CRAN*'s *"rolling release,"* which mandates software projects to reference the latest versions of third-party libraries. **(c)** During the statistical analysis spanning 2012–2017, the ecosystems of *Cargo* and *CPAN* exhibited a consistent number of library version updates. Researchers speculate that this may be due to the age and activity level of the communities, with Cargo being the youngest ecosystem and *CPAN* being the oldest. In comparison, the ecosystems of *npm*, *NuGet*, *RubyGems*, and *Packagist* demonstrated a significantly higher number of software library version updates.
- ***Frequency of Library Version Updates:*** Literature [4, 38] has conducted investigations and comparisons of the frequency of software library version updates in various ecosystems, including *CRAN*, *Cargo*, *RubyGems*, and *Packagist*. The findings indicate that the *npm* ecosystem exhibits the highest level of continuous updates, while the *NuGet* ecosystem demonstrates a significant and increasing trend in continuous updates. Overall, in each ecosystem, approximately one-third

of the software libraries undergo five or more version updates within a year, while another one-third of the libraries do not release any new versions. Research [49–57] has revealed a close relationship between the update frequency of software libraries and their popularity, with libraries that have higher update frequencies generally enjoying greater popularity.
- ***Lag in Library Version Updates:*** By synthesizing empirical investigations from literature [3, 4, 6, 13, 58–74] on the lag in software library version updates across different programming language communities, it is evident that, apart from the *CRAN* ecosystem with its *"rolling release"* rule, other ecosystems exhibit varying degrees of lag in version updates. This lag contributes significantly to the rampant spread of security vulnerabilities within open-source software library ecosystems, as timely dissemination of patch updates to downstream software projects becomes challenging. To address these challenges, a plethora of research studies [75–97] have emerged in recent years to assist developers in effectively and securely upgrading third-party software libraries to their latest versions.
- ***Library Migration:*** During the software evolution process, when defects cannot be resolved by upgrading the version of a third-party library, the library needs to be completely removed and replaced by another software library with similar functionalities. Existing research has proposed various approaches for identifying library migration in open-source software ecosystems [98, 99], as well as methods for establishing migration evolution rules [75, 100, 101]. Empirical investigations on library migration trends have been conducted in the literature [76], and comprehensive analysis frameworks have been developed to quantify dependency changes and library migration, capturing the evolutionary behavior characteristics of migrations. Moreover, researchers have introduced a wide range of techniques and tools [77–94] in recent years to assist developers in addressing code modifications and compatibility issues arising from library migration, facilitating the completion of migration operations.

2.3.3 Complexity Increases

With the growth and continuous updates of open-source software library ecosystems, their complexity inevitably increases. Existing literature has conducted investigations on the increase in complexity, focusing on the following two aspects:

- ***Number of Direct Dependencies/Transitive Dependencies:*** The complexity of open-source software library ecosystems is most evident in the transitive dependency relationships among libraries. Research from literature [3, 6, 11, 13, 38, 41, 43, 95, 102] indicates that during the evolution of software, the number of direct dependencies on software libraries typically grows slowly, while the number of transitive dependencies shows a rapid growth trend. In each programming language community, the modest linear growth of direct library dependencies results in an exponential increase in the number of transitive library dependencies. Researchers have provided statistics on the *npm*, *CRAN*, and *RubyGems* ecosystems between 2007 and 2016:

- (a) In the *npm* ecosystem, half of the software libraries introduce at least 22 transitive library dependencies, while a quarter of them have at least 95 transitive dependencies. By 2018, the average number of transitive dependencies per software reached 80, showing exponential growth. On average, a software library has 22.1 times more transitive dependencies than direct dependencies.
- (b) In the *CRAN* ecosystem, half of the software libraries have a maximum of five direct library dependencies, and on average, the number of transitive dependencies is 3.64 times higher than the number of direct dependencies.
- (c) In the *RubyGems* ecosystem, half of the software libraries have a maximum of eight direct library dependencies. On average, the number of transitive dependencies is 6.35 times higher than the number of direct dependencies. Compared to the *RubyGems* ecosystem, *npm* software possesses a greater number of transitive dependency libraries but fewer direct library dependencies.

- ***Number of Downstream Projects:*** The exponential growth of downstream software projects serves as an indicator of the complexity within open-source software library ecosystems. Studies [6, 11, 102] reveal that in many programming language communities, the average number of downstream software projects (i.e., projects depending on a software library) increases at a faster rate compared to the average number of upstream software projects (i.e., transitive dependencies relied upon by a software library). This trend is observed in ecosystems such as *RubyGems* and *npm*. Despite the significantly lower number of library releases in the *RubyGems* ecosystem compared to *npm*, the average number of downstream software projects per library is higher in *RubyGems*. Consequently, the emergence of a software library with a vulnerability leads to a more pronounced *"ripple effect"* within the ecosystem. Furthermore, research indicates a continual decrease in the proportion of isolated software libraries within the *npm*, *RubyGems*, and *CRAN* ecosystems. These ecosystems exhibit extensive interconnected graphs of software libraries, covering 96.1% of libraries in the *CRAN* community, 98.2% in the *npm* community, and 100% in the *RubyGems* community.

With the growth in scale, version evolution, and complexity of open-source software library ecosystems, there are significant challenges in selecting appropriate third-party software libraries and utilizing them correctly from the vast repositories of software [96, 97, 103–111]. Introducing a large number of third-party software libraries into a software project also entails risks such as reduced understandability [112], maintainability [112–115], performance degradation [116, 117], and build failures [118], leading to diverse dependency issues.

2.4 Conclusion

Existing research has utilized graph theory to construct dependency models for various programming language communities, such as *Maven*, *NuGet*, *PyPI*, *npm*, and several other software library ecosystems. In these models, software libraries are represented as nodes, and the dependency relationships between libraries are depicted as directed edges. The determination of dependency relationships takes into account both the version constraint ranges and the syntax rules of dependency resolution.

Based on modeling open-source software library ecosystems, researchers conducted empirical studies to observe library evolutionary behaviors. Out of the 383 papers collected in Chap. 1, 95 papers specifically describe the evolutionary behaviors of open-source software library ecosystems. These studies focus on different programming language communities and investigate three key aspects: the growth in scale, continuous updates, and the increasing complexity of these ecosystems. In the upcoming chapters, we will thoroughly explore the intricate relationship between the evolutionary behaviors of open-source software library ecosystems and the issues associated with dependencies in modern software projects.

References

1. Abate P, Di Cosmo R, Boender J, et al. Strong dependencies between software components. In: 2009 3rd international symposium on empirical software engineering and measurement. Piscataway: IEEE; 2009. p. 89–99.
2. Bavota G, Canfora G, Di Penta M, et al. The evolution of project inter-dependencies in a software ecosystem: the case of apache. In: 2013 IEEE international conference on software maintenance. Piscataway: IEEE; 2013. p. 280–89.
3. Decan A, Mens T, Claes M. An empirical comparison of dependency issues in OSS packaging ecosystems. In: 2017 IEEE 24th international conference on software analysis, evolution and reengineering (SANER). Piscataway: IEEE; 2017. p. 2–12.
4. Decan A, Mens T, Grosjean P. An empirical comparison of dependency network evolution in seven software packaging ecosystems. Empir Softw Eng 2019;24(1):381–416.
5. German DM, Gonzalez-Barahona JM, Robles G. A model to understand the building and running inter-dependencies of software. In: 14th working conference on reverse engineering (WCRE 2007). Piscataway: IEEE; 2007. p. 140–49.
6. Kikas R, Gousios G, Dumas M, et al. Structure and evolution of package dependency networks. In: 2017 IEEE/ACM 14th international conference on mining software repositories (MSR). Piscataway: IEEE; 2017. p. 102–112.
7. Kula RG, De Roover C, German DM, et al. A generalized model for visualizing library popularity, adoption, and diffusion within a software ecosystem. In: 25th international conference on software analysis, evolution and reengineering (SANER). Piscataway: IEEE; 2018. p. 288–299.
8. Lertwittayatrai N, Kula RG, Onoue S, et al. Extracting insights from the topology of the JavaScript package ecosystem. In: 2017 24th Asia-Pacific software engineering conference (APSEC). Piscataway: IEEE; 2017. p. 298–307.

9. Mora-Cantallops M, Sánchez-Alonso S, García-Barriocanal E. A complex network analysis of the comprehensive R Archive Network (CRAN) package ecosystem. J Syst Softw 2020;170:110744.
10. Tantisuwankul J, Nugroho YS, Kula RG, et al. A topological analysis of communication channels for knowledge sharing in contemporary GitHub projects. J Syst Softw 2019;158:110416.
11. Wittern E, Suter P, Rajagopalan S. A look at the dynamics of the JavaScript package ecosystem. In: Proceedings of the 13th international conference on mining software repositories; 2016. p. 351–361.
12. Zheng X, Zeng D, Li H, Wang F. Analyzing open-source software systems as complex networks. Phys A Stat Mech Appl. 2008;387(24):6190–6200.
13. Zimmermann M, Staicu CA, Tenny C, et al. Small world with high risks: a study of security threats in the npm ecosystem. In: 28th USENIX security symposium (USENIX Security 19); 2019. p. 995–1010.
14. Nielsen BB, Torp MT, Møller A. Modular call graph construction for security scanning of Node.js applications. In: Proceedings of the 30th ACM SIGSOFT international symposium on software testing and analysis; 2021. p. 29–41.
15. Huang J, Xue B, Jiang J, et al. Scalably detecting third-party Android libraries with two-stage bloom filtering. IEEE Trans Softw Eng 2022;49(4):2272–2284.
16. Libraries.io monitors open source packages across 32 different package managers. https://libraries.io/
17. Apache Maven is a software project management and comprehension tool. https://maven.apache.org/
18. Gradle is the open source build system for Java, Android, and Kotlin. https://gradle.org/
19. pip is the package installer for Python. https://pypi.org/project/pip/
20. The Python Package Index (PyPI) is a repository of software for the Python programming language. https://pypi.org/
21. Go Module Mirror, Index, and Checksum Database, proxy.golang.org
22. npm is committed to making JavaScript development elegant, productive, and safe. https://www.npmjs.com/
23. Cargo is a professional site building platform for designers and artists. https://cargo.site/
24. The Rust community's crate registry. https://crates.io/
25. https://cran.r-project.org/
26. NuGet is the package manager for .NET. https://www.nuget.org/downloads
27. https://www.nuget.org/
28. A Dependency Manager for PHP. https://getcomposer.org/
29. Packagist is the main Composer repository. https://packagist.org/
30. Bundler provides a consistent environment for Ruby projects by tracking and installing the exact gems and versions that are needed. https://bundler.io/
31. https://rubygems.org/
32. https://www.gnu.org/software/make/
33. CMake is the de-facto standard for building C++ code. https://cmake.org/
34. https://www.gnu.org/software/automake/manual/html_node/Why-Autotools.html
35. https://ubuntu.com/server/docs/package-management
36. https://www.redhat.com/sysadmin/how-manage-packages
37. Bavota G, Canfora G, Di Penta M, et al. How the apache community upgrades dependencies: an evolutionary study. Empir Softw Eng 2015;20:1275–1317.
38. Mora-Cantallops M, Sicilia M , García-Barriocanal E, et al. Evolution and prospects of the comprehensive R archive network (CRAN) package ecosystem. J Softw Evolut Process. 2020;32(11):e2270.
39. Hornik K. Are there too many R packages? Austr J Stat 2012;41(1):59–66.
40. Caneill M, Germán DM, Zacchiroli S. The debsources dataset: two decades of free and open source software. Empir Softw Eng. 2017;22:1405–37.

41. Massacci F, Pashchenko I. Technical leverage in a software ecosystem: development opportunities and security risks. In: 2021 IEEE/ACM 43rd international conference on software engineering (ICSE). Piscataway: IEEE; 2021. p. 1386–1397.
42. Caneill M, Zacchiroli S. Debsources: live and historical views on macro-level software evolution. In: Proceedings of the 8th ACM/IEEE international symposium on empirical software engineering and measurement; 2014. p. 1–10.
43. Gonzalez-Barahona JM, Robles G, Michlmayr M, et al. Macro-level software evolution: a case study of a large software compilation. Empir Softw Eng. 2009;14(3):262–85.
44. Chen X, Abdalkareem R, Mujahid S, et al. Helping or not helping? Why and how trivial packages impact the npm ecosystem. Empir Softw Eng. 2021;26:1–24.
45. Chowdhury MAR, Abdalkareem R, Shihab E, et al. On the untriviality of trivial packages: an empirical study of npm JavaScript packages. IEEE Trans Softw Eng. 2021;48(8):2695–708.
46. Abdalkareem R, Oda V, Mujahid S, et al. On the impact of using trivial packages: an empirical case study on npm and PyPi. Empir Softw Eng. 2020;25:1168–204.
47. Abdalkareem R, Nourry O, Wehaibi S, et al. Why do developers use trivial packages? an empirical case study on npm. In: Proceedings of the 2017 11th joint meeting on foundations of software engineering; 2017. p. 385–395.
48. Bommarito E, Bommarito M. An empirical analysis of the python package index (PyPi). arXiv preprint arXiv:1907.11073; 2019.
49. De La Mora FL, Nadi S. An empirical study of metric-based comparisons of software libraries. In: Proceedings of the 14th international conference on predictive models and data analytics in software engineering; 2018. p. 22–31.
50. Lima C, Hora A. What are the characteristics of popular APIs? A large-scale study on Java, Android, and 165 libraries. Softw Qual J. 2020;28(2):425–58.
51. Mileva YM, Dallmeier V, Zeller A. Mining API popularity. Testing–practice and research techniques. In: 5th international academic and industrial conference, TAIC PART 2010, Windsor, September 3–5, 2010. Proceedings. Berlin: Springer; 2010. p. 173–180.
52. Piccioni M, Furia CA, Meyer B. An empirical study of API usability. In: 2013 ACM/IEEE international symposium on empirical software engineering and measurement. Piscataway: IEEE; 2013. p. 5–14.
53. Raemaekers S, Nane GF, van Deursen A, et al. Testing principles, current practices, and effects of change localization. In: 2013 10th working conference on mining software repositories (MSR). Piscataway: IEEE; 2013. p. 257–266.
54. Raemaekers S, van Deursen A, Visser J. Measuring software library stability through historical version analysis. In: 2012 28th IEEE international conference on software maintenance (ICSM); 2012. p. 378–387.
55. Sajnani H, Saini V, Ossher J, et al. Is popularity a measure of quality? an analysis of maven components. In: 2014 IEEE international conference on software maintenance and evolution. Piscataway: IEEE; 2014. p. 231–240.
56. Nguyen R, Holt R. Life and death of software packages: an evolutionary study of Debian. In: Proceedings of the 2012 conference of the center for advanced studies on collaborative research; 2012. p. 192–204.
57. Soto-Valero C, Benelallam A, Harrand N, et al. The emergence of software diversity in maven central. In: 2019 IEEE/ACM 16th international conference on mining software repositories (MSR). Piscataway: IEEE; 2019. p. 333–343.
58. Wang Y, Chen B, Huang K, et al. An empirical study of usages, updates and risks of third-party libraries in java projects. In: 2020 IEEE international conference on software maintenance and evolution (ICSME). Piscataway: IEEE; 2020. p. 35–45.
59. Almanee S, Ünal A, Payer M, et al. Too quiet in the library: an empirical study of security updates in android apps' native code. In: 2021 IEEE/ACM 43rd international conference on software engineering (ICSE). Piscataway: IEEE; 2021. p. 1347–1359.
60. Yasumatsu T, Watanabe T, Kanei F, et al. Understanding the responsiveness of mobile app developers to software library updates. In: Proceedings of the Ninth ACM conference on data and application security and privacy; 2019. p. 13–24.

61. Derr E, Bugiel S, Fahl S, et al. Keep me updated: an empirical study of third-party library updatability on android. In: Proceedings of the 2017 ACM SIGSAC conference on computer and communications security; 2017. p. 2187–2200.
62. McDonnell T, Ray B, Kim M. An empirical study of API stability and adoption in the android ecosystem. In: 2013 IEEE international conference on software maintenance. Piscataway: IEEE; 2013. p. 70–79.
63. Chinthanet B, Kula RG, McIntosh S, et al. Lags in the release, adoption, and propagation of npm vulnerability fixes. Empir Softw Eng. 2021:26:1–28.
64. Zerouali A, Constantinou E, Mens T, et al. An empirical analysis of technical lag in npm package dependencies.In: International conference on software reuse. Cham: Springer International Publishing; 2018. p. 95–110.
65. Decan A, Mens T, Constantinou E. On the evolution of technical lag in the npm package dependency network. In: 2018 IEEE international conference on software maintenance and evolution (ICSME). Piscataway: IEEE; 2018. p. 404–414.
66. Alfadel M, Costa DE, Shihab E. Empirical analysis of security vulnerabilities in python packages. Empir Softw Eng. 2023;28(3):59.
67. Decan A, Mens T, Constantinou E. On the impact of security vulnerabilities in the npm package dependency network. In: Proceedings of the 15th international conference on mining software repositories; 2018. p. 181–191.
68. Zerouali A, Mens T, Decan A, et al. On the impact of security vulnerabilities in the npm and RubyGems dependency networks. Empir Softw Eng. 2022;27(5):107.
69. Zerouali A, Mens T, Gonzalez-Barahona J, et al. A formal framework for measuring technical lag in component repositories—and its application to npm. J Softw Evolut Process. 2019:31(8):e2157.
70. Huang K, Chen B, Xu C, et al. Characterizing usages, updates and risks of third-party libraries in Java projects. Empir Softw Eng. 2022;27(4):90.
71. Kula RG, German DM, Ouni A, et al. Do developers update their library dependencies? An empirical study on the impact of security advisories on library migration. Empir Softw Eng. 2018;23:384–417.
72. Prana GAA, Sharma A, Shar LK, et al. Out of sight, out of mind? How vulnerable dependencies affect open-source projects. Empir Softw Eng. 2021;26:1–34.
73. Cox J, Bouwers E, Van Eekelen M, et al. Measuring dependency freshness in software systems. In: 2015 IEEE/ACM 37th IEEE international conference on software engineering. Piscataway: IEEE; 2015. p. 109–118.
74. Stringer J, Tahir A, Blincoe K, et al. Technical lag of dependencies in major package managers. In: 2020 27th Asia-Pacific software engineering conference (APSEC). Piscataway: IEEE; 2020. p. 228–237.
75. Wang C, Jiang J, Li J, et al. Transforming programs between APIs with many-to-many mappings. In: 30th European conference on object-oriented programming (ECOOP 2016). Schloss-Dagstuhl-Leibniz Zentrum für Informatik; 2016.
76. He H, He R, Gu H, et al. A large-scale empirical study on Java library migrations: prevalence, trends, and rationales. In: Proceedings of the 29th ACM joint meeting on european software engineering conference and symposium on the foundations of software engineering; 2021. p. 478–490.
77. Henkel J, Diwan A. Catchup! capturing and replaying refactorings to support API evolution. In: Proceedings of the 27th international conference on Software engineering; 2005. p. 274–283.
78. Dig D, Johnson R. The role of refactorings in API evolution. In: 21st IEEE international conference on software maintenance (ICSM'05). Piscataway: IEEE; 2005. p. 389–398.
79. Lämmel R, Pek E, Starek J. Large-scale, AST-based API-usage analysis of open-source Java projects. In: Proceedings of the 2011 ACM symposium on applied computing; 2011. p. 1317–1324.
80. Alrubaye H, Alshoaibi D, Alomar E, et al. How does library migration impact software quality and comprehension? an empirical study. In: International conference on software and software reuse. Cham: Springer International Publishing; 2020. p. 245–260.

81. Teyton C, Falleri JR, Blanc X. Mining library migration graphs. In: 2012 19th working conference on reverse engineering. Piscataway: IEEE; 2012. p. 289–298.
82. Xing Z, Stroulia E. API-evolution support with Diff-CatchUp. IEEE Trans Softw Eng. 2007;33(12):818–36.
83. Teyton C, Falleri JR, Blanc X. Automatic discovery of function mappings between similar libraries. In: 2013 20th working conference on reverse engineering (WCRE); 2013. p.192–201.
84. Alrubaye H, Mkaouer MW. Automating the detection of third-party Java library migration at the function level. In: CASCON; 2018. p. 60–71.
85. Alrubaye H, Mkaouer MW, Ouni A. On the use of information retrieval to automate the detection of third-party java library migration at the method level. In: 2019 IEEE/ACM 27th international conference on program comprehension (ICPC). Piscataway: IEEE; 2019. p. 347–357.
86. Balaban I, Tip F, Fuhrer R. Refactoring support for class library migration. ACM SIGPLAN Notices 2005;40(10):265–79.
87. Chen C, Xing Z, Liu Y, et al. Mining likely analogical APIs across third-party libraries via large-scale unsupervised API semantics embedding. IEEE Trans Softw Eng. 2019;47(3):432–47.
88. Winter VL, Mametjanov A, Winter VL, Mametjanov A. Generative programming techniques for Java library migration. In: Proceedings of the 6th international conference on generative programming and component engineering; 2007. p. 185–196.
89. Cossette BE, Walker RJ. Seeking the ground truth: a retroactive study on the evolution and migration of software libraries. In: Proceedings of the ACM SIGSOFT 20th international symposium on the foundations of software engineering; 2012. p. 1–11.
90. Ni A, Ramos D, Yang AZH, et al. Soar: a synthesis approach for data science API refactoring. In: 2021 IEEE/ACM 43rd international conference on software engineering (ICSE); 2021. p. 112–124.
91. Robillard MP, Kutschera K. Lessons learned while migrating from swing to JavaFX. IEEE Softw. 2019;37(3):78–85.
92. Suwa H, Ihara A, Kula RG, et al. An analysis of library rollbacks: a case study of Java libraries. In: 2017 24th Asia-Pacific software engineering conference workshops (APSECW); 2017. p. 63–70.
93. Brito A, Xavier L, Hora A, et al. Why and how Java developers break APIs. In: 2018 IEEE 25th international conference on software analysis, evolution and reengineering (SANER); 2018. p. 255–265.
94. Bartolomei TT, Czarnecki K, Lämmel R, et al. Study of an API migration for two XML APIs. In: Software language engineering: second international conference, SLE 2009, Denver, CO, October 5–6, 2009. Berlin: Springer; 2010. p. 42–61.
95. Tang W, Xu Z, Liu C, et al. Towards understanding third-party library dependency in C/C++ ecosystem. In: Proceedings of the 37th IEEE/ACM international conference on automated software engineering; 2022. p. 1–12.
96. Robillard MP, Bodden E, Kawrykow D, et al. Automated API property inference techniques. IEEE Trans Softw Eng. 2012;39(5):613–37.
97. Acharya M, Xie T, Pei J, et al. Mining API patterns as partial orders from source code: from usage scenarios to specifications. In: Proceedings of the 6th joint meeting of the European software engineering conference and the ACM SIGSOFT symposium on The foundations of software engineering; 2007. p. 25–34.
98. Teyton C, Falleri JR, Palyart M, et al. A study of library migrations in Java. J Softw Evolut Process. 2014;26:1030–52.
99. Lamothe M, Shang W, Chen THP. A3: assisting android API migrations using code examples. IEEE Trans Softw Eng. 2020;48(2):417–31.
100. Meng S, Wang X, Zhang L, et al. A history-based matching approach to identification of framework evolution. In: 2012 34th international conference on software engineering (ICSE). Piscataway: IEEE; 2012. p. 353–363.

101. Cogo FR, Oliva GA, Hassan AE. Deprecation of packages and releases in software ecosystems: a case study on npm. IEEE Trans Softw Eng. 2022;48(7):2208–23.
102. Plakidas K, Schall D, Zdun U. Evolution of the R software ecosystem: metrics, relationships, and their impact on qualities. J Syst Softw. 2017;132:119–46.
103. Borges HS, Valente MT. Mining usage patterns for the Android API. PeerJ Comput Sci. 2015;1:e12.
104. Holmes R, Walker RJ, Murphy GC. Approximate structural context matching: an approach to recommend relevant examples. IEEE Trans Softw Eng. 2006;32(12):952–70.
105. Saied MA, Sahraoui H, Dufour B. An observational study on API usage constraints and their documentation. In: 2015 IEEE 22nd international conference on software analysis, evolution, and reengineering (SANER). Piscataway: IEEE; 2015. p. 33–42.
106. Saied MA, Abdeen H, Benomar O, et al. Could we infer unordered API usage patterns only using the library source code? In: 2015 IEEE 23rd international conference on program comprehension. Piscataway: IEEE; 2015. p. 71–81.
107. Saied MA, Sahraoui H. A cooperative approach for combining client-based and library-based API usage pattern mining. In: 2016 IEEE 24th international conference on program comprehension (ICPC). Piscataway: IEEE; 2016. p. 1–10.
108. Niu H, Keivanloo I, Zou Y. API usage pattern recommendation for software development. J Syst Softw. 2017;129:127–39.
109. Saied MA, Ouni A, Sahraoui H, et al. Improving reusability of software libraries through usage pattern mining. J Syst Softw. 2018;145:164–79.
110. Nguyen HA, Nguyen TT, Wilson Jr G, et al. A graph-based approach to API usage adaptation. ACM Sigplan Notices 2010;45(10):302–21.
111. Nielebock S, Heumüller R, Schott KM, et al. Guided pattern mining for API misuse detection by change-based code analysis. Autom Softw Eng. 2021;28(2):15.
112. Bauer V, Heinemann L, Deissenboeck F. A structured approach to assess third-party library usage. In: 2012 28th IEEE international conference on software maintenance (ICSM). IEEE, Piscataway; 2012. p. 483–492.
113. Yoon IC, Sussman A, Memon A, et al. Prioritizing component compatibility tests via user preferences. In: 2009 IEEE international conference on software maintenance; 2009. p. 29–38.
114. Yoon I, Sussman A, Memon A, et al. Testing component compatibility in evolving configurations. Inf Softw Technol. 2013;55(2):445–58.
115. Dogguy M, Glondu S, Le Gall S, et al. Enforcing type-safe linking using inter-package relationships. Stud Inform Univ. 2011;9(1):129–57.
116. Mitchell N, Schonberg E, Sevitsky G. Four trends leading to Java runtime bloat. IEEE Softw. 2009;27(1):56–63.
117. Tan J, Chen Y, Liu Z, et al. Toward efficient interactions between Python and native libraries. In: Proceedings of the 29th ACM joint meeting on european software engineering conference and symposium on the foundations of software engineering; 2021. p. 1117–1128.
118. Macho C, McIntosh S, Pinzger M. Automatically repairing dependency-related build breakage. In: 2018 IEEE 25th international conference on software analysis, evolution and reengineering (SANER). Piscataway: IEEE; 2018. p. 106–117.

Part III
Dependency Issues in Software Supply Chain

Chapter 3
Common Types of Dependency Issues

Abstract The interplay and constraints of asynchronous evolution in open-source software libraries, along with build environment restrictions and complex dependency configurations, result in five common dependency issues. These include compatibility problems arising from API breaking changes, violations of open-source license agreements, conflicts due to multiple library versions, bloated dependencies with excessive or redundant components, and the propagation of vulnerable dependencies through outdated dependencies. Figure 3.1 depicts the causal relationship between evolutionary behaviors and these dependency issues. Extensive research has been conducted to understand and address these issues, emphasizing the importance of careful dependency management, resolving conflicts, and actively updating dependencies to ensure software functionality, compliance, performance, and security.

3.1 Compatibility Issues

Software projects and their dependencies on third-party libraries are typically developed and maintained by different developers. This can result in asynchronous evolution between the software projects and their dependencies, leading to frequent compatibility issues. The evolution of software libraries encompasses not only the addition of new features but also changes in various aspects such as method signatures, licenses, and configuration files. Over the past few years, there has been significant research interest, with nearly 40 publications, focusing on the problem of API breaking changes during the evolution of software libraries. By analyzing and extracting relevant concepts and descriptions from these publications, we provide a comprehensive definition and introduction to compatibility issues (Fig. 3.1).

Issue Definition During the process of version evolution, four types of API breaking changes can disrupt the backward compatibility of software libraries. These include *API signature changes*, *API implementation changes*, *API deprecations*, and *API removals*. When software projects upgrade to a new version of a third-

Y. Wang et al., *Managing Software Supply Chains*,
https://doi.org/10.1007/978-981-96-1797-5_3

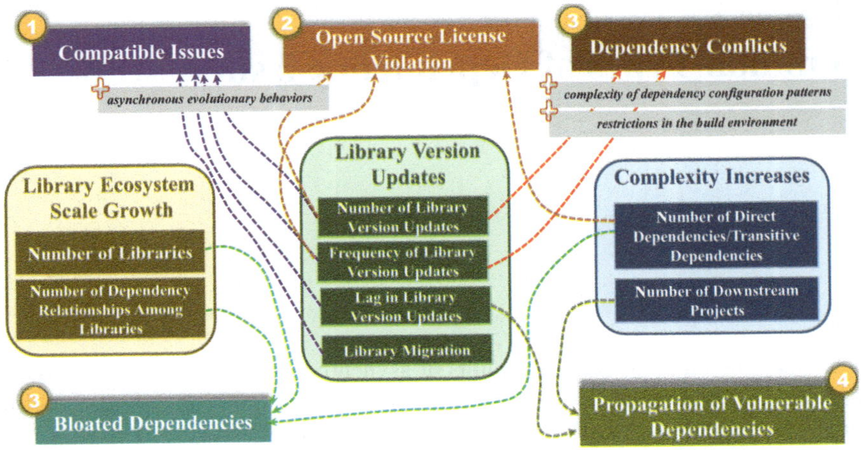

Fig. 3.1 Causal relationship between evolutionary behaviors and dependency issues

party library, these changes can easily lead to unexpected behaviors during build or runtime [1, 2].

3.1.1 Issue Impacts

Regarding the impact of API breaking changes during software library evolution, we analyze the issue from two perspectives: the ecosystem and software projects.

Impact on the Ecosystem Research conducted by Brito et al. [3] indicates that the *NuGet* ecosystem has the highest occurrence of API breaking changes, followed by *npm* and *Maven*. Notably, the *npm* build rules allow different versions of the same software library to coexist within a software project, thereby mitigating the *"ripple effect"* of API breaking changes in that language community. Zhang et al. [4] discovered that API breaking changes are more frequent in Python projects and can occur at any stage of software evolution. The dynamic nature and flexibility of Python make it challenging to detect such changes, resulting in a broader impact on client applications. Conversely, Java is relatively less affected by these issues.

Impact on Software Developers Different programming language ecosystems have varying dependency management mechanisms, which influence developers' willingness to address API breaking changes. While library developers strive to avoid such changes, they inevitably make backward-incompatible API modifications under the guise of evolution, continually dealing with technical debt. Literature [5] highlights the distinction of the *CRAN* software repository for the ***R*** language, which requires library developers to notify dependent projects before making API breaking changes. This approach allows downstream developers to update according to their own development plans, with a more lenient approach to version numbering. This coordinated approach to asynchronous version evolution facilitates continuous synchronization among developers and effectively mitigates compatibility issues. The governance strategies and experiences of the ***R*** language community in managing API breaking changes are valuable and can be promoted to developers in other language communities.

3.1.2 Issue Types

According to the ways in which API changes occur during software library version evolution, we can categorize the causes of compatibility issues into three types:

- ***API Signature Changes:*** Changes in API signatures (including method names, parameter types, parameter declaration order, and return value types) in software libraries can result in binary or source code incompatibility. Binary incompatibility occurs when errors arise during program linking, while source code incompatibility occurs during program compilation [6, 7].
- ***API Implementation Changes:*** When the API signatures remain unchanged in software libraries, altering the implementation of methods or fields (such as preconditions or default values) can also lead to backward incompatible program behaviors [8]. Research conducted by Mostafa et al. [9] classified the reasons for API implementation changes, considering factors such as incompatible behaviors and invocation conditions. They found that backward incompatibility issues are prevalent in Java software libraries. Similarly, Dig et al. [10] investigated the evolutionary history of API implementations in popular Java frameworks and software libraries, revealing that 80% of API breaking changes were a result of software refactoring operations.
- ***API Deprecation and Deletion:*** During the process of software version evolution, deprecating and removing APIs can lead to compatibility issues and even cause a *"ripple effect"* within the open-source software library ecosystem [11]. Essentially, API deprecation serves as a warning to downstream developers before its removal. However, in practice, many software library developers do not strictly provide deprecation warnings for APIs, resulting in software crashes during execution. Robbes et al. [12] were the pioneering researchers who investigated the impact of API changes on the compatibility of downstream software projects that depend on them. Through their study of the *Squeak* and *Pharo* software ecosystems, they concluded that API deprecation can have a destructive impact on the open-source software library ecosystem. Qiu et al. [13], through analysis of a large number of Java projects, found that 51.1% of deprecated classes, 43.5% of deprecated APIs, and 18.1% of deprecated fields were still used in actual development, causing significant compatibility issues. Additionally, Sawant et al. [14, 15], building upon the work of Robbes et al. [12], conducted further research on the Java ecosystem and confirmed that most client

software projects do not respond to deprecated entities. Even if they do respond, they tend to resolve the issue by removing problematic API calls. They also argue that the deprecation mechanism in Java does not provide the correct incentives for developers.

In the case of the aforementioned three types of API breaking changes, developers should adhere to semantic versioning rules to prevent the propagation of compatibility issues within the open-source software library ecosystem. Semantic versioning employs major, minor, and patch version numbers to signify API breaking changes, non-breaking changes, and bug fixes [16]. However, the lack of standardized updates to library semantic versions is a primary cause for exposing compatibility problems during software evolution. Studies conducted by Raemaekers et al. [17, 18] and Zhang et al. [18] highlight the prevalence of incorrect semantic version updates in software ecosystems. Investigations have revealed an average of 30 backward compatibility issues per popular software, with API breaking changes occurring even in patch and minor versions where backward compatibility should have been maintained.

3.2 Open-Source License Violation

Out of the 383 papers collected in Chap. 1 on the open-source software supply chain, 29 papers specifically focus on studying open-source license violations. Based on the existing literature, we provide an overview of these issues.

Issue Definition Open-source licenses are legal permissions included in open-source software, typically through copies or statements, granting users the freedom to use, modify, and share the copyrighted software [19]. The main differences between open-source licenses are in the restrictions they impose on distributing derivative software, particularly the requirements for sharing modified and extended code. These licenses are generally categorized into three types based on their restrictions: ***permissive***, ***copyleft***, and ***weak copyleft*** [20]. ***Permissive licenses*** have minimal redistribution requirements and impose fewer restrictions on derivative software, allowing it to be used in proprietary projects. Examples include the *BSD family*, *MIT*, *Apache 2.0*, and *MulanPSL-2.0*. ***Copyleft licenses*** mandate that modifications and extensions must be released under the same license as the original software. The *GPL family* is an example of copyleft licenses. ***Weak copyleft licenses*** require modifications and redistributions to be licensed under the same terms, but larger works combining these components can be kept proprietary. The *MPL license* is an example. Asynchronous evolution of open-source software libraries can introduce conflicts due to license-related operations such as adding/removing licenses, upgrading/downgrading licenses, or changing licenses in upstream and downstream software. These operations can introduce source files or third-party libraries with conflicting licenses, leading to compliance issues [21, 22].

3.2.1 Issue Impacts

Due to the frequent occurrence of open-source license violations, software project developers face three significant impacts:

- ***Legal disputes:*** Open-source licenses serve as legally binding contracts between the authors of third-party libraries and software project developers. When developers misuse or misunderstand the license agreements and use the libraries in violation of legal terms, it exposes development organizations or companies to legal risks. For example, *CoKinetic* filed a lawsuit against *Panasonic Avionics* in 2017, accusing them of violating the *GPL 2.0* open-source license agreement. Panasonic Avionics, whose software development relied on the Linux operating system that complies with the *GPL*, chose not to release its operating system source code as open-source, which raised concerns about competition. *CoKinetic* claimed deliberate violation of the *GPL 2.0* license and demanded $100 million in copyright fees [23].
- ***Selection of software project licenses:*** Open-source license agreements convey the terms of software copyrights from software project developers to downstream users. Once a license is selected for a software project, it typically remains unchanged throughout the project's life cycle. Therefore, the selection of license can significantly impact the success or failure of the software project. Developers often face challenges in selecting the appropriate license [24]. A study by Sen et al. [25] found that developers who invest more thought and effort into license selection have a higher likelihood of obtaining an unrestricted software project license in subsequent evolution. This finding holds true even if most open-source developers tend to prefer restrictive or weakly restrictive license agreements.
- ***Selection of third-party library licenses:*** When software project developers decide to use third-party libraries, they must ensure that the license terms align with their intended use. In the complex ecosystem of interdependencies among open-source libraries, understanding the impact and constraints of diverse license agreements from third-party libraries becomes increasingly challenging. Researchers such as Almeida et al. [26, 27] conducted a survey among software practitioners to assess the usage of popular open-source licenses. The results indicated that only about 62% of developers provided the same judgments as legal experts in instances of license usage. Developers often struggle to provide clear answers when multiple licenses from different software libraries are involved, despite having a good understanding of the implications of using individual licenses.

3.2.2 Issue Types

With the introduction and evolution of third-party libraries, software projects face two common types of open-source license violations:

- ***Compatibility issues with multiple licenses:*** During the development of a software project, it is typical to incorporate multiple license agreements from different source files or third-party libraries. When conflicting terms arise among these licenses, compatibility issues emerge. Moraes et al. [28] conducted a study on the prevalence of multiple licenses in the npm ecosystem, analyzing millions of software libraries used in 1,552 JavaScript projects. They found that around 61% of projects utilized more than one open-source license. On average, each software project introduced 4.7 licenses (with a maximum of 256). Among them, 373 projects encountered conflicts between pairs of open-source licenses, highlighting the widespread occurrence of compatibility issues with multiple licenses.
- ***Inconsistencies in licenses:*** If the license agreement of a third-party library used by downstream software projects is inconsistent with the license under which the library is distributed, it can lead to infringement in the usage of the third-party software library. The causes of such inconsistencies can be categorized into two scenarios [29]: (1) The developers of the software library update the license agreement, but older versions of the library, which still include the original license, continue to be used by downstream software projects. (2) Downstream software projects unauthorizedly remove or modify the original license agreement in the third-party library. The first type of license inconsistency issue can be resolved by upgrading to newer versions of the third-party library. However, the second type of license inconsistency issue can result in infringement if it lacks approval or authorization from the copyright owner. For example, in the case of *XimpleWare* suing *Versata* Software, *Versata* was accused of including *GPL-licensed* code in its product but removing the copyright and usage agreements required by the *GPL* [30].

3.3 Dependency Conflicts

Among the 383 research papers collected in Chap. 1 related to open-source software supply chain, 12 of them discussed the dependency conflict issues. We provide the following definition for this problem:

Issue Definition During the evolution of software projects, dependency conflict issues can arise due to direct and transitive dependencies: (1) the presence of different versions of the same software library, (2) conflicts arising from classes with identical fully qualified names across different software libraries, (3) conflicts between classes with the same fully qualified name in both the software project and the software library, and (4) conflicts arising from version ranges between the software library and the platform framework. Under the constraints of the build environment, the project is limited to arbitrating and loading only one version from multiple versions of the software library, effectively masking off the remaining versions. If the installed library version is not the expected version to be utilized, it can result in build failures or runtime crashes [31].

3.3.1 Issue Impacts

The impact of dependency conflicts on the open-source software library ecosystem can be examined from three key perspectives:

- ***Pervasiveness:*** Empirical studies have revealed the widespread occurrence of dependency conflict issues in popular programming language ecosystems, including Python, Java, C#, and Rust. These ecosystems have amassed millions of reported instances of dependency conflicts within their respective GitHub version control systems [32, 33].
- ***Diversity:*** The manifestation of dependency conflict issues is influenced by various factors, such as the order of declaration for different software library versions in configuration scripts, the topology of the dependency tree, platform versions within the build environment, and the rules governing dependency manager installations. Modifications to any of these conditions can lead to different approaches in resolving dependencies, thereby impacting program behaviors accordingly [34].
- ***Severity:*** Dependency conflicts can result in software build failures, particularly in languages like Python and C#. Moreover, they can give rise to more severe consequences, including `ClassNotFoundException`, `NoSuchMethodException`, program crashes, or inconsistencies in program semantics, particularly in Java software [31].

3.3.2 Issue Types

During the evolution of software projects, upgrading, downgrading, or migrating third-party libraries and platform frameworks often trigger dependency conflict issues. As shown in Fig. 3.2, based on the causes of conflicts, we can categorize the problems into four types:

- ***Multiple versions of the same software library:*** If multiple versions of the same software library are directly or transitively introduced into a software project, dependency manager will load one of the versions based on a specific dependency resolving strategy (such as *"shortest path first"* in *Maven*, *"newest version first"* in *Gradle*, and *"direct dependency first"* in *NuGet*), thereby overshadowing the other versions. Research indicates that for Java projects, if the loaded version does not include the required classes or methods called by the software project, it can lead to runtime crashes [31]. Similarly, for C# and Python projects [34, 35], if the installed version of the conflicting library does not satisfy

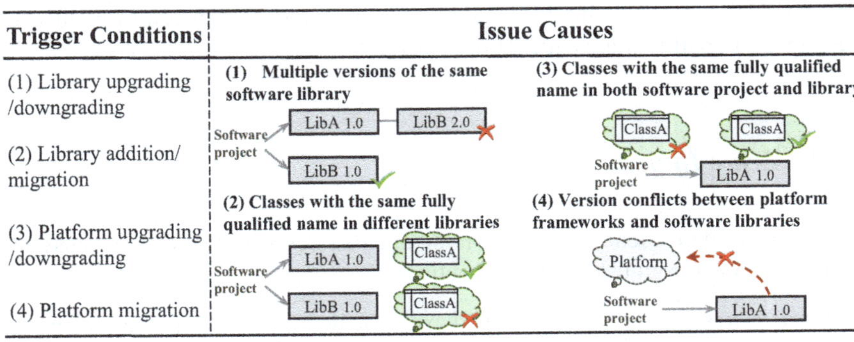

Fig. 3.2 Issue types of dependency conflicts

the dependency constraints of the overshadowed version, it can result in build failures.

- ***Classes with the same fully qualified name in different libraries:*** If different libraries contain multiple class files with the same fully qualified name, dependency manager will load the class file declared first in the configuration script, overshadowing the other ones. If the loaded class file lacks the methods actually called by the software project, it can lead to runtime crashes [31].
- ***Classes with the same fully qualified name in both software project and third-party library:*** When both the software project and a third-party software library have class files with identical fully qualified names, conflicts may arise. In situations where the project is built using the *UberJar* method, which involves packaging the project code and the third-party software library together, the class files from the third-party library take precedence over those with the same names in the project itself. Consequently, if the loaded class file does not contain the methods that are actually called by the software project, it can result in runtime crashes [31].
- ***Version conflicts between platform frameworks and software libraries:*** In programming language communities such as C# and C/C++ that rely on platform frameworks, software libraries often impose restrictions on the compatible versions of the platform frameworks they can be installed on. During the evolution of software projects, this can easily lead to conflicts between the versions of the platform framework and the software library, resulting in build failures [34, 35].

3.4 Bloated Dependencies

The investigation revealed that 18 recently published papers discussed the issue of software bloated dependencies. By extracting relevant concepts and descriptions from the literature, we provide the following definition for this problem.

Issue Definition Third-party libraries are introduced into a software project either directly or transitively through dependencies. However, only a portion of their features or functions is actually utilized. We refer to the unnecessary code dependencies in the software project during the build and runtime processes as bloated dependencies [36].

3.4.1 Issue Impacts

The presence of bloated dependencies in a software project brings about several significant impacts [37]:

- ***Build efficiency:*** Bloated dependencies increase the size of build files, leading to slower build times and deployment processes. On resource-constrained devices, the excessive file size can hinder software deployment. Larger build files also consume more network bandwidth during distribution, further hampering build efficiency.
- ***Maintenance cost:*** Bloated dependencies introduce additional testing and maintenance burdens for developers. With a larger codebase due to unnecessary dependencies, developers need to allocate more time and resources to ensure that all dependencies are up-to-date, compatible, and free of vulnerabilities. This involves monitoring and managing a larger set of dependencies, performing more extensive testing, and addressing potential conflicts or issues that may arise. The increased maintenance workload can potentially slow down development cycles and increase the overall cost of maintaining the software project.
- ***Security risks:*** Bloated dependencies increase the attack surface of a software project, thereby elevating the security risks. Unused dependencies may contain vulnerabilities that could be exploited by attackers. By including these bloated dependencies, the software project introduces additional avenues for potential security breaches. It becomes crucial to keep all dependencies updated and secure, but managing a large number of dependencies increases the complexity and the likelihood of overlooking critical updates or security patches. Consequently, the presence of bloated dependencies amplifies the overall security risks faced by the software project.

3.4.2 Issue Types

Based on the code granularity, bloated dependencies can be categorized into the following three types:

- ***Bloated libraries:*** Dependency managers play a crucial role in automatically downloading and installing software libraries, both direct and transitive, by parsing project dependency configuration scripts. However, this convenient process comes with a downside—the introduction of bloated software libraries. Current research primarily focuses on exploring this issue within the Maven ecosystem. Studies [38–40] have qualitatively and quantitatively analyzed the prevalence of bloated dependencies in Java projects, revealing that a staggering 75.1% of software projects suffer from this problem. It is worth noting that the root causes extend beyond inadequate modularization and dependency configuration by library developers. Project developers themselves contribute to the problem by mistakenly configuring dependency scopes in `pom.xml`, such as *compile*, *runtime*, and *test*, thereby introducing unnecessary bloated dependencies [36].

- ***Bloated class files:*** During the evolution of software libraries, they often introduce new features, leading to larger library sizes and a departure from their original functional focus. However, in practical scenarios, software projects typically utilize only a subset of class files from third-party libraries. By removing bloated class files, it is still possible to ensure the correct building and functionality of the software. Studies [41, 42] have extensively examined the intricate inter-library dependencies, inter-package dependencies, and interclass dependencies in software projects to explore effective strategies for eliminating unnecessary class files. Fan et al. [37] specifically investigated the issue of bloated dependencies stemming from inconsistencies between declared dependencies in configuration scripts and imported dependencies in source files, with the aim of enhancing software build efficiency. Additionally, research [43] has been dedicated to reducing security vulnerabilities in web applications by eliminating bloated and high-risk source files.
- ***Bloated functions/code blocks:*** When it comes to loaded class files, only a fraction of functions/code blocks are actually used. Therefore, selectively removing unnecessary functions/code blocks from class files offers a more precise approach to eliminating bloated dependencies. This allows developers to further reduce the size of software projects, surpassing conservative debloating strategies that mainly focus on software libraries/class files. Third-party libraries often include a wide range of features to meet complex user requirements or support different client software, leading to larger file sizes. Vázquez et al. [44] analyzed bundled third-party software libraries in JavaScript applications and successfully improved webpage loading speed by eliminating bloated functions. Recent research has also explored reducing unnecessary code or functions to mitigate security risks in various contexts, including large-scale browsers [45], commercial software [46], web applications [43], and Unix applications [47].

3.5 Propagation of Vulnerable Dependencies

Among the 383 research papers collected in Chap. 1 in the field of software supply chain, 90 papers discussed the propagation of vulnerable dependencies. By extracting relevant concepts and descriptions from the literature, we provide the following interpretation of the problem.

Issue Definition Attackers frequently inject malicious code into widely used software libraries or exploit vulnerabilities in poorly designed libraries with the intention to steal user privacy information [48, 49], engage in unauthorized profit-making activities [50], escalate privileges [49], or execute denial-of-service attacks [51]. Third-party libraries with security risks may harbor undisclosed vulnerabilities or known vulnerabilities. These risks propagate to numerous downstream software projects through the dependency relationships within the open-source software library ecosystem, posing a significant threat to the overall trustworthiness of the community [3, 52, 53].

3.5.1 Issue Impacts

The impact of vulnerable dependency propagation on the open-source software library ecosystem can be analyzed from the following three aspects:

- ***Security risks:*** Introducing vulnerable dependencies into software projects can result in large-scale privacy breaches, such as the disclosure of user information, passwords, or abnormal behaviors, leading to major accidents or economic losses. For example, the *Heartbleed* vulnerability (`CVE-2014-0160`), publicly disclosed in 2012, in the *OpenSSL* open-source *cryptographic* library, exposed 24–55% of popular websites using the *Transport Layer Security* protocol to attacks [54–57]. This security vulnerability allowed attackers to remotely access private keys and passwords [196]. Furthermore, attackers can replace ad libraries to add malicious functionality from the perspective of application developers and steal information from application users, causing financial losses [58]. Research indicates that around 50.6% of vulnerabilities are only patched after public disclosure, which may increase the likelihood of exploitation by attackers [59].
- ***Impact scope:*** Popular software libraries have a broad impact, not only on the software projects directly dependent on them but also through transitive dependencies, affecting a large number of downstream software [6]. According to a study by Zimmermann et al. [33], in the open-source software library ecosystem, an average single package impacts 230 downstream software projects. The top five ranked libraries impact a varying number of downstream software projects, ranging from 134,774 to 166,086, ultimately leading to ecosystem-level security vulnerability issues. The significant number of transitive dependencies has resulted in the widespread propagation of security vulnerabilities across various programming language communities [60].
- ***Remediation cost:*** For software developers, the solutions for addressing vulnerability issues may include (1) upgrading/downgrading the directly or transitively introduced vulnerable dependencies [61], (2) migrating to reliable software libraries with similar functionalities [61], and (3) developers fixing the vulnerabilities and maintaining the software library by themselves [62]. Most vulnerabilities can be resolved by updating the directly dependent libraries.

However, updating or migrating third-party libraries can introduce compatibility issues, requiring developers to put in greater effort for testing [63–66]. For large enterprise software systems that are critical for business operations, any changes can potentially cause system downtime and bring unforeseen losses and risks.

3.5.2 Issue Types

Based on whether vulnerabilities in the software library have been publicly disclosed, we categorize the issues into the following two types:

- ***0-Day Vulnerabilities:*** 0-day vulnerabilities refer to undisclosed security vulnerabilities in a software library that can be exploited by attackers. Common attack methods for 0-day vulnerabilities include (1) attackers stealing the credentials of the software library developers and maliciously injecting vulnerable code [67–69], (2) attackers disguising their own vulnerable software libraries with names similar to popular ones [70–73], and (3) attackers exploiting the inherent vulnerable code characteristics of popular software libraries [74, 75]. Vulnerable code that is commonly exploited by attackers includes **(a)** *Field Exposure* [76, 77]: reading or modifying private fields through method invocations, **(b)** *Privilege Escalation* [50, 63, 65, 78–89]: accessing excessive methods or data, **(c)** *Life Cycle Abuse* [75]: accessing data objects after service deregistration (or before service registration), and **(d)** *Denial of Service* [60]: disrupting normal access to clients or servers.
- ***1-Day Vulnerabilities:*** 1-day vulnerabilities refer to publicly disclosed security vulnerabilities in a software library that can be exploited by attackers. When vulnerability is disclosed in a software library, developers may delay the release of patch versions, or the released patch versions may get blocked in the open-source software library dependency chain due to the lags of upstream software version updates. As a result, the vulnerabilities remain a security threat to software projects, unable to propagate widely [90–92].

3.6 Conclusion

The interplay and constraints of asynchronous evolution in open-source software libraries, along with the restrictions imposed by the build environment and the complexity of dependency configurations, contribute to five common dependency issues. Extensive research has been conducted in the existing literature to understand these problems:

- ***Compatibility issues:*** Forty studies have focused on addressing compatibility problems that arise due to API breaking changes during the evolution of software libraries. These issues can result in incompatibilities between different library versions or with other components, leading to functionality errors or failures.

- ***Open-source license violations:*** Twenty-nine studies have delved into issues related to violations of open-source license agreements. These violations encompass conflicts and inconsistencies in license terms, such as improper attribution, unauthorized modifications, or the use of incompatible licenses. Such violations can have legal consequences and impact the compliance and distribution of the software.
- ***Dependency conflicts:*** Twelve studies have examined conflicts that occur when multiple versions of the software library are introduced in a software project. These conflicts can lead to runtime crashes or build failures due to incompatible dependencies or conflicting requirements. Resolving these conflicts often requires careful management of dependency versions and resolving dependency hierarchies.
- ***Bloated dependencies:*** Eighteen studies have explored the problem of unnecessary or redundant dependencies. Bloated dependencies refer to the inclusion of excessive or redundant software components, libraries, or packages in a project. This can increase the size and complexity of the software, leading to performance issues, longer build times, and difficulties in maintenance and troubleshooting.
- ***Vulnerable dependency propagation:*** Nineteen studies have investigated the propagation of security vulnerabilities through dependencies. Outdated or vulnerable software components used as dependencies can serve as entry points for attacks, potentially compromising the security of the entire software system. These studies emphasize the risks associated with using outdated or unpatched dependencies and highlight the importance of actively managing and updating dependencies to mitigate security risks.

In the subsequent chapters, we present effective diagnosis techniques tailored to different programming language ecosystems to combat the aforementioned dependency issues.

References

1. Jezek K, Dietrich J, Brada P. How Java APIs break–an empirical study. Inf Softw Technol. 2015;65:129–46.
2. Hora A, Robbes R, Anquetil N, et al. How do developers react to API evolution? the Pharo ecosystem case. In: 2015 IEEE international conference on software maintenance and evolution (ICSME). Piscataway: IEEE; 2015. p. 251–260.
3. Brito A, Valente MT, Xavier L, et al. You broke my code: understanding the motivations for breaking changes in APIs. Empir Softw Eng. 2020;25:1458–92.
4. Zhang Z, Zhu H, Wen M, et al. How do python framework APIs evolve? an exploratory study. In: 2020 IEEE 27th international conference on software analysis, evolution and reengineering (SANER). Piscataway IEEE; 2020. p. 81–92.

5. Bogart C, Kästner C, Herbsleb J, et al. When and how to make breaking changes: policies and practices in 18 open source software ecosystems. ACM Trans Softw Eng Methodol. 2021;30(4):1–56.
6. Dietrich J, Jezek K, Brada P. Broken promises: an empirical study into evolution problems in Java programs caused by library upgrades. In: IEEE conference on software maintenance, reengineering, and reverse engineering (CSMR-WCRE); 2014. p. 64–73.
7. Dietrich J, Jezek K, Brada P. What Java developers know about compatibility, and why this matters. Empir Softw Eng. 2016;21:1371–96.
8. Jia Z, Li S, Yu T, et al. DepOwl: detecting dependency bugs to prevent compatibility failures. In: International conference on software engineering (ICSE); 2021. p. 86–98.
9. Mostafa S, Rodriguez R, Wang X. Experience paper: a study on behavioral backward incompatibilities of Java software libraries. In: Proceedings of the 26th ACM SIGSOFT international symposium on software testing and analysis; 2017. p. 215–225.
10. Dig D, Johnson R. How do APIs evolve? A story of refactoring. J Softw Maint. Evolut Res Pract. 2006;18(2):83–107.
11. Sawant AA, Huang G, Vilen G, et al. Why are features deprecated? an investigation into the motivation behind deprecation. In: 2018 IEEE international conference on software maintenance and evolution (ICSME); 2018. p. 13–24.
12. Robbes R, Lungu M, Röthlisberger D. How do developers react to API deprecation? The case of a Smalltalk ecosystem. In: Proceedings of the ACM SIGSOFT 20th international symposium on the foundations of software engineering; 2012. p. 1–11.
13. Qiu D, Li B, Leung H. Understanding the API usage in Java. Inf Softw Technol. 2016;73:81–100.
14. Sawant AA, Robbes R, Bacchelli A. On the reaction to deprecation of 25,357 clients of 4+1 popular Java APIs. In: 2016 IEEE international conference on software maintenance and evolution (ICSME). Piscataway: IEEE; 2016. p. 400–410.
15. Sawant AA, Robbes R, Bacchelli A. To react, or not to react: patterns of reaction to API deprecation. Empir Softw Eng. 2019;24:3824–70.
16. Mezzetti G, Møller A, Torp MT. Type regression testing to detect breaking changes in NodeJS libraries. In: 32nd European conference on object-oriented programming (ECOOP 2018).
17. Raemaekers S, Van Deursen A, Visser J. Semantic versioning versus breaking changes: a study of the maven repository. In: 2014 IEEE 14th international working conference on source code analysis and manipulation. Piscataway: IEEE; 2014. p. 215–224.
18. Raemaekers S, van Deursen A, Visser J. Semantic versioning and impact of breaking changes in the Maven repository. J Syst Softw. 2017;129:140–58.
19. Di Penta M, German DM, Guéhéneuc YG, et al. An exploratory study of the evolution of software licensing. In: Proceedings of the 32nd ACM/IEEE international conference on software engineering-volume 1; 2010. p. 145–154.
20. Kapitsaki GM, Kramer F. Open source license violation check for SPDX files. In: Software reuse for dynamic systems in the cloud and beyond. 14th international conference on software reuse; 2014. p. 90–105.
21. Mlouki O, Khomh F, Antoniol G. On the detection of licenses violations in the android ecosystem. In: 2016 IEEE 23rd international conference on software analysis, evolution, and reengineering (SANER), vol. 1; 2016. p. 382–392.
22. Meloca R, Pinto G, Baiser L, et al. Understanding the usage, impact, and adoption of non-OSI approved licenses. In: Proceedings of the 15th international conference on mining software repositories; 2018. p. 270–280.
23. CoKinetic Systems Pursues $100 Million GPL License Violation Case Against Panasonic Avionics. WP Tavern. https://wptavern.com/cokinetic-systems-pursues-100-million-gpl-license-violation-case-against-panasonic-avionics
24. Vendome C, Linares-Vásquez M, Bavota G, et al. When and why developers adopt and change software licenses. In: 2015 IEEE international conference on software maintenance and evolution (ICSME). Piscataway: IEEE; 2015. p. 31–40.

25. Sen R, Subramaniam C, Nelson ML. Open source software licenses: strong-copyleft, non-copyleft, or somewhere in between? Decision Supp Syst. 2011;52(1):199–206.
26. Almeida DA, Murphy GC, et al. Do software developers understand open source licenses? In: 25th international conference on program comprehension (ICPC); 2017. p. 1–11.
27. Almeida DA, Murphy GC, et al. Investigating whether and how software developers understand open source software licensing. Empir Softw Eng. 2019;24(1):211–39.
28. Moraes JP, Polato I, Wiese I, et al. From one to hundreds: multi-licensing in the JavaScript ecosystem. Empir Softw Eng. 2021;26(3):39.
29. Viseur R, Robles G. First results about motivation and impact of license changes in open source projects. In: Open source systems: adoption and impact: 11th IFIP WG 2.13 international conference; 2015. p. 137–145.
30. Wu Y, Manabe Y, Kanda T, et al. Analysis of license inconsistency in large collections of open source projects. Empir Softw Eng. 2017;22:1194–222.
31. Wang Y, Wen M, Liu Z, et al. Do the dependency conflicts in my project matter? In: Proceedings of the 2018 26th ACM joint meeting on European software engineering conference and symposium on the foundations of software engineering; 2018. p. 319–330.
32. Wang Y, Wen M, Wu R, et al. Could I have a stack trace to examine the dependency conflict issue? In: 2019 IEEE/ACM 41st international conference on software engineering (ICSE); 2019. p. 572–583.
33. Wang Y, Qiao L, Xu C, et al. Hero: on the Chaos when PATH meets modules. In: 2021 IEEE/ACM 43rd international conference on software engineering (ICSE). Piscataway: IEEE; 2021. p. 99–111.
34. Wang Y, Wen M, Liu Y, et al. Watchman: monitoring dependency conflicts for python library ecosystem. In: Proceedings of the ACM/IEEE 42nd international conference on software engineering; 2020. p. 125–135.
35. Li Z, Wang Y, Lin Z, et al. Nufix: escape from NuGet dependency maze. In: Proceedings of the 44th international conference on software engineering; 2022. p. 1545–1557.
36. Jezek K, Dietrich J. On the use of static analysis to safeguard recursive dependency resolution. In: 2014 40th EUROMICRO conference on software engineering and advanced applications. Piscataway: IEEE; 2014. p. 166–173.
37. Fan G, Wang C, Wu R, et al. Escaping dependency hell: finding build dependency errors with the unified dependency graph. In: Proceedings of the 29th ACM SIGSOFT international symposium on software testing and analysis; 2020. p. 463–474.
38. Soto-Valero C, Harrand N, Monperrus M, et al. A comprehensive study of bloated dependencies in the maven ecosystem. Empir Softw Eng. 2021;26(3):45.
39. Soto-Valero C, Durieux T, Baudry B. A longitudinal analysis of bloated java dependencies. In: Proceedings of the 29th ACM joint meeting on European software engineering conference and symposium on the foundations of software engineering; 2021. p. 1021–1031.
40. Song X, Wang Y, Cheng X, et al. Efficiently trimming the fat: streamlining software dependencies with Java reflection and dependency analysis. In: Proceedings of the IEEE/ACM 46th international conference on software engineering; 2024. p. 1–12.
41. Matos AS, Ferreira Filho JB, Rocha LS. Splitting APIs: an exploratory study of software unbundling. In: IEEE/ACM 16th international conference on mining software repositories (MSR). Piscataway: IEEE; 2019. p. 360–370.
42. Shah SMA, Dietrich J, McCartin C. On the automation of dependency-breaking refactorings in Java. In: 2013 IEEE international conference on software maintenance; 2013. p. 160–169.
43. Azad BA, Laperdrix P, Nikiforakis N. Less is more: quantifying the security benefits of debloating web applications. In: 28th USENIX security symposium (USENIX security 19); 2019. p. 1697–1714.
44. Vázquez HC, Bergel A, Vidal S, et al. Slimming JavaScript applications: an approach for removing unused functions from JavaScript libraries. Inf Softw Technol. 2019;107:18–29.
45. Qian C, Koo H, Oh CS, et al. Slimium: debloating the chromium browser with feature subsetting. In: Proceedings of the 2020 ACM SIGSAC conference on computer and communications security; 2020. p. 461–476.

46. Qian C, Hu H, Alharthi M, et al. RAZOR: a framework for post-deployment software debloating. In: 28th USENIX security symposium (USENIX Security 19); 2019. p. 1733–1750.
47. Heo K, Lee W, Pashakhanloo P, et al. Effective program debloating via reinforcement learning. In: Proceedings of the 2018 ACM SIGSAC conference on computer and communications security; 2018. p. 380–394.
48. Grace MC, Zhou W, Jiang X, et al. Unsafe exposure analysis of mobile in-app advertisements. In: Proceedings of the fifth ACM conference on Security and Privacy in Wireless and Mobile Networks; 2012. p. 101–112.
49. Yang W, Li J, Zhang Y, et al. APKLancet: tumor payload diagnosis and purification for android applications. In: Proceedings of the 9th ACM symposium on Information, computer and communications security; 2014. p. 483–494.
50. Shekhar S, Dietz M, Wallach DS. AdSplit: separating smartphone advertising from applications. In: 21st USENIX Security Symposium (USENIX Security 12); 2012. p. 553–567.
51. Parrend P, Frénot S. Classification of component vulnerabilities in java service oriented programming (sop) platforms. In: International symposium on component-based software engineering. Berlin; 2008. p. 80–96.
52. Decan A, Mens T, Claes M. An empirical comparison of dependency issues in OSS packaging ecosystems. In: 2017 IEEE 24th international conference on software analysis, evolution and reengineering (SANER). Piscataway: IEEE; 2017. p. 2–12.
53. Vasilakis N, Benetopoulos A, Handa S, et al. Supply-chain vulnerability elimination via active learning and regeneration. In: Proceedings of the 2021 ACM SIGSAC conference on computer and communications security; 2021. p. 1755–1770.
54. Decan A, Mens T, Constantinou E. On the impact of security vulnerabilities in the npm package dependency network. In: Proceedings of the 15th international conference on mining software repositories; 2018. p. 181–191.
55. Dashevskyi S, Brucker AD, Massacci F. A screening test for disclosed vulnerabilities in FOSS components. IEEE Trans Softw Eng. 2018;45(10):945–66.
56. Decan A, Mens T, Constantinou E. On the impact of security vulnerabilities in the npm package dependency network. In: Proceedings of the 15th international conference on mining software repositories; 2018. p. 181–191.
57. Gkortzis A, Feitosa D, Spinellis D. A double-edged sword? Software reuse and potential security vulnerabilities. In: Reuse in the big data era: 18th international conference on software and systems reuse, ICSR 2019; 2019. p. 187–203.
58. Mojica IJ, Adams B, Nagappan M, et al. A large-scale empirical study on software reuse in mobile apps. IEEE Softw. 2013;31(2):78–86.
59. Alfadel M, Costa DE, Shihab E. Empirical analysis of security vulnerabilities in python packages. Empir Softw Eng. 2023;28(3):59.
60. Prana GAA, Sharma A, Shar LK, et al. Out of sight, out of mind? How vulnerable dependencies affect open-source projects. Empir Softw Eng. 2021;26(4):59.
61. Walden J. The impact of a major security event on an open source project: the case of OpenSSL. In: Proceedings of the 17th international conference on mining software repositories; 2020. p. 409–419.
62. Massacci F, Neuhaus S, Nguyen VH. After-life vulnerabilities: a study on Firefox evolution, its vulnerabilities, and fixes. In: International symposium on engineering secure software and systems. Berlin; 2011. p. 195–208.
63. Massacci F, Pashchenko I. Technical leverage in a software ecosystem: development opportunities and security risks. In: 2021 IEEE/ACM 43rd international conference on software engineering (ICSE). Piscataway: IEEE; 2021. p. 1386–1397.
64. Zerouali A, Mens T, Gonzalez-Barahona J, et al. A formal framework for measuring technical lag in component repositories — and its application to npm. J Softw Evolut Process. 2019;31(8):20.

65. Stringer J, Tahir A, Blincoe K, et al. Technical lag of dependencies in major package managers. In: 2020 27th Asia-Pacific software engineering conference (APSEC). Piscataway: IEEE; 2020. p. 228–237.
66. Zerouali A, Mens T, Gonzalez-Barahona J, et al. A formal framework for measuring technical lag in component repositories and its application to npm. J Softw Evolut Process. 2019;31(8):20.
67. Duan R, Alrawi O, Pai Kasturi R , et al. Towards measuring supply chain attacks on package managers for interpreted languages. In: Proceedings of network and distributed system security symposium; 2021.
68. Ferreira G, Jia L, Sunshine J, et al. Containing malicious package updates in npm with a lightweight permission system. In: 2021 IEEE/ACM 43rd international conference on software engineering (ICSE). Piscataway: IEEE; 2021. p. 1334–1346.
69. Nikiforakis N, Invernizzi L, Kapravelos A, et al. You are what you include: large-scale evaluation of remote JavaScript inclusions. In: Proceedings of the 2012 ACM conference on Computer and communications security; 2012. p. 736–747.
70. Sejfia A, Schäfer M. Practical automated detection of malicious npm packages. In: Proceedings of the 44th international conference on software engineering; 2022. p. 1681–1692.
71. Ohm M, Plate H, Sykosch A, et al. Backstabber's knife collection: a review of open source software supply chain attacks. In: Detection of intrusions and malware, and vulnerability assessment: 17th international conference, Lisbon, Portugal; 2020. p. 23–43.
72. Taylor M, Vaidya R, Davidson D, et al. Defending against package typosquatting. In: International conference on network and system security; 2020. p. 112–131.
73. Kwon T, Su Z. Automatic detection of unsafe dynamic component loadings. IEEE Trans Softw Eng. 2011;38(2):293–313.
74. Hu W, Octeau D, McDaniel PD, et al. Duet: library integrity verification for android applications. In: Proceedings of the 2014 ACM conference on Security and privacy in wireless & mobile networks; 2014. p. 141–152.
75. Parrend P. Enhancing automated detection of vulnerabilities in java components. In: Proceedings of 2009 international conference on availability, reliability and security; 2009. p. 216–223.
76. Demetriou S, Merrill W, Yang W, et al. Free for all! assessing user data exposure to advertising libraries on android. In: NDSS; 2016.
77. Musch M, Steffens M, Roth S, et al. Script protect: mitigating unsafe third-party JavaScript practices. In: Proceedings of the 2019 ACM Asia conference on computer and communications security; 2019. p. 391–402.
78. Stevens R, Gibler C, Crussell J, et al. Investigating user privacy in android ad libraries. In: Workshop on mobile security technologies (MoST), Published online 2012.
79. Wang F, Zhang Y, Wang K, et al. Stay in your Cage! a sound sandbox for third-party libraries on android. In: European symposium on research in computer security; 2016. p. 476.
80. Son S, Kim D, Shmatikov V. What mobile ads know about mobile users. In: Network and distributed system security symposium (NDSS); 2016. p. 14.
81. Paturi A, Kelley P, Mazumdar S. Introducing privacy threats from ad libraries to android users through privacy granules. In: Proceedings of NDSS workshop on usable security (USEC'15); 2015.
82. Wang Y, Hariharan S, Zhao C, et al. Compac: enforce component-level access control in Android. In: Proceedings of the 4th ACM conference on data and application security and privacy; 2014. p. 25–36.
83. Sun M, Tan G. NativeGuard: Protecting android applications from third-party native libraries. In: Proceedings of the 2014 ACM conference on Security and privacy in wireless & mobile networks; 2014. p. 165–176.
84. Felt AP, Chin E, Hanna S, et al. Android permissions demystified. In: Proceedings of the 18th ACM conference on computer and communications security; 2011. p. 627–636.
85. Politz JG, Eliopoulos SA, Guha A, et al. ADsafety: type-based verification of JavaScript sandboxing. In: 20th USENIX security symposium (USENIX Security 11); 2011. p. 1–16.

86. Narayan S, Disselkoen C, Garfinkel T, et al. Retrofitting fine grain isolation in the Firefox renderer. In: 29th USENIX security symposium (USENIX Security 20); 2020. p. 699–716.
87. Vasilakis N, Staicu CA, Ntousakis G, et al. Preventing dynamic library compromise on Node.js via RWX-based privilege reduction. In: Proceedings of the 2021 ACM SIGSAC conference on computer and communications security; 2021. p. 1821–1838.
88. De Groef W, Massacci F, Piessens F. NodeSentry: least-privilege library integration for server-side JavaScript. In: Proceedings of the 30th annual computer security applications conference; 2014. p. 446–455.
89. Shin I, Seo J. FlexDroid: enforcing in-app privilege separation in Android. In: Network and distributed system security symposium (NDSS); 2016.
90. Almanee S, Unal A, Payer M, et al. Too quiet in the library: an empirical study of security updates in android apps' native code. In: ICSE; IEEE; 2021. p. 1347–1359.
91. McDonnell T, Ray B, Kim M. An empirical study of API stability and adoption in the android ecosystem.In: ICSM; 2013. p. 70–79.
92. McDonnell T, Ray B, Kim M. An empirical study of API stability and adoption in the android ecosystem. In: 2013 IEEE international conference on software maintenance; 2013. p. 70–79.

Part IV
Ecosystem-Level Techniques Combating Dependency Issues

Chapter 4
Detecting Compatibility Issues for Machine Learning Libraries

Abstract A Machine Learning (ML) pipeline configures the workflow of a learning task using the APIs provided by ML libraries. However, a pipeline's performance can vary significantly across different configurations of ML library versions. Misconfigured pipelines can result in inferior performance, such as inefficient *executions*, *numeric errors*, and even *crashes*. A pipeline is subject to misconfiguration if it exhibits significantly inconsistent performance upon changes in the versions of its configured libraries or the combination of these libraries. We refer to such performance inconsistency as an *ML library compatibility (MLC) issue*. A systematic understanding of MLC issues helps configure effective ML pipelines and identify misconfigured ones. To this end, we conduct the first empirical study of MLC issues' pervasiveness, impact, and root causes. To facilitate scalable in-depth analysis, we develop *Piecer*, an infrastructure that automatically generates a set of pipeline variants by varying different version combinations of ML libraries and detects their performance inconsistencies. We apply *Piecer* to the 3,380 pipelines that can be deployed out of the 11,363 ML pipelines collected from multiple ML competitions at *Kaggle* platform. The empirical study results show that 1,092 (32.3%) of the 3,380 pipelines manifest significant performance inconsistencies on at least one variant. We find that 399, 243, and 440 pipelines can achieve better competition scores, execution time, and memory usage, respectively, by adopting a different configuration. Based on our findings, we construct a repository containing 164 defective APIs and 106 API combinations from 418 library versions. The defective API repository facilitates future studies of automated detection techniques for MLC issues. Leveraging the repository, we captured MLC issues in 309 real-world ML pipelines.

4.1 Introduction

Machine Learning (ML) libraries (e.g., *TensorFlow* and *PyTorch*) have gained much attention in both academia and industry, which are used in a wide range of domains, including natural language processing, image processing, autonomous driving, etc. [1–5]. These libraries provide off-the-shelf ML solutions, optimized

Y. Wang et al., *Managing Software Supply Chains*,
https://doi.org/10.1007/978-981-96-1797-5_4

numerical computations, efficient data structures, visualization, and other handy utilities, to facilitate application development.

In practice, the calls to ML library APIs are often organized by means of an ML pipeline, which automates the workflow of an ML task in nine stages as shown in Fig. 4.1. To timely incorporate support for new hardware, algorithms, and bug fixes, ML libraries keep evolving rapidly. However, different combinations of ML library versions can cause inconsistencies in pipelines' performances, crashes, and *NaN* bugs, as demonstrated by the real-life example in Sect. 4.2.2. In this chapter, we refer to the performance inconsistencies of ML pipelines induced by varying ML library versions as an *ML library compatibility (MLC) issue*.

Despite the widespread use of ML pipelines, there have been no prior systematic studies on MLC issues. We have little knowledge of MLC issues, such as their pervasiveness in real-world ML pipelines, their impact on ML tasks' performances, and their root causes. The deficient knowledge can hinder effective deployment of ML pipelines in various ways: (1) *ML library vendors* lack awareness of the need to test the interactions between specific library versions that could be concurrently deployed by a pipeline, (2) *ML pipeline developers* lack advice on good and bad practices in ML pipeline configuration, and (3) *tool builders* lack scientific criteria to recommend appropriate versions of ML libraries to pipeline developers when maintaining and evolving ML libraries.

To fill the knowledge gap, we conduct a large-scale empirical study to understand the status quo of MLC issues. To facilitate scalable analysis, we develop *Piecer*,

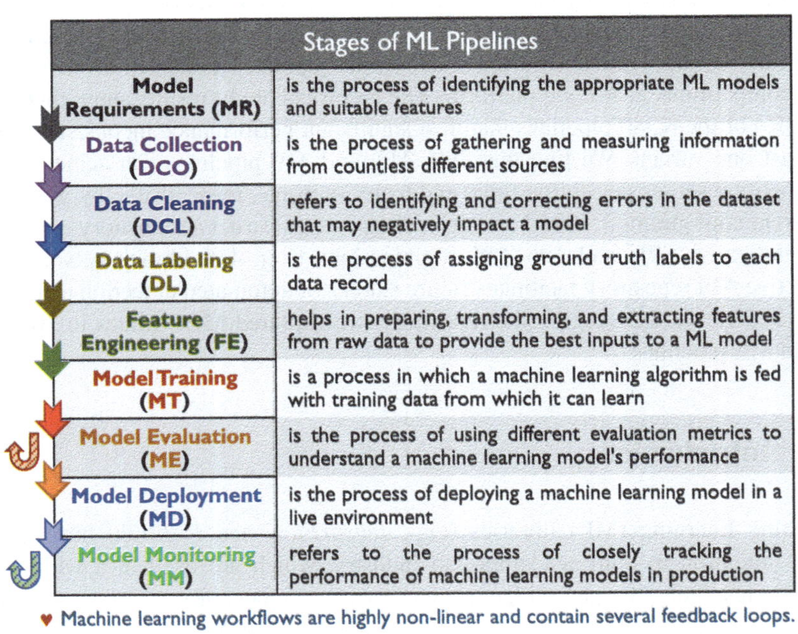

Fig. 4.1 Description of the stages in ML pipeline

which automatically generates a set of pipeline variants by varying version combinations of ML libraries and compares three aspects of performance inconsistencies: *execution time*, *memory usage*, and *prediction performance* (*precision* and *recall*). To understand the status quo of MLC issues, we leverage *Piecer* to analyze 11,363 ML pipelines from various competition categories on *Kaggle* platform. The pipelines utilize 112 popular ML libraries. We investigate the pervasiveness and severity of MLC issues in ML pipelines and analyze their root causes of inducing performance inconsistencies. The main empirical findings are:

(1) We identify 601 library combinations commonly adopted by the 11,363 ML pipelines in our dataset.
(2) Among the 3,380 ML pipelines that we are able to deploy, 1,092 (32.3%) manifest significant performance inconsistencies on at least one variant. We find that 399, 243, and 440 pipelines among the deployable pipelines could achieve higher competition scores, shorter execution time, and lower memory usage, respectively, using a different configuration of the library versions available at the time of competition.
(3) By analyzing the historical evolution data of 577 defective APIs that induce MLC issues, we identify four types of issue root causes. Specifically, MLC issues exposed in 164 defective APIs are affected by one library version. MLC issues in 3,720 pipeline variants are caused by combinations of APIs from different library versions.

4.2 Preliminaries

4.2.1 Background

ML Libraries Machine learning comprises several kinds of learning algorithms such as *supervised learning*, *unsupervised learning*, *deep learning*, and *reinforcement learning*. To provide fast access to these algorithms and facilitate the complicated data analysis process, the open-source community developed two types of ML libraries: ***ML frameworks*** and ***data science libraries***. *ML Frameworks* (e.g., *Scikit-Learn* [6] and *PyTorch* [7]) provide ready-made algorithms and allow developers to easily apply ML-based solutions to applications. *Data science libraries* provide data visualization (e.g., *Matplotlib* [8]), efficient data structures (e.g., *Pandas* [9]), scientific computing functions (e.g., *Numpy* [10]), or other utilities.

ML Pipelines The term *pipeline* corresponds to the *pipes-and-filter* design pattern that decomposes the software architecture into several stages with processing units (filters) and ordered connections (pipes). By the *ML pipeline*, we are referring to a nine-stage pipeline that goes through **data oriented** (*collection, cleaning, and labeling*) and **model oriented** (*model requirements*, *feature engineering*, *training*, *evaluation*, *deployment*, and *monitoring*) stages.

Figure 4.1 explains each ML stage. According to the investigation results in studies [11, 12], most performance issues or crashes occurred in the *DCO*, *DCL*, *FE*, *MT*, and *ME* stages of ML pipelines. The five stages are commonly implemented based on various ready-made algorithms encapsulated in ML libraries.

4.2.2 Motivation

Since ML libraries rapidly evolve to add/remove/change features and fix bugs, various version combinations may dramatically affect pipelines' performance. Figure 4.2 shows an illustrative example of an MLC issue, which participates in the competition *MNIST* [13] hosted on *Kaggle* platform. This pipeline aims to identify digits from a dataset of tens of thousands of handwritten images, leveraging two ***TensorFlow*** APIs and eight ***Keras*** APIs to implement *DCL* and *MT* stages, respectively. Interestingly, when using different version combinations of ***TensorFlow*** and ***Keras***, the categorization accuracy of the pipeline varies from 0.559 to 0.997, leading to a rise in competition ranking from 523th to 1st. Even worse, some version combinations cause crashes due to API breaking changes.

Similar situations can be found in many issue reports. In the *MLC* issue#20642 [14] of project ***Sklearn***, a developer complained that the execution time of API ***Sklearn****.cluster.KMeans()* in their ML pipeline varies significantly when using different versions of ***Numpy***. This issue attracted 34 comments from experienced developers to diagnose the root causes and was linked to four

{Keras, Tensorflow} Versions	Score (AUC)	Ranking	Time (ms)	Memory (MB)
{2.7.1, 2.7.0}	Crash	Crash	Crash	Crash
{2.4.3, 2.4.1}	0.768	522	1895.656	1244.446
{2.4.3, 2.3.1}	0.737	521	1882.099	1241.001
{2.4.3, 2.2.0}	0.559	523	1926.980	1248.518
{2.3.1, 2.4.1}	Crash	Crash	Crash	Crash
{2.3.1, 2.3.1}	Crash	Crash	Crash	Crash
{2.3.1, 2.2.0}	0.997	1	1877.330	1199.130
{2.3.1, 2.1.0}	0.997	1	1888.612	1202.602
{2.3.1, 2.0.0}	Crash	Crash	Crash	Crash
{2.3.1, 1.15.2}	0.997	1	1989.861	1194.425
{2.3.1, 1.14.0}	0.997	1	1853.423	1196.269
{2.3.1, 1.13.1}	0.997	1	1901.693	1183.123

Fig. 4.2 An illustrative example of an MLC issue

similar performance bugs induced by ML library versions (i.e., ***scipy***#15050, ***Sklearn***#21729, ***scipy***#15129, and ***Sklearn***#21808). The above examples motivate us to conduct a large-scale empirical study to investigate the impacts of different combinations of ML library versions on ML pipelines' performances, which can shed light on approaches for detecting or repairing MLC issues.

Our study aims to answer the following three research questions:

- **RQ1 (Common ML Library Combinations):** ***What combinations of ML libraries do developers commonly use?*** To answer RQ1, we collect 11,363 published ML pipelines and analyze their library usage to identify common library combinations.
- **RQ2 (Impacts of Different ML Library Version Combinations):** ***Do different version combinations of ML libraries affect pipelines' performances?*** To answer RQ2, for each ML pipeline, we generate a series of variants with different ML library version combinations to inspect their performance inconsistencies. In particular, we define the generation rules of ML library version combinations, to systematically explore their impacts on pipelines' performances.
- **RQ3 (Root Causes of Performance Inconsistencies):** ***What are the root causes of pipelines' performance inconsistencies when adopting different version combinations of ML libraries?*** To answer RQ3, we consider the pipeline variants that induce (1) significant performance inconsistencies, (2) crashes, and (3) *NaN* bugs as subjects, to analyze the corresponding root causes and triggering conditions.

4.2.3 Piecer

To scale up the impact analysis of possible ML library version combinations on pipelines' performances, we develop an infrastructure, *Piecer* (*PI*p*E*line *C*onfiguration Explo*R*e), to automate such a process. Figure 4.3 shows an overall architecture of *Piecer*. It mainly consists of three components:

4.3 Empirical Study

Component 1: Constructing ML Library Version Pool For a given ML pipeline, *Piecer* constructs a dependency pool $Dp = \{V_{Lib_1}, V_{Lib_2}, \cdots, V_{Lib_n}\}$ to collect all the installable version candidates $V_{Lib_i} = \{v_1, v_2, \cdots, v_m\}$ of referenced ML libraries Lib_i. To achieve this, it first parses the pipeline's dependency management script (*Requirement.txt*, *Setup.py*, or *METADATA*) to identify all the versions of direct dependencies that satisfy the specified version constraints. For each version of direct dependency, it iteratively collects the version constraints of the required transitive dependencies. If a library Lib_i corresponds to multiple version constraints,

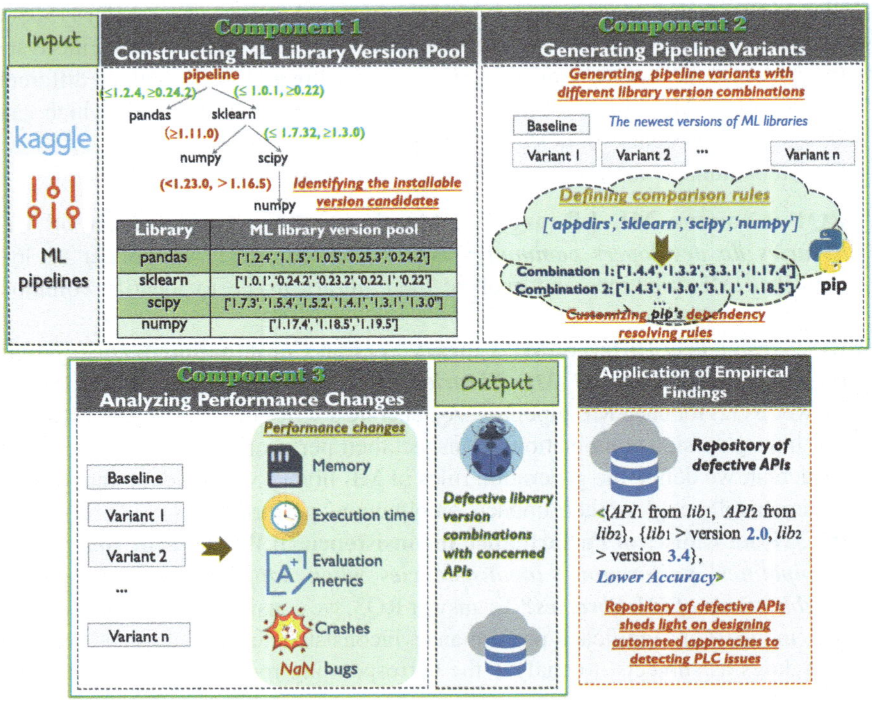

Fig. 4.3 The overall architecture of *Piecer*

Piecer considers their intersection as installable version candidates V_{Lib_i}. In the cases where a library Lib_i is specified with incompatible version constraints, we remove the versions of direct dependencies that induce such dependency conflicts from Dp.

Component 2: Generating Pipeline Variants with Different ML Library Version Combinations To explore the impacts of library versions on a pipeline's performance, *Piecer* generates a set of pipeline variants with different version combinations of ML libraries selected from our dependency pool Dp. For a given ML pipeline, it considers the newest versions of referenced ML libraries as ***a version combination baseline.*** By defining a series of comparison rules (see definitions in Sect. 4.3.3), *Piecer* generates a set of ML library version combinations by varying the versions of concerned libraries and keeping the remaining library versions be consistent with the baseline.

According to the dependency resolution rules of Python build tool *pip*, it installs the newest library versions from PyPI central repository that satisfies the corresponding version constraint. To enable the installation of an expected version combination of ML libraries, *Piecer* customizes the dependency resolution rules of *pip* to select our specified library version candidates (satisfying the corresponding version constraints) from our dependency pool Dp.

Component 3: Analyzing Performance Inconsistencies For each ML pipeline, *Piecer* runs the baseline and all the variants to check their performance inconsistencies across various library version combinations. It focuses on three aspects of performance inconsistencies: *execution time*, *memory usage*, and *evaluation metrics* (e.g., *Precision* and *Recall*). Specifically, *Piecer* performs two tasks:

- *Measuring performance inconsistencies:* For each library API referenced by the pipeline, it leverages measurement functions to capture the performance inconsistencies between the variant and baseline. For example, *Piecer* adopts functions ***timeit***.*default_timer()*, ***tracemalloc***.*get_traced_memory()*, and ***pynvml***.*nvmlDeviceGet-MemoryInfo()* to measure the execution time and CPU and GPU memory usage of the changed APIs, respectively. The evaluation metrics can be implemented with the aid of functions ***sklearn***.*metrics.accuracy_score()*, ***sklearn***.*metrics.recall_score()*, etc. For the pipelines involving deep learning models, *Piecer* retrains the model to capture the impacts of library version changes precisely. To reduce the interference of random factors, it runs each pipeline five times and averages the outcomes.
- *Recording the problematic library version combinations:* Compared with the baseline, *Piecer* records the library version combinations (with the concerned APIs) that (1) induce significant performance inconsistencies of pipelines (see definitions in Sect. 4.3.3) and (2) cause program crashes or *NaN* bugs, for further analysis.

4.3.1 Data Collection

We collected pipelines from *Kaggle* [15], the most popular crowdsourced platform for ML competitions. We select *Kaggle* pipelines as subjects to conduct our empirical study for four reasons: (1) All the ML pipelines in a competition correspond to the unified evaluation metrics for ranking, which enable us to compare the outcomes across different combinations of library versions, (2) each pipeline provides its corresponding source code and dataset, which facilitate our reproduction, (3) competitions in *Kaggle* platform cover a wide range of domains and techniques, which guarantee the diversity of ML tasks, and (4) the small size pipelines on *Kaggle* have few interference factors (e.g., environmental dependencies), which enables our analysis for the root causes of MLC issues. We did not select open-source large-scale ML pipelines as subjects because they rarely provide (1) detailed training steps in documentation, (2) complete datasets, and (3) all the required dependencies. Therefore, we face challenges on deploying the complex pipelines. However, the common ML library version combinations identified in Kaggle pipelines are also adopted by large-scale ML pipelines (see statistics in Sect. 4.4). As such, the empirical findings identified in Kaggle pipelines can scale to more complex ML-based projects.

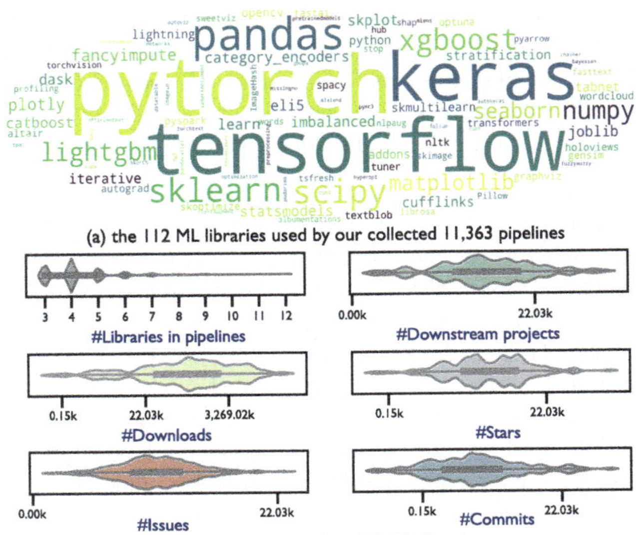

(a) the 112 ML libraries used by our collected 11,363 pipelines

(b) demographics of the 112 ML libraries

Fig. 4.4 Description of the stages in ML pipeline

We collected the ML pipelines from *Kaggle* competitions that satisfy three criteria. First, the competitions were hosted in the last 3 years (from January 1, 2019 to July 31, 2021). The search returned 168 competitions that involve 14,772 pipelines. Second, we only kept the competitions that contain more than 100 competing pipelines (i.e., popularity). Third, the pipelines should depend on more than three ML libraries, including both ML frameworks and data science libraries (i.e., complexity). With the above process, we finally obtained 11,363 pipelines from 42 competitions.

In total, our collected pipelines depend on 112 ML libraries, including 23 ML frameworks and 89 data science libraries. Among them, the top five most frequently used libraries are *Pandas* (13,054), *Sklearn* (7,821), *Numpy* (6,967), *TensorFlow* (3,279), and *PyTorch* (2,836). Figure 4.4 shows the demographics of the 112 ML libraries. On average, each ML library has 29,156 $\pm$ 338 downstream projects, 4,094,010 $\pm$ 3,285 monthly downloads, 7,460 $\pm$ 121 stars, and 603 $\pm$ 45 issues and 4,358 $\pm$ 198 commits in their GitHub repositories. According to a ranked list of awesome ML libraries provided by a popular GitHub project (updated weekly) [16], the 112 libraries cover 25 categories (including image and video processing, etc.). The above statistics demonstrate that the ML libraries used in *Kaggle* pipelines are also widely used in large amounts of open-source ML pipelines, indicating their representativeness.

4.3.2 RQ1: Common ML Library Combinations

Study Methodology A combination of ML libraries is typically used in certain stages of ML pipeline workflows [3]. To granularly identify common library combinations, we analyze the library usage in pipeline workflow stages. Specifically, we perform two tasks in the investigation: (1) Leveraging *Jedi* [17], a static analysis tool for Python, we located 8,853 unique ML library APIs invoked by our collected 11,363 pipelines, and (2) two Ph.D. students assigned label of workflow stages for each ML library API. The labels were assigned based on the code comments in ML pipelines for stating the API usage, or the description of the package (or sub-package), in which the API was declared. For example, we considered API ***xgboost**.score()* worked in the *ME* stage, since its declaration was accompanied by an explanatory code comment "*#Evaluate model performance*" in the ML pipeline. We did not assign labels for the APIs that (*i*) did not have a description in its package or (*ii*) the two Ph.D. students could not reach a consensus on the descriptions. We employed *Cohen's Kappa* [18] to measure the consistencies between the two Ph.D. students. If the *Kappa* value was less than 0.9, the students needed to discuss to resolve disagreements. This iterative process would stop once the *Kappa* value was equal to or greater than 0.9, indicating substantial agreement. Eventually, we obtained 7,983 labeled ML library APIs. The labeling process took 2 months for the two students who have over 2 years of experience in ML development to analyze and perform cross validation. We released the dataset on the website for public scrutiny.

Results By inspecting the 7,983 labeled ML library APIs, we observed that the pipelines from *Kaggle* platform only involved five stages of workflows: *DCO*, *DCL*, *FE*, *MT*, and *ME*. As aforementioned, recent empirical studies [11, 12] revealed that the majority of performance issues or crashes occurred in the five stages. In our study, we focus on these core stages of pipeline workflows, to identify their common combinations of library usage.

Table 4.1 summarizes the occurrences of ML library combinations in the single stage/multistages of pipeline workflows. We identified 176, 112, and 32 library combinations in the *DCO*, *DCL*, and *ME* stages, respectively. Since the open-source community provides various solutions to help developers extract critical features from raw data and automatically train their ML models, 480 and 513 library combinations were identified in the *FE* and *MT* stages of our collected pipelines. Our results reveal that 16/176, 13/112, 55/480, 56/513, and 2/32 of library combinations were commonly adopted by the majority of ML pipelines to implement *DCO*, *DCL*, *FE*, *MT*, and *ME* stages, respectively (occurrences $\geq Avg$). The combinations may include both ML frameworks and data science libraries. Table 4.2 illustrates the top five common library combinations in single stage. For example, 3,858 pipelines use *Pandas* in *DCO* stage, while 807 pipelines combine *Numpy* and *Pandas* with *PyTorch* for data collection.

As shown in Table 4.1, during the synthesis of the data oriented stages (*DCO*, *DCL*, and *FE*), we identified the use of 2,316 library combinations. 372 out of the

Table 4.1 Occurrences of ML library combinations in the pipelines

Occurrences	DCO	DCL	FE	MT	ME	Data oriented stages	Model oriented stages
[1,10)	125	80	386	425	23	2,124	641
[10,50)	34	13	66	60	5	161	73
[50,100)	10	6	9	8	0	18	16
[100,500)	2	11	16	14	2	11	21
[500, ∞)	4	1	2	5	1	2	4
Avg	59	90	21	20	275	5	14
#Common	16	13	55	56	2	372	87

Note: *Data Oriented Stages* = *DCO* + *DCL* + *FE*; *Model Oriented Stages* = *MT* + *ME*
Avg denotes the average occurrences of ML library combinations in each stage
#Common denotes the number of common library combinations
We consider a library combination is commonly adopted by ML pipelines
If its occurrences in each stage are above ***Avg***

Table 4.2 Statistics of top five common ML library combinations in single stage

Rank	*Data COllection*		*Data CLeaning*		*Feature Engineering*		*Model Training*		*Model Evaluation*	
	Combinations	*N*	*Combinations*	*N*	*Combinations*	*N*	*Combinations*	*N*	*Combinations*	*N*
1	Pandas	3,858	Numpy	1,745	Sklearn	1,295	Sklearn	1,503	Sklearn	5,940
2	Numpy, Pandas, PyTorch	807	PyTorch	428	Numpy	701	Tensorflow	1,422	Tensorflow	284
3	Pandas, PyTorch	553	Nltk	358	Keras	385	PyTorch	993	Sklearn, Tensorflow	258
4	Nltk, Pandas	521	Tensorflow	332	Tensorflow	359	Keras	851	Keras, Sklearn	12
5	OpenCV, Numpy, Pandas, PyTorch	487	Pandas	277	Pandas	357	Lightgbm	519	Pytorch-lightning, Sklearn	11

The top common ML library combinations in multi-stages are provided on our website **http://piecer-plc.github.io**
N denotes Occurrences

2,316 combinations occurred in more than five pipelines. We also identified 755 ways of implementing model oriented stages (*MT* and *ME*) using combinations of libraries. Of those 87 were commonly used in our collected pipelines. The top common ML library combinations used in multistages are provided on our website. We observed that 1,134 pipelines adopt a combination of *Pandas*, *Numpy*, and *Sklearn* for data oriented stages, and 725 pipelines combine *TensorFlow* with *Sklearn* for modeling oriented stages.

Answer to RQ1: *We identified 16, 13, 55, 56, and 2 common ML library combinations in the DCO, DCL, FE, MT, and ME stages, respectively. In the data oriented stages (DCO, DCL, and FE) and model oriented stages (MT and ME), we identified 372 and 87 common ML library combinations, respectively. Such common ML library combinations are adopted by the majority of ML pipelines.*

4.3.3 *RQ2: Impacts of Different ML Library Version Combinations*

Study Methodology We present the study methodology of RQ2 in three aspects: *Subject selection*, *Generation rules of library version combinations*, and *Experiment setup*.

Subject Selection Since each pipeline corresponds to a series of variants, the comparison experiment is time-consuming and would take lots of machine resources. To guarantee the feasibility of our RQ2 study, we set three filter conditions to select subjects from our collected 11,363 pipelines:

- 1,490 pipelines that do not use common ML library combinations in the single- or multistages are filtered out.
- 4,299 pipelines that involve the private datasets (not published on *Kaggle*) are filtered out.
- 157 pipelines that use the private libraries (could not be found from PyPI or GitHub repositories) are filtered out.
- We restrict the dataset size of pipelines to 100 GB. 2,037 pipelines are filtered out according to this condition.

Eventually, we obtained 3,380 pipelines, involving 13 ML frameworks and 77 data science libraries. The 90 ML libraries cover 80.4% of popular ones we presented in Fig. 4.4.

Generation Rules of Library Version Combinations We deployed *Component 1* of *Piecer* to take each pipeline as an input to construct a dependency pool $Dp = \{V_{Lib_1}, V_{Lib_2}, \cdots, V_{Lib_n}\}$, by collecting all the installable version candidates of the referenced ML libraries. To reduce the computation complexity, in our study, we only considered popular versions of each ML library in Dp that are widely used by downstream users (the popularity of library versions is provided on *Libraries.io* website). Leveraging *Component 2* of *Piecer*, we generate a set of pipeline variants with different ML library version combinations. To this end, we define two generation rules of ML library version combinations, to systematically explore their impacts on pipelines' performances:

- ***Rule 1****: Varying version combinations of ML libraries in the single stage:* For a given ML pipeline, *Piecer* iteratively varies the version combinations of ML libraries used in each workflow stage (*DCO*, *DCL*, *FE*, *MT*, and *ME*), while it keeps the remaining libraries to be the newest versions in our dependency pool Dp. Let $L = \{Lib_1, Lib_2, \cdots, Lib_m\}$ be an ML library combination (direct dependencies) used in a certain workflow stage. Each library $Lib_i \in L$ corresponds to a set of version candidates $V_{Lib_i} = \{v_1, v_2, \cdots, v_t\}$ in our dependency pool Dp. *Piecer* determines a set of version combinations of ML libraries used in a certain workflow stage as $LV = V_{Lib_1} \times V_{Lib_2} \cdots \times V_{Lib_m}$, where $Lib_i \in L$ and the symbol "×" denotes *Cartesian product.*

- ***Rule 2**: Varying version combinations of ML libraries in the multistages: Piecer* iteratively varies the version combinations of ML libraries used in data oriented stages (*DCO*, *DCL*, and *FE*) and model oriented stages (*MT* and *ME*), while it keeps the remaining libraries to be the newest versions in our dependency pool Dp.

  Let $LV(DCO)$, $LV(DCL)$, $LV(FE)$, $LV(MT)$, and $LV(ME)$ be the sets of installable version combinations of ML libraries used in *DCO*, *DCL*, *FE*, *MT*, and *ME* workflow stages, respectively (generated based on *Rule 1*). *Piecer* determines the ML library version combinations in the multistages as follows: (1) *data oriented stages*: $LV(Data) = LV(DCO) \times LV(DCL) \times LV(FE)$, (2) *model oriented stages*: $LV(Model) = LV(MT) \times LV(ME)$, and (3) *overall architecture*: $LV(Overall) = LV(Data) \times LV(Model)$.

Table 4.3 shows the statistics of pipeline variants. In total, *Piecer* generated 74,373 variants for the 3,380 pipelines, based on the generation rules of library version combinations. On average, each pipeline corresponds to 22 ± 8 variants.

Experiment Setup For an ML pipeline, *Piecer* considers the newest versions of referenced ML libraries as a version combination baseline. Using *Component 3*, we run the baseline and all its corresponding variants, to capture the performance inconsistencies. Based on confidence interval analysis [19], we consider the library version combinations induce performance inconsistencies, if

$$\exists Metric_b \mid Metric_v \notin [\bar{x} - z\frac{s}{\sqrt{n}}, \bar{x} + z\frac{s}{\sqrt{n}}] \tag{4.1}$$

where $Metric_b$ and $Metric_v$ denote the *execution time*, *memory usage*, or *competition scores* of baseline and a pipeline variant, respectively; $\bar{x}$ and s are the average value and standard deviation of $Metrics_v$, respectively; and n denotes the total number of pipeline variants. According to the parameter setting and z table provided in approach [20], we calculate the 99.9% confidence interval of the mean, and the z value is taken as 3.29053. Note that *competition scores* (e.g., *Precision* and *Recall*) are the metrics provided by *Kaggle* for evaluating the pipelines' outcomes.

We use *Cohen*'s d [21] to measure how far the performance inconsistent outcomes exceed the confidence interval. According to formula (2), we divide the outcomes into two groups: performance inconsistency group and normal group. *Cohen*'s d is used to describe the standardized mean difference between two group means.

Table 4.3 Statistics of pipeline variants generated by *Piecer*

		#Variants generated by *Rule 1*					#Variants generated by *Rule 2*		
#Pipeline	#Variant	DCO	DCL	FE	MT	ME	Data oriented	Model oriented	Overall architecture
3,380	74,373	357	447	867	4,333	530	12,741	21,359	33,639

Note: *We filtered out the overlapping pipeline variants generated by Rules 1 and 2.*

$$d = \frac{\bar{x_1} - \bar{x_2}}{\sqrt{\frac{(n_1-1)s_1^2+(n_2-1)s_2^2)}{n_1+n_2-2}}} \tag{4.2}$$

In this formula, $\bar{x_1}$ and $\bar{x_2}$ are the mean values of performance inconsistency group and normal group, respectively, n_i is the sample size (i.e., number of outcomes in each group), and s_i is the sample variance of each group. According to approach [22], *Cohen*'s d interprets effect sizes in the meta-analysis: small effect = 0.2–0.5, medium effect = 0.5–0.8, and large effect = 0.8 and higher. In our study, we consider the outcomes with large effect size as the ***significant performance inconsistencies*** induced by pipeline variants.

Our study is conducted on three machines with the same configuration: Intel Xeon Silver 4110 machine with 128 GB RAM, Ubuntu 16.04.7 LTS, and two NVIDIA Tesla V100 GPUs. The comparison experiments took about 8 months for three Ph.D. students to deploy and run the 74,373 variants of 3,380 pipelines.

Results Among the 3,380 pipelines, 1,092 (32.3%) manifest significant performance inconsistencies on at least one variant. 42,488 and 536 variants (involving 2,323 pipelines) induce program crashes and *NaN* bugs, respectively.

Figure 4.5 and Table 4.4 summarize the performance inconsistencies of the 1,092 pipelines. We can observe that:

- For 399, 243, and 440 pipelines, changing the version combinations of ML libraries from the baselines (i.e., the newest versions) could achieve better performances in *competition scores*, *execution time*, and *memory usage*, respectively. The variants of 109 pipeline manifested over 50% of performance differences compared with the baselines. For example, *CFEC#1254* [23] adopts the APIs of library *Sklearn* ***sklearn****.neighbors.KNeighborsClassifier()* and ***sklearn****.naive_bayes.GaussianNB()* in *MT* workflow stage. Combining older version *Sklearn* 0.19.2 with other ML libraries' newest versions, the pipeline achieves significant improvement in *execution time* and *memory usage*, compared with the baseline (22.6 s and 409.8 MB ***vs.*** 451.2 s and 2,337.9 MB).
- For 252, 340, and 209 pipelines, the baselines outperform all the other ML library version combinations in *competition scores*, *execution time*, and *memory usage*, respectively. In 496 pipelines, the newest versions of ML libraries manifested over 50% of performance differences, compared with the average outcomes of variants. For example, *TPS-#839* [24] uses the API of library *Catboost* ***Catboost****.CatBoostRegressor()* in *MT* workflow stage. The baseline significantly outperforms the other pipeline variants in *execution time* (14.0 s ***vs.*** 141.6 s).
- As shown in Table 4.4, compared with baselines, the variants of 1,057 pipelines achieved gain on certain performance metrics, with a drop of other ones. The variants of 141 and 151 pipelines manifest an overall rise and fall in performance metrics, respectively. The results indicate that a significant proportion of performance changes are the issues deserved further investigations, rather than trade-offs between different measurements.

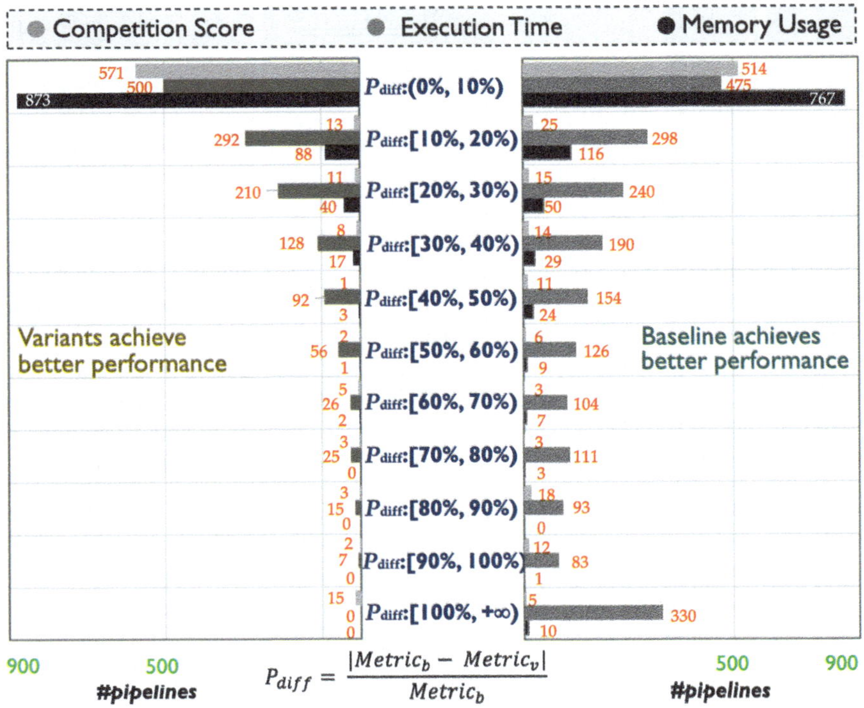

Fig. 4.5 Performance inconsistencies: *Baseline vs. Variants*

Table 4.4 Performance inconsistencies: *Baseline vs. Variants*

Competition Score	Execution Time	Memory Usage	#Pipeline	#Variants
⇑	⇑	⇑	141	596
⇑	⇑	⇓	97	318
⇑	⇓	⇑	158	742
⇑	⇓	⇓	125	471
⇑	⇓	-	143	404
⇑	⇑	-	128	367
⇓	⇑	⇑	144	570
⇓	⇑	⇓	115	329
⇓	⇓	⇑	184	960
⇓	⇓	⇓	151	526
⇓	⇓	-	154	406
⇓	⇑	-	125	346
⇑	-	-	249	587
⇓	-	-	275	614
-	⇑	-	465	1,535
-	⇓	-	597	1,566
-	-	⇑	644	2,488
-	-	⇓	652	2,422

"⇑/⇓" denotes that at least one pipeline variant achieves better/worse performance than the baseline; "-" denotes unchanged performances.

Table 4.5 Impacts of library versions on competition ranking

Competitions	Rise /Fall	#pipeline variants that affect competition rankings									
		R: 0%–10%	*R: 10%–20%*	*R: 20%–30%*	*R: 30%–40%*	*R: 40%–50%*	*R: 50%–60%*	*R: 60%–70%*	*R: 70%–80%*	*R: 80%–90%*	*R: 90%–100%*
Competition 1 [61]	↑	219	5	2	3	17	2	0	0	0	0
	↓	262	0	7	124	0	32	22	0	0	0
Competition 2 [62]	↑	184	67	29	15	3	1	0	1	0	0
	↓	120	38	20	30	8	22	16	5	0	0
Competition 3 [63]	↑	142	38	12	0	0	0	0	0	0	0
	↓	77	21	18	1	2	0	0	0	0	0
Competition 4 [64]	↑	705	17	0	0	0	8	0	2	6	0
	↓	677	35	9	2	0	7	12	0	0	0
Competition 5 [57]	↑	1,144	62	4	13	10	12	35	18	1	0
	↓	1,230	218	81	59	87	110	145	238	45	0
Competition 6 [65]	↑	126	0	0	0	0	0	0	0	0	0
	↓	52	0	71	0	0	0	0	0	0	0
Competition 7 [66]	↑	188	1	0	1	0	0	0	0	11	0
	↓	348	14	10	16	0	1	0	0	0	0
Competition 8 [67]	↑	54	23	18	11	12	0	0	0	0	0
	↓	59	17	5	1	0	4	3	1	0	0
Competition 9 [59]	↑	24	2	2	0	0	0	0	0	0	0
	↓	14	2	2	0	24	0	0	3	0	0
Competition 10 [60]	↑	4	2	3	0	0	0	0	55	0	0
	↓	0	9	0	0	0	0	0	0	0	0

R = ($Rank_b$ - $Rank_v$) / $Rank_b$, where $Rank_b$ and $Rank_v$ are competition rankings of the baseline and variant, respectively.

In general, ML pipelines with different library combinations more easily induce significant inconsistencies of *execution time* and *memory usage*. 60.0% of 653 pipelines still manifest the inconsistencies of *competition scores* on the variants. Table 4.5 illustrates ten competitions whose rankings (determined by competition scores) can be affected by changing the ML library versions in pipelines. Interestingly, we observed that the rankings in *Competitions 5* [25], *9* [26], and *10* [27] even changed dramatically on the pipeline variants. For example, among the 4,668 variants generated by *Piecer* for the 249 pipelines in *Competitions 5* [25], 1,299 and 2,213 variants can cause the rise and fall in ranking, respectively. In particular, MNIST#85 [28] moved up from 201*th* to 5*th* place in the ranking, after changing the versions of libraries Keras 2.7.0 and TensorFlow 2.7.0 to Keras 2.3.1 and TensorFlow 2.1.1, respectively.

Piecer exposed MLC issues in 37 ML libraries, involving 890 APIs. Table 4.6 shows statistics of the ML libraries whose versions significantly affect pipelines' performances. We can observe that:

- The defective ML libraries include both ML frameworks and data science libraries. For each ML library, a proportion of APIs perform best in the newest versions, while the other APIs achieve the optimal performances in their old versions. For example, *TensorFlow* provides 41, 125, and 65 APIs whose newest

Table 4.6 Statistics of the ML libraries whose varied versions significantly affect pipelines' performances

Metrics	Type	ML Libraries × #pipelines	#Problematic APIs				
			DCO	DCL	FE	MT	ME
Competition Score	Baseline better	Pandas × 1, Opencv-python × 1, Nltk × 1, Numpy × 1, Torchvision × 1, Autokeras × 1, Catboost × 2, Sklearn × 39, Keras × 52, Tensorflow × 72	6	3	20	109	6
	Baseline worse	Pandas × 1, Transformers × 1, Numpy × 2, Opencv-python × 2, Sklearn × 9, Keras × 12, Tensorflow × 24	5	4	11	61	4
Execution Time	Baseline better	Scipy × 3, Sklearn × 135, Opencv-python × 18, Nltk × 31, Category_encoders × 13, Numpy × 12 Pandas × 10, Gensim × 3, Transformers × 11, Catboost × 40, Xgboost × 63, TensorFlow × 191 Lightgbm × 58, Keras × 146, Spacy × 22	15	22	80	348	28
	Baseline worse	Autokeras × 1, Torchvision × 3, Numpy × 7, Opencv-python × 7, Catboost × 9, Nltk × 12 Pandas × 18, Keras × 682, Tensorflow × 789, Sklearn × 795	5	14	42	159	14
Memory Usage	Baseline better	Optuna × 1, Spacy × 1, Catboost × 1, Numpy × 2, Nltk × 2, Transformers × 2, Pytorch × 3 Lightgbm × 3, Pandas × 4, Keras × 4, Xgboost × 5, Sklearn × 11,Tensorflow × 14	4	9	16	92	6
	Baseline worse	Keras × 1, Numpy × 1, Xgboost × 1, Pandas × 2, Sklearn × 3	3	4	3	7	5

#pipeline denotes the number of pipelines that adopt the ML libraries.

versions negatively affect the pipelines' *competition scores*, *execution time*, and *memory usage*, respectively. Besides, the three metrics reward the 200 APIs of *TensorFlow* in the newest versions.

- Among the five workflow stages, *MT* involves the most library APIs (479 APIs from 22 libraries) that can induce MLC issues into 892 ML pipelines.

Answer to RQ2: *Among the 3,380 deployable ML pipelines, 1,092 (32.3%) manifest significant performance inconsistencies on at least one variant. For 399, 243, and 440 pipelines, changing the version combinations of ML libraries from the baselines (i.e., the newest versions) could achieve better performances in competition scores, execution time, and memory usage, respectively. For 252, 340, and 209 pipelines, the baselines outperform all the other ML library version combinations in competition scores, execution time, and memory usage, respectively.*
Implication: *Due to the version constraints between dependencies or the limitations of the installation environment, various library version combinations are likely to be adopted in ML pipelines. Understanding their impacts on pipeline performances helps developers avoid MLC issues.*

4.3.4 RQ3: Root Causes of Performance Inconsistencies

Study Methodology To further analyze the root causes of MLC issues, we randomly sampled (a) 294 out of the 1,092 pipelines that induced significant performance inconsistencies after varying library versions, (b) 329 out of the 2,276 pipelines causing crashes, and (c) 42 out of the 47 pipelines inducing *NaN* bugs. This sampling approach [29] guarantees that the root causes distilled from the sampled pipelines can be generalized to the whole dataset with a 95% confidence level and a 5% confidence interval. Specifically, we performed four tasks as follows:

- For each pipeline variant, we identified a collection of ML library APIs $A = \{a_1, a_2, \cdots, a_n\}$ that induced MLC issues, using *Component 3* of *Piecer*. Let $a_1.Libv$ be the ML library version that contains API $a_i \in A$. In total, we obtained 577 APIs from 452 library versions in the 19,048 pipeline variants.
- We performed an in-depth analysis on defective APIs by inspecting their *historical evolution data* across the ML library versions, including release notes, issues, code commits, and code comments (on GitHub repositories). To understand whether the MLC issue of an API $a_i \in A$ was affected by a combination of library versions, we divided the APIs into two groups:
  - ***Group 1***: We consider an MLC issue is ***induced by the individual library***, if it satisfies that (1) the issue is exposed in API $a_i \in A$, and (2) among the library versions used by the pipeline variant, only $a_i.Libv$ is inconsistent with that in baseline. 295 APIs $a_i \in A$ inducing MLC issues in 9,055 pipeline variants fall into *Group 1*. We considered the MLC issues were induced by the evolution of library $a_i.Libv$ and focused on its historical data for inspection.
  - ***Group 2***: As shown in Fig. 4.6, we divided the MLC issues ***induced by combinations of library versions*** into two types:

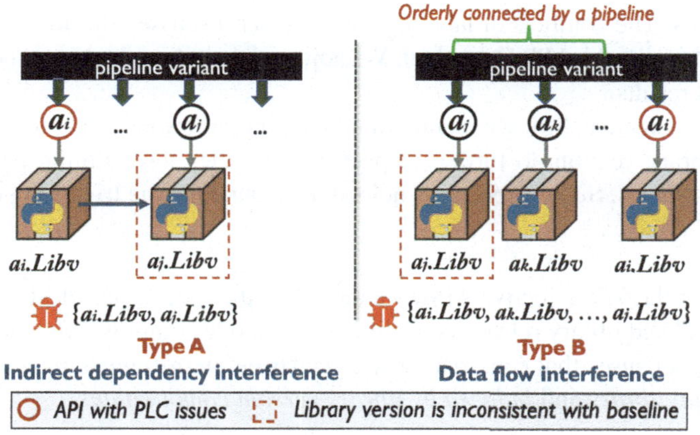

Fig. 4.6 Usage patterns of defective library version combinations

Type A. Suppose a pipeline variant directly uses APIs a_i and a_j from different ML libraries, and a_i transitively invokes the APIs from library $a_j.Libv$. We consider an MLC issue is induced by ***indirect dependency interference***, if it satisfies that (1) the issue is exposed in API $a_i \in A$, and (2) among the library versions used by the pipeline variant, only $a_j.Libv$ is inconsistent with that in baseline. We then consider $\{a_i.Libv, a_j.Libv\}$ is a defective library version combination. For the 98 defective APIs in 3,799 pipeline variants falling into *Type A*, we inspected their historical evolution data.

Type B. Suppose APIs a_j, a_k, $\cdots$, a_u and a_i from different libraries are orderly connected by a pipeline, and the outcomes of APIs a_j, a_k, $\cdots$, a_u can affect the inputs of a_i. We consider an MLC issue is induced by ***data flow interference***, if it satisfies that (1) the issue is exposed in API $a_i \in A$, (2) among the library versions used by the pipeline variant, only $a_j.Libv$ is inconsistent with that in baseline, and (3) a_i does not invoke APIs from $a_j.Libv$. We then consider $\{a_j.Libv, a_k.Libv, \cdots, a_u.Libv, a_i.Libv\}$ is a defective library version combination. We inspected the historical evolution data of defective API a_j and analyzed the impacts of defective library version combination.

- We followed an *open coding procedure* [79], a widely used approach for qualitative research, to distill and categorize the root causes of performance inconsistencies. Initially, two Ph.D. students, who had over 2 years of ML development experience, independently analyzed the release notes, issues, code commits, and code comments of 577 defective APIs across the library versions in variant and baseline. After the first round of analysis and labeling, the two students gathered to compare and discuss their results, in order to adjust the taxonomy, with the help of a third Ph.D. student to resolve conflicts. In this manner, we constructed the pilot taxonomy. This led to a more clear-cut labeling strategy. Next, the first two Ph.D. students continued to label the root causes of the remaining 306 APIs' performance inconsistencies and iteratively refined the results. The conflicts of labeling were further discussed during meetings and resolved by the third Ph.D. student. We adjusted the pilot taxonomy and obtained the final results.
- For each defective API, we identified all the pipeline variants that use it from the same library version, to further inspect whether they have similar performance inconsistencies. Such inspections helped us understand the triggering conditions of MLC issues.

Results For the 577 defective APIs, we identified the root causes of MLC issues by analyzing related library release notes, issues, and code commits. We identified four common root causes that can arise in two scenarios: *performance impacts induced by individual library* and *induced by library version combinations*.

Performance Impacts Induced by Individual ML Library MLC issues of 164 defective APIs were affected by one library version. The issues share four common root causes below.

- ***API Optimization*** (96/164 = 58.5%). For 96 defective APIs, we found descriptions in the historical evolution data for declaring the optimization for *hardware support*, *data processing*, *calculations*, etc. For example, in NLPDT#plyger [30], the memory usage of API ***Transformers****.trainer()* is changed from 2 to 91 MB, when downgrading library ***Transformers*** to 4.11.3 or lower versions. In commit log *7a0adbb* [31], developers stated that they added support for gradient checkpointing in BERT since ***Transformers*** 4.12.0 for optimizing memory performance. The API optimization results in the improvement of execution time (36/96), memory usage (32/96), and competition scores (28/96). On average, the library versions containing nonoptimized APIs still have 45,647 monthly downloads in PyPI.
- ***Default Hyperparameter Changes*** (16/164 = 9.8%). For 16 defective APIs, developers added, deleted, or changed the values of default hyperparameters for training ML models, leading to performance inconsistencies across different library versions. The above clues can be located in the historical evolution data of libraries. For example, the release note [32] of library ***Sklearn*** 0.22.0 states that developers change a default hyperparameter "*gamma*" in API ***Sklearn****.svm.SVC()*. We observed that the accuracy of MNIST#85 [28] rose from 0.143 to 0.986 after upgrading ***Sklearn*** to 0.22.0 or higher versions.

  The symptoms of changing default hyperparameters are manifested as the improvement of execution time (5/16), memory usage (7/16), competition scores (2/16), or cause *NaN* bugs (2/16). For each API with changed default hyperparameters, all the pipeline variants using it could reproduce the symptoms of performance changes, in the cases that developers did not customize the arguments. However, such library versions with poor performances still have 905,851 monthly downloads on average.
- ***Technical Debts*** (5/164 = 3%). For five defective APIs, we found declarations in their code comments stating that there are technical debts in the old library versions. Developers considered them as either experimental APIs or incomplete implementations. For example, in the code comments of API ***Sklearn****.ensemble.HistGradientBoostingClassifier()*, developers explained that they improved this experimental API since ***Sklearn*** 0.24.2. We observed that the memory usage of CFECII#385 [33] reduced from 105 to 55 MB, after upgrading ***Sklearn*** to 0.24.2 or higher versions.

  The symptoms of technical debts are manifested in the bad performance of execution time (2/5), memory usage (2/5), or competition scores (1/5). By inspection, for each API with technical debts, all the pipeline variants adopting it could manifest the similar performance changes. This means that such MLC issues can be easily triggered if any ML pipeline uses our identified defective APIs. On average, the above library versions with technical debts have 589,3827 monthly downloads.
- ***API Breaking Changes*** (47/164 = 28.7%). For 47 defective APIs, developers introduced breaking changes (i.e., *API addition*, *removal*, and *signature changes*) during library evolution. They induced 41,204 crashes and 492 *NaN* bugs in the

pipeline variants. Digging out the above API breaking changes in the popular library versions can help developers avoid compatibility issues.

Performance Impacts Induced by ML Library Version Combinations According to the definition of *Types A* and *B* issues in Group 2, *for the defective library version combinations, the root causes of problems may arise from one ML library, but the MLC issues are actually exposed in the APIs from other libraries, due to the interactions between libraries in the pipelines.* By inspecting historical evolution data of the concerned defective APIs, we observed that the root causes can be *API Optimization, Default Hyperparameter Changes, Technical Debts*, or *API Breaking Changes*. In total, we identified MLC issues in 3,720 pipeline variants that are affected by 106 defective API combinations from different ML library versions.

- *Type A: Indirect Dependency Interference (41/106 = 38.7%).* We located 41 *Type A* library version combinations, involving 57 APIs from 10 ML libraries. 2,511 pipeline variants adopting the defective library version combinations manifested the poor performance of execution time (15/41), memory usage (11/41), competition scores (5/41) or induced crashes (7/41), and *NaN* bugs (3/41). For example, pipeline CFEC#1211 [34] directly depends on ML libraries {***Sklearn*** 1.0.1, ***Pandas*** 0.25.0} in the *MT* stage. The pipeline invokes API ***Sklearn****.logisticRegression()*, which transitively depends on API ***Pandas****.rolling()* from library ***Pandas***. We observed the memory usage of ***Sklearn****.logisticRegression()* changed from 593MB to 1,329MB after downgrading ***Pandas*** to version 0.24.2. After investigation, we found an issue ***Pandas***#25893 [35] that API ***Pandas****.rolling()* suffered from memory bugs in ***Pandas*** 0.24.2. The combination of ***Sklearn*** and ***Pandas*** is used by 19,774 pipelines on *Kaggle*, and 1,616 of them invoke ***Sklearn****.linear_model.logisticRegression()*. Such defective versions are liable to induce MLC issues.
- *Type B: Data Flow Interference (65/106 = 61.3%).* We located 96 *Type B* library version combinations from 4,972 pipeline variants, involving 121 APIs from 15 ML libraries. The above defective library version combinations caused inferior performance of execution time (24/96), memory usage (16/96), competition scores (19/96) or induced crashes (3/96), and *NaN* bugs (3/96). For example, pipeline NLPDT#785 [36] invokes APIs ***Nltk****.stem.porter.PorterStemmer()*, ***Sklearn****.extraction. text.TfidfVectorizer()*, and ***Catboost****.CatBoostClassifier()* from libraries {***Nltk*** 3.6, ***Sklearn*** 1.0.1, ***Catboost*** 1.0.3}. The outcomes of former two APIs can affect the inputs of ***Catboost****.CatBoostClassifier()* via data flow interactions in the pipeline, while the former two APIs are not invoked by the latter one. After downgrading ***Nltk*** to version 3.5, we observed the execution time of ***Catboost****.CatBoostClassifier()* varied from 16 s to 36 s. The combination of ***Nltk***, ***Sklearn***, and ***Catboost*** is adopted by 310 pipelines on *Kaggle*, 42% of them invoked the concerned three APIs. Such MLC issues can be easily triggered since the buggy version ***Nltk*** 3.5 has 831,749 monthly downloads.

Answer to RQ3: *By analyzing the historical evolution data of 577 defective APIs, we identified four types of essential root causes of inducing MLC issues. MLC issues exposed in 164 defective APIs are affected by one library version. MLC issues in 3,720 pipeline variants are caused by combinations of APIs from different library versions.*
Implication: *Future research may focus on designing approaches to detecting and repairing MLC issues by automatically mining and monitoring the evolution of defective ML library APIs.*

4.4 Application of Empirical Findings

Repository of Defective APIs Let a 3-tuple $D =< A, LV, P >$ be a defective API (combination) whose invocation(s) potentially trigger MLC issues, where A denotes the signature(s) of API (combination), LV denotes the defective library version range, and P denotes the aspects of performance changes (e.g., execution time, memory usage, and *Precision*). For example, < {**Nltk**.$stem.porter.PorterStemmer()$, **Catboost**.$CatBoostClassifier()$}, {**Catboost** = 1.0.3, **Nltk** = 3.5}, $Executiontime$ > denotes an API combination of **Nltk**.$stem.$ $porter.PorterStemmer()$ and **Catboost**.$CatBoostClassifier()$ in libraries *Catboost* 1.0.3 and *Nltk* 3.5, respectively, which achieves worse performance in execution time. Based on our empirical findings in RQs1–3, we construct a repository containing 164 defective APIs and 109 API combinations, involving 19 ML libraries. Leveraging the defective API repository, we can capture the MLC issues in real-world ML pipelines and ML libraries. Our study aims to answer the following two research questions:

- **RQ4:** ***Do real-world ML complex pipelines use the identified defective library APIs?***
- **RQ5:** ***Can the repository of defective APIs help capture real MLC issues?***

Experiment Setup To answer RQ4, we collected large-scale representative ML pipelines from GitHub and *Hugging Face* [37] platforms released by leading IT companies (including *Microsoft*, *Google*, *Tencent*, and *Alibaba*) as subjects. The large-scale industrial pipelines typically handle real-world challenging tasks, which are typically more complex than the specific competition tasks implemented by *Kaggle* pipelines. We selected *Hugging Face* platform because it is the most popular AI model repository, where users can share pretrained models, datasets, and demos of ML projects [38, 39]. To achieve this, we formulated search keywords as {***topic***: machine-learning, ***topic***: deep-learning} × {***org***: *Microsoft*, ***org***: *Google*, ***org***: *Tencent*, ***org***: *Aalibaba*}. The search returns 124 and 34 ML pipelines from GitHub and *Hugging Face*, respectively. Table 4.7 shows the statistics of collected large-scale

Table 4.7 Statistics of collected real-world large-scale pipelines

	Stars/downloads			KLOC			# ML libraries			# ML library APIs		
	Min	Max	Avg	Min	Max	Avg	Min	Max	Avg	Min	Max	Avg
GitHub pipelines	9	20,249	1,660	31	2,543,862	59,513	1	18	4	2	1,510	110
Hugging face pipelines	107	6,057,167	262,248	691	447,470	47,653	1	29	6	1	1,499	161

Microsoft: 86 pipelines, *Google*: 48 pipelines, *Tencent*: 5 pipelines, *Alibaba*: 19 pipelines

pipelines. On average, they achieve 1,660 stars on GitHub and 262,248 downloads on *Hugging Face* (popular), have 53,583 KLOC (large in scale), and depend on 5 ML libraries and 136 ML library APIs (complex). As we discussed in Sect. 4.3.1, we face challenges on deploying large-scale pipelines, due to lacking detailed training steps in documentation, complete datasets, or required dependencies. For the collected ML pipelines, we investigate whether they use defective APIs in the problematic library version combinations identified in our repository.

To answer RQ5, we collected 1,064 pipelines as subjects from the 17 competitions hosted between August 1, 2021 and June 1, 2022 on *Kaggle* platform. Eventually, 497 out of 1,064 pipelines have been successfully deployed. Among them, 303 and 194 pipelines invoke 80 (80/164 = 48.8%) defective APIs and 69 (69/106 = 65.1%) API combinations in our repository, respectively. For each pipeline using defective APIs, we checked if the performance inconsistencies, crashes, and *NaN* bugs can be exposed on the corresponding problematic library versions. Since *Kaggle* platform has no issue trackers, we posted the validated results (i.e., performance changes across various library versions) as comments on the pipelines' websites to warn pipeline developers/users against MLC issues. For the 43 defective APIs invoked by 17 pipelines that achieve worse performances on ML libraries' newest versions, we also reported the MLC issues to their issue trackers to ask library developers for validation.

Results of RQ4 Table 4.8 reports the experiment results of RQ4. Among the collected 158 large-scale ML pipelines, 142 (89.9%) of them depend on the identified defective ML library version combinations in our repository, and 69 of them invoke the corresponding defective APIs (combinations). In total, the collected large-scale ML pipelines involve 18 defective library version combinations (75%) and 184 defective APIs (combinations) (67.4%) in our repository. For example, API *cv2.imread*() from library *OpenCV* is used by 19 ML pipelines in *DCO* stage, which may induce significant performance inconsistencies in execution time. The results indicate that our empirical findings identified in *Kaggle* pipelines can scale to more complex industrial pipelines.

Results of RQ5 Table 4.9 reports the statistics of our experiment results. In total, we exposed MLC issues in 309 out of 497 real-world pipelines. 208 (67.3%) of them were induced by one ML library version, while the remaining 101 (32.7%)

Table 4.8 Experiment results of RQ4

	M_1	M_2	M_3	M_4
GitHub pipelines	101	55	18	123
Hugging Face pipelines	31	14	14	73
Sum	142	69	18	184

M_1: *#Pipelines using defective ML library version combinations in our repository*
M_2: *#Pipelines using the defective APIs (combinations) in our repository*
M_3: *#Defective library version combinations used by the pipelines*
M_4: *#Defective APIs (combinations) used by the pipelines*

Table 4.9 Results of RQ5: MLC issues identified in real-world pipelines and ML libraries

309 MLC Issues Identified in Real Pipelines (*#pipeline ID*)		
Performance Impacts Induced by One ML Library Version		#36502↓↓↓, #36523↑↑↑, #36544↓↓, #36567↓↑, #36575↓↑↑, #36577↑↓↑, #36586↓↓, #36590↓, #36594↑, #36600↑↓↑, #36616↑↓↓, #36618↓↓, #36625↑↑↓, #36630↓↑↓, #11094↓↓↓, #11119↑↓, #11167↑↑↓, #11169↑, #31772↓↓↓, #31773↓↓, #31776↑↓↑, #31784↑↑, #31785↓↓↑, #31824↓↓↓, #31856↑↑, #31870↓↓↑, #31883↓, #31902↑↓, #37112↓↑↓, #37117↓↑, #37124↓↑↑, #37258↓↓, #37259↓, #37261↓↓↑, #37297↓↓↓, #37298↑↓, #37317↓↓↓, #37321↓↓↑, #37335↑, #37403↓, #37410↓↓↑, #37426↓↓↓, #36151↓↑↑, #36153↓↓↑, #36169↓↓↓, #36173↓↑↓, #36199↓↓, #36209↓↓, #36237↓↑↑, #36326↓↓, #36333↑, #36335↓, #36471↑↑↑, #36476↓↓, #36488↓↑, #36501↑↑, #36634↓↑↓, #36635↑↑, #36637↑, #36639↑↑, #36641↓↑, #36642↑↓↑, #36647↓↑↑, #36649↓, #36690↑↑↑, #36734↓↑↑, #36916↓↓, #36938↑↓↑, #37107↑↑, #37111↑↑, #33431↑↓, #33445↓↑, #33468↓↑↑, #33472↑↓, #33487↓↓, #33514↓↑↓, #33600↓↓↑, #33602↓, #33603↓↑↑, #33620↓, #33659↑↓↓, #33668↑↓↑, #33704↑↓, #33705↓↓, #33125↑↓, #33129↓↑, #33147↓, #33171↓↑↓, #33176↓↓↑, #33185↓↑, #33194↓↓, #33253↓↓, #33275↓, #33288↓↑, #33325↓↑↓, #33372↓↓, #33377↑↓, #33409↑↓↑, #34197↓↓, #34198↓↓↓, #34207↓↓, #34215↓↑↓, #34220↑↓↓, #34229↑↓, #34241↓↓, #34243↓, #34248↓, #34327↓↓↓, #34328↓, #34331↑, #34333↓↑↑, #31920↓↓↑, #31950↓↑, #31975↓↓↑, #32053↑↑, #32292↑, #32347↓, #32427↑↑↓, #32449↑↑↓, #32532↑, #32564↓, #32569↑↑↑, #32574↓, #32835↓↑, #33123↓↓, #33797↓↓↑, #33801↓↑, #33807↓↓, #33823↑↓↓, #33941↑↓, #33948↑↓↑, #33981↑↑↓, #34150↓↑, #34154↓↑, #34159↑↓↓, #34185↑↑↓, #34186↓↓↓, #34187↓↓↓, #34334↑, #34367↓↑↑, #34388↓, #34442↓, #34463↓↓↑, #34474↑↓↓, #34601↑↑, #34658↓↑↑, #34789↓↓, #35760↑↓, #35776↓, #36124↓↑, #36128↓↓, #36146↓↓, #37445↓↓↓, #37652↓↑↓, #37731↓↑, #38020↑↑↑, #38107↑↓↑, #38150↓, #31915↓↑, #33423↓, #33789↓↑↓, #34767, #34923, #36172, #36252, #36187, #36214, #33335, #11180, #31900, #31947, #31997, #32009, #32253, #32518, #32560, #32566, #32607, #32923, #32928, #33138, #33193, #33335, #33346, #33721, #33724, #33346, #33742, #33754, #33770, #33776, #33790, #33796, #33811, #33812, #33877, #33878, #33913, #33886, #34068, #34116, #34332, #34336, #34352, #37763
Performance Impacts Induced by Combinations of ML Library Versions	***Type A***	#11087↓↓↓, #11166↓↓, #11193↓↓↑, #11195↑↓↑, #11224↓↓, #31751↑↑, #31753↓↑↑, #31770↑↑, #32490↑↑, #33247↑↓↑, #33274↑↑↑, #33302↓↑, #33303↓↓↑, #33329↑↑, #33341↓↓, #33342↓↓↑, #33394↓↑↑, #33395↓↓↑, #33398↑↓↓, #33437↑↓↑, #33439↓↓↑, #33539↓↓↑, #33744↑↑↓, #33805↓↓↓, #33837↑↓↑, #33839↓↓, #33853↑↓↓, #33959↑↓↓, #33963↓↓↓, #33994↓↑, #34177↓↑↑, #34226↓↑↑, #34712↓↓↓, #35699↓↑↑, #36157↑↓↑, #36174↑↓↑, #36188↓↑↓, #36198↓↑↓, #36211↑↓↓, #36265↑↓, #36306↓↑↑, #36316↓↓↓, #36563↑↓↑, #36572↑↑, #36582↓, #36728↑↑↓, #36729↓↓↓, #37061↓↓, #37359↓↑↑, #37448↑↓↓, #37758↓↑, #37832↑↑, #37913↓↑, #36267↓↑↑, #33939↓↓↑, #36267↓↑↑, #36487, #36557, #36624, #36650, #36662, #34249, #34300, #36552
	Type B	#32522↓, #33734↓↑, #33735↓, #33775↓↓↑, #33794↓↓↓, #33850↓↓↑, #33857↓↓, #33896↓, #33910↓↑↓, #33935↓, #34344↑↓↑, #34374↓↓, #34637↑↓, #34646↑↓↓, #34650↑↓, #34693↑↓, #34699↓, #34702↑↓, #36239↑, #36264↑, #36284↓↓, #36574↓↓, #36587↑↓, #36664↑, #36848↓, #37343↑↑, #37360↑↓, #37543↓↓↓, #37552↓↑, #37768↑↓, #37776↑↑, #38067↓↓, #38126↓↓, #38162↑, #38230↑↓, #36695, #36879, #36907, #34299, #34322, #36621
18 MLC Issues Repored to ML libraries (*Report ID, #Problematic APIs*)		
[*Catboost*#2142, 2 APIs]♠,[*ImbalancedLearn*#923, 2 APIs]♠, [*Keras*#17217, 8 APIs]♠, [*OpenCV*#22472, 2 APIs]♠, [*Optuna*#3976, 2 APIs]♠, [*Sklearn*#23427, 3 APIs]♠,[*Xgboost*#8033, 2 APIs]♠,[*CategoryEncoders*#362, 2 APIs]♣,[*CategoryEncoders*#364, 2 APIs]♣,[*LightGBM*#5336, 3 APIs]♣, [*LightGBM*#5475, 3 APIs]♣,[*Sklearn*#24138, 1 APIs]♣, [*Transformers*#18950, 3 APIs]♣, [*Tensorflow*#56600, 4 APIs]♣,[*Tensorflow*#56958, 7 APIs]♣, [*Shap*#2644, 1 APIs]♠, [*Shap*#2644, 1 APIs]♠		

MLC issues were manifested in performance changes (rise↑ / fall↓) of three aspects: Competition scores, Execution time and Memory usage, and Crashes/ NaN bugs; ♠ *Confirmed issues under fixing;* ♣ *Acknowledged by developers (Developers considered the issues were worthy of further investigation);* ♠ *Not bugs;* ♣ *Not bugs in the latest versions;* ♠ *Pending Issues.*

of pipelines were caused by the combinations of ML library versions. The MLC issues involve 58 defective APIs and 42 API combinations. Specifically, 251, 50, and 9 pipelines manifested in performance inconsistencies, crashes, and *NaN* bugs, respectively. We can observe that 188 (37.8%) pipelines invoking the defective API (combination) did not reveal MLC issues. The conditions of triggering such issues may be affected by many factors, such as hyperparameters and dataset size, which deserve further investigations in the future research.

Encouragingly, 20 pipeline developers show their great interests in our detailed diagnosis info of MLC issues generated by *Piecer*. For example, as shown in Fig. 4.7, *Piecer*'s testing results pointed out that the execution time of pipeline *GoogleBrain-VPP*#1686 [40] changed dramatically across different version combinations of ***Sklearn*** and ***Xgboost***. Developers confirmed the issue and left a comment: "*Thanks for this valuable information. I will surely try and compare different versions.*"

For the 43 defective APIs that achieve worse performance on ML libraries' newest versions, we filed them into 17 issue reports on GitHub. Seven (41.2%) of them had been quickly confirmed by developers and were being fixed based on our testing results. Six issues (35.3%) were acknowledged by the developers to be worthy of further investigation. Developers considered Xgboost#8033 were

{Sklearn, xgboost} Versions	Score	Time (ms)	Memory (MB)	{Sklearn, xgboost} Versions	Score	Time (ms)	Memory (MB)
{1.0.1, 1.5.1}	0.622	3755.792	2330.385	{0.22.1, 1.4.2}	0.650	4207.324	2354.084
{1.0.1, 1.2.1}	0.653	3807.698	2649.305	{0.22.1, 1.1.1}	0.652	7974.568	2648.538
{1.0.1, 1.1.1}	0.652	8151.661	2649.224	{0.22.1, 1.0.2}	0.656	7451.785	2647.906
{1.0.1, 1.0.2}	0.656	7783.346	2649.181	{0.22.1, 0.90}	0.654	4743.717	2329.738
{1.0.1, 0.90}	0.654	4634.113	2649.073	{0.22.0, 1.5.1}	0.622	3752.547	2357.178
{0.24.2, 1.5.1}	0.621	3763.312	2330.292	{0.22.0, 1.4.2}	0.650	4168.140	2354.079
{0.24.2, 1.1.1}	0.652	7926.313	2651.979	{0.22.0, 1.0.2}	0.657	7664.165	2647.902
{0.24.2, 1.0.2}	0.655	7645.457	2651.979	{0.22.0, 0.90}	0.654	4683.703	2330.310
{0.22.1, 1.5.1}	0.622	3772.575	2357.182	{0.20.3, 1.0.2}	0.652	406.435	2649.010

Fig. 4.7 An MLC issue *GoogleBrain-VPP*#1686 [40] reported by us

not bugs. They had to improve some aspects of performance at the cost of other metrics. The remaining reports are pending probably because of inactive project maintenance.

For example, we reported an MLC issue to library ***Catboost*** whose API ***Catboost****.CatBoostClassifier()* in the latest version nearly consumes five times memory, compared with that in versions ≤0.10.3. Developers quickly confirmed this issue and commented that "*I could reproduce your results and saw a jump in RAM consumption from 34 MB to 150 MB.*"

The experiment results demonstrate that our defective API repository shed light on designing automated approaches to detecting MLC issues on real-world pipelines and ML libraries.

4.5 Implications

For ML Pipeline Developers Our empirical study reveals the pervasiveness and seriousness of MLC issues in ML pipelines. Developers can utilize *Piecer* or our provided defective API repository to select version combinations of ML libraries when optimizing the performance of their pipelines.

For ML Library Vendors Our empirical findings show that an ML library may achieve worse performance on its latest version when working with other ML libraries in the pipelines. ML library developers should consider common library combinations and perform integration testing before releasing new versions.

For SE Researchers For SE researchers, future research can focus on designing promising techniques to detect and repair MLC issues.

For Tool Builders Tool builders can leverage our defective API repository and *Piecer* to recommend appropriate version combinations of ML libraries to pipeline developers when maintaining/evolving ML libraries.

We hope that this chapter can inspire a symbiotic ecosystem where researchers, tool builders, and library vendors work together to assist developers combat MLC issues.

4.6 Threats to Validity

Internal Validity Our empirical study involved manual effort, which might introduce subjectivity and bias. To mitigate this threat, we followed an open coding scheme where two Ph.D. students independently checked and cross-validated all the results. We employed *Cohen's Kappa* [18] to measure the consistencies between the two students. If the *Kappa* value was less than 0.9, the students needed to discuss to resolve disagreements. To enhance transparency and accountability, we made our dataset publicly accessible for scrutiny.

External Validity The external validity concerns about the generality of our results. To mitigate such a threat, we collected 11,363 high-quality ML pipelines from *Kaggle* platform as subjects to conduct our empirical study. The pipelines depend on 112 popular ML libraries, including 23 ML frameworks and 89 data science libraries. On average, each ML library has 29,156 $\pm$ 338 downstream projects, 4,094,010 $\pm$ 3,285 monthly downloads, 7,460 $\pm$ 121 stars, and 603 $\pm$ 45 issues and 4,358 $\pm$ 198 commits in their GitHub repositories. Besides, we also collected large-scale representative ML pipelines from GitHub and *Hugging Face* [37] platforms released by leading IT companies as subjects, to investigate whether they use defective APIs in the problematic library version combinations identified in our repository. Our empirical findings obtained based on such a representative dataset can be generalized to more ML pipelines.

4.7 Related Work

Machine Learning Libraries There have been a lot of work focusing on the performance enhancement and quality assurance of ML frameworks. Zhang et al. [11] conducted an empirical study on the common bugs of ML applications using *TensorFlow*. Nargiz et al. [41] and Islam et al. [12] further conducted studies on *Keras*, *TensorFlow*, *PyTorch*, *Caffe*, and *Theano* with a taxonomy of bugs. Han et al. [42] performed an exploratory study on the dependency networks of deep learning libraries. They studied the application domains, dependency degrees, and version update behaviors of ML applications that depend on *TensorFlow*, *PyTorch*, and *Theano*. Dilhata et al. [3] conducted a quantitative and qualitative empirical study to investigate the ML library usage and evolution. They only focused on the ML frameworks and explored how developers used these libraries (e.g., common library combinations) and how the usage evolved over the projects' lifetime. Wang et al. [43], Guo et al. [44], and Phamet et al. [45] proposed novel mutation testing/differential techniques to detect behavioral inconsistencies across multiple

ML frameworks. Georgiou et al. [46] presented an in-depth empirical analysis to investigate and compare the energy consumption and runtime performance of DL frameworks (*PyTorch* and *TensorFlow*).

Our study distinguishes from the existing work in three aspects: (1) We focus on various types of common ML libraries including both ML frameworks and data science libraries, (2) we conduct the first empirical study to explore the impacts of different library version combinations on ML pipelines' performances, and (3) with the aid of our identified defective API repository, we detect many MLC issues in real-world ML applications.

Machine Learning Applications Several SE researchers presented comprehensive empirical studies on real bugs and technical challenges of ML applications. Islam et al. [47], Guo et al. [48], Han et al. [49], Zhang et al. [50], and Chen et al. [51] collected a set of high-quality DL questions and answers on Stack Overflow and summarized the main challenges in developing and deploying ML applications, respectively. Approaches [52, 53] presented a root cause taxonomy of deep learning specific failures to facilitate future software development. Shen et al. [54] studied the bugs rising in the popular deep learning compilers and provided a series of valuable guidelines for deep learning compiler bug detection and debugging. Phamet et al. [55] studied the variance of DL systems and the awareness of this variance among researchers and practitioners. Existing and new testing techniques [56–75] were also proposed for and adapted to machine learning applications to expose real bug. The works by Ma et al. [76, 77] and Shen et al. [78] proposed mutation operators specific to deep learning applications. Humbatova et al. [56] followed a systematic process to extract mutation operators from existing bug taxonomies to simulate the effects of real DL bugs. In this chapter, we capture the performance inconsistencies of ML pipelines using differential testing across various library version combinations.

4.8 Conclusion and Future Work

In this chapter, we empirically studied 11,363 ML pipelines from diverse competitions on *Kaggle* to explore the impacts of different ML library version combinations on their performances. Our study reveals the pervasiveness and severity of MLC issues in ML pipelines. Our findings can motivate the establishment of a symbiotic ecosystem where researchers, tool builders, and library vendors work together to assist developers in combating MLC issues.

References

1. Liu C, Gao C, Xia X, Lo D, Grundy J, Yang X. On the reproducibility and replicability of deep learning in software engineering. ACM Trans Softw Eng Methodol. 2021;31(1):1–46. https://doi.org/10.1145/3477535

2. Lu Q, Zhu L, Xu X, Whittle J, Xing Z. Towards a roadmap on software engineering for responsible AI. In: Proceedings of the 1st international conference on AI engineering: software engineering for AI; 2022. p. 101–112. https://doi.org/10.1145/3522664.3528607
3. Dilhara M, Ketkar A, Dig D. Understanding software2.0: a study of machine learning library usage and evolution. ACM Trans Softw Eng Methodol. 2021;30(4):1–42. https://doi.org/10.1145/3453478
4. Liblit B, Luo L, Ramirez AM, Mukherjee R, Patterson Z, Piskachev G, Schäf M, Tripp O, Visser W. Shifting left for early detection of machine-learning bugs. In: International symposium on formal methods. https://doi.org/10.1007/978-3-031-27481-7-33
5. Xiu M, Jiang ZMJ, Adams B. An exploratory study of machine learning model stores. IEEE Softw. 2020;38(1):114–122. https://doi.org/10.1109/MS.2020.2975159
6. 2021. Scikit-Learn. https://scikit-learn.org/stable/. Accessed: 01 Aug 2021.
7. 2021. PyTorch. https://pytorch.org/. Accessed: 01 Aug 2021.
8. 2021. Matplotlib. https://matplotlib.org/. Accessed: 01 Aug 2021.
9. 2021. Pandas. https://pandas.pydata.org/. Accessed: 01 Aug 2021.
10. 2021. Numpy. https://numpy.org/. Accessed: 01 Aug 2021.
11. Guo Q, Chen S, Xie X, Ma L, Hu Q, Liu H, Liu Y, Zhao J, Li X. An empirical study towards characterizing deep learning development and deployment across different frameworks and platforms. In: 2019 34th IEEE/ACM international conference on automated software engineering (ASE). IEEE; 2019. p. 810–822. https://doi.org/10.1109/ASE.2019.00080
12. Islam MJ, Nguyen G, Pan R, Rajan H. A comprehensive study on deep learning bug characteristics. In Proceedings of the 2019 27th ACM joint meeting on european software engineering conference and symposium on the foundations of software engineering; 2019. p. 510–520. https://doi.org/10.1145/3338906.3338955
13. 2022. MNIST. https://www.kaggle.com/c/Kannada-MNIST. Accessed: 01 Jul 2022.
14. 2022. Sklearn#20642. https://github.com/scikit-learn/scikit-learn/issues/20642. Accessed: 01 Jul 2022.
15. 2021. Kaggle. https://www.kaggle.com/. Accessed: 01 Aug 2021.
16. 2021. A ranked list of awesome ML library. https://github.com/ml-tooling/bestof-ml-python. Accessed: 01 Aug 2021.
17. 2021. Kaggle. https://jedi.readthedocs.io//. Accessed: 01 Aug 2021.
18. Viera AJ, Garrett JM, et al. Understanding interobserver agreement: the kappa statistic. Fam Med. 2005;37(5):360–63.
19. Loftus GR, Masson MEJ. Using confidence intervals in within-subject designs. Psychon Bull Rev. 1994;1(4):476–490. https://doi.org/10.3758/BF03210951
20. Yin C, Li B, Yin Z. A distributed sensing data anomaly detection scheme. Comput Secur. 2020;97:101960. https://doi.org/10.1016/j.cose.2020.101960
21. Cohen J. Statistical power analysis for the behavioral sciences. Milton Park: Routledge; 2013. https://doi.org/10.4324/9780203771587
22. Sawilowsky SS. New effect size rules of thumb. J Modern Appl Stat Methods 2009;8(2):6. https://doi.org/10.22237/jmasm/1257035100
23. 2022. CFEC#1254. https://www.kaggle.com/dskagglemt/categorical-featureencoding-challenge. Accessed: Jul 2022.
24. 2022. TPS-Jul#839. https://www.kaggle.com/code/tps-july-2021-simple-fastcode. Accessed: 01 Jul 2022.
25. 2022. Competition 5. https://www.kaggle.com/c/Kannada-MNIST. Accessed: 01 Jul 2022.
26. 2022. Competition 9. https://www.kaggle.com/c/optiver-realized-volatility-prediction. Accessed: 01 Jul 2022.
27. 2022. Competition 10. https://www.kaggle.com/c/champs-scalar-coupling. Accessed: 01 Jul 2022.
28. 2022. MNIST#85. https://www.kaggle.com/joesmithkaggle/the-simple-kernelfor-kannada-mnist. Accessed: 01 Jul 2022.
29. Krejcie RV, Morgan DW. Determining sample size for research activities. Edu Psychol. Measurem. 1970;30(3):607–610. https://doi.org/10.1177/001316447003000308

30. 2022. NLPDT#plyger. https://www.kaggle.com/code/plyger/notebook268f8a3109/notebook. Accessed: 01 Jul 2022.
31. 2022. Commit log 7a0adbb. https://github.com/huggingface/transformers/pull/4659/commits/7a0adbb56ae719a784f781bb2d80edf856e71916. Accessed: 01 Jul 2022.
32. 2022. Release note of Sklearn 0.22.0. https://scikit-learn.org/stable/modules/generated/sklearn.svm.SVC.html. Accessed: 01 Jul 2022.
33. 2022. CFECII#385. https://www.kaggle.com/nandhuelan/let-s-tickle-the-catmeow. Accessed: 01 Jul 2022.
34. 2022. CFEC#1211. https://www.kaggle.com/code/nandhuelan/catembed/notebook. Accessed: 01 Jul 2022.
35. 2022. Issue Pandas#25893. https://www.kaggle.com/dskagglemt/categoricalfeature-encoding-challenge. Accessed: Jul 2022.
36. 2022. NLPDT#785. https://www.kaggle.com/code/onuraydere/decisiontreeandbernoullinb. Accessed: 01 Jul 2022.
37. 2021. Hugging Face. https://huggingface.co/models. Accessed: 01 Aug 2021.
38. Wolf T, Debut L, Sanh V, Chaumond J, Delangue C, Moi A, Cistac P, Rault T, Louf R, Funtowicz M, et al. Transformers: state-of-the-art natural language processing. In: Proceedings of the 2020 conference on empirical methods in natural language processing: system demonstrations; 2020. p. 38–45. https://doi.org/10.18653/v1/2020.emnlp-demos.6
39. Tunstall L, Von Werra L, Wolf T. Natural language processing with transformers. Sebastopol: "O'Reilly Media"; 2022.
40. 2022. GoogleBrain-VPP#1686. https://www.kaggle.com/code/ranjeetshrivastav/ventilator-pressure-prediction-xgboost/comments. Accessed: 01 Jul 2022.
41. Humbatova N, Jahangirova G, Bavota G, Riccio V, Stocco A, Tonella P. Taxonomy of real faults in deep learning systems. In: Proceedings of the ACM/IEEE 42nd international conference on software engineering; 2020. p. 1110–1121. https://doi.org/10.1145/3377811.3380395
42. Han J, Deng S, Lo D, Zhi C, Yin J, Xia X. An empirical study of the dependency networks of deep learning libraries. In: 2020 IEEE international conference on software maintenance and evolution (ICSME). IEEE; 2020. p. 868–878. https://doi.org/10.1109/ICSME46990.2020.00116
43. Wang Z, Yan M, Chen J, Liu S, Zhang D. Deep learning library testing via effective model generation. In: Proceedings of the 28th ACM joint meeting on european software engineering conference and symposium on the foundations of software engineering; 2020. p. 788–799. https://doi.org/10.1145/3368089.3409761
44. Guo Q, Xie X, Li Y, Zhang X, Liu Y, Li X, Shen C. Audee: automated testing for deep learning frameworks. In: 2020 35th IEEE/ACM international conference on automated software engineering (ASE). IEEE; 2020. p. 486–498. https://doi.org/10.1145/3324884.3416571
45. Pham HV, Lutellier T, Qi W, Tan L. CRADLE: cross-backend validation to detect and localize bugs in deep learning libraries. In: 2019 IEEE/ACM 41st international conference on software engineering (ICSE). IEEE; 2019. p. 1027–1038. https://doi.org/10.1109/ICSE.2019.00107
46. Georgiou S, Kechagia M, Sharma T, Sarro F, Zou Y. Green AI: do deep learning frameworks have different costs? In: Proceedings of the 44th international conference on software engineering; 2022. p. 1082–1094. https://doi.org/10.1145/3510003.3510221
47. Islam MJ, Pan R, Nguyen G, Rajan H. Repairing deep neural networks: fix patterns and challenges. In: Proceedings of the ACM/IEEE 42nd international conference on software engineering; 2020. p. 1135–1146. https://doi.org/10.1145/3377811.3380378
48. Guo Q, Chen S, Xie X, Ma L, Hu Q, Liu H, Liu Y, Zhao J, Li X. An empirical study towards characterizing deep learning development and deployment across different frameworks and platforms. In: 2019 34th IEEE/ACM international conference on automated software engineering (ASE). IEEE; 2019. p. 810–822. https://doi.org/10.1109/ASE.2019.00080
49. Han J, Shihab E, Wan Z, Deng S, Xia X. What do programmers discuss about deep learning frameworks. Empir Softw Eng. 2020;25:2694–747. https://doi.org/10.1007/s10664-020-09819-6

50. Zhang T, Gao C, Ma L, Lyu M, Kim M. An empirical study of common challenges in developing deep learning applications. In: 2019 IEEE 30th international symposium on software reliability engineering (ISSRE); 2019. p. 104–115. https://doi.org/10.1109/ISSRE.2019.00020
51. Chen Z, Cao Y, Liu Y, Wang H, Xie T, Liu X. A comprehensive study on challenges in deploying deep learning based software. In: Proceedings of the 28th ACM joint meeting on european software engineering conference and symposium on the foundations of software engineering; 2020. p. 750–762. https://doi.org/10.1145/3368089.3409759
52. Han J, Deng S, Lo D, Zhi C, Yin J, Xia X. An empirical study of the dependency networks of deep learning libraries. In: 2020 IEEE international conference on software maintenance and evolution (ICSME). IEEE; 2020. p. 868–878. https://doi.org/10.1109/ICSME46990.2020.00116
53. Liang Y, Lin Y, Song X, Sun J, Feng Z, Dong JS. gDefects4DL: a dataset of general real-world deep learning program defects. In: Proceedings of the ACM/IEEE 44th international conference on software engineering: companion proceedings; 2022. p. 90–94. https://doi.org/10.1145/3510454.3516
54. Shen Q, Ma H, Chen J, Tian Y, Cheung S-C, Chen X. A comprehensive study of deep learning compiler bugs. In: Proceedings of the 29th ACM joint meeting on european software engineering conference and symposium on the foundations of software engineering; 2021. p. 968–980. https://doi.org/10.1145/3468264.3468591
55. Pham HV, Qian S, Wang J, Lutellier T, Rosenthal J, Tan L, Yu Y, Nagappan N. Problems and opportunities in training deep learning software systems: an analysis of variance. In: Proceedings of the 35th IEEE/ACM international conference on automated software engineering; 2020. p. 771–783. https://doi.org/10.1145/3324884.3416545
56. Humbatova N, Jahangirova G, Tonella P. DeepCrime: mutation testing of deep learning systems based on real faults. In: Proceedings of the 30th ACM SIGSOFT international symposium on software testing and analysis; 2021. p. 67–78. https://doi.org/10.1145/3460319.3464825
57. Riccio V, Jahangirova G, Stocco A, Humbatova N, Weiss M, Tonella P. Testing machine learning based systems: a systematic mapping. Empir Softw Eng. 2020;25:5193–254. https://doi.org/10.1007/s10664-020-09881-0
58. Hu Q, Guo Y, Xie X, Cordy M, Ma L, Papadakis M, Le Traon Y. Efficient testing of deep neural networks via decision boundary analysis. arXiv preprint arXiv:2207.10942 (2022). https://doi.org/10.48550/arXiv.2207.10942
59. Tambon F, Khomh F, Antoniol G. A probabilistic framework for mutation testing in deep neural networks. Inf Softw Technol. 2023;155:107129. https://doi.org/10.1016/j.infsof.2022.107129
60. Wei M, Huang Y, Yang J, Wang J, Wang S. Cocofuzzing: testing neural code models with coverage-guided fuzzing. IEEE Trans Reliabil. 2022;72:1276–89. https://doi.org/10.1109/TR.2022.3208239
61. Zhang JM, Harman M, Ma L, Liu Y. Machine learning testing: survey, landscapes and horizons. IEEE Trans Softw Eng. 2020;48:1–36. https://doi.org/10.1109/TSE.2019.2962027
62. Pei K, Cao Y, Yang J, Jana S. DeepXplore: automated whitebox testing of deep learning systems. In: Proceedings of the 26th symposium on operating systems principles; 2017. p. 1–18. https://doi.org/10.1145/3132747.3132785
63. Tian Y, Pei K, Jana S, Ray B. DeepTest: automated testing of deep-neural-network-driven autonomous cars. In: Proceedings of the 40th international conference on software engineering, 2018. p. 303–314. https://doi.org/10.1145/3180155.3180220
64. Ma L, Juefei-Xu F, Zhang F, Sun J, Xue M, Li B, Chen C, Su T, Li L, Liu Y, et al. DeepGauge: multi-granularity testing criteria for deep learning systems. In: Proceedings of the 33rd ACM/IEEE international conference on automated software engineering; 2018. p. 120–131. https://doi.org/10.1145/3238147.3238202
65. Sun Y, Wu M, Ruan W, Huang X, Kwiatkowska M, Kroening D. Concolic testing for deep neural networks. In: Proceedings of the 33rd ACM/IEEE international conference on automated software engineering; 2018. p. 109–119. https://doi.org/10.1145/3238147.3238172

66. Zhang M, Zhang Y, Zhang L, Liu C, Khurshid S. DeepRoad: GAN-based metamorphic testing and input validation framework for autonomous driving systems. In: 2018 33rd IEEE/ACM international conference on automated software engineering (ASE). IEEE; 2018. p. 132-142. https://doi.org/10.1145/3238147.3238187
67. Kim J, Feldt R, Yoo S. Guiding deep learning system testing using surprise adequacy. In: 2019 IEEE/ACM 41st international conference on software engineering (ICSE). IEEE; 2019. p. 1039–1049. https://doi.org/10.1109/ICSE.2019.00108
68. Xie X, Ma L, Juefei-Xu F, Xue M, Chen H, Liu Y, Zhao J, Li B, Yin J, See S. DeepHunter: a coverage-guided fuzz testing framework for deep neural networks. In: Proceedings of the 28th ACM SIGSOFT international symposium on software testing and analysis; 2019. p. 146–157. https://doi.org/10.1145/3293882.3330579
69. Du X, Xie X, Li Y, Ma L, Liu Y, Zhao J. DeepStellar: model-based quantitative analysis of stateful deep learning systems. In: Proceedings of the 2019 27th ACM joint meeting on european software engineering conference and symposium on the foundations of software engineering; 2019. p. 477–487. https://doi.org/10.1145/3338906.3338954
70. Xie X, Ma L, Wang H, Li Y, Liu Y, Li X. DiffChaser: detecting disagreements for deep neural networks. In: International joint conferences on artificial intelligence organization; 2019. https://doi.org/10.24963/ijcai.2019/800
71. Ma L, Juefei-Xu F, Xue M, Li B, Li L, Liu Y, Zhao J. DeepCT: tomographic combinatorial testing for deep learning systems. In: 2019 IEEE 26th international conference on software analysis, evolution and reengineering (SANER). IEEE; 2019. p. 614–618. https://doi.org/10.1109/SANER.2019.8668044
72. Deng Y, Yang C, Wei A, Zhang L. Fuzzing deep-learning libraries via automated relational API inference. In: Proceedings of the 30th ACM joint european software engineering conference and symposium on the foundations of software engineering; 2022. p. 44–56. https://doi.org/10.1145/3540250.3549085
73. Braiek HB, Khomh F. DeepEvolution: a search-based testing approach for deep neural networks. In: 2019 IEEE international conference on software maintenance and evolution (ICSME). IEEE; 2019. p. 454–458. https://doi.org/10.1109/ICSME.2019.00078
74. Zhou J, Li F, Dong J, Zhang H, Hao D. Costeffective testing of a deep learning model through input reduction. In: 2020 IEEE 31st international symposium on software reliability engineering (ISSRE). IEEE; 2020. p. 289–300. https://doi.org/10.1109/ISSRE5003.2020.00035
75. Hong Kang J, Rattanukul P, Haryono SA, Nguyen TG, Ragkhitwetsagul C, Pasareanu C, Lo D. SkipFuzz: active learning-based input selection for fuzzing deep learning libraries. arXiv preprint arXiv:2212.04038 (2022). https://doi.org/10.48550/arXiv.2212.04038
76. Ma L, Zhang F, Sun J, Xue M, Li B, Juefei-Xu F, Xie C, Li L, Liu Y, Zhao J, et al. DeepMutation: Mutation testing of deep learning systems. In: 2018 IEEE 29th international symposium on software reliability engineering (ISSRE). IEEE; 2018. p. 100–111. https://doi.org/10.1109/ISSRE.2018
77. Hu Q, Ma L, Xie X, Yu B, Liu Y, Zhao J. DeepMutation++: a mutation testing framework for deep learning systems. In: 2019 34th IEEE/ACM international conference on automated software engineering (ASE). IEEE; 2019. p. 1158–1161. https://doi.org/10.1109/ASE.2019.00126
78. Shen W, Wan J, Chen Z. Munn: mutation analysis of neural networks. In: 2018 IEEE international conference on software quality, reliability and security companion (QRS-C). IEEE; 2018. p. 108–115. https://doi.org/10.1109/QRS-C.2018.00032
79. Creswell JW. Qualitative inquiry and research design: choosing among five approaches. 3rd ed. London: Sage Publications; 2013. https://doi.org/10.1177/1524839915580941

Chapter 5
Diagnosing NuGet Dependency Conflicts

Abstract Developers usually suffer from **d**ependency **c**onflict (DC) issues, i.e., package dependency constraints are violated when a project's platform or dependencies are changed. This problem is especially serious in .NET ecosystem due to its fragmented platforms (e.g., .NET Framework, .NET Core, and .NET Standard). Fixing DC issues is challenging due to the complexity of dependency constraints: Multiple DC issues often occur in one project, solving one DC issue usually causes another DC issue cropping up, and the exponential search space of possible dependency combinations is also a barrier.

In this chapter, we aim to help .NET developers tackle the DC issues. First, we empirically studied a set of real DC issues, learning their common fixing strategies and developers' preferences in adopting these strategies. Based on these findings, we propose *NuFix*, an automated technique to repair DC issues. *NuFix* formulates the repair task as a binary integer linear optimization problem to effectively derive an optimal fix in line with the learnt developers' preferences. The experiment results and expert validation show that *NuFix* can generate high-quality fixes for all the DC issues with 262 popular .NET projects. Encouragingly, 20 projects (including affected projects such as `Dropbox`) have approved and merged our generated fixes and shown great interests in our technique.

5.1 Introduction

.NET is an open-source development platform for building various types of projects (e.g., mobile apps, microservices) implemented using C#, F#, and VB [2]. Microsoft provides a tool, NuGet, for building projects and sharing packages on multiple .NET platforms at a central repository *nuget.org* [3]. As of August 2021, *nuget.org* maintains over 3 million package versions.

With the rapid evolution of the .NET ecosystem, managing dependencies in .NET projects becomes a critical challenge. This is mainly due to the fragmentation of .NET ecosystem, which makes dependency constraints between packages especially complicated: (1) There are nine actively used and updated platform variations (e.g., .NET Framework, .NET Core), involving 220 platform versions [4]. Most .NET

Y. Wang et al., *Managing Software Supply Chains*,
https://doi.org/10.1007/978-981-96-1797-5_5

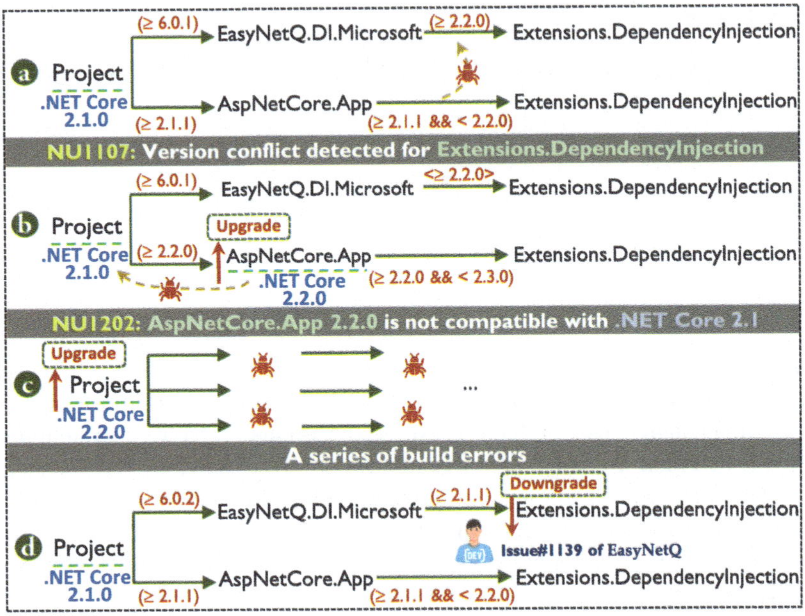

Fig. 5.1 An illustrative example of issue#1139 [5] in `EasyNetQ`

packages are specified to some target platform versions while incompatible with other ones. (2) At different target platform versions, a package typically requires different transitive dependencies. As a package evolves, new versions may require different dependencies or support different target platforms.

Due to fragmentation of .NET ecosystem, a project's dependency graph can be greatly changed when developers upgrade/migrate its .NET platform or depended packages. These changes can easily introduce build errors. Based on NuGet's build rules, the package installations of a project will be blocked if there are conflicting constraints (e.g., constraints on package versions and target platforms) imposed by the project or its depended packages. In this chapter, we refer to such build errors as ***dependency maze*** (DC) issues.

Figure 5.1 shows a real DC issue and illustrates the complication in fixing it. In Fig. 5.1a, a .NET project received a build error when upgrading its direct dependency `EasyNetQ.DI` to version 6.0.1. This is because the upgrade introduced a new dependency of `DependencyInjection` version (≥2.2.0). The new dependency, however, conflicted with the dependency of `DependencyInjection` version (≥2.1.1 && <2.2.0) introduced by `AspNetCore.App`. As a result, the upgrade failed with an error code of NU1107.

To resolve the conflicts, developers first tried to upgrade `AspNetCore.App` to version 2.2.0, which depends on a newer `DependencyInjection` version (≥2.2.0 && <2.3.0) as shown in Fig. 5.1b. However, a new DC issue arose because `AspNetCore.App` 2.2.0 targets .NET Core 2.2.0 platform, which is incompatible with the project's target platform .NET Core 2.1.0. Therefore, they had to upgrade project's target platform to .NET Core 2.2.0 to resolve such a conflict as shown in Fig. 5.1c. However, the platform upgrade induced many changes to the project's dependencies.

A series of new build errors arose. It is difficult to figure out a solution to resolve all these DC issues, the developers finally rolled back all the changes and filed an issue report #1139 [5] to `EasyNetQ.DI`'s developers, seeking for assistance to downgrade its dependency of `DependencyInjection` to ($\geq$2.1.1)) as shown in Fig. 5.1d. The example illustrates the complexity of DC issues. It also shows that DC issues can manifest themselves in multiple types with respect to different root causes (see Sect. 5.2.2).

Fixing a DC issue can be challenging. Multiple DC issues often occur in a project at the same time. For those projects with large dependency graphs, fixing such issues is a time-consuming and error-prone process that exercises a series of changes in dependency constraints in response to newly induced DC issues.

Among our collected 169 DC issue reports from 500 representative .NET projects, 42.6% of them involve more than five simultaneous build errors (error count varied from 1 to 150), and 24.9% of them involve more than two error types (see Sect. 3.1). Out of the 169 issues, 124 have documented fixes. On average, each fix requires a combination of 8.8 dependency changes, and each change involves 27.5 possible choices in package version constraints, which involves a large solution search space. More importantly, when deciding a fixing solution, developers often consider their desired properties of configuration (e.g., inducing fewer risky build warnings), which are echoed by the discussions in many issues such as #5696 of `aspnetcore` [6]. However, it is difficult for developers to imagine all possible dependency graphs affected by dependency changes, to figure out an optimal solution that satisfies their preferences.

In this chapter, we aim to develop a technique to help .NET developers tackle DC issues. We can formulate a DC issue scenario (including installed and available package versions and user upgrade requirements), build rules, and developers' preferences as a linear optimization problem to find feasible DC issue fixing solutions. To achieve this, three technical challenges should be carefully studied: (1) How to formally define the configuration preferences in line with .NET developers' practices, (2) how to rigorously assign weights for the preferences encoded in a linear programming model, and (3) how to find an acceptable fixing solutions that can induce build warnings (based on NuGet's build rules) if the fully safe solutions do not exist. The existing work [7] adopted a linear programming model to resolve the package upgradeability problem for GNU/Linux-based distributions. However, it cannot be directly adapted to repair DC issues since the three challenges are still unresolved in this approach (see baseline comparisons in Sect. 5.2).

To address the above challenges, we propose an effective technique, *NuFix*, to repair DC issues. *NuFix* is built on top of our comprehensive study of developers' preferences in fixing DC issues.

Since deriving a developer preferred solution typically requires rich domain knowledge of dependency configurations, we first empirically studied a collection of real DC issue reports, to learn the characteristics of fixing strategies. By encoding the empirical findings into a linear optimization model, *NuFix* seeks for the global optimal fixing solution.

Furthermore, we proposed a variant optimization model based on NuGet's build rules, to seek an optimal sub-solution when a fully safe solution does not exist. Finally, we collected a set of real documented fixes of DC issues by .NET developers as a training dataset to learn the role played by each preference in determining a solution.

Our evaluation shows that *NuFix* can generate high-quality fixes for the DC issues with 262 popular .NET projects.

We invited ten experienced .NET experts working at Microsoft to evaluate the quality of our generated fixes. Their feedback indicates that the generated fixes meet the developers' desired properties for the build management. In particular, we further reported our generated fixes to the corresponding project developers for validation. Encouragingly, 20 project developers (including affected projects such as `Dropbox` [8]) have replaced their real fixes with the ones derived by *NuFix* and shown great interests in our technique.

5.2 Background

5.2.1 Fragmentation of .NET Ecosystem

Two types of fragmentations exist in the .NET ecosystem.

- ***Platform-level fragmentation.*** .NET supports nine platform variations, which are actively updated. For instance, five .NET platforms, including .NET Framework, .NET Core, .NET Standard, Mono, and Universal Windows Platform (UWP), were introduced to support Windows OS. By August 2021, the five platforms have released 60 versions [4]. Two evolution characteristics across these versions lead to the platform-level fragmentation problem:

  (1) *Installing a different .NET platform version can introduce changes in transitive package dependencies with specific version constraints to a project's local environment.* Figure 5.2a gives an example of the change in transitive dependencies introduced by .NET core platform to the local environment from 38 packages to 3 packages after upgrading the platform from version 1.1.1 to 2.1.0.
  (2) *A .NET platform may be incompatible with the packages that target other .NET platforms or other versions of the same .NET platform.* For instance, packages targeting one of the four platforms, including .NET Framework, .NET Core, Mono, and UWP, are incompatible with the other three platforms. As shown in Fig. 5.2b, package `Log4net` 2.0.12 is incompatible with .NET Core, since it only supports the .NET Framework ≤ 4.0. To broaden

the .NET package ecosystem, since 2016, Microsoft introduced .NET Standard platform for package developers, to provide a unified class library that is available for different .NET variations. Hence the packages targeting .NET Standard can be installed on multiple platforms. Nevertheless, the uniformity of ecosystem has not been realized, since each .NET Standard version only supports limited versions of .NET platforms. Figure 5.2c gives an illustrative example. Based on .NET Standard's documentation [9], a package targeting .NET Standard 2.1 can be installed on .NET Core 3.0 and 3.1, Mono 6.4, and UWP TBD, while it is incompatible with other platforms.

- ***Package-level fragmentation.*** Packages in the .NET ecosystem are mostly platform-specific, which target only specific versions of some .NET platform variants. Each package version provides an isolated *assembly* for each supported platform version. When building a package version, NuGet selectively installs an assembly compatible with the target .NET platform version. The set of dependencies required by each isolated assembly varies. Consider package `Nlog` 4.7.0 described in Fig. 5.2d. Its assemblies that target .NET Framework 3.5 and 4.0 require no dependencies, whereas its assemblies that target .NET Standard 1.3 and 1.5 require three and six different dependencies, respectively. Moreover, different versions of a package may (1) provide assemblies requiring different dependencies for the same target platform and (2) support different .NET platforms. For instance, `Nlog` 4.6.6 and `Nlog` 4.6.7 require different dependencies for the same target platform .NET Standard 1.5. In another example, the upgrade of `RF.Contracts` from 4.3.0 to 4.3.1 migrates its target platform from .NET Standard 2.1 to .NET 5.0. These package characteristics induce many variations across various .NET platforms.

5.2.2 *NuGet Dependency Maze*

We briefly describe the DC issues numbered by NuGet:

- NU1605 (*Downgrading dependency due to the direct dependency priority rule*): Suppose that different version constraints of the same package are introduced into a project as a direct dependency and transitive dependencies, respectively. Based on NuGet's *direct dependency priority* rule, it installs such a package based on the direct dependency's version constraint. NuGet will report an NU1605 error, if the resolved package version is lower than its transitively introduced version constraint(s).
- NU1107 (*Unable to resolve dependency constraints between transitive packages*): If different version constraints of the same package are introduced into a project as transitive dependencies, NuGet will report an NU1107 error when it cannot resolve a version satisfying all the constraints of conflicting dependencies.

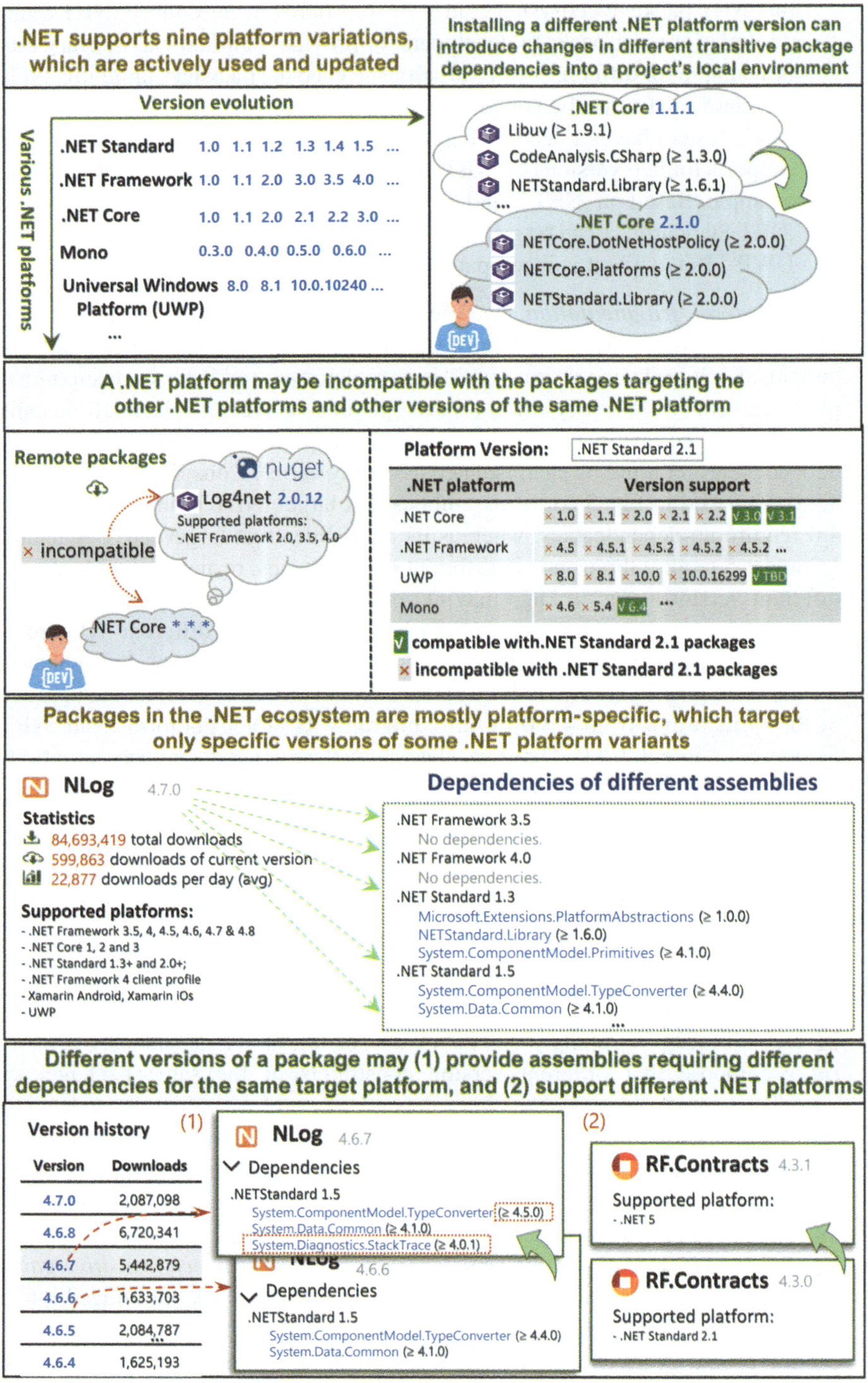

Fig. 5.2 The severity of fragmentation in the .NET ecosystem

- NU1202 (*Package does not contain any assemblies compatible with the client project's target platform*): If a package does not contain any assemblies compatible with the client project's target platform, NuGet will report an NU1202 error when installing it.
- NU1203 (*Package does not support the OS where the client project runs*): .NET packages can use configuration attribute *Runtime Identifier* to designate on which OS they can be installed. NuGet will report an NU1203 error, if the *Runtime Identifier* of a required assembly is inconsistent with the OS where client project runs.
- NU1108 (*Circular dependency is not allowed*): NuGet will report an NU1108 error, if a circular dependency (e.g., $\text{PKG}_a \rightarrow \text{PKG}_b \rightarrow \text{PKG}_a$) is introduced into the project.

5.3 Empirical Study

We empirically study the characteristics of DC issue fixing solutions, with the aim to answer two research questions:

- **RQ1 (Fixing Strategies):** *What are common practices for fixing DC issues? What are challenges of figuring out a fix?*
- **RQ2 (Configuration Preferences):** *What are developers' preferences when determining fixes for DC issues?*

To answer RQ1-2, we collected top popular 3,000 .NET projects on GitHub (by *Star* count) and randomly selected 500 subjects (denoted as $subjectSet_1$) to mine DC issue reports from their issue trackers. We focused on the build failures due to conflicting constraints imposed by build rules. To identify the fixing strategies of DC issues, we analyzed their issue descriptions, developers' discussions, and fixes. Note that the rest 2,500 collected .NET projects not used in RQ1-2 (denoted as $subjectSet_2$) were adopted to evaluate our DC issue repair technique later (see Sect. 5.5).

5.3.1 Data Collection

Step1: Collecting .NET Projects We collected top popular 3,000 .NET projects from GitHub based on their *Star* counts, and from which we randomly selected 500 subjects as $subjectSet_1$. Figure 5.3 shows the 500 projects' demographics. They are (1) nontrivial in size (on average having 63.1 KLOC), (2) well maintained (on average having 239 code commits), (3) popular (63% of them have over 300 stars), (4) complicated in dependencies (74.1% of them have more than 15 direct dependencies), and (5) diverse (concerning projects targeting nine types of .NET platforms).

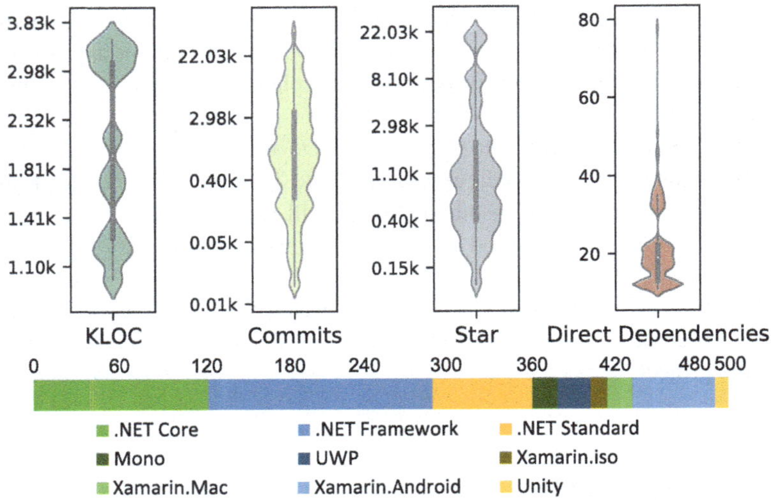

Fig. 5.3 Demographics of the 500 subjects (log scale)

Step2: Collecting DC Issues We collected DC issues from the 500 projects in $subjectSet_1$. To locate DC issues, we searched the projects for the issue reports filed between May 2018 and May 2021 (i.e., in the past 3 years) using keywords "version conflicts," "incompatible target platform," and build error numbers (e.g., "NU1107"). Those issue reports that do not have a clear error number were found by the first two keywords. Keywords "version conflicts," "incompatible target platform" and installation error numbers returned 1,631, 922 and 1,012 issue reports, respectively. We removed duplicated reports from the search results and then retained those that explain the issues and their root causes.

Eventually, we collected 169 DC issue reports, covering 116 .NET projects. Among them, 124 issues have fixes, and 45 issues have clear fixing plans agreed by developers. There are 72 (42.6%) issues that can cause over five build errors. Note that these reports may not contain the new build errors introduced by the fixing process. Figure 5.4 shows statistics of the 167 issue reports, where N_{IR} denotes the number of issue reports containing each type of DC issues. For each issue type, Max and Avg denote the maximum and average issue count in an issue report, respectively. Each report on average describes 7.1 issues, where 42 (24.9%) reports describe more than two issue types. For the 124 issue reports with fixes, the number of involved dependency changes varies from 1 to 69 (i.e., 8.8 ± 8.4).

Step3: Data Analysis To answer RQ1-2, we performed an in-depth analysis on (1) fixes of the 124 issues, (2) planned solutions of the remaining 45 issues, and (3) comments in the issue reports. We followed an open coding procedure [10], a widely used approach for qualitative research, to categorize the fixing strategies and configuration preferences discussed in issue reports. Initially, two Ph.D. students, who have over 3 years of .NET development experience, independently analyzed the

	NU1605	NU1107	NU1202	NU1203	NU1108
N_{IR}	62	89	62	12	6
Max	150	63	16	8	1
Avg	3.58	1.97	1.56	0.18	0.04

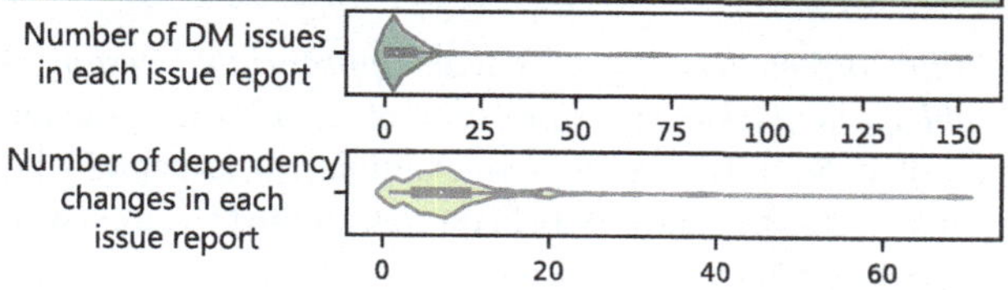

Fig. 5.4 Statistics of the 169 DC issue reports (log scale)

fixes and developers' discussions of 85 issue reports. After the first round of analysis and labeling, the two students gathered to compare and discuss their results, in order to adjust the taxonomy, with the help of a third author to resolve conflicts. In this manner, we constructed the pilot taxonomy. Next, the first two students continued to label the fixes or discussions of the remaining 84 issue reports and iteratively refined the results and the labeling strategy. The conflicts of labeling were again discussed during meetings and resolved by the third Ph.D. student. We adjusted the pilot taxonomy and obtained the final result.

5.3.2 RQ1: Fixing Strategies

Via analyzing our collected data, we observed three fixing strategies.

Strategy 1: *Upgrading/downgrading the direct dependencies that directly or transitively introduce the problematic package versions* (116/169). This strategy was adopted by 116 (68.6%) of issue reports to resolve five types of DC issues. For example, in issue#81 [11], project `Installer` directly references package `NETCore.App` with constraint (≥2.1.0) and transitively depends on `NETCore.App` again with (≥2.1.2) via package `ReverseProxy`. NuGet resolves `NETCore.App`'s version as 2.1.0, based on the direct dependency's constraint (≥2.1.0) (i.e., *direct dependency priority* rule). It then reports an NU1605 error, since `ReverseProxy` has to reference a lower version of `NETCore.App` than it expects. Developers faced the choice of two possible solutions: (1) upgrading `NETCore.App` to 2.1.2 and (2) downgrading `ReverseProxy` to a version that was compatible with `NETCore.App` 2.1.0. They adopted solution (2), as their project was incompatible with `NETCore.App` 2.1.2.

While Strategy 1 can fix the original DC issues, it may introduce multiple types of new DC issues. Each direct dependency update can affect the rest of a project's dependency graph, introducing multiple types of new DC issues (e.g., issue#1139 [5] of `EasyNetQ` as discussed in Sect. 5.1). As a result, developers may need to change more dependencies to resolve the new DC issues.

Problem 5.1 (💡 Finding 1:) *Upgrading/downgrading the direct dependencies that introduce the problematic package versions is the most common strategy to fix all types of DC issues. The fixes can induce new DC issues.*

***Strategy** 2: Adding direct dependencies with appropriate version constraints to override the problematic package versions* (61/169). 36.1% of issue reports adopted this strategy to solve NU1107 issues. For example, in issue#886 [12], two conflicting constraints (≥10.0.1) and (=9.0.1) on `Newtonsoft.Json` were transitively introduced by direct dependencies `Tokens.Jwt` 5.2.1 and `Sdk.Functions` 1.0.8, respectively. With the aid of NuGet's *direct dependency priority* rule, developers explicitly declared `Newtonsoft .Json` 10.0.1 as a direct dependency to override its other required versions. After the overriding, these packages can be successfully installed. While the original NU1107 issue was resolved, NuGet generated a new NU1608 warning that the installed version (10.0.1) of `Newtonsoft.Json` exceeded the constraint (=9.0.1) specified by `Sdk.Functions` 1.0.8. At the end, the developers chose to ignore the warning and enable the `<NoWarn>` property for NU1608 in the configuration file.

We observed that all the 61 issue reports solved NU1107 issues using *Strategy 2* at the cost of inducing NU1608 warnings. As discussed in issue#18 of `ServiceFabric` [13], since its developers could not figure out how to fix their NU1107 issues using *Strategy 1*, they temporarily tolerated the NU1608 warnings induced by *Strategy 2*.

Problem 5.2 (💡 Finding 2:) *Adding direct dependencies is a common strategy to fix NU1107 issues. However, it often causes NU1608 warnings.*

***Strategy** 3: Upgrading/migrating the client project's target platform* (34/169). Thirty-four (20.1%) of the issue reports solved NU1202 issues by upgrading/migrating the client project's target platform. For example, in issue#11 [14] of `Unmocakable`, a project got an error when installing `Unmocakable` 3.0.89. The above package only supports .NET Standard 2.1, which is not compatible with the project's target platform .NET Core 2.2.0. By analyzing the interactive compatibility matrix [9] of .NET Standard, developers upgraded their target platform to .NET Core 3.0.0 (compatible with .NET Standard 2.1) in order to work with the desired `Unmocakable` version.

Since packages contain multiple assemblies with different transitive dependencies that support different target platform versions, *Strategy 3* may greatly affect client project's dependency graph. We observed that 8 out of 10 issue reports adopting *Strategy 3* to solve NU1202 issues introduced a series of new DC issues (e.g., issue#1039 of `refit` [15]). In such cases, developers continued to fix the new issues using a combination of *Strategies 1*, *2*, and *3*.

Problem 5.3 (💡 Finding 3:) *Upgrading/migrating target platform is sometimes adopted to fix DC issues. However, the fixes can have large impact to dependencies and tend to induce new DC issues.*

Finally, in 30 out of 169 issue reports, developers cannot figure out fixing solutions. They have to coordinate with the developers of problematic packages to adjust their configurations. We do not consider this solution as a recommended strategy, since it requires developer coordination and is not subject to full automation.

5.3.3 RQ2: Configuration Preferences

For RQ2, we found clues for developers' configuration preferences in 54 issue reports and summarized as follows:

Avoid Inducing Incompatibility Issues In 16 of the 54 issue reports (29.6%), to avoid inducing incompatibility issues at runtime, developers tend to adopt a combination of fixing strategies with two preferences below.

- ***Preference 1:*** *Fewer upgrades/downgrades of dependencies' major versions (6/16).* Based on the *semantic versioning strategy* [16], developers are suggested to increase their projects' major version number, if they make incompatible API changes. When exploring DC issue solutions, developers tried to make fewer upgrades/downgrades that change direct dependencies' major versions to avoid incompatibility issues. The above viewpoint was discussed in six issue reports, e.g., issue#972 of `EasyNetQ` [17].
- ***Preference 2:*** *Fewer changes in direct dependencies' versions (10/16).* Developers favored fixing solutions with fewer changes in the version constraints of direct dependencies because this can usually lower the chances that incompatibilities arise after resolving DC issues. Moreover, upgrading is preferable to downgrading if either of them can resolve DC issues. Developers expressed such a preference in ten issue reports, e.g., issue#153 of `AndroidX` [18].

Avoid Affecting Project Maintainability We observed the following three preferences used in 38 of the 54 issue reports (70.4%) for the sake of project maintainability.

- ***Preference 3:*** *Fewer installed packages (15/38).* Introducing too many packages into a project will complicate the topological structure of its dependency graph. Hence, developers prefer to install the package versions with fewer transitive dependencies, to prevent potential DC issues. Such preference was echoed by discussions in seven reports, e.g., issue#545 of `standard` [19].
- ***Preference 4:*** *Fewer installed packages targeting inconsistent .NET platform with client project (7/38).* Many .NET Standard packages can be directly or transitively introduced into the .NET Core/.NET Framework/UWP/Mono projects,

while the projects targeting .NET Standard 2.0 and above can install specific versions of .NET Framework packages. Since each .NET Standard version supports limited versions of other .NET platforms, introducing more packages targeting inconsistent platform with client project would be more likely to cause DC issues when the projects upgrade/migrate their target platforms in future. To ease maintenance, developers try to ensure that more packages introduced in their projects support the same .NET platform as the local ones. Such preference was revealed in seven issue reports, e.g., issue#14393 of `aspnetcore` [20].

- ***Preference 5:*** *Fewer risky build warnings (16/38).* In 16 issue reports, developers expressed that they did not want to adopt the solutions inducing the build warnings below into their projects:

  (1) ⚠ NU1608 (*Package version is outside of dependency constraint*): When different version constraints of a package are introduced as a direct dependency and transitive dependencies, respectively, NuGet resolves such a package version based on the direct one. An NU1608 warning will be reported if the resolved version of a package is outside of its other dependency constraints. We observed that developers rolled back fixing *Strategy 2* when exploring solutions for NU1107 issues in five issue reports (e.g., issue #5696 of `aspnetcore` [6]), because they could not tolerate the risky NU1608 warnings induced by such solutions.

  (2) ⚠ NU1103 (*No stable package versions are found in the version constraint*): If there are no stable versions within a package's specified version constraint but only prerelease versions (e.g., *3.0.0-beta-00032*), NuGet will report an NU1103 warning. Since the prerelease package versions were not reliable, developers did not adopt the fixing solutions introducing such NU1103 warnings in six issue reports (e.g., issue#36550 of `corefx` [21]).

  (3) ⚠ NU1701 (*Package does not specify its target platforms*): If an introduced package does not specify its target platforms, NuGet will report an NU1701 warning as its assemblies may not be 100% compatible with the client project. To avoid potential incompatibility issues, developers gave up the fixing solutions that caused new NU1701 warnings and adopted other ones in five issue reports (e.g., issue#425 of `GoogleCloudPlatform` [22]).

5.4 Methodology

From our empirical study, we understand the pervasiveness and seriousness of the problem and learn the atomic fixing strategies and developers' preferences from real DC issue fixes. Motivated by our empirical findings (Sect. 5.3), the solution design is expected to meet four properties: (1) modeling ability to represent various dependency constraints (Sect. 5.2.2), problematic projects with multiple DC issues (Sect. 5.3.1), and potential fixes composed of multiple atomic fixing strategies

(Sect. 5.3.2), (2) learning ability to better adapt developers' preferences by distilling characteristics of real DC issue fixes (Sect. 5.3.3), and (3) online inference efficiency to derive the fixes within users' acceptable waiting time.

Based on the above analysis, we propose *NuFix*, a novel technique to derive fixes for DC issues. The key idea is to leverage binary integer linear programming, upon which we can systematically reformulate this task and encode our empirical findings (i.e., fixing strategies and developers' preferences) into linear constraints and optimization functions. Binary integer linear programming is a well-studied technique that meets our efficiency requirements. Moreover, to tune hyperparameters rigorously by learning from real documented fixes, we incorporate Bayesian optimization into our model to optimize the hyperparameters in a non-gradient manner.

5.4.1 Overall Architecture

Figure 5.5 gives the overall architecture of *NuFix*. We list the inputs of *NuFix* as follows:

- *Problematic dependency configuration file (i.e., ∗.csproj)*. It configures the client project's direct dependencies and the specified version constraints on them.
- *Candidate target .NET platforms*. It is an ordered list of acceptable platforms, since one of our fixing strategies is to upgrade/migrate client project's target platform (*Strategy 3*).
- *Candidate range of direct dependencies' versions (developers' requirements)* (optional). *NuFix* allows developers to customize their package upgrade requirements or the search scope of package versions to avoid inducing undesired program behaviors. For example, developers may want to specify the version

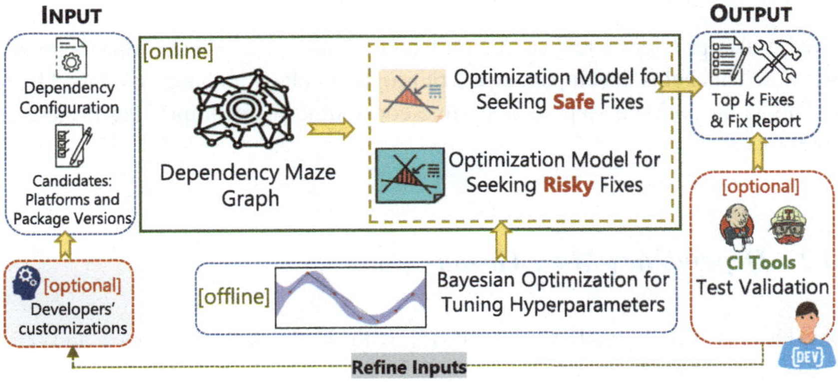

Fig. 5.5 Architecture of *NuFix*

of `Lucene.Net` to be limited within [3.0.3, 4.0.0), if they are already aware of the incompatible versions (≥4.0.0) through experience. One alternative design is to only consider the package versions without introducing API breaking changes, but this is too strict: It is a common practice that developers may be willing to resolve the DC issues at an acceptable cost of adapting the API changes.

NuFix mainly consists of five modules:

- ***Generating Dependency Maze Graph*** (Sect. 5.4.2). Given a target platform and the dependency configuration with customized package versions, this module generates a dependency maze graph consisting of all possible dependencies (both direct and transitive) and the constraints among them.
- ***Seeking Safe Fixes*** (Sect. 5.4.3). Given a DC graph, this module tries to seek the fixes that do not introduce risky build warnings (refer to as *safe fixes*). These fixes are based on *Strategy 1* (upgrading/downgrading direct dependencies), the most commonly adopted strategy in our empirical study (*Finding 1*). To address the combinatorial explosive search space problem, we first propose to formulate the repair task as a binary integer linear programming model, and then we can obtain the fixes using mathematical optimization solvers (in *NuFix* we use `python-mip` [23]).
- ***Seeking Risky Fixes*** (Sect. 5.4.4). Sometimes there is no safe fix. Therefore, we propose a variant optimization model to seek fixes that may introduce some risky build warnings (NU1608, NU1103, and NU1701). This model allows not only *Strategy 1* but also *Strategy 2* (adding direct dependencies to override the problematic package versions).
- ***Tuning Hyperparameters*** (Sect. 5.4.5). The aforementioned two optimization models involve some hyperparameters. In this module, we tune these hyperparameters based on Bayesian optimization. Note that this is an offline step.
- ***Generating Fix Reports***. For each DC graph, this module reports the top k fixes. To help developers understand the derived fixes, *NuFix* also reports their properties (e.g., *a list of build warnings induced by this fix*). The developers can review these fix reports to choose their preferred one.

NuFix also provides a test validation feature that triggers client project's bundled test cases. This helps developers aware of program behavior changes induced by the fix. This is an optional step, as it is time-consuming to recompile the project and trigger its tests.

5.4.2 Dependency Maze Graph

Consider a directed graph $G = (V, E)$ with V the set of vertices and $E = \{(i, j) | i, j \in V\}$ the set of edges:

- Each vertex $v \in V$ denotes a package version (e.g., `NLog` 4.6.7). We use two attributes, v.PKG and v.VER to denote the package and the version, respectively.

Each edge $e = (i, j) \in E$ indicates that i directly depends on j.PKG, and j.VER satisfies the version constraint specified by i. We exclude the package versions that may lead to NU1202/1203/1108 errors or NU1103/1701 warnings.

- We use a special vertex $v^* \in V$ to represent the client project. For each vertex v satisfying $(v^*, v) \in E$, it means that this project depends on v.PKG, and v.VER is a candidate version of v.PKG for this project. For each $v \in V$, there is always at least one path from v^* to v. Moreover, to handle the transitive dependencies of platform (Fig. 5.2a), the specified platform will also be added as a successor vertex of v^*.

Given G, our main task is to find a set $\hat{V} \subseteq V$, which represents a dependency (both direct and transitive) configuration of the client project that can resolve DC issues. For each $\hat{V}$, *NuFix* automatically generates the corresponding fix.

5.4.3 Seeking Safe Fixes

We formulate the repairing task as a binary integer linear programming model as follows.

Variables For each $v \in V$, we introduce a binary variable $v.\delta$ (i.e., $v.\delta \in \{0, 1\}$), representing whether v should be a dependency (either direct or transitive) in the fix:

$$\hat{V} = \{v | v \in V \wedge V.\delta = 1\} \tag{5.1}$$

Constraints First, $v^*.\delta = 1$. Second, each project will not depend on more than one version of the same package (according to NuGet's build rules):

$$\sum_{i \in V}^{i.\text{PKG}=p} i.\delta \leq 1, \qquad \forall p \in \{v.\text{PKG} | v \in V\} \tag{5.2}$$

Third, for each vertex in $\hat{V}$ (i.e., the variable of this vertex takes the value 1), we divide its successors into several groups by the PKG attribute. For each group, there should be one and only one vertex that is in $\hat{V}$. These constraints guarantee that: For each package in the final solution, its dependency requirements will always be satisfied. Formally, we have

$$\sum_{i \in V}^{\substack{(v,i) \in E, \\ i.\text{PKG}=p}} i.\delta \geq v.\delta, \quad \forall v \in V, p \in \{v'.\text{PKG} | (v, v') \in E\} \tag{5.3}$$

Last, transitive dependencies should conform to the *"lowest applicable version"* rule in NuGet dependency resolution:

$$\sum_{j \in V}^{(j,i)\in E} j.\delta * I_{\mathrm{LB}}(j,i) \geq i.\delta, \quad \forall i \in \{v|(v^*, v) \notin E\} \setminus v^* \tag{5.4}$$

where I_{LB} is an indicator function of whether or not i.VER is a lowest application version of i.PKG for j. This constraint guarantees that dependency configuration $\hat{V}$ is entirely based on *Strategy 1* (upgrading/downgrading the direct dependencies).

Objective Function We design the objective function based on the identified preferences discussed in Sect. 5.3.3.

To encourage *Preference 1* (developers prefer fewer dependency upgrades/downgrades crossing their major versions), we incorporate it into our objective function as a factor:

$$\max z_1 = \sum_{v \in V} v.\delta * I_{\mathrm{MV}}(v) \tag{5.5}$$

where I_{MV} is an indicator function of whether or not v.PKG is a direct dependency and v.VER shares the same major version as the original version.

To encourage *Preference 2* (developers prefer fewer changes on direct dependencies' versions), we have

$$\max z_2 = -\sum_{v \in V} v.\delta * I_{\mathrm{U}}(v), \quad \max z_3 = -\sum_{v \in V} v.\delta * I_{\mathrm{D}}(v) \tag{5.6}$$

where $I_{\mathrm{U}}/I_{\mathrm{D}}$ is an indicator function of whether or not v.PKG is a direct dependency and v.VER is greater/lower than its original version in the problematic configuration file. We use indicator functions I_{U} and I_{D} to distinguish between upgrades and downgrades.

To encourage *Preference 3* (developers prefer to introduce fewer packages in project's dependency graph), we have

$$\max z_4 = -\sum_{v \in V} v.\delta \tag{5.7}$$

To encourage *Preference 4* (fewer installed packages targeting inconsistent .NET platform with client project), we have

$$\max z_5 = -\sum_{v \in V} v.\delta * \mathrm{i}_C(v) \tag{5.8}$$

where I_C is an indicator function of whether or not v targets inconsistent .NET platform with client project.

In this section, we ignore *Preference 5* (introducing fewer warnings) because this model will never introduce warning.

We define our overall objective function as

$$\max z = \sum_{k=1}^{5} \alpha_k * z_k \tag{5.9}$$

where $(\alpha_1, \alpha_2, \alpha_3, \alpha_4, \alpha_5) \in [0, 1](\sum_{i=1}^{5} \alpha_i = 1)$ are hyperparameters. Section 5.4.5 details the tuning hyperparameter procedure.

5.4.4 Seeking Risky Fixes

Sometimes it is infeasible to find safe fixes. Therefore, in this section we propose a variant model that can seek risky fixes (i.e., fixes that may introduce build warnings). As introduced in Sect. 5.3.3, we need to consider three types of build warnings: (1) NU1608 (*package version is outside of dependency constraint*), (2) NU1103 (*no stable package versions are found in the version constraint*), and (3) NU1701 (*package does not specify its target platforms*).

To find fixes with NU1103 and NU1701, we allow unstable versions (denoted as V_{NU1103}) and versions that do not specify their target platforms (denoted as V_{NU1701}) in G. We have

$$\max z_6 = -\sum_{v \in V_{\text{NU1103}}} v.\delta, \quad \max z_7 = -\sum_{v \in V_{\text{NU1701}}} v.\delta \tag{5.10}$$

It is challenging to find fixes with NU1608, because NU1608 means that some constraints in Eq. 5.3 will be violated. Concretely, Eq. 5.3 should be relaxed as

$$\sum_{i \in V}^{i.\text{PKG}=p} i.\delta \geq v.\delta \tag{5.11}$$

This relaxation makes the model intractable because the search space explodes, and we cannot trace the number of violated constraints in Eq. 5.3. To address this problem, we introduce an auxiliary binary variable $x_{v,p}$ for each $v \in V \setminus v^*$ and $p \in \{v'.\text{PKG} | (v, v') \in E\}$. This variable indicates whether or not v's dependency constraint on p is violated. Then we have another relaxation for Eq. 5.3:

$$x_{v,p} + \sum_{i \in V}^{\substack{(v,i) \in E, \\ i.\text{PKG}=p}} i.\delta \geq v.\delta \tag{5.12}$$

We want to violate constraints in Eq. 5.3 as few as possible:

$$\max z_8 = -\sum_{v,p} x_{v,p} \tag{5.13}$$

Similar to z (Eq. 5.9), the overall objective function of the variant model for seeking risky fixes is

$$\max z' = \sum_{k=1}^{8} \alpha'_k * z_k \tag{5.14}$$

5.4.5 *Tuning Hyperparameters*

We use Bayesian optimization to tune the hyperparameters $\boldsymbol{\alpha}$ in our models: $\boldsymbol{\alpha} = (\alpha_1, \ldots, \alpha_5)$ for safe fixes, and $\boldsymbol{\alpha} = (\alpha'_1, \ldots, \alpha'_8)$ for risky fixes. Bayesian optimization is a global optimization algorithm built upon Bayesian inference and Gaussian process, which attempts to find the maximum/minimum value of a *black box* function in as few iterations as possible. Here *black box* means that we do not have access to the gradient of our models with respect to $\boldsymbol{\alpha}$.

To start a Bayesian optimization task, we need to specify the function f to be optimized. Intuitively, we wish to find an $\boldsymbol{\alpha}$ that makes the fixes returned by our model as similar as possible to real fixes provided by developers. Concretely, consider a training dataset $\mathcal{D}$ consisting of some pairs in the form of $(G, \hat{V})$: G is a dependency maze graph, and $\hat{V}$ is the real fix (this training dataset is detailed in Sect. 5.5.3). Then we have

$$\min f(\boldsymbol{\alpha}) = \sum_{(G,\hat{V})\in\mathcal{D}} (z^*(G, \boldsymbol{\alpha}) - z(G, \hat{V}, \boldsymbol{\alpha})) \tag{5.15}$$

where $z^*(G, \boldsymbol{\alpha})$ is the maximum value of the objective function z that our model solves (given G and $\boldsymbol{\alpha}$).

5.5 Evaluation

We study two research questions in our evaluation section:

- **RQ3 (Effectiveness of** *NuFix*)**:** *How effective is NuFix in fixing DC issues for .NET projects?*
- **RQ4 (Usefulness of** *NuFix*) *Do the fixes generated by NuFix make sense from practitioners' perspectives?*

To answer RQ3, we constructed a high-quality benchmark, to evaluate *NuFix*'s capability of fixing DC issues.

To answer RQ4, we invited ten experienced .NET experts from industry to manually validate the fixes generated by *NuFix* and further reported our generated fixes to the corresponding project developers in open-source community for validation.

5.5.1 Benchmark Construction

We considered the 2,500 .NET projects in $subjectSet_2$ as subjects. By mining these projects' code commits on GitHub, we constructed a high-quality benchmark consisting of real commits for resolving DC issues. Specifically, we filtered commits based on four criteria:

- Commits with $\leq$10 dependency changes were filtered out.
- We only kept the commits whose logs explicitly stated that the revisions aimed to upgrade/migrate the projects' platforms. This is based on our empirical finding that platform changes often trigger more complicated DC issues.
- For each project, we manually upgraded/migrated the project to the specified new platform. Only commits that could reveal DC issues were kept.

The final benchmark consists of 392 $\langle Input, Fix \rangle$ instances:

- *Input* is a 4-tuple $\langle C, P_0, P_1, R \rangle$. Specifically, C is a set of packages paired with their specified versions, extracted from the problematic configuration file before merging the commit; P_0 is the original .NET platform before updating; P_1 is the target .NET platform after merging the commit; and R is the constraints of package versions. Note that, to be fair in comparison with real fixes, R excludes all package versions that were released after the timestamp of code commit.
- *Fix* is a set of dependency changes. We should not directly use all changed dependencies of the commit as *Fix*, because not all these changes are to resolve the DC issues. As such, we define *Fix* as the minimum subset of dependency changes in a code commit, satisfying that the subset can tackle the DC issue in P_1.

As shown in Fig. 5.6 and Table 5.1, the instances in benchmark cover five types of DC issues and involve the projects targeting nine types of platforms. Each instance concerns 8.2 DC issues on average. The number of dependency changes concerned in each fix varies from 3 to 50 (i.e., 8.4 $\pm$ 5.9).

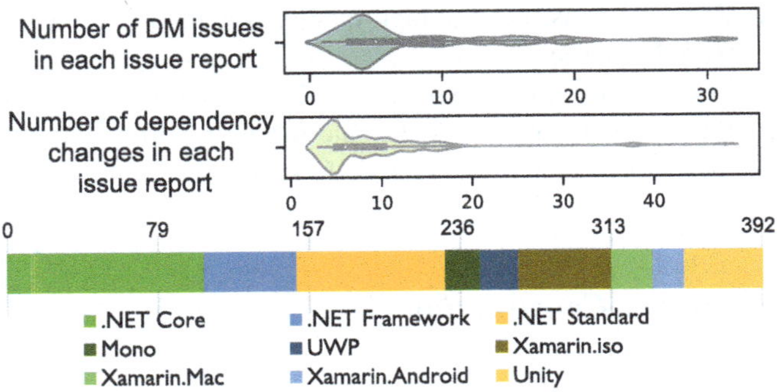

Fig. 5.6 Statistics of 392 instances in our benchmark (log scale)

Table 5.1 Statistics of 392 documented fixes in our benchmark

	NU1605	NU1107	NU1202	NU1203	NU1108
N_{IR}	192	61	365	12	6
Max	39	5	24	3	1
Avg	2.66	1.79	3.67	0.07	0.02

Table 5.2 Statistics of our training and test datasets

Training dataset			
# Fixes inducing warnings[a] (39)			# Fixes not inducing warnings
NU1608	NU1103	NU1701	91
17	26	4	
Test dataset			
# Fixes inducing warnings[a] (62)			# Fixes not inducing warnings
NU1608	NU1103	NU1701	200
36	57	7	

[a]Some fixes induce more than one type of warnings

5.5.2 *RQ3: Effectiveness of NuFix*

We briefly describe the experiment design and results in this section. To ease presentation, we refer to the fixes derived by *NuFix* as *N-fix* and a fix derived by developers in our benchmark as a *real fix*.

Data Splits According to approaches [24–28], a sample size ten times the number of hyperparameters is reasonable for training. Since *NuFix* requires 13 hyperparameters, we randomly held out 130 of the 392 instances as the training dataset for tuning hyperparameters. The rest of them are regarded as the test dataset. Statistics of two datasets are described in Table 5.2.

Evaluation Metrics We define four evaluation metrics below:

- *FR* (Fixing Ratio): the proportion of DC issue cases for which the technique can derive fixes

- *SFR* (Safely Fixing Ratio): the proportion of DC issue cases for which the technique can derive safe fixes
- *TPR* (Test Passing Ratio): the proportion of derived fixes that can pass the projects' bundled tests
- *Similarity*: how similar are the derived fixes to the corresponding real fixes. We define *Similarity* based on *IoU*:

$$Similarity = \frac{|Changes_N \cap Changes_R|}{|Changes_N \cup Changes_R|} \tag{5.16}$$

where $Changes_N$ and $Changes_R$ are the changes induced by the derived and real fixes, respectively. We define two types of similarity metrics based on the changes in the equivalence operator between two dependencies: (a) *Type A*: Two changes will be regarded as equivalent if they share the same package, major version, and direct dependency constraints and (b) *Type B*: Two changes will be regarded as equivalent if they share the same package and major version. For each instance in our benchmark, we averaged the *Similarity* values of the top $k = 5$ derived fixes as the result.

Comparison Two baseline approaches are considered in our study:

- ***CUDF for .NET***: CUDF [7] is proposed to resolve the package upgradeability problem for GNU/Linux-based distributions using a linear programming model. We adapt it to derive DC issue fixes (denoted as *C-fixes*) by encoding NuGet's build rules. It defines five user preferences to explore configurations. We only consider three of them: *fewer newly installed packages*, *fewer changes in direct dependencies*, and *fewer packages that are not up-to-date*, while the rest two preferences are not applicable to NuGet's build rules. In CUDF, the weights of user preferences are not rigorously defined. As such, we adopt the empirical weights assigned for the above three user preferences in approach [7]: 1, 1, and $|V|+1$, where $|V|$ is available the version count of required packages.
- *PyDFix* ***for .NET***: *PyDFix* [29] is proposed to fix unreproducibility in Python builds caused by dependency version errors. We adopt it to derive fixes for DC issues (denoted as *P-fixes*) based on NuGet's build rules. *PyDFix* considers the available versions of packages that cause DC issues as the search space of fixing strategies. Such strategies are sorted by the highest version priority. It iteratively tries out each fixing strategy and then adds it into a documented fix if such a strategy can repair at least one unresolved DC issue. This procedure continues until all the DC issues are resolved, or all the fixing strategies have been tested. Note that in each iteration, it rebuilds the project to verify the fixing strategy. Since such a process is computationally expensive, we set *PyDFix*'s time budget to be 120 minutes.

Hyperparameters Table 5.2 shows the tuned hyperparameters, by applying Bayesian optimization algorithm to our training dataset. To understand how *NuFix* balances the developers' preferences, we compared the average value of each weighted preference-based factor (i.e., $\alpha_k * z_k$ and $\alpha'_k * z_k$ for our two optimization models, respectively), which indicates the factor influence for seeking fixes.

From Table 5.3, we can tell that for .NET practitioners: (1) Ensuring the compatibility of packages (indicated by $k = 1, 2, 3$) plays a leading role in DC issue fixing; in practice, dependency upgrades ($k = 2$) are preferable to downgrades ($k = 3$), (2) NU1608 warnings (indicated by $k = 8$) are much more intolerable than NU1103 and NU1701 warnings for developers, and (3) developers indeed prefer to install packages as few as possible ($k = 4$) and introduce fewer packages targeting inconsistent .NET platform with their client projects ($k = 5$), but these two preferences are not the top priority.

Results Table 5.4 shows the evaluation results. To ease discussion, we further divided our testing dataset into three groups based on their difficulties (by #dependency changes N_s in real fixes). *NuFix* generates fixes for each .NET project within 12.5 seconds and achieves a 100% *FR* for the instances with different difficulties. 77.5% N-fixes are safe fixes, of which the safely fixing ratio is higher than real fixes (59.2%). While CUDF achieves $FR = SFR = 77.5\%$, since it does not support a variant model to seek risky fixes if safe fixes do not exist. In contrast, *PyDFix* exhibits poor performance in our evaluation. The primary reason is that DC issues in the .NET ecosystem are significantly more complex than those in the Python ecosystem (on average 2.4 dependency changes for fixing unreproducibility in a Python build [29] **vs.** 8.4 ± 5.9 dependency changes in a real fix of our benchmark); thus the iterative search methodology of *PyDFix* is insufficient to deal with the exponentially large search space.

For the 192 out of 262 instances having bundled test cases, we deployed their CI tools to further evaluate whether N-fixes would cause test failures. Encouragingly, *NuFix* achieves 73.3% *TPR* on average, owing to its well-defined objective function (prefer fewer upgrades/downgrades of dependencies' major versions and fewer changes in direct dependency versions). The above *TPR* can be improved via iteratively refining the search scope of package versions by developers. However, CUDF and *PyDFix* do not restrict their algorithms to seek solutions with fewer package upgrades/downgrades crossing major versions. Instead, they reward the

Table 5.3 Tuned hyperparameters used in our object functions

Seeking safe fixes				
$\alpha = (\alpha_1, ..., \alpha_5) = (0.73, 0.14, 0.12, 0.01, 0.03)$				
$\lvert\alpha_1 * z_1\rvert$	$\lvert\alpha_2 * z_2\rvert$	$\lvert\alpha_3 * z_3\rvert$	$\lvert\alpha_4 * z_4\rvert$	$\lvert\alpha_5 * z_5\rvert$
2.19	1.36	1.23	0.81	0.78

Seeking risky fixes							
$\alpha = (\alpha'_1, ..., \alpha'_8) = (0.06, 0.01, 0.01, 4*10^{-4}, 1.2*10^{-3}, 0.01, 0.08, 0.83)$							
$\lvert\alpha'_1 * z_1\rvert$	$\lvert\alpha'_2 * z_2\rvert$	$\lvert\alpha'_3 * z_3\rvert$	$\lvert\alpha'_4 * z_4\rvert$	$\lvert\alpha'_5 * z_5\rvert$	$\lvert\alpha'_6 * z_6\rvert$	$\lvert\alpha'_7 * z_7\rvert$	$\lvert\alpha'_8 * z_8\rvert$
0.20	0.19	0.17	0.07	0.06	0.02	0.02	0.15

Table 5.4 *NuFix*'s effectiveness on DC issue fixing

	FR			SFR				TPR		
	NuFix	CUDF	*PyDFix*	*NuFix*	CUDF	*PyDFix*	Benchmark	*NuFix*	CUDF	*PyDFix*
Difficult	100%	60.2%	0.0%	60.2%	60.2%	0.0%	43.9%	69.4%	32.2%	0.0%
Moderate	100%	87.9%	28.8%	87.9%	87.9%	22.7%	67.4%	75.3%	35.6%	15.1%
Easy	100%	87.5%	65.6%	87.5%	87.5%	53.1%	71.9%	76.1%	38.0%	31.2%
Average	100%	77.5%	41.9%	77.5%	77.5%	33.5%	59.2%	73.3%	34.6%	20.8%
Time (Avg)	*NuFix*: 12.5 seconds			CUDF: 10.2 seconds				*PyDFix*: 115.4 minutes		

Similarity

	NuFix		CUDF		*PyDFix*	
	Type A	Type B	Type A	Type B	Type A	Type B
Difficult	50.1%	68.2%	18.5%	38.8%	0.0%	0.0%
Moderate	57.5%	76.2%	23.4%	39.8%	13.5%	14.2%
Easy	64.9%	85.1%	20.6%	35.3%	25.4%	32.5%
Average	55.7%	74.3%	21.2%	38.9%	16.8%	19.8%

† #Difficult cases (N_s: >=8): 98; #Moderate cases (N_s: 4–8): 132; #Easy cases (N_s: <4): 32

fixes with more up-to-date packages. As result, on average, they achieve 34.6% and 20.8% *TPR*, respectively.

NuFix achieves *Type A* and *Type B* similarities of 55.7% and 74.3%, respectively, which significantly outperforms the baseline approaches. Figure 5.7 shows the distribution of five properties of the generated fixes. We can observe that (1) N-fixes can better satisfy *Preferences* 1 and 2 than real fixes, which is indicated by the fact that P_1'/P_1 and P_2'/P_2 are significantly greater than 1. (2) For *NuFix*, *Preference 3* is a secondary factor comparing to *Preference 1 and 2*, as P_3'/P_3 varies from 0 to 7. (3) For CUDF, most of P_2'/P_2 and P_3'/P_3 are greater than 1 and close to those of N-fixes, since it considers *Properties 2* and *3* as user preferences. (4) CUDF and *PyDFix* prefer to install newest package versions and do not take *Properties 1* and *4* into account. As such, its P_1'/P_1 and P_4'/P_4 are significantly lower than those of N-fixes. (5) P_5 and P_5' indicate that N-fixes induced far fewer build warnings than C-fixes, P-fixes, and real fixes. (6) Low *Similarity* does not necessarily mean that N-fixes are not good, as the above phenomena are more significant when the *Similarity* is low. To further understand these N-fixes with low *Similarity*, we performed expert validation in Sect. 5.5.3.

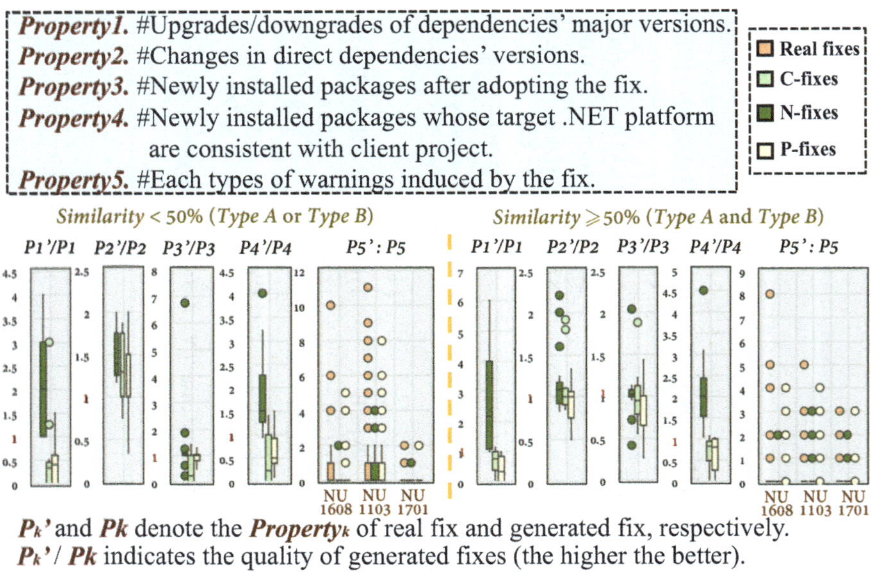

Fig. 5.7 Distribution of five properties of N-fixes and real fixes

5.5.3 RQ4: Usefulness of *NuFix*

In this research question, we aim to validate the usefulness of *NuFix* by means of the feedback from .NET experts and project developers.

Setup for Expert Validation A DC issue can have multiple fixing solutions. As such, we want to evaluate if a fix generated by *NuFix* is valid even if it differs significantly from the real fix. To conduct the evaluation, we invited .NET experts from industry to manually assess the generated fixes.

- *Participants.* We invited ten .NET experts with over 3 years of development experience from Microsoft to participate in our study.
- *Subjects.* All the top fixes generated by *NuFix* in Sect. 5.5.2 were selected if (1) their *Similarity* (either *Type A* or *Type B*) with the corresponding real fixes is less than 50% and (2) they do not result in test failures. 123 pairs of N-fixes and real fixes were selected.
- *Procedure.* The formal study session was supervised by two authors. We provided a 10-minute briefing to the ten participants on the two tasks before starting the tasks.
  - *Task 1. Background information collection.* We collected from the participants (1) their experience in years, (2) the .NET platforms that they have worked on, and (3) whether they have encountered DC issues in their projects in the past 3 months. We collected the information to investigate whether the participants had experience in dealing with DC issues.
  - *Task 2. Fix assessment.* Each participant was assigned to examine 12 or 13 fix pairs. The participant was asked to choose the preferred fix in each fix pair. To facilitate that, the participant was given the original dependency configuration and the DC issues arose for each fix pair. We also provided each participant a visualization of the package dependency graph after adopting a fix. The graph contains the updated packages and the information of their five properties (Fig. 5.7) as auxiliary info. To avoid biased results, we did not disclose to participants which of the fix in a fix pair is the real fix or the N-fix.

Setup for Project Developer Validation We further validated the usefulness of N-fixes by checking if the project developers would replace their real fixes with N-fixes. We wanted to focus on the N-fixes of those projects whose developers were more likely to give us feedback. Therefore, from the 123 N-fixes (selected in expert validation), we chose the ones if they satisfy the following: (1) Their code repositories have commit records in the past month (actively maintained) and (2) there are no dependency updates since these real fixes are merged (ensuring the current configurations equal the real fixes). Following these two criteria, we finally chose 25 N-fixes. We made pull requests (PRs) to revise their configurations based on the N-fixes. The PRs also explained the improvements of our suggested configurations in terms of the five properties (e.g., inducing fewer packages).

Ethical Considerations We provided all .NET experts with a form that informed them about the study purpose, the data we collected and stored, and email to contact us in case they had concerns. Additionally, before making PRs to project developers for validation, we have thoroughly tested the fixes derived by *NuFix*, to avoid spamming the open-source community. All PRs were submitted in compliance with projects' contribution guidelines and licenses.

Results of Expert Validation Figure 5.8(1) and (2) shows the experience background of our participants. 40% of participants have 10–15 years of experience in .NET development, and 70% of them are proficient with more than four types of platforms. In particular, they all have experience with DC issues in the past 3 months.

The expert validation results are described in Fig. 5.8(3). In 70.7% of the cases, participants preferred the fixes generated by *NuFix* to the real fixes. While in 22.8% of cases, they confirmed that either of the two fixes was acceptable for them, since the fixes were evenly matched in practitioners' desired properties. In particular, an expert commented on a pair of fixes for resolving DC issues (2 NU1107 and 12 NU1202 errors) in commit#*3bb49c4* of `h5` [30]: "*One fix (real fix) addressed the issues at the cost of inducing two NU1608 warnings. While the other fix (N-fix) is excellent because it did not cause any warnings with one more upgrade of package's major version.*"

In eight cases (6.5%), experts only adopted the real fixes. We further analyzed these instances and found that to guarantee fewer upgrades/downgrades of dependencies' major versions (higher weight in *NuFix*'s objective function), *NuFix* derived the fixes at the expense of introducing numerous additional packages. For example, to resolve eight NU1202 issues in commit#*008e928* of project `Restaurant` [31], developers changed four direct dependencies' major versions in the real fix. While *NuFix* fix only upgrades two dependencies' major versions, it induces 75 more packages.

Results of Project Developer Validation Among our 25 submitted PRs that suggested project developers to replace their real fixes with the ones derived

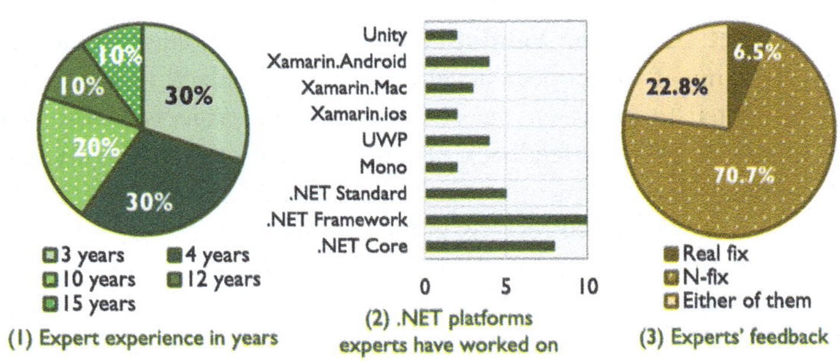

Fig. 5.8 Results of expert validation

by *NuFix*, 20 PRs (80.0%) have been quickly merged. Most of the fixes are confirmed by the affected projects such as `Dropbox` [8]. The remaining five PRs are pending. Developers of these projects have not made decisions. We have not received rejection of our suggestions. The results indicate that N-fixes can resolve the encountered DC issues better than or as good as the original fixes. A developer specially left a comment in PR#43 [32] of `charlessolar`: "*At the time configuration had issues, but I believe that they were fixed by these commits.*"

Developers also showed interest in the *NuFix* tool. For example, one developer commented "*For my own curiosity, what is the name of the tool you used to generate the fixes? Please do share it once you are ready!*" in `Fortnox`'s PR #41 [33]. Details of our PRs can be found on *NuFix*'s website.

5.6 Threats to Validity

Subjectivity of Inspection In our empirical study, we adopted manual analysis to construct the taxonomy of fixing strategies and discuss developers' configuration preferences. The manual analysis may pose threats to the validity of empirical findings. To minimize this threat, we adopted an open coding procedure [10], to categorize the results. Each issue report was inspected and labeled by two co-authors independently. Any discrepancy was discussed and resolved by the third author, until consensus was reached.

Bias in Expert Validation The data from expert validation may be subject to bias. To limit this bias, we investigated participants' profiles and ensured they have over 3 years of .NET development experience. In particular, they have dealt with DC issues in the past 3 months. To guarantee that they fully understand the tasks, we gathered ten experts and gave them a 10-minute briefing at the beginning of study session. We did not disclose to participants who fix was the real fix/N-fix in each given fix pair.

5.7 Related Work

Build-Failure Repair Studies on automated program repair [34–59] are emerging in recent years, especially the build-failure repair techniques [29, 60–66]. For example, *Bart* [63] is a tool that summarizes *Maven* build logs and provides relevant online links to reduce developers' resolution efforts. *HireBuild* [64] uses historical build fix information to generate fixes for build scripts that have led to similar types of build failures. *HoBuff* [65] applies dataflow analysis to build logs and generating fixes for the faults analyzed. *BuildMedic* [66] repairs dependency-related build failures for Maven projects based on three common fixing strategies. *PyDFix* [29] is the latest technique proposed to detect and fix unreproducibility in Python builds caused by dependency version errors. *BuildMedic* [66] and *PyDFix* [29] share a common workflow: They considered the possible package version updates as the search space of fixing strategies. They iteratively try out each fixing strategy and then add it into a documented fix if such a strategy can repair at least one unresolved build error. This procedure continues until all the build errors are resolved, or all the fixing strategies have been tested. Such a process is computationally expensive since it rebuilds the project in each iteration to verify the fixing strategy. However, the search space of possible fixes for DC issues in .NET ecosystem is exponentially large. Our comparison results (see Sect. 5.5.2) show that the above iterative search methodology exhibits poor performance in repairing DC issues.

Dependency Solving Various studies have been made on dependency management [67–81]. Studies [11, 82–85] mainly focus on detecting dependency issues rather than fixing. In this chapter, we focus on resolving dependency issues arising from software evolution. Approaches [1], [7, 86–91] aim to resolve the package upgradeability problem for GNU/Linux-based distributions. Vouillon et al. [86, 87] identify a set of packages that cannot be installed/upgraded together, using graph-theoretic transformations. Mancinelli et al. [88] propose an approach that formulates the resolution of dependencies and inter-package conflicts as a linear optimization problem among feasible upgrade solutions. Recent techniques [7, 89, 90] make further enhancement in the consideration of developer preferences.

However, these existing works are inapplicable to resolve the DC issues in .NET projects because they lack (1) empirical supports for the defined user preferences, (2) a rigorous process to assign weights for user preferences, and (3) providing an optimal sub-solution when a perfect solution fixing all issues does not exist. In this chapter, we address these limitations and propose an effective technique to derive DC issue fixes, in which developers' preferences are empirically investigated and systematically explored.

5.8 Conclusion and Future Work

In this chapter, we empirically studied DC issues in .NET projects, which are prevalent and challenging for developers to address. We investigated their fixing strategies and developers' configuration preferences. To help developers repair DC issues, we developed the *NuFix* tool, by formulating this task as a binary integer optimization problem. The evaluation confirmed the effectiveness of *NuFix*, as its derived fixes were in line with developers' desired properties. In the future, we plan to use effective testing/static analysis techniques to efficiently validate *NuFix*'s generated fixes.

References

1. Abate P, Di Cosmo R, Gousios G, Zacchiroli S. Dependency solving is still hard, but we are getting better at it: In: 2020 IEEE 27th International Conference on Software Analysis, Evolution and Reengineering (SANER). IEEE; 2020. p. 547–551.
2. Troelsen A. C# and the .NET Platform. Berlin: Springer; 2003.
3. NuGet central repository[EB/OL]. [2021-02-01]. https://www.nuget.org/
4. Introduction for .NET platforms in Microsoft documentation[EB/OL]. [2021-06-01]. https://docs.microsoft.com/en-us/dotnet/standard/components
5. Issue #1139 of project EasyNetQ[EB/OL]. [2021-06-01]. https://github.com/EasyNetQ/EasyNetQ/issues/1139
6. 2021. Issue#5696 of project aspnetcore. https://github.com/dotnet/aspnetcore/issues/5696. Accessed: 01 Jun 2021.
7. Abate P, Di Cosmo R, Treinen R, Zacchiroli S. Dependency solving: a separate concern in component evolution management. J Syst Softw. 2012;85(10):2228-40.
8. Project Dropbox[EB/OL]. [2021-06-01]. https://github.com/dropbox/dropbox-sdk-dotnet
9. 2021. Interactive compatibility matrix of .NET Standard. https://docs.microsoft.com/en-us/dotnet/standard/net-standard#net-implementation-support. Accessed: 01 Feb 2021.
10. Creswell JW. Qualitative inquiry and research design: choosing among five approaches, 3rd ed. Thousand Oaks: SAGE Publications; 2013.
11. Issue #81 of project Installer[EB/OL]. [2021-06-01]. https://github.com/dotnet/installer/issues/81
12. Issue #886 of project AzureAD[EB/OL]. [2021-06-01]. https://github.com/AzureAD/azure-activedirectory-identitymodel-extensions-for-dotnet/issues/886
13. Issue #18 of project ServiceFabric[EB/OL]. [2021-06-01]. https://github.com/autofac/Autofac.ServiceFabric/issues/18
14. Issue #11 of project Unmockable[EB/OL]. [2021-06-01]. https://github.com/riezebosch/Unmockable/issues/11
15. Issue #1039 of project refit[EB/OL]. [2021-06-01]. https://github.com/reactiveui/refit/issues/1039
16. 2021. Semantic versioning strategy. https://semver.org/. Accessed: 01 Jun 2021.
17. 2021. Issue#972 of project EasyNetQ. https://github.com/EasyNetQ/EasyNetQ/issues/972. Accessed: 01 Jun 2021.
18. 2021. Issue#153 of project AndroidX. https://github.com/xamarin/AndroidX/issues/153. Accessed: 01 Jun 2021.
19. 2021. Issue#545 of project standard. https://github.com/dotnet/standard/issues/545. Accessed: 01 Jun 2021.
20. 2021. Issue#14393 of project aspnetcore. https://github.com/dotnet/aspnetcore/issues/14393. Accessed: 01 Jun 2021.
21. 2021. Issue#36550 of project corefx. https://github.com/dotnet/corefx/pull/36550. Accessed: 01 Jun 2021.
22. 2021. Issue#425 of project GoogleCloudPlatform. https://github.com/GoogleCloudPlatform/dotnet-docs-samples/issues/425. Accessed: 01 Jun 2021.
23. 2021. python-mip. https://pypi.org/project/mip/. Accessed: 01 Feb 2021.
24. Kohli MD, Summers RM, Geis JR. Medical image data and datasets in the era of machine learning—whitepaper from the 2016 C-MIMI meeting dataset session. J Digital Imag. 2017;30(4):392–99.
25. Kalayeh HM, Landgrebe DA. Predicting the required number of training samples. IEEE Trans Pattern Analy Mach Intell. 1983;6:664–67.
26. Mukherjee S, Tamayo P, Rogers S, Rifkin R, Engle A, Campbell C, Golub TR, Mesirov JP. Estimating dataset size requirements for classifying DNA microarray data. J Comput Biol. 2003;10(2):119–42.

27. Caballero Y, Bello R, Taboada A, Nowe A, Maria M Garcia, Casas G. A new measure based in the rough set theory to estimate the training set quality. In: 2006 eighth international symposium on symbolic and numeric algorithms for scientific computing. IEEE; 2006. p. 133–140.
28. Figueroa RL, Zeng-Treitler Q , Kandula S, Ngo LH. Predicting sample size required for classification performance. BMC Med Inf Decis Making 2012;12(1):1–10.
29. Mukherjee S, Almanza A, Rubio-González C. Fixing dependency errors for python build reproducibility. In: Proceedings of the 30th ACM SIGSOFT international symposium on software testing and analysis (ISSTA 2021); 2021. p. 439–451.
30. 2021. Project h5. https://github.com/theolivenbaum/h5. Accessed: 01 Feb 2021.
31. 2021. Project Restaurant. https://github.com/chayxana/Restaurant-App. Accessed: 01 Feb 2021.
32. 2021. PR#43 of charlessolar. https://github.com/charlessolar/eShopOnContainersDDD/pull/43. Accessed: 01 Jun 2021.
33. PR #41 of project fortnox.NET[EB/OL]. [2021-06-01]. https://github.com/zenta-ab/fortnox.NET/pull/41
34. Jia Z, Li S, Yu T, Zeng C, Xu E, Liu X, Wang J, Liao X. DepOwl: detecting dependency bugs to prevent compatibility failures. In: 2021 IEEE/ACM 43rd international conference on software engineering (ICSE); 2021. p. 86–98.
35. Wang Y, Wen M, Liu Z, Wu R, Wang R, Yang B, Yu H, Zhu Z, Cheung S-C. Do the dependency conflicts in my project matter?. In: Proceedings of the 2018 26th ACM joint meeting on European software engineering conference and symposium on the foundations of software engineering; 2018. p. 319–330.
36. Dong R-Z, Peng X, Yu Y-J, Zhao W-Y. Requirements-driven self-repairing against environmental failures. In: 2013 international symposium on theoretical aspects of software engineering. IEEE; 2013. p. 241–244
37. Yu T, Pradel M. Pinpointing and repairing performance bottlenecks in concurrent programs. Empir Softw Eng. 2018;23(5):3034–71.
38. DeMarco F, Xuan J, Berre DL, Monperrus M. Automatic repair of buggy if conditions and missing preconditions with SMT. In: Proceedings of the 6th international workshop on constraints in software testing, verification, and analysis; 2014. p. 30–39.
39. Tufano M, Watson C, Bavota G, Penta MD, White M, Poshyvanyk D. Learning how to mutate source code from bug-fixes. In: 2019 IEEE international conference on software maintenance and evolution (ICSME). IEEE; 2019. p. 301–312.
40. Wu M, Guo S, Schaumont P, Wang C. Eliminating timing side-channel leaks using program repair. In: Proceedings of the 27th ACM SIGSOFT international symposium on software testing and analysis; 2018. p. 15–26.
41. Tan SH, Yi J, Mechtaev S, Roychoudhury A, et al. Codeflaws: a programming competition benchmark for evaluating automated program repair tools. In: 2017 IEEE/ACM 39th international conference on software engineering companion (ICSE-C). IEEE; 2017. p. 180–182.
42. Yi J, Ahmed UZ, Karkare A, Tan SH, Roychoudhury A. A feasibility study of using automated program repair for introductory programming assignments. In: Proceedings of the 2017 11th joint meeting on foundations of software engineering; 2017. p. 740–751.
43. Monperrus M, Urli S, Durieux T, Martinez M, Baudry B, Seinturier L. Repairnator patches programs automatically. Ubiquity 2019;2019:1–12.
44. Koyuncu A, Liu K, Bissyandé TF, Kim D, Monperrus M, Klein J, Traon YL. iFixR: bug report driven program repair. In: Proceedings of the 2019 27th ACM joint meeting on European software engineering conference and symposium on the foundations of software engineering; 2019. p. 314–325.
45. Yi J, Tan SH, Mechtaev S, Böhme M, Roychoudhury A. A correlation study between automated program repair and test-suite metrics. Empir Softw Eng. 2018;23(5):2948–979.
46. Gao Z, Chen Z, Zou Y, Memon AM. SITAR: GUI test script repair. IEEE Trans Softw Eng. 2015;42(2):170–186.

47. Hussain I, Csallner C. Dynamic symbolic data structure repair. In: 2010 ACM/IEEE 32nd international conference on software engineering, vol. 2. IEEE; 2010. p. 215–218
48. Fischer B, Saabas A, Uustalu T. Program repair as sound optimization of broken programs. In: 2009 third IEEE international symposium on theoretical aspects of software engineering. IEEE; 2009. p. 165–173.
49. Li X, d'Amorim M, Orso A. Intent-preserving test repair. In: 2019 12th IEEE conference on software testing, validation and verification (ICST). IEEE; 2019. p. 217–227.
50. Tian H, Liu K, Kaboré AK, Koyuncu A, Li L, Klein J, Bissyandé TF. Evaluating representation learning of code changes for predicting patch correctness in program repair. In: The 35th IEEE/ACM international conference on automated software engineering (ASE 2020); 2020.
51. Daniel B, Gvero T, Marinov D. On test repair using symbolic execution. In: Proceedings of the 19th international symposium on software testing and analysis; 2010. p. 207–218.
52. Ren X, Yu B, Qi H, Juefei-Xu F, Li Z, Xue W, Ma L, Zhao J. Few-shot guided mix for DNN repairing. In: 2020 IEEE international conference on software maintenance and evolution (ICSME). IEEE; 2020. p. 717–721.
53. Wong C-P, Santiesteban P, Kästner C, Goues CL. VarFix: balancing edit expressiveness and search effectiveness in automated program repair. In: Proceedings of the 29th ACM joint meeting on European software engineering conference and symposium on the foundations of software engineering; 2021. p. 354–366.
54. Afzal A, Motwani M, Stolee K, Brun Y, Goues CL. SOSRepair: expressive semantic search for real-world program repair. IEEE Trans Softw Eng. 2019;47:2162–81.
55. Le XBD, Lo D, Goues CL. History driven program repair. In 2016 IEEE 23rd international conference on software analysis, evolution, and reengineering (SANER), vol. 1. IEEE; 2016. p. 213–224.
56. Murphy-Hill E, Zimmermann T, Bird C, Nagappan N. The design space of bug fixes and how developers navigate it. IEEE Trans Softw Eng. 2014;41(1):65–81.
57. Adamsen CQ, Møller A, Karim R, Sridharan M, Tip F, Sen K. Repairing event race errors by controlling nondeterminism. In: 2017 IEEE/ACM 39th international conference on software engineering (ICSE). IEEE; 2017. p. 289–299.
58. Franz P, Berger T, Fayaz I, Nadi S, Groshev E. ConfigFix: interactive configuration conflict resolution for the linux kernel. In: 2021 IEEE/ACM 43rd international conference on software engineering: software engineering in practice (ICSE-SEIP). IEEE; 2021. p. 91–100.
59. Kim D, Tao Y, Kim S, Zeller A. Where should we fix this bug? a two-phase recommendation model. IEEE Trans Softw Eng. 2013;39(11):1597–1610.
60. Zhang C, Chen B, Chen L, Peng X, Zhao W. A large-scale empirical study of compiler errors in continuous integration. In: Proceedings of the 2019 27th ACM joint meeting on european software engineering conference and symposium on the foundations of software engineering; 2019. p. 176–187.
61. Jafar Al-Kofahi, Hung Nguyen V, and Tien N Nguyen. Fault localization for build code errors in makefiles. In Companion proceedings of the 36th international conference on software engineering; 2014. p. 600–601.
62. Lou Y, Chen Z, Cao Y, Hao D, Zhang L. Understanding build issue resolution in practice: symptoms and fix patterns. In: Proceedings of the 28th ACM joint meeting on european software engineering conference and symposium on the foundations of software engineering; 2020. p. 617–628.
63. Vassallo C, Proksch S, Zemp T, Gall HC. Unbreak my build: assisting developers with build repair hints. In: 2018 IEEE/ACM 26th international conference on program comprehension (ICPC). IEEE; 2018. p. 41–4110.
64. Hassan F, Wang X. HireBuild: an automatic approach to history-driven repair of build scripts. In: 2018 IEEE/ACM 40th international conference on software engineering (ICSE). IEEE; 2018. p. 1078–1089.
65. Lou Y, Chen J, Zhang L, Hao D, Zhang L. History-driven build failure fixing: how far are we?. In: Proceedings of the 28th ACM SIGSOFT international symposium on software testing and analysis; 2019. p. 43–54.

66. Macho C, McIntosh S, Pinzger M. Automatically repairing dependency-related build breakage. In: IEEE 25th international conference on software analysis, evolution and reengineering (SANER). IEEE; 2018. p. 106–117.
67. Dietrich J, Pearce D, Stringer J, Tahir A, Blincoe K. Dependency versioning in the wild. In: 2019 IEEE/ACM 16th international conference on mining software repositories (MSR); 2019. p. 349–359.
68. Decan A, Mens T. What do package dependencies tell us about semantic versioning? IEEE Trans Softw Eng. 2021;47(6):1226–40.
69. Jia Z, Li S, Yu T, Zeng C, Xu E, Liu X, Wang J, Liao X. DepOwl: detecting dependency bugs to prevent compatibility failures. In: 2021 IEEE/ACM 43rd international conference on software engineering (ICSE); 2021. p. 86–98.
70. Soto-Valero C, Benelallam A, Harrand N, Barais O, Baudry B. The emergence of software diversity in maven central. In: 2019 IEEE/ACM 16th international conference on mining software repositories (MSR); 2019. p. 333–343.
71. César S-V, Nicolas H, Martin M, Benoit B. A comprehensive study of bloated dependencies in the Maven ecosystem. Empir Softw Eng. 2021;26:45.
72. Decan A, Mens T, Constantinou E. On the evolution of technical lag in the npm package dependency network. In: 2018 IEEE international conference on software maintenance and evolution (ICSME). IEEE; 2018. p. 404–414.
73. Decan A, Mens T, and Grosjean P. An empirical comparison of dependency network evolution in seven software packaging ecosystems. Empir Softw Eng. 2019;24(1):381–416.
74. Hejderup J, van Deursen A, Gousios G. Software ecosystem call graph for dependency management. In: 2018 IEEE/ACM 40th international conference on software engineering: new ideas and emerging technologies results (ICSE-NIER). IEEE; 2018. p. 101–104.
75. Valiev M, Vasilescu B, Herbsleb J. Ecosystem-level determinants of sustained activity in open-source projects: a case study of the PyPI ecosystem. In: Proceedings of the 2018 26th ACM joint meeting on european software engineering conference and symposium on the foundations of software engineering; 2018. p. 644–655.
76. Abate P, Cosmo RD. Predicting upgrade failures using dependency analysis. In: 2011 IEEE 27th international conference on data engineering workshops. IEEE; 2011. p. 145–150.
77. Bavota G, Canfora G, Di Penta M, Oliveto R, Panichella S. How the apache community upgrades dependencies: an evolutionary study. Empir Softw Eng. 2015;20(5):1275–1317.
78. Li L, Li D, Bissyandé TF, Klein J, Cai H, Lo D, Le Traon Y. Automatically locating malicious packages in piggybacked android apps. In: 2017 IEEE/ACM 4th international conference on mobile software engineering and systems (MOBILESoft). Piscataway: IEEE; 2017. p. 170–174.
79. Decan A, Mens T, Constantinou E. On the evolution of technical lag in the npm package dependency network. In: 2018 IEEE international conference on software maintenance and evolution (ICSME). IEEE; 2018. p. 404–414.
80. Zerouali A, Constantinou E, Mens T, Robles G, González-Barahona J. An empirical analysis of technical lag in npm package dependencies. In: International conference on software reuse. Springer; 2018. p. 95–110.
81. Kula RG, German DM, Ouni A, Ishio T, Inoue K. Do developers update their library dependencies?. Empir Softw Eng. 2018;23(1):384–417.
82. Wang Y, Wen M, Wu R, Liu Z, Shin Tan H, Zhu Z, Yu H, Cheung S-C. Could I have a stack trace to examine the dependency conflict issue?. In: 2019 IEEE/ACM 41st international conference on software engineering (ICSE). IEEE; 2019. p. 572–583.
83. Huang K, Chen B, Shi B, Wang Y, Xu C, Peng X. Interactive, effort-aware library version harmonization. In: Proceedings of the 28th ACM joint meeting on european software engineering conference and symposium on the foundations of software engineering; 2020. p. 518–529.
84. Wang Y, Wen M, Liu Y, Wang Y, Li Z, Wang C, Yu H, Cheung S-C, Xu C, Zhu Z. Watchman: monitoring dependency conflicts for Python library ecosystem. In: Proceedings of the ACM/IEEE 42nd international conference on software engineering; 2020. p. 125–135.

85. Patra J, Dixit PN, Pradel M. ConflictJS: finding and understanding conflicts between JavaScript libraries. In: Proceedings of the 40th international conference on software engineering; 2018. p. 741–751.
86. Vouillon J, Di Cosmo R. On software component co-installability. ACM Trans Softw Eng Methodol. 2013;22(4):34.
87. Vouillon J, Di Cosmo R. Broken sets in software repository evolution. In: Proceedings of the 2013 international conference on software engineering; 2013. p. 412–421.
88. Mancinelli F, Boender J, Di Cosmo R, Vouillon J, Durak B, Leroy X, Treinen R. Managing the complexity of large free and open source package-based software distributions. In: 21st IEEE/ACM international conference on automated software engineering (ASE'06). IEEE; 2006. p. 199–208.
89. Trezentos P, Lynce I, Oliveira AL. Apt-pbo: solving the software dependency problem using pseudo-Boolean optimization. In: Proceedings of the IEEE/ACM international conference on automated software engineering; 2010. p. 427–436.
90. Argelich J, Le Berre D, Lynce I, Marques-Silva J, Rapicault P. Solving Linux upgradeability problems using Boolean optimization. In: LoCoCo 2010: logics for component configuration; 2010.
91. Tucker C, Shuffelton D, Jhala R, Lerner S. OPIUM: Optimal package install/uninstall manager. In: 29th international conference on software engineering (ICSE'07); 2007. p. 178–188.

Chapter 6
Streamlining Software Bloated Dependencies

Abstract Numerous third-party libraries introduced into client projects are not actually required, resulting in modern software being gradually bloated. Software developers may spend much unnecessary effort to manage the bloated dependencies: keeping the library versions up-to-date, making sure that heterogeneous licenses are compatible, and resolving dependency conflict or vulnerability issues.

However, the prior debloating techniques can easily produce false alarms of bloated dependencies since they are less effective in analyzing Java reflections. Besides, the solutions given by the existing approaches for removing bloated dependencies may induce new issues that are not conducive to dependency management. To address the above limitations, in this chapter, we developed a technique, *Slimming*, to remove bloated dependencies from software projects reliably. *Slimming* statically analyzes the Java reflections that are commonly leveraged by popular frameworks (e.g., *Spring Boot*) and resolves the reflective targets via parsing configuration files (`*.xml`, `*.yml`, and `*.properties`). By modeling string manipulations, *Slimming* fully resolves the string arguments of our concerned reflection APIs to identify all the required dependencies. More importantly, it helps developers analyze the debloating solutions by weighing the benefits against the costs of dependency management. Our evaluation results show that the static reflection analysis capability of *Slimming* outperforms all the other existing techniques with 97.0% of *Precision* and 98.8% of *Recall*. Compared with the prior debloating techniques, *Slimming* can reliably remove the bloated dependencies with a 100% test passing ratio and improve the rationality of debloating solutions. In our large-scale study in the Maven ecosystem, *Slimming* reported 484 bloated dependencies to 66 open-source projects. Thirty-eight reports (57.6%) have been confirmed by developers.

6.1 Introduction

Dependency management tools (e.g., Maven for Java and Cargo for Rust) boost software reuse by automatically fetching all the direct and transitive third-party dependencies required to compile, test, and deploy a client project. In practice,

Y. Wang et al., *Managing Software Supply Chains*,
https://doi.org/10.1007/978-981-96-1797-5_6

however, numerous introduced third-party libraries are not actually used by client code, resulting in gradually bloating software projects. A recent study [1] on 435 open-source projects showed that the number of transitive dependencies in 2011 was 1,695, and by the end of 2020, this number grew up to 286,228 (increase > 250×). Bloated software negatively affects code performance on resource-constrained devices with limited memory. Additionally, it poses a direct security threat since unused libraries increase security attack surfaces and introduces an extra burden for dependency management. Software developers may spend much effort to manage unnecessary dependencies: keeping the library versions up-to-date, making sure that heterogeneous licenses are compatible, and resolving dependency conflicts or vulnerability issues.

To promote dependency management, developers urgently need an effective technique to help them remove the bloated third-party libraries from dependency configurations. Many existing debloating techniques [2–12] are proposed for reducing the size of software at fine granularity (i.e., method/statement level), to improve the efficiency of installations and executions on resource-constrained hardware. Soto-Valero [1] et al. develop a coarse-grained debloating technique, *DepClean*, which constructs the complete dependency tree of a project and determines the presence of bloated libraries by statically analyzing the bytecode. However, the prior approaches have the following limitations:

- *Less effective in analyzing Java reflections.* Dynamic language features are widely adopted in developing modern software projects, which are also leveraged by projects to facilitate flexible integration with the code from third-party libraries. To avoid false alarms of bloated dependencies, a debloating technique should be empowered by effective reflection analysis. However, reflection analysis is a long-standing hard open problem. Previous debloating techniques consider Java reflection as a separate assumption, and they either handle it partially based on dynamic analysis techniques [6] or cannot resolve it well based on the existing static analysis tools [4, 5, 7, 13]. The dynamic analysis techniques heavily depend on the test coverage rate of the given projects, which is not scalable for all the subjects. The static analysis techniques cannot resolve the reflection code well since dynamic behaviors of reflective calls are mainly specified by their string arguments, with some string values being intra-procedurally and inter-procedurally manipulated, read from configuration files, or even retrieved from the Internet. The challenges of static reflection analyses are illustrated in Sect. 6.2.1.
- *Removing bloated libraries may induce new issues that are not conducive to dependency management.* In many cases, although the client project does not actually use a bloated dependency, the libraries transitively introduced by the bloated dependency can be invoked by client code via certain direct dependencies. After removing the bloated library from a configuration file, the referenced transitive dependencies should be declared as the client project's

direct dependencies to ensure the program can run correctly. At the cost of the above changes, developers would spend much effort to keep their versions up-to-date. However, their updated version can easily induce incompatibility issues with the libraries depending on them. There is no existing technique to help developers analyze the solutions for removing bloated dependencies by weighing the benefits against the costs of dependency management. The challenges of removing bloated dependencies are illustrated in Sect. 6.2.2.

To address the above limitations, in this chapter, we developed a technique, *Slimming*, to help developers reliably remove bloated dependencies from software projects. Our work focuses on the Maven ecosystem, the most popular package manager, and an automatic build system for Java programming language. *Slimming* is empowered by effective static reflection analyses, which can precisely resolve (1) the reflections that are synthesized by dependency injections, annotations, and configurations in popular Java frameworks (e.g., *Java EE Servlets, Java Beans, Apache Struts, Spring, Spring Boot*, and *Tomcat*) and (2) nonconstant arguments of reflection APIs that are undergone a series of complex string manipulations. Leveraging static reflection analyses, *Slimming* captures all the bloated dependencies not actually used by the client projects. Furthermore, our tool derives debloating solutions by making a trade-off between the benefits (e.g., removal of bloated dependencies can also resolve the issues of vulnerabilities/dependency conflicts/incompatible licenses/outdated dependencies) and the costs (e.g., potentially inducing more maintenance effort) of dependency management.

To evaluate *Slimming*, we conduct a systematic study to assess the effectiveness of reflection analysis and the reliability of debloating solutions. We first construct a high-quality benchmark including 3,520 reflective calls captured by dynamic techniques from a collection of framework-based Java projects. *Slimming* achieves a *Precision* of 97.0% and a *Recall* of 98.8% on reflection resolution, which significantly outperforms all the state-of-the-art reflection analysis techniques. By collecting a set of Java projects with a 100% test coverage for their byte code instructions, we further validate whether the derived debloating solutions will induce new issues. The experiment results indicate that *Slimming* can reliably remove bloated dependencies with a 100% test passing ratio and 0 false alarm. Moreover, leveraging *Slimming*, we conducted a large-scale study on Java projects to reveal the landscapes of bloated dependencies in the Maven ecosystem. To evaluate the usefulness of our tool, we configure *Slimming* to report 484 bloated dependencies to 66 open-source projects. Thirty-eight reports (57.6%) have been confirmed by developers. The above feedback demonstrates the rationality of debloating solutions, which conform to developers' viewpoints on software maintenance.

6.2 Motivation and Challenges

6.2.1 Resolving Java Reflections

To precisely locate bloated dependencies, project developers should identify all the usage of third-party libraries. However, modern Java projects heavily leverage frameworks (e.g., *Spring Boot*) in their development. These frameworks commonly employ dynamic techniques (e.g., dependency injection), based on Java reflections, annotations, and configurations in `*.xml`, `*.yml`, and `*.properties` files. Such dynamic patterns resist static reflection analysis, leading to false alarms of bloated dependencies.

Figure 6.1 shows an illustrative example of challenges in resolving Java reflections. Figure 6.1a extracts a code snippet from the open-source project `Mall`, which is implemented for sending messages to servers. As shown in Fig. 6.1b, the *SpringBoot* framework leverages API `SpringApplication.run()` (`Line 14`) to inject the information from annotation (`Line 10`) and configuration file `messageBean.xml` (`Line 11`) to the container instance *application* via *dependency*

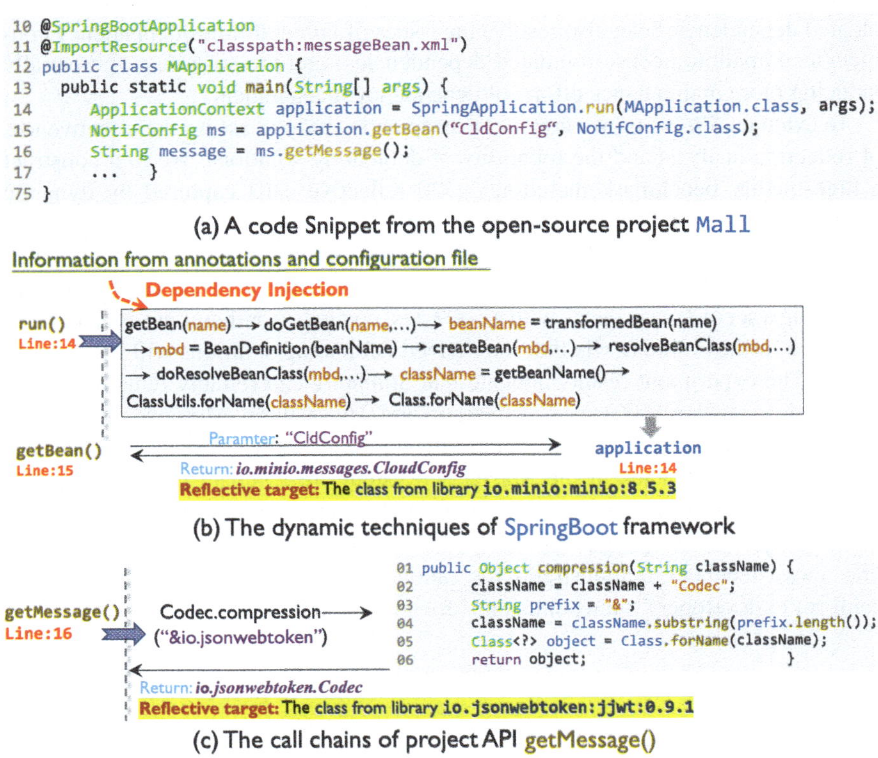

Fig. 6.1 An illustrative example of challenges in resolving Java reflections

injection technique. The call chain triggered by `SpringApplication.run()` involves Java reflection, which accesses *class-retrieving method* `Class::forname` to return a set of class objects. The reflective target *io.minio.messages.CloudConfig* is returned by *SpringBoot* framework API `ApplicationContext.get-Bean()` (`Line 15`) via argument `"CldConfig"` from the container instance *application*. Unfortunately, the values of return types and API arguments can only be captured from data flow at runtime, rather than resolved by static reflection analysis. Since class *io.minio.messages.CloudConfig* belongs to the third-party library `io.minio:minio:8.5.3`, failing to resolve this reflective target may result in a false alarm regarding bloated dependencies.

In addition, the call chain triggered by API `NotifConfig.get-Messgae()` (`Line 16`) also involves reflective calls. As shown in Fig. 6.1c, the *class-retrieving method* `Class::forname` (`Lines 05`) returns a class object representing a class that is specified by the value of its string argument `"className"`. The reflective target *io.jsonwebtoken.Code* has undergone two string operations `"+"` and `"substring()"` in `Lines 02` and `04`, respectively, which can only be resolved by precise string analysis. However, existing static reflection analysis techniques built on top of *Doop* [14] model simple string operations including `"+"` and `"append()"` to resolve reflective targets, but they cannot deal with the other complex string operations. Missed inferring such a reflective target from a third-party library `io.jsonwebtoken:jjwt:0.9.1` can also result in a false alarm of bloated dependency.

> ***Challenge #1:*** *The frameworks (e.g., SpringBoot) commonly employ dynamic techniques combining Java reflections with annotations/configuration files. The reflective targets can involve the usage of third-party libraries, which are difficult to be resolved statically.*
> ***Challenge #2:*** *Existing reflection analyses resolve class-level reflective targets by statically analyzing the string arguments of* class-retrieving method *calls. The arguments can be nonconstant strings that undergo both intra-procedurally and inter-procedurally string operations (e.g., `"append()"`), which cannot be fully resolved by the existing techniques.*

6.2.2 Removing Bloated Dependencies

Removing the identified bloated dependencies from configuration files (`POM.xml`) may induce new issues, since the solutions are not conducive to long-term dependency management for client projects. Figure 6.2 illustrates the dependency graph of a popular open-source project `Spring-amqp` (566 Stars on GitHub). In issue report `Spring-amqp#65` [15], developers noticed that library *springframework:context:*

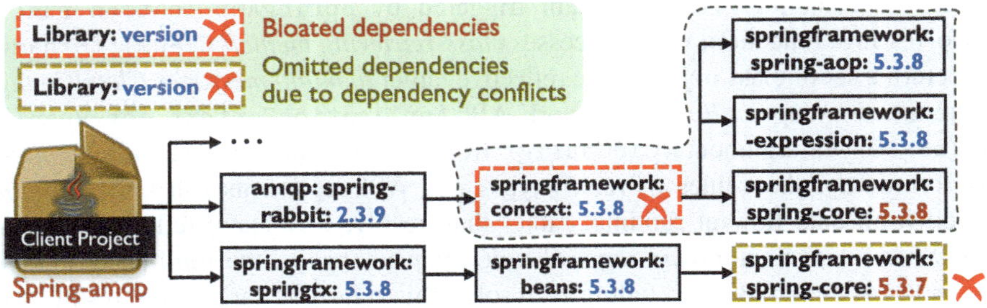

Fig. 6.2 An illustrative example of challenges in removing bloated dependencies

5.3.8 is a bloated dependency, which is not actually invoked by the client project. However, three libraries *spring-aop: 5.3.8*, *expression: 5.3.8*, and *spring-core: 5.3.8* introduced by *springframework:context: 5.3.8* are used by project `Spring-amqp` through its direct dependency *amqp: spring-rabbit: 2.3.9*. To ensure that the program can run correctly, after removing the bloated library *springframework:context: 5.3.8* from `POM.xml`, developers should declare its three dependencies as project `Spring-amqp`'s direct dependencies. In the subsequent maintenance process, potential issues come with the above changes:

- After declaring the three libraries *spring-aop: 5.3.8*, *expression: 5.3.8*, and *spring-core: 5.3.8* as direct dependencies, developers should spend much effort to keep their versions up-to-date. However, their updated versions may be incompatible with the asynchronously evolved version of library *amqp: spring-rabbit*.
- As shown in Fig. 6.2, two versions of library *spring-core* are introduced in the dependency graph. The build tool loads version 5.3.8 while shadows version 5.3.7. Due to such a dependency conflict issue, library *springframework:beans: 5.3.8* actually invokes the loaded version *spring-core 5.3.8*. If developers declare library *spring-core* as a direct dependency, its updated version may also induce incompatibility issues with *springframework:beans*.

In this scenario, developers abandoned such a solution, since they thought the removal of bloated dependency would bring greater maintenance costs to their project. Interestingly, by inspection, we noticed similar cases happened in project `Jax-rs2-guide` (`Jax-rs2-guide`#203 [16]). However, since the bloated dependency exposed a high-severity level vulnerability (`CVE-2022-22976`), `Jax-rs2-guide`'s developer finally decided to remove it at the expense of a higher maintenance burden, after making a trade-off on dependency management.

> ***Challenge #3:*** *Removing bloated dependencies can easily induce new issues that are not conducive to dependency management. There is no existing technique to help developers analyze the solutions of removing bloated dependencies, by weighing the benefits (e.g., removal of bloated dependencies can also resolve the issues of vulnerabilities/dependency conflicts/incompatible licenses/outdated dependencies) against the costs (e.g., potentially induce more maintenance effort) on dependency management.*

6.3 Slimming Approach

To address the limitations of prior debloating approaches, we developed a technique, *Slimming*, to help developers reliably remove the bloated dependencies. Figure 6.3 shows the overall architecture of *Slimming*. To precisely identify bloated dependencies, our tool is empowered by effective ***static reflection analyses*** that can overcome *Challenges#1* and *#2*. As illustrated in Section 2.1, the frameworks encapsulate a set of publicly accessible APIs to deal with dynamic language

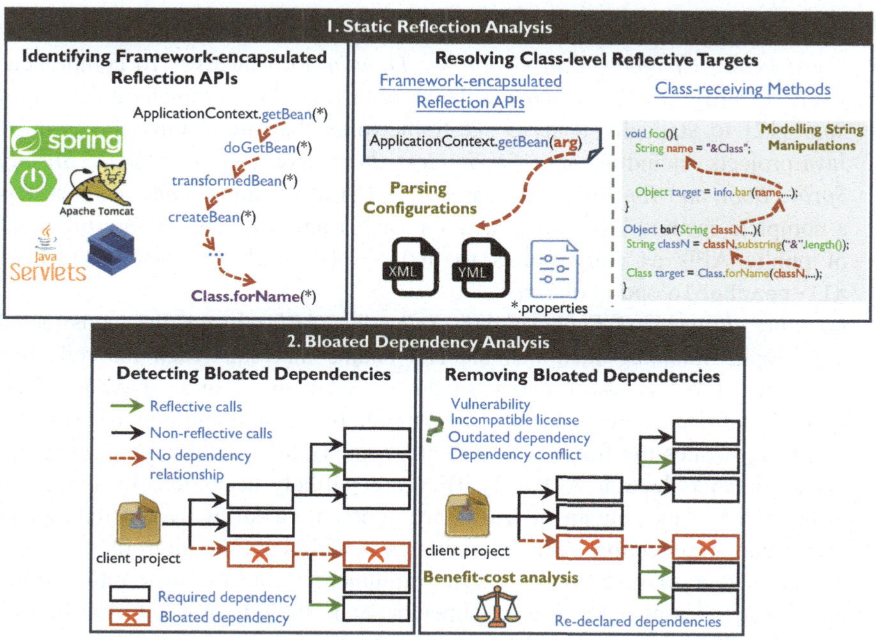

Fig. 6.3 The overall architecture of *Slimming*

features, which transitively reach reflective call sites (we refer to such public APIs as ***framework-encapsulated reflection APIs***). In this chapter, to address *Challenge #1*, *Slimming* leverages a scalable technique to identify all the framework-encapsulated reflection APIs from popular frameworks. Based on static analysis, our tool further parses the arguments of framework-encapsulated reflection APIs combined with framework configuration files (`*.xml`, `*.yml`, and `*.properties`) to resolve the class-level reflective targets. To address *Challenge #2*, *Slimming* models all the string operations defined by JDK (e.g., *String.substring*()) for inferring nonconstant strings of class-receiving methods.

Based on static reflection analysis, *Slimming* captures all the bloated dependencies not actually used by the client project. To address *Challenge #3* regarding removing bloated dependencies, our tool generates the solutions by weighing the benefits (e.g., removal of bloated dependencies can also resolve the issues of vulnerabilities/dependency conflicts/incompatible licenses/outdated dependencies) against the costs (e.g., potentially inducing more maintenance effort) of dependency management.

6.3.1 Static Reflection Analysis

Slimming performs the static reflection analysis in two steps:

Step 1: Identifying Framework-Encapsulated Reflection APIs This step involves two tasks:

- *Constructing Complete Call Graph for Popular Frameworks.* To comprehensively identify framework-encapsulated reflection APIs, *Slimming* leverages *Soot* [17] to statically analyze six frameworks that are commonly used by Java projects, including *Java EE Servlets*, *Java Beans*, *Apache Struts*, *Spring*, *Spring Boot*, and *Tomcat*. Based on *Soot*'s CHA algorithm, *Slimming* constructs a complete method-level call graph for each framework by configuring a set of public APIs as entry points to find all the reachable methods (setting `all-reachable` option of *Soot*).
- *Locating Framework-Encapsulated Reflection APIs.* From the constructed call graph, *Slimming* identifies the call chains that can reach the reflective call sites (i.e., class-retrieving methods, such as `Class::forname` and `ClassLoader::load-Class`). Furthermore, on these identified call chains, *Slimming* locates the framework APIs that satisfy three criteria as framework-encapsulated reflection APIs: (1) They are publicly accessible by the client projects, (2) they contain at least one argument of string type (framework-encapsulated reflection APIs communicate with configuration files `*.xml`, `*.yml`, and `*.properties` via string arguments), and (3) their return types are abstract classes, interfaces, or superclasses in the inheritance hierarchy (the instantiated class objects are determined by the reflective targets).

Based on the above process, *Slimming* eventually identifies 294 framework-encapsulated reflection APIs from the six popular Java frameworks. Among them, 40, 32, 42, 65, 79, and 36 APIs are located from *Java EE Servlets*, *Java Beans*, *Apache Struts*, *Spring*, *Spring Boot*, and *Tomcat*, respectively.

Step 2: Resolving Class-Level Reflective Targets Since we aim to identify the bloated dependencies at the library level from configurations, for static analysis, *Slimming* resolves the reflective targets at the class level. Resolving reflective targets mainly relies on analyzing the string arguments to Java reflection APIs. For a given Java project, *Slimming* statically analyzes its call graph and performs the following tasks to deal with framework-encapsulated reflection APIs and class-retrieving methods separately.

(a) Analyzing Framework-Encapsulated Reflection APIs On the call graph of the project under analysis, *Slimming* first locates the framework-encapsulated reflection APIs. Furthermore, leveraging framework configuration files, it analyzes the API arguments to resolve the class-level reflective targets in the following two steps:

- *Parsing Configuration Files.* Typically, framework configuration files (`*.xml`, `*.yml`, and `*.properties`) record the fully qualified class name as the reflective targets, and each class name corresponds to a string literal. Framework-encapsulated reflection APIs return the reflective targets using the string literals as their arguments to map the class names from configuration files. For example, in the code snippet of Fig. 6.1a, the framework-encapsulated reflection API `ApplicationContext.getBean(*)` communicates with the container instance *application* (whose information is injected by configuration file `messageBean.xml`) via the string argument `"CldConfig"` to return the corresponding reflective target *io.minio.messages.CloudConfig*. The mapping of reflective target and string literal `"CldConfig"` is configurated in `messageBean.xml` file. Therefore, to perform static reflection analysis, *Slimming* collects and parses three types of configuration files in a given project to extract the mappings of the fully qualified class name and its corresponding string literal. The parsing patterns of *Slimming* for configuration files are described in Fig. 6.4. Each pattern identifies the concerned mappings $attr_1 \rightarrow attr_2$, according to the syntax rules of `*.xml`, `*.yml`, and `*.properties`, where $attr_1$ is a string attribute extracted from the configuration files, and $attr_2$ is $attr_1$'s attribute value in the format of class name.
- *Resolving Reflective Targets.* For each identified framework-encapsulated reflection API, *Slimming* checks if its string arguments map a fully qualified class name in the configuration file. Our tool considers the mapped class name as a reflective target returned by the framework-encapsulated reflection API.

(b) Analyzing Class-Retrieving Methods In addition to the framework-encapsulated reflection APIs, *Slimming* deals with four class-retrieving methods that are most widely used by modern Java projects [18]: `Class::forName`,

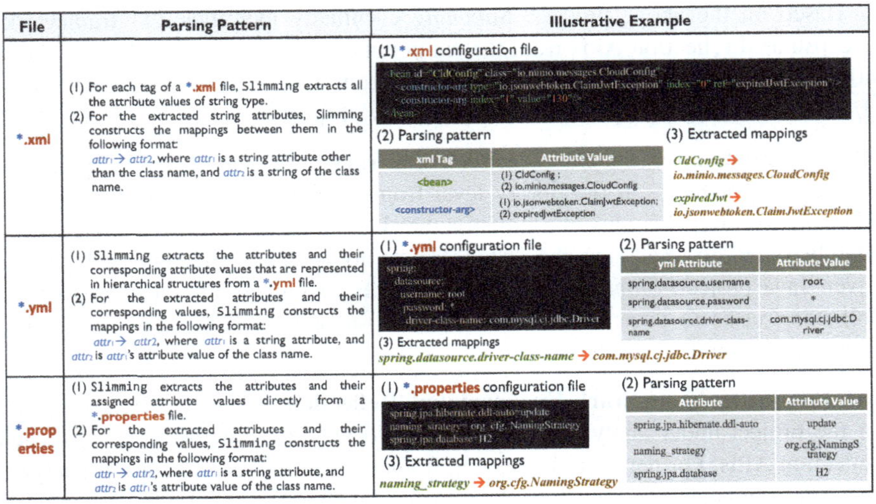

Fig. 6.4 Parsing patterns of *Slimming* for configuration files

ClassLoader::load-Class, Object::getClass, and .class. Java reflection begins with class objects, which are returned by calling class-retrieving methods. Note that the class object returned by O.getClass() and A.class represents the dynamic type (class) of O and A, respectively. *Slimming* can efficiently resolve the reflective targets by statically analyzing these two class-retrieving methods. However, Class::forName and ClassLoader::loadClass return a class object representing a class that is specified by the value of their string arguments. Therefore, resolving reflective targets depends on analyzing the string arguments of the above two class-retrieving methods.

If the string arguments of Class::forName and ClassLoader::loadClass are constant strings, *Slimming* considers the arguments of class names as reflective targets. However, according to an investigation on reflection usage in popular Java projects [18], in practice, nearly 65.3% of reflection API arguments are nonconstant strings that are undergone intra-procedural and inter-procedural string manipulations. To precisely resolve the nonconstant string arguments, *Slimming* models all the string operations defined by JDK (e.g., String.length(), String.substring()) for inferring string manipulations, which involves three tasks:

- *Tagging the end location of string manipulations. Slimming* identifies each class-receiving method with string arguments and tags its first string argument as the end location of string manipulations. The first string argument of class-receiving methods Class::forName and ClassLoader::loadClass is the outcome of string manipulations.
- *Tagging the start location of string manipulations.* From each tagged end location, *Slimming* performs pointer analysis to trace the data flow and locates a

```
Algorithm 1: Modelling string manipulations
   Input: start_location; end_location
   Output: model_result
1  Initiate model_result;
2  start_variable ← start_location;
3  stringOperations ← [String:String:subString(int),String:int:length(),...];
4  while start_variable ≠ end_location do
5      tmp_statement = get_statement(start_variable);
6      if tmp_statement.Contains(stringOperations) then
7          (instanceObject, APIsignature, arg) ← method_analysis(tmp_statement);
8          if instanceObject's type ∈ {Integer, String, Char} then
9              model_result ← valueOfObject(instanceObject).APIsignature(arg);
10         else
11             model_result ← instanceObject.APIsignature(arg);
12         start_variable ← update_variable(model_result);
13     else
14         start_variable ← pointer_analysis(tmp_statement);
15 return model_result;
```

Fig. 6.5 Modeling string manipulations

string assignment statement that satisfies two conditions: (1) The value assigned is a string constant, and (2) the assigned string variable is not an argument of the function in which it is defined. *Slimming* tags this string variable as the corresponding start location of string manipulations.

- *Modeling string manipulations.* The algorithm of modeling string manipulations is described in Fig. 6.5, which takes the tagged start location (*start_location*) and end location (*end_location*) of string manipulations as inputs and returns the manipulation outcome (*model_result*). The algorithm works as follows. It first initiates *model_result* and assigns the *start_location* to *start_variable* (`Lines 1-2`). To fully resolve the nonconstant string arguments of reflection APIs, our tool collects 72 types of string operations that are defined by JDK and assigns the signature array to *StringOperations* (`Line 3`). *Slimming* iteratively analyzes each statement *tmp_statement* invoked between *start_location* and *end_location* and utilizes *start_variable* to point to the current statement under analysis (`Line 5`). If *tmp_statement* involves a string operation API (e.g., *String.substring()*), *Slimming* then extracts the API's signature and arguments and the instance object of string manipulation (`Lines 6-7`). Next, our tool invokes the corresponding string operation API with the above extracted arguments to simulate the string manipulations (the simulated outcome is assigned to *model_result*) (`Lines 8-11`). Furthermore, *Slimming* assigns the current value of *model_result* to the concerned string argument/variable referenced by the subsequent string manipulation relevant statement (`Line 12`). If the *tmp_statement* does not involve a string operation API, *Slimming* traces the data flow based on pointer analysis (`Lines 13-14`). Our tool iteratively performs the above tasks until its pointer moves to the end location of string manipulations.

6.3.2 Bloated Dependency Analysis

Based on the dependency relationships captured by static reflection analysis, *Slimming* removes the bloated dependencies in two steps:

Step 1: Detecting Bloated Dependencies Leveraging *Soot*, *Slimming* first obtains the class-level dependency graph of a given project based on static analysis. Our tool further adds the dependencies between classes that are captured by reflection analysis to construct a complete dependency graph. *Slimming* considers a library as a bloated dependency if none of its defined classes exists in the dependency graph.

Step 2: Removing Bloated Dependencies *Slimming* performs a benefit-cost analysis to remove the bloated dependencies reasonably. It takes the following factors into consideration:

- *Factors that bring additional benefit to dependency management: Slimming* considers a solution that brings additional benefit to dependency management if removing bloated dependencies can also resolve four types of issues:
  - *Vulnerability issues:* The bloated dependencies contain the vulnerabilities that have been disclosed in vulnerability databases. *Slimming* collects the vulnerable library information from two recognized databases *GitHub Advisory DB* [19] and *Snyk Vulnerability DB* [20], as the basis for assessment.
  - *Incompatible license issues:* The open-source licenses declared by bloated dependencies are incompatible with that of a client project. *Slimming* checks the incompatible license issues based on compatible relationships among 389 popular open-source licenses provided on *Free Software Foundation* website [21].
  - *Outdated dependency issues:* The bloated dependencies are the libraries that have not been maintained by developers for more than N years. Based on the outdated dependencies defined by approach [22], *Slimming* sets $N = 3$ and collects the last updated date of each project in *Maven Central Repository* when performing analysis.
  - *Dependency conflict issues:* Multiple versions of a library that are directly or transitively introduced into a client project are all identified as bloated dependencies. *Slimming* captures the dependency conflict issues leveraging the warnings reported by `maven-dependency-tree` plugin [23].
- *Factors that induce costs on dependency management:* Let $BD = \{lib_1, lib_2, \cdots, lib_n\}$ be a collection of identified bloated dependencies of a given project, $TD_i = \{lib_1, lib_2, \cdots, lib_m\}$ be a set of libraries transitively introduced by a bloated dependency $lib_i \in BD$, and $RD_i \subseteq TD_i$ be a set of libraries in TD_i that are referenced by the client project. We refer to a library $lib_k \in RD_i$ as the ***over-dependency management cases***, *which needs to be additionally declared as the client project's direct dependency after removing the bloated library $lib_i \in BD$ to avoid inducing runtime errors.* At the cost of the above changes, developers would spend the effort to keep the additionally

declared library versions up-to-date. However, their updated versions can easily induce incompatibility issues with the libraries depending on them.

A Benefit-Cost Analysis for a Debloating Solution For a bloated dependency $lib_i \in BD$, *Slimming* performs a benefit-cost analysis to generate a reliable debloating solution as follows:

- *Case 1:* If $TD_i = \emptyset$, *Slimming* removes the bloated dependency lib_i from configuration file.
- *Case 2:* If $TD_i \neq \emptyset$ and $RD_i = \emptyset$, *Slimming* removes the bloated dependency lib_i from configuration file.
- *Case 3:* Suppose that $TD_i \neq \emptyset$, $RD_i \neq \emptyset$, and the bloated dependency lib_i also induces the issues of vulnerabilities/dependency conflicts/incompatible licenses/outdated dependencies. Since removing lib_i can bring additional benefits to dependency management, *Slimming* suggests developers perform such a debloating solution at a cost of additionally declaring its dependencies $lib_k \in RD_i$ as direct dependencies of the client project.

According to the syntax rules of Maven dependency configurations, if the bloated dependencies are inherited from the parent module, *Slimming* removes them with the aid of *<provided>* tag of `POM.xml` file. Otherwise, *Slimming* performs debloating solutions using *<exclusion>* tag. *Slimming* triggers projects' bundled tests to validate whether the debloating solution will cause program errors. Our tool finally reports a collection of bloated dependencies and the corresponding debloating solution if all the tests are passed.

6.4 Evaluation

We study two research questions in our evaluation section:

- **RQ1 (Effectiveness of Reflection Analysis)**: ***How effective is*** *Slimming* ***in analyzing Java reflections?*** To answer RQ1, we constructed a high-quality benchmark and compare *Slimming* with three state-of-the-art reflection analysis techniques to evaluate their effectiveness.
- **RQ2 (Reliability of Debloating Solutions)**: ***Can*** *Slimming* ***reliably remove the bloated dependencies without inducing new issues?*** To answer RQ2, we collected 40 Java projects with 100% test coverage for their byte code instructions, to validate whether removing bloated dependencies will induce new issues.

Table 6.1 Demographics of collected Java projects for RQ1 and RQ2

Metrics \ Statistics	Max.	Min.	Avg.	Med.
#Tests	737	1	27	4
#Stars	34,200	5	4,527	55
#Modules	14	1	5	4
#Direct Dependencies	30	6	13	10

6.4.1 Data Collection

Following the prior approaches [18, 24], we adopt six large *DaCapo* datasets (2006-10-MR2) [25] and 3,520 reflective calls captured by dynamic techniques from 37 framework-based Java projects as benchmarks, to evaluate *Slimming*'s effectiveness in reflection analysis (**RQ1**). The benchmark construction process involves two steps:

- *Collecting Framework-Based Java Projects:* Since the subjects in *DaCapo* datasets (collected in 2006) do not rely on the frameworks such as *Spring Boot*, etc., they cannot comprehensively reflect the reflection resolving capability of *Slimming*. As such, we extend the datasets by collecting more representative framework-based Java projects. The project collection satisfies ***four criteria***: (1) The projects have more than 5 Stars (i.e., popularity), (2) the projects have more than five direct dependencies (i.e., complexity), (3) the projects' bundled tests achieve 100% of instruction coverage.[1] Such high test coverage for Java byte code instructions enables us to completely capture the reflective targets, leveraging the dynamic program analysis tool *TamiFlex* [27], and (4) the projects depend on at least one popular framework.

  With the above process, we obtained 37 Java projects (37.8%, 21.6%, 13.5%, 8.1%, 13.5%, and 5.4% of them rely on *Spring Boot*, *Spring*, *Tomcat*, *Java EE Servlets*, *Java Beans*, and *Apache Struts* frameworks, respectively). Table 6.1 describes the demographics of the collected Java projects. On average, each project has 27.3 ± 81.5 tests, 4,579.5 ± 11,023.4 Stars, 5.4 ± 4.6 modules, and 12.8 ± 6.1 direct dependencies.
- *Identifying All the Reflective Targets Using TamiFlex: TamiFlex* is an effective dynamic analysis tool proposed by approach [27], which inserts runtime checks into the program to capture the reflective calls triggered by program execution. Leveraging *TamiFlex*, we execute the tests bundled with the 37 Java projects (100% test coverage for byte code instructions), to precisely and completely obtain the reflective targets.

[1] We leverage a popular Java code coverage library *JaCoCo* [26] to measure the instruction coverage. Instruction coverage provides information about the amount of code that has been executed or missed.

Table 6.2 Statistics of our constructed benchmark

	Type 1	Type 2	Type 3	Type 4	Others	Sum
DaCaPo	143	84	0	4	10	241
37 Java projects	1,888	84	1,082	213	12	3,279
Sum	**2,031**	**168**	**1,082**	**217**	**22**	**3,520**

Table 6.2 shows the statistics of our constructed benchmark. In total, *TamiFlex* captures 3,520 reflective targets. Among them, 2,032 (57.7%) are received from nonconstant string arguments of class-receiving methods (***Type 1***), which are undergone a series of string manipulations; 168 (4.8%) are received from constant string arguments of class-receiving methods (***Type 2***); 1,082 (30.7%) are recorded in the framework configuration files, which need to communicate with framework-encapsulated reflection APIs (***Type 3***); 217 (6.2%) are embellished with annotations (***Type 4***); and 22 (0.6%) are implemented in other manners (e.g., retrieving from the Internet).

6.4.2 RQ1: Effectiveness of Reflection Analysis

Study Methodology We compare *Slimming* with three state-of-the-art reflection analysis techniques to evaluate their effectiveness:

- *Doop* [28] is a state-of-the-art framework for Java pointer and taint analysis. In addition to the basic options (e.g., "`reflection-classic`") provided by *Doop* for reflection analysis, we also turned on the option "`reflection-substring-analysis`" proposed by approach [24] (***APLAS 2015***) to resolve reflective targets based on string-flow analysis.
- *JackEE* [29] is a static analysis framework relying on the context of *Doop* (***PLDI 2020***), to resolve the reflections that are synthesized by *dependency injections*, *Java annotations*, and *configurations* in Enterprise Frameworks including *Java EE Servlets*, *Java Beans*, *Spring*, and *Apache Struts*.
- *Soot* [17] is the best-known static analysis framework to construct dependency graphs for Java programs. We turn on the options "`Safe forName`" and "`Safe newInstance`" provided by *Soot* for reflection resolution.

All the baseline approaches extract the dependency relationships at method granularity; in our study, we only consider the resolved reflective class names to make the comparisons.

Evaluation Metrics Leveraging our constructed benchmark, we consider six metrics in the evaluation: (1) ***True Positive (TP)***: the reflective targets resolved by *Slimming* are recorded in the benchmark by *TamiFlex*, (2) ***False Positive (FP)***: the reflective targets resolved by *Slimming* are not recorded in the benchmark by

TamiFlex, and (3) ***False Negative (FN)***: the reflective targets are recorded in the benchmark by *TamiFlex* but not resolved by *Slimming*.

Based on the above three metrics, we can obtain the *Precision*, *Recall*, and *F-measure* as follows: (a) ***Precision*** = *TP* / (*TP* + *FP*), (b) ***Recall***: *TP* / (*TP* + *FN*), and (c) ***F-measure***: 2 × *Precision* × *Recall* / (*Precision* + *Recall*). *Precision* evaluates whether *Slimming* can resolve reflective targets precisely. *Recall* evaluates the capability of *Slimming* in resolving all the reflective targets. *F-measure* combines the *Precision* and *Recall* together [30].

Results Table 6.3 shows the experiment results of RQ1. *Slimming* resolves 3,584 reflective targets with a *Precision* of 97.0%, a *Recall* of 98.8% and an *F-measure* of 97.9%. In contrast, *Doop*, *JackEE*, and *Soot* report a large number of false positive and negative cases, resulting in *Precision* = 44.8%, 52.7%, and 34.8% and *Recall* = 80.7%, 85.8%, and 76.5% respectively. By checking the analytic effectiveness for different types of reflective targets (as shown in Table 6.4), we found that *Slimming* can resolve 1,982 out of 2,031 (97.6%) nonconstant string arguments of class-receiving methods by modeling string manipulations (***Type 1***) and 1,075 out of 1,082 (99.4%) class names recorded in framework configuration files (`*.xml`, `*.yml`, and `*.properties`) by analyzing framework-encapsulated reflection APIs (***Type 3***). Based on the results, we can conclude that *Slimming* can effectively resolve different types of reflective targets, significantly outperforming all the baselines.

FP Analysis For all the static reflection analysis techniques, if they cannot resolve the nonconstant string arguments of class-receiving methods, they will mock the return types of class-receiving methods as reflective targets. In the cases that the class-receiving methods' return types are abstract classes, interfaces, or superclasses, the techniques will infer all the potential types of instantiated class objects as the results. "*Type Inference*" column of Table 6.4 shows *#return types*

Table 6.3 Experiment results of RQ1

Baselines \ Metrics	TP	FP	FN	Precision	Recall	F-measure
Doop [28]	2,840	3,507	680	44.8%	80.7%	57.6%
JackEE [29]	3,020	2,709	500	52.7%	85.8%	65.3%
Soot [17]	2,693	5,042	827	34.8%	76.5%	47.9%
Slimming	**3,477**	**107**	**43**	**97.0%**	**98.8%**	**97.9%**

Table 6.4 Effectiveness of analyzing different types of reflective targets

Baselines \ Types	Type 1	Type 2	Type 3	Type 4	Others	Type inference
Doop [28]	728	168	0	165	0	1,779
JackEE [29]	728	168	828	217	0	1,079
Soot [17]	623	168	0	217	0	1,685
Slimming	**1,982**	**168**	**1,075**	**217**	**0**	**35**

of class-receiving methods that are mocked by these techniques. *Doop*, *JackEE*, and *Soot* report 3,507, 2,709, and 5,042 *FPs*, respectively, because they are less effective in dealing with ***Types 1*** and ***3*** cases.

FN Analysis *Slimming* produces 43 *FNs* since it cannot resolve 14 nonconstant string arguments of class-receiving methods (***Type 1***), 7 classes recorded in the framework configuration files (***Type 3***), and 22 classes received from Internet (***Others***). For the 14 ***Type 1*** cases, *Slimming* is unable to simulate the string manipulations that involve string arrays. For the seven ***Type 3*** cases, these framework-based projects use customized types of files to configure reflective targets rather than `*.xml`, `*.yml`, or `*.properties`. Moreover, the three baselines can only deal with simple string operations including "+" and "`append()`" to resolve reflective targets, as such they produce many *FNs* for ***Type 1*** cases. *JackEE* can handle few framework-encapsulated reflection APIs and analyze `*.xml` configurations in two popular frameworks including *Java Beans* and *Spring*, resulting in 254 *FNs* for ***Type 3*** cases.

Conclusion: *Slimming achieves a Precision of 97.0% and a Recall of 98.8%, which significantly outperforms all the baselines.*

6.4.3 RQ2: Reliability of Debloating Solutions

Study Methodology We adopt the 40 collected Java projects that satisfy the ***Selection Criteria (1–3)*** defined in Sect. 6.4.1 as a dataset for RQ2, since their 100% test coverage for Java byte code instructions can help validate whether removing the identified bloated dependencies will cause program errors. Two state-of-the-art debloating tools are considered as baselines to compare their reliability of debloating solutions:

- ***Maven Dependency Analyzer (MDA)*** [31] is an official Maven plugin that is actively maintained by the Maven team (supported by the *Apache Software Foundation*) for identifying undeclared or unused libraries of Java projects.
- *DepClean* [13] is proposed to identify bloated dependencies of Maven projects (***ESE 2021***), including both direct/transitive dependencies declared in `POM.xml` and inherited dependencies declared in parent `POM.xml`.

Evaluation Metrics We define four evaluation metrics:

- ***TPR (Test Passing Ratio)***: Proportion of the debloated projects that can pass bundled tests.

- ***#FA (Number of False Alarms)***: Number of the removed dependencies that are invoked by client project via Java reflections.
- ***#IDC (Number of Induced Dependency Conflicts)***: Number of dependency conflict issues induced by the debloating solutions.
- ***#ODMC (Number of Over-Dependency Management Cases)***: Number of additionally declared direct dependencies that are derived by the debloating solutions.

In order to calculate *#IDC*, we leverage *Decca* [32], a state-of-the-art detection tool to capture dependency conflicts. Specially, we are only concerned with the dependency conflict issues that can cause runtime errors (e.g., `NoSuchMethodError`).

Results Table 6.5 shows the experiment results of RQ2. For the 40 collected Java projects, on average, the debloating solutions generated by *Slimming* reliably remove seven bloated dependencies with a **100%** test passing ratio and **0** false alarms. In contrast, on average, *Mda* and *DepClean* remove 7 and 13 bloated dependencies with the 57.5% and 73.6% test passing ratios and 1 and 2 false alarms, respectively. *Slimming* outperforms the other two baselines on all the evaluation metrics.

#FA Analysis Owing to *Slimming*'s effective static reflection analysis, it precisely identifies all the usage of third-party libraries without producing false alarms. *DepClean* is implemented as a Maven plugin that extends the *Mda*. Both of them rely on the *Asm* library [33] to perform the static analysis, which visits all the `.class` files of the compiled projects in order to register bytecode calls toward classes, methods, and fields among projects and their dependencies. Since *Asm* cannot deal with reflection calls well, these two baselines can produce false alarms for bloated dependencies.

Table 6.5 Experiment results of RQ2

	#BD			*TPR (%)*			*#FA*			*#IDC*			*#ODMC*		
	Max.	*Min.*	*Avg.*	*Max.*	*Min.*	*Avg.*	*Max.*	*Min.*	*Avg.*	*Max.*	*Min.*	*Avg.*	*Max.*	*Min.*	*Avg.*
MDA	25	0	7	100	0	57.5	6	0	1	5	0	2	-	-	-
DepClean	50	0	13	100	40.0	73.6	8	0	2	3	0	1	168	0	30
Slimming	32	0	7	100	100	100	0	0	0	0	0	0	3	0	1

Distribution

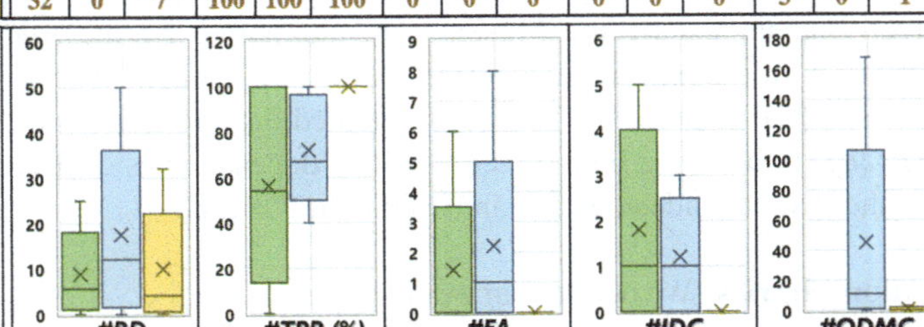

***#BD** denotes the number of bloated dependencies reported by the tools*

#IDC and #ODMC Analyses Due to its effective benefit-cost analysis, the solutions do not induce dependency conflict issues and on average only additionally declare one direct dependency, after removing the bloated dependencies. *DepClean* adopts an alternative debloating solution: It first adds all the used transitive dependencies as direct dependencies and then excludes all the bloated dependencies. As such, *DepClean* induces many over-dependency management cases, which potentially induce new issues (e.g., dependency conflicts) and bring much maintenance burden to project developers. Since *Mda* does not provide solutions for removing bloated dependencies, we cannot calculate its *#ODMC* metric.

Conclusion: *On our collected Java projects, on average, the debloating solutions generated by Slimming reliably remove seven bloated dependencies with a* ***100%*** *TPR and* ***0*** *FAs. Due to its effective benefit-cost analysis, the solutions do not induce dependency conflict issues and only additionally declare a few direct dependencies after removing the bloated dependencies.*

6.5 Large-Scale Analysis

Leveraging *Slimming*, we conducted a large-scale study on Java projects to reveal the landscapes of bloated dependencies in the Maven ecosystem. Besides, we further study the research question:

- **RQ3 (Usefulness of** *Slimming***):** ***Can*** *Slimming* ***provide useful solutions to assist developers remove bloated dependencies? Do the debloating solutions conform to developers' viewpoints on software maintenance?*** To answer RQ3, we report the bloated dependencies with detailed diagnosis info and feasible solutions to projects' issue trackers. We assess the usefulness of *Slimming* based on developers' feedback.

6.5.1 Landscapes of Bloated Dependencies

Study Methodology For a large-scale empirical study, we queried the GitHub API on March 1, 2023 to obtain a list of GitHub URLs, including all projects that use Java as the primary programming language. From this list, we kept the projects as subjects if they (1) achieve more than 5 Stars (*popularity*) and (2) have more than five direct dependencies (*complexity*). The initial dataset contains a total of 21,200 Java projects. In the second step, we compiled the newest release version of each collected Java project using Maven. This compilation process is a challenging task involving resolving and downloading dependencies. To increase the ratio of

Table 6.6 Statistics of the 4,035 projects in our large-scale study

Metrics \ Statistics	Max.	Min.	Avg.	Med.
#Stars	25,530	6	425.1	22
#Modules	134	1	12.4	3
#Direct dependencies	97	6	11.3	9
#Transitive dependencies	467	0	59.1	45

successful compilations, we tried to compile the projects using Java 8 if they did not compile with Java 11. Unfortunately, 17,165 Java projects still failed to compile due to (1) lacking dependencies (parts of dependencies were only provided in private repositories) and (2) resolving the incompatible dependency versions (developers did not explicitly declare their version constraints). Eventually, we obtained 4,035 Java projects (including 8,337 modules) that passed the compilations as the definitive dataset for our empirical study could be further analyzed by *Slimming*.

Table 6.6 shows the descriptive statistics of the 4,035 Java projects. Of those 991 projects are multi-module projects, and the number of modules ranges from 1 to 134 (*Avg.* = 12.4, *Med.* = 3). The last two lines in the table give the number of direct dependencies (*Avg.* = 11.3, *Med.* = 9) and transitive dependencies (*Avg.* = 59.1, *Med.* = 45).

Results Table 6.7 summarizes the statistics of our investigation results. With a longitudinal analysis of 4,035 Java projects, *Slimming* identified 152,711 bloated dependencies from 2,503 projects (62.0%). On average, each project contains 30.5 $\pm$ 22.7 bloated dependencies (0.4 $\pm$ 0.7 bloated direct dependencies and 27.9 $\pm$ 21.3 bloated transitive dependencies), accounting for 39.7% of the total number of their third-party libraries. For the 775 multi-module projects, nearly 8.1% of bloated dependencies are inherited from parent `POM.xml`.

We identified 10,800 dependencies only invoked by client projects via Java reflections. Specifically, the 16,200 reflective targets resolved by *Slimming* involve complicated implementations, including nonconstant string arguments (58.3%) and constant string arguments (4.8%) of class-receiving methods, classes recorded in the framework configuration files (30.7%), and classes embellished with annotations (0.6%). These libraries can easily be mistaken for bloated dependencies by state-of-the-art debloating tools. *Slimming* precisely resolves the reflective calls to avoid false alarms due to its effective static analysis capability.

By further inspecting the 152,711 bloated dependencies, we found that 37,027 (24.3%) were outdated libraries, 3,157 (2.1%) were vulnerable libraries, 901 (0.6%) induced license conflicts, and 13,823 (9.1%) induced dependency conflict issues. However, we observed that many project developers invested nontrivial effort to upgrade these libraries and resolve the warnings of vulnerabilities/license conflicts/dependency conflicts caused by bloated dependencies, which was not required. For example, a popular project `Logisland` [34] (106 Stars on GitHub)

Table 6.7 Statistics of bloated dependencies in our large-scale study

Statistics in Each Project	*Max.*	*Min.*	*Avg.*	*Med.*	
#Bloated dependencies	198	1	30.1	25	
Proportion of bloated dependencies to all the introduced dependencies (%)	75.9	3.3	41.9	38.3	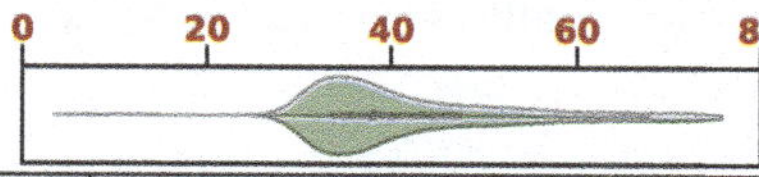
#Bloated direct dependencies	6	0	0.38	0	
#Bloated transitive dependencies	193	0	27.9	23	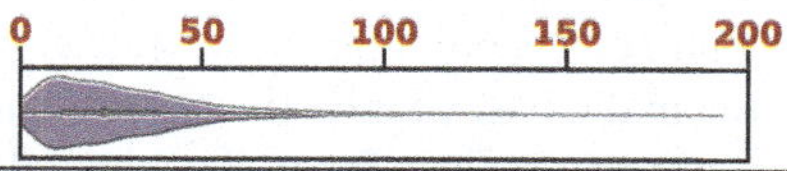
#Bloated dependencies inherited from parent POM	156	0	2.2	0	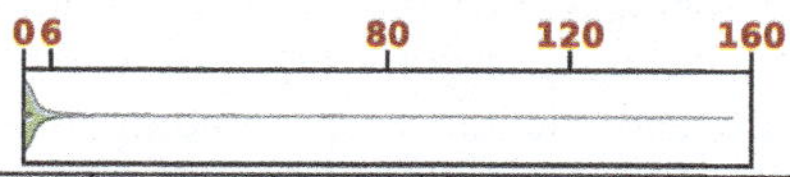
#Dependencies only invoked by client project via Java reflections	26	0	2.2	2	
#Bloated Dependencies that are outdated libraries	153	0	7.4	4	
#Bloated Dependencies that are vulnerable libraries	15	0	0.6	0	
#Bloated Dependencies that induce license conflicts	19	0	0.2	0	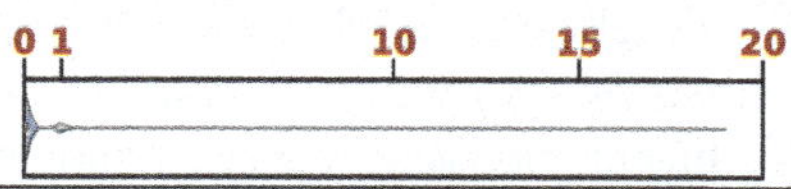
#Bloated Dependencies that induce dependency conflicts	94	0	2.8	1	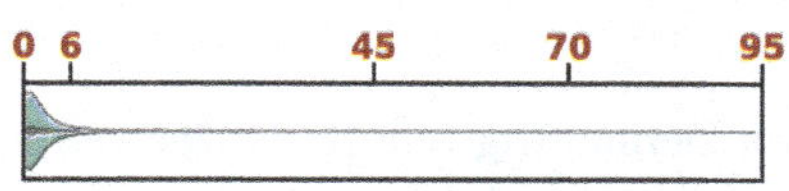

introduced 152 bloated dependencies. However, during the maintenance process, developers submitted four commits to the GitHub repository with the purpose of keeping the bloated library versions up-to-date. Since 14 bloated dependencies were vulnerable libraries, project `Logisland` [34] continually received high-severity vulnerability warnings against them from build tools. Reliably removing the bloated dependencies can help developers save unnecessary maintenance costs and reduce the frequent false alarms warned by build tools for vulnerability issues and license/version conflicts between dependencies.

6.5.2 RQ3: Usefulness of *Slimming*

Study Methodology From the 2,503 Java projects with bloated dependencies detected by *Slimming* in Sect. 6.5.1, we selected the ones that satisfy two criteria to report to their corresponding issue trackers: (1) Their code repositories have commit records in the past year (actively maintained), and (2) the number of bloated dependencies is greater than 5, or the bloated dependencies induce dependency management issues (e.g., vulnerabilities). Following the criteria, we finally chose 66 subjects. Our issue reports describe the bloated dependencies with detailed diagnosis info and file the corresponding feasible debloating solutions as *Pull Requests* (PRs) to code repositories. To allow developers better understand the benefit-cost analysis of debloating solutions, we also provide a figure to visualize the library dependency graph with labeled additionally declared dependencies and bloated dependencies (marking out their dependency management issues: vulnerabilities/dependency conflicts/incompatible licenses/outdated dependencies). We evaluate the usefulness of *Slimming* based on developers' feedback.

Results Table 6.8 summarizes the statuses of our reported issues. Among our submitted 66 issue reports, the developers quickly confirmed 38 of them (57.6%), and 36 confirmed reports (54.5%) were later fixed or under-fixing using our debloating solutions. In two confirmed reports (3.0%), the developer did not merge our PRs since their projects were planning to use the bloated dependencies in their subsequent versions as the extension of functionalities. In our four reported issues (6.1%), developers said they did not care about bloated dependencies. The other 24 reports (36.4%) were still pending, likely due to the less active project maintenance. In our 59 issue reports, removing bloated dependencies can also resolve 20 vulnerabilities, 8 license incompatibilities, 11 dependency conflicts, and 243 outdated dependencies.

Feedback on Debloating Solutions Derived by *Slimming* We discuss the representative cases that reveal the usefulness and rationality of our debloating solutions in three aspects:

Table 6.8 Experiment results of RQ3

66 Issue Reports Submitted by Slimming
Jax-rs2#203♠🟪🟩🟫; TarsJava#170♠; Small-spring#56♠🟫; Immutables#1382♠🟧🟫;
Tomee#852♠🟪🟫; Azure-iot#1543♠🟧🟫; Quickstart#388♠🟧🟫; JavaNotes#1♠🟫;
Lemon#210♠🟧; Karate-grpc#23♠🟧 ; Camel-kafka#1352♠🟧🟫; Linkis#1716♠🟪🟫;
Ysomap#18♠🟫; XChange#4200♠; Swagger-parser#1590♠; Vertx#429♠🟫;
Mycat2#694♠🟫; Yuzhouwan#343♠; Openapi-gen#9768♠🟫; Jax#36♠🟫;
Nerdronix#3♠🟪🟫; Spring-boot#32♠🟪🟫; CombatLogX#191♠🟪🟫; Tutorials#13568♠🟫;
Jetcache#565♠🟪🟫; Wso2-syn#1771♠🟫; Tesseract4java#61♠🟫; Openimaj#317♠🟫;
Azure#19070♠🟫; QuickBooks#158♠🟫; Dubbo#278♠🟫; Deeplearning4j#9190♠;
Springboot#34♣; Alldata#50♣🟫; Tez#127♣🟪🟫; Amazon#135♣🟫;
OSM2World#174●🟫; Kafka#83●🟫; Skywalking#172★🟪🟫; Jmeter#523★🟩🟫;
Java-sec#75★🟫; Jeecg#4819★🟫; Ice4j#258▲🟩🟫; DataSphereStudio#584▲🟫;
Notebook#24▲🟫; Shardingsphere#153▲🟪🟫; Scouter#925▲🟫; Myblog#8▲🟫;
Yshopmall#23▲🟪🟫; X-SpringBoot#31▲🟫; Itstack#57▲; Pay-java#92▲🟪🟫;
Kontraktor#119▲🟩🟫; Jprotobuf#84▲🟫; Spring-amqp#65▲; Milton2#176▲🟩🟫;
Ninja#746▲🟧🟫; Protege#1051▲🟧🟫; Aws#3192▲🟧🟫; JacORB#299▲🟧🟫; Mall4j#18▲🟫;
Asterisk#383▲🟧🟫; Msf4j#582▲🟫; DataX#973▲🟫; Karamel#206▲🟫; RuoYi#36▲🟪🟫;

♠: Confirmed issues were fixed with our debloating solutions;
♣: Confirmed issues were under fixing with our debloating solutions;
●: Confirmed issues but developers plan to use bloated dependencies in future;
★: Rejected issues in which developers did not care about bloated dependencies;
▲: Pending issues; ***Removing the bloated dependencies can also resolve: vulnerabilities*** 🟪, ***license incompatibilities*** 🟩, ***dependency conflicts*** 🟧 ***outdated dependencies*** 🟫. Detailed info is on **https://slimming-fat.github.io/**

- *The confirmed reports cover many popular projects.* The confirmed reports involve many popular projects, such as `Apache/Linkis#1716` [35] (3.1k Stars) and `Apache/Tomee#852` [36] (419 Stars).
- *Many projects were willing to remove bloated libraries to streamline software dependencies.* For example, *Slimming* identified 32 bloated dependencies in `Linkis#1716` [35], accounting for 78% of the project's third-party libraries. Especially, two dependencies are invoked by client code through Java reflections. Developers adopted our debloating suggestions since our PR passed all the tests. In report `Tez#127` [37], the bloated dependency *org.codehaus.jettison:jettison:1.3.4* contains vulnerability `#CVE-2022-45693`. Although removing this bloated library at the cost of additionally declaring its transitive dependency *stax:stax-api:1.0.1* as project `Tez`'s direct dependency, developers quickly merged the PR submitted by *Slimming*.
- *Developers showed great interest in our Slimming tool.* For example, one developer left a comment in report `quickstart#388` [38]: "*Thanks very much*

for the contribution, extremely useful. What tool did you use to do the analysis?" A developer appreciated our PR for `mapstruct#134` [39] and commented that "*Can you please tell us how you did your analysis? It seems to me like this PR has been created in an automated way.*"

Impacts of Debloating Solutions on Dependency Management By inspecting the code repositories of 38 projects that confirmed our submitted issues, we found 60 commit records submitted by developers for upgrading the bloated dependencies and 20 vulnerability warnings from *GitHub Advisory* against the bloated dependencies. For example, in report `Linkis#1716` [35], project developers updated ten versions for bloated dependencies *commons-io:commons-io*, *com.google.code.gson:gson*, and *commons-net:commons-net* in the past 3 years and continually received high-severity vulnerability warnings (`#CVE-2021-29425`, `#CVE-2022-25647` and `#CVE-2021-37533`) against this library from build tools. The results indicate that debloating solutions derived by *Slimming* help developers remove unused dependencies and reduce unnecessary maintenance costs.

Conclusion: Slimming reported 484 bloated dependencies to 66 open-source projects. Thirty-eight reports (57.6%) were confirmed by developers. The feedback indicates the usefulness and rationality of our debloating solutions.

6.6 Discussions

Limitations (1) For static analysis, *Slimming* resolves the dynamic behaviors of reflective calls leveraged by six popular Java frameworks (*Java EE Servlets*, *Java Beans*, *Apache Struts*, *Spring*, *Spring Boot*, and *Tomcat*), rather than all the existing frameworks, which may lead to few false alarms for bloated dependencies. (2) Before reporting the identified bloated dependencies, *Slimming* triggers projects' bundled tests to validate their debloating solutions. In practice, such a validation heavily depends on the test coverage ratio of given projects, which cannot guarantee the reliability of debloating solutions.

Threats to Validity One possible threat is the representativeness of our study Java projects. In our experiments, we only consider the open-source Java projects, not cover the industrial projects. To minimize the threat, we conducted a large-scale study in the Maven ecosystem to collect the projects in various scales and complexity. Another threat comes from evaluating *Slimming*'s usefulness. We rely on developers' feedback to validate our submitted bug reports. In general, there may be disagreement between the developers on the validity of the bug reports. However, we did not encounter such disagreement for all the evaluated subjects. Therefore, the positive feedback is a strong indication of the usefulness of our approach.

6.7 Related Work

6.7.1 Java Reflection Analysis

There are two directions of research on Java reflection analysis: *Static Reflection Analysis* [14, 18, 24, 40–45] and *Dynamic Reflection Analysis* [27, 46]. Livshits et al. [40] introduce the first static reflection analysis for Java. By interleaving with a pointer analysis, this reflection analysis discovers constant string values by performing regular string inference and infers the types of reflectively created objects. Many modern pointer analysis frameworks such as Doop [14], Wala [41], and Chord [42] adopt a similar approach to analyze Java reflection statically, and many subsequent reflection analyses [18, 24, 43–45] are also inspired by the same work. Hirzel et al. [46] propose an online pointer analysis for handling some dynamic features in Java at runtime. To tackle reflection, their analysis instruments a program to generate constraints dynamically when the injected code is triggered at runtime. Sridharan et al. [47] and Antoniadis et al. [29] proposed approaches that exploit domain knowledge to automatically generate a specification of framework-related behaviors (e.g., reflection usage) by processing both application code and configuration files.

In addition to a pointer analysis for resolving reflection targets, our *Slimming* leverages a scalable approach to identify the specifications of framework-related reflection usage patterns (including *Spring Boot*, *Spring*, *Tomcat*, *Java EE Servlets*, *Java Beans*, and *Apache Struts*) in a systematic manner. It outperforms the existing reflection analysis approaches in the metrics of both *Precision* and *Recall*.

6.7.2 Software Debloating

In the past few years, several fine-grained debloating techniques have been proposed for reducing binary code size for efficient installations and executions on embedded hardware with limited memory. These fine-grained debloating techniques are designed for various domains, including JavaScript programs [2, 3], Java applications [4–7], application containers (e.g., docker) [8], or native C programs [9–12]. These range from static analysis [2, 4, 5, 7, 12] to load/runtime techniques [6, 8, 9, 11] and machine learning [10]. For promoting dependency management, Soto-Valero proposed two coarse-grained debloating approaches [1, 13] at library granularity, which are the most relevant research to *Slimming*. They first developed a tool *DepClean* [13], which constructs the complete dependency tree of a project and statically analyzes the bytecode to determine the presence of bloated dependencies. Leveraging *DepClean*, they conducted an empirical study [1]to learn the evolution and impact of bloated dependencies in the Maven software ecosystem.

However, all the existing debloating techniques that rely on static analysis do not consider dynamic language features. The effectiveness of prior debloating techniques that use dynamic analysis approaches heavily depends on the test coverage ratio of the given projects. *This unsoundness makes debloating unreliable: removing dynamically invoked code and inducing subsequent runtime errors.* In addition, the coarse-grained debloating tool *DepClean* removes the unused libraries without considering its impacts on a project's dependency graph structure. *Such solutions make debloating unreasonable: removing libraries may induce new issues that are not conducive to dependency management.* In this chapter, we address these limitations, propose an effective technique to resolve Java reflections, and systematically analyze the library dependency graph to remove the bloated dependencies reliably.

6.8 Conclusion and Future Work

In this chapter, we present an effective technique, *Slimming*, to help developers reliably remove bloated dependencies from Java projects. Practical static reflection analyses empower our tool and drive debloating solutions by weighing the benefits against the costs of dependency management. The evaluation results indicate the effectiveness of *Slimming* in deriving debloating solutions. In the future, we plan to improve the static analysis capability and generalize *Slimming* to other programming ecosystems to help more developers streamline software dependencies.

References

1. Soto-Valero C, Durieux T, Baudry B. A longitudinal analysis of bloated Java dependencies. In: Proceedings of the 29th ACM joint meeting on European software engineering conference and symposium on the foundations of software engineering; 2021. p. 1021–1031.
2. Vázquez HC, Bergel A, Vidal S, Díaz Pace JA, Marcos C. Slimming JavaScript applications: an approach for removing unused functions from JavaScript libraries. Inf Softw Technol. 2019;107(2019):18–29.
3. Qian C, Koo H, Oh C, Kim T, Lee W. Slimium: debloating the chromium browser with feature subsetting. In: Proceedings of the 2020 ACM SIGSAC conference on computer and communications security; 2020. p. 461–476.
4. Bruce BR, Zhang T, Arora J, Xu GH, Kim M. Jshrink: in-depth investigation into debloating modern Java applications. In Proceedings of the 28th ACM joint meeting on European software engineering conference and symposium on the foundations of software engineering; 2020. p. 135–146.

5. Jiang Y, Wu D, Liu P. JRed: program customization and bloatware mitigation based on static analysis. In: 2016 IEEE 40th annual computer software and applications conference (COMPSAC), vol. 1. IEEE; 2016. p. 12–21.
6. Soto-Valero C, Durieux T, Harrand N, Baudry B. Coverage-based debloating for Java bytecode. ACM Trans Softw Eng Methodol. 2023;32(2):1–34.
7. Macias K, Mathur M, Bruce BR, Zhang T, Kim M. WebJShrink: a web service for debloating Java bytecode. In: Proceedings of the 28th ACM joint meeting on european software engineering conference and symposium on the foundations of software engineering; 2020. p. 1665–1669.
8. Rastogi V, Davidson D, De Carli L, Jha S, McDaniel P. Cimplifier: automatically debloating containers. In: Proceedings of the 2017 11th joint meeting on foundations of software engineering; 2017. p. 476–486.
9. Quach A, Prakash A, Yan L. Debloating software through piece-wise compilation and loading. In: 27th USENIX security symposium (USENIX Security 18); 2018. p. 869–886.
10. Heo K, Lee W, Pashakhanloo P, Naik M. Effective program debloating via reinforcement learning. In: Proceedings of the 2018 ACM SIGSAC conference on computer and communications security; 2018. p. 380–394.
11. Qian C, Hu H, Alharthi M, Chung SPH, Kim T, Lee W. Razor: a framework for post-deployment software debloating. In USENIX Security Symposium; 2019. p. 1733–1750.
12. Sharif H, Abubakar M, Gehani A, Zaffar F. TRIMMER: application specialization for code debloating. In Proceedings of the 33rd ACM/IEEE international conference on automated software engineering; 2018. p. 329–339.
13. Soto-Valero C, Harrand N, Monperrus M, et al. A comprehensive study of bloated dependencies in the maven ecosystem. Empir Softw Eng. 2021;26(3):45.
14. Bravenboer M, Smaragdakis Y. Strictly declarative specification of sophisticated points-to analyses. In: Proceedings of the 24th ACM SIGPLAN conference on object oriented programming systems languages and applications; 2009. p. 243–262.
15. 2023. Issue spring-amqp#65. https://github.com/spring-projects/spring-amqp-samples/pull/65. Accessed: 26 Mar 2023.
16. 2023. Issue jax-rs2-guide#203. https://github.com/feuyeux/jax-rs2-guide-II/pull/203. Accessed: 26 Mar 2023.
17. 2023. Soot. http://soot-oss.github.io/soot/. Accessed: 26 Mar 2023.
18. Li Y, Tan T, Xue J. Understanding and analyzing Java reflection. ACM Trans Softw Eng Methodol. 2019;28(2):1–50.
19. 2023. GitHub Advisory DB. https://github.com/advisories. Accessed: 26 Mar 2023.
20. 2023. Snyk Vulnerability DB. https://security.snyk.io/vuln/maven. Accessed: 26 Mar 2023.
21. 2023. Free Software Foundation website. http://www.gnu.org/licenses/license-list.en.html. Accessed: 26 Mar 2023.
22. Huang K, Chen B, Xu C, Wang Y, Shi B, Peng X, Wu Y, Liu Y. Characterizing usages, updates and risks of third-party libraries in Java projects. Empir Softw Eng. 2022;27(4):87.
23. 2023. maven-dependency-tree. https://maven.apache.org/plugins/maven-dependency-plugin/tree-mojo.html. Accessed: 26 Mar 2023.
24. Smaragdakis Y, Balatsouras G, Kastrinis G, Bravenboer M. More sound static handling of Java reflection. In: Programming Languages and Systems: 13th Asian Symposium, APLAS 2015, Pohang, South Korea, November 30-December 2, 2015, Proceedings 13; 2015. p. 485–503.
25. 2023. DaCaPo (2006-10-MR2). https://sourceforge.net/projects/dacapobench/files/archive/2006-10-MR2/dacapo-2006-10-MR2.jar. Accessed: 26 Mar 2023.
26. 2023. JaCoCo. https://www.eclemma.org/jacoco/trunk/doc/counters.html. Accessed: 26 Mar 2023.
27. Bodden E, Sewe A, Sinschek J, Oueslati H, Mezini M. Taming reflection: Aiding static analysis in the presence of reflection and custom class loaders. In: Proceedings of the 33rd International Conference on Software Engineering; 2011. p. 241–250.
28. 2023. Doop. https://github.com/plast-lab/doop-mirror. Accessed: 26 Mar 2023.

29. Antoniadis A, Filippakis N, Krishnan P, Ramesh R, Allen N, Smaragdakis Y. Static analysis of Java enterprise applications: frameworks and caches, the elephants in the room. In: Proceedings of the 41st ACM SIGPLAN conference on programming language design and implementation; 2020. p. 794–807.
30. Wu R, Zhang H, Kim S, Cheung S-C. Relink: recovering links between bugs and changes. In: Proceedings of the 19th ACM SIGSOFT symposium and the 13th European conference on Foundations of software engineering; 2011. p. 15–25.
31. 2023. Maven Dependency Analyzer. https://github.com/apache/maven-dependency-analyzer. Accessed: 26 Mar 2023.
32. Wang Y, Wen M, Liu Z, Wu R, Wang R, Yang B, Yu H, Zhu Z, Cheung S-C. Do the dependency conflicts in my project matter? In: Proceedings of the 2018 26th ACM joint meeting on European software engineering conference and symposium on the foundations of software engineering; 2018. p. 319–330.
33. 2023. ASM. https://asm.ow2.io/. Accessed: 26 Mar 2023.
34. 2023. Logisland. https://github.com/Hurence/logisland. Accessed: 24 Jan 2023.
35. 2023. Apache/Linkis#1716. https://github.com/apache/linkis/pull/1716. Accessed: 26 Mar 2023.
36. 2023. Apache/Tomee#852. https://github.com/apache/tomee/pull/852. Accessed: 26 Mar 2023.
37. 2023. Apache/Tez#127. https://github.com/apache/tez/pull/127. Accessed: 26 Mar 2023.
38. 2023. quickstart#388. https://github.com/jbosstm/quickstart/pull/388. Accessed: 26 Mar 2023.
39. 2023. mapstruct#134. https://github.com/mapstruct/mapstruct-examples/pull/134. Accessed: 26 Mar 2023.
40. Livshits B, Whaley J, Lam MS. Reflection analysis for Java. In Programming languages and systems: third asian symposium, APLAS 2005, Tsukuba, November 2–5, 2005. Proceedings 3. Berlin: Springer; 2005. p. 139–160.
41. 2023. WALA UserGuide: PointerAnalysis. https://wala.sourceforge.net/wiki/index.php/UserGuide:PointerAnalysis#Contexts-for-Reflection. Accessed: 26 Mar 2023.
42. Naik M, Aiken A, Whaley J. Effective static race detection for Java. In: Proceedings of the 27th ACM SIGPLAN conference on programming language design and implementation; 2006. p. 308–319.
43. Li Y, Tan T, Sui Y, Xue J. 2014. Self-inferencing reflection resolution for Java. In: ECOOP 2014–object-oriented programming: 28th European conference, Uppsala, July 28–August 1, 2014. Proceedings 28. Berlin: Springer; 2014. p. 27–53.
44. Li Y, Tan T, Xue J. Effective soundness-guided reflection analysis. In: Static analysis: 22nd international symposium, SAS 2015, Saint-Malo, September 9–11, 2015, Proceedings 22. Berlin: Springer; 2015. p. 162–180.
45. Zhang Y, Tan T, Li Y, Xue J. Ripple: reflection analysis for android apps in incomplete information environments. In: Proceedings of the seventh ACM on conference on data and application security and privacy; 2017. p. 281–288.
46. Hirzel M, Von Dincklage D, Diwan A, Hind M. Fast online pointer analysis. ACM Trans Programm Languages Syst. 2007;29(2):11–es.
47. Sridharan M, Artzi S, Pistoia M, Guarnieri S, Tripp O, Berg R. F4F: taint analysis of framework-based web applications. In: Proceedings of the 2011 ACM international conference on object oriented programming systems languages and applications; 2011. p. 1053–1068.

Chapter 7
Exploring Cross Ecosystem Vulnerability Impacts

Abstract Vulnerabilities, referred to as CLV issues, are induced by cross-language invocations of vulnerable libraries. Such issues greatly increase the attack surface of Python/Java projects due to their pervasive use of C libraries. Existing Python/Java build tools in PyPI and Maven ecosystems fail to report the dependency on vulnerable libraries written in other languages such as C. CLV issues are easily missed by developers. In this chapter, we conduct the first empirical study on the status quo of CLV issues in PyPI and Maven ecosystems. It is found that 82,951 projects in these ecosystems are directly or indirectly dependent on libraries compiled from the C project versions that are identified to be vulnerable in CVE reports. Our study arouses the awareness of CLV issues in popular ecosystems and presents related analysis results.

The study also leads to the development of the first automated mechanism, *Insight*, which provides a turn-key solution to the identification of CLV issues in PyPI and Maven projects based on published CVE reports of vulnerable C projects. *Insight* automatically identifies if a PyPI or Maven project is using a C library compiled from vulnerable C project versions in published CVE reports. It also deduces the vulnerable APIs involved by analyzing the usage of various foreign function interfaces such as *CFFI* and *JNI* in the concerned PyPI or Maven project. *Insight* achieves a high detection rate of 88.4% on a popular CLV issue benchmark. Contributing to the open-source community, we report 226 CLV issues detected in the actively maintained PyPI and Maven projects that are directly dependent on vulnerable C library versions. Our reports are well received and appreciated by developers with queries on the availability of *Insight*. A total of 127 reported issues (56.2%) were quickly confirmed by developers, and 74.8% of them were fixed/under fixing by popular projects, such as `Mongodb` (2022. https://www.mongodb.com/. Accessed: 2022-03-01) and `Eclipse/Sumo` (2022. https://www.eclipse.org/sumo/. Accessed: 2022-03-01).

Y. Wang et al., *Managing Software Supply Chains*,
https://doi.org/10.1007/978-981-96-1797-5_7

7.1 Introduction

Foreign function interfaces (FFIs) like *CFFI* [1] and *JNI* [2] provide powerful bridging mechanisms that allow a project implementing in one language to access libraries written in another language. The use of FFIs by Python and Java projects in the PyPI and Maven ecosystems is common. Our investigation shows that, as of March 1 2022, 46.7% and 32.1% of projects in PyPI and Maven ecosystems directly or transitively use C libraries. However, existing library managers and dependency management tools (e.g., `Maven` [3], `Pip` [4], and `DependencyBot` [5]) in these ecosystems fail to warn developers against the use of vulnerable libraries written in another language. As a result, Python and Java developers can easily miss the security risks induced by the use of vulnerable C libraries, as demonstrated by the real-life example in Sect. 7.2.2. In this chapter, we refer to the vulnerability issues induced by cross-language invocations as *CLV issues*.

To understand the status quo of cross-ecosystem vulnerabilities, we conduct an empirical study on the CLV issues in the PyPI and Maven ecosystems induced by vulnerable C libraries. We select PyPI, Maven, and C because of their popularity. The results of our study would be of relevancy to many developers. It finds that 24,605 projects in PyPI, and Maven ecosystems are directly or indirectly dependent on libraries compiled from the C project versions that are identified to be vulnerable in CVE reports.

Our study also leads to the development of an automated tool, *Insight*, that complements existing dependency management tools to identify the projects suffering from CLV issues. The development of *Insight* needs to resolve two challenges.

(1) Gaps between CVE reports and the build scripts of PyPI or Maven projects. CVE reports identify vulnerable C project versions, whereas PyPI or Maven projects build scripts identify the C library versions used. However, C libraries and their corresponding C projects have different naming and versioning schemes. In practice, a C project version is often compiled into multiple published C library versions. However, CVE (**C**ommon **V**ulnerabilities and **E**xposures) reports only indicate the C project versions that contain the vulnerabilities. Nontrivial analysis effort is required to track down the vulnerable C library versions from CVE reports.

Figure 7.1 presents an illustrative scenario of the version number differences. `OpenSSL` is a C project compiled into two C libraries `libcrypto.so` and `libssl.so`. It is reported by *CVE-2021-3711* that the `OpenSSL` project versions 1.1.1-1.1.1k are vulnerable. The vulnerability is reported to be fixed in `OpenSSL` project version 1.1.1L. However, the version number of the `libssl.so` library evolves separately from that of its OpenSSL project. It is also true for the `libvorbis` project and its libraries. C developers may not necessarily use a separate version number for a library after code updates or fixes. Indeed, `libssl.so.1.1` in `OpenSSL` 1.1.1L contains the fix for `libssl.so.1.1` in `OpenSSL` 1.1.1-1.1.1k. As discussed in Sect. 7.2, nearly 80% of C libraries violate the semantic versioning rules in Linux community. The version number of libraries, therefore, cannot

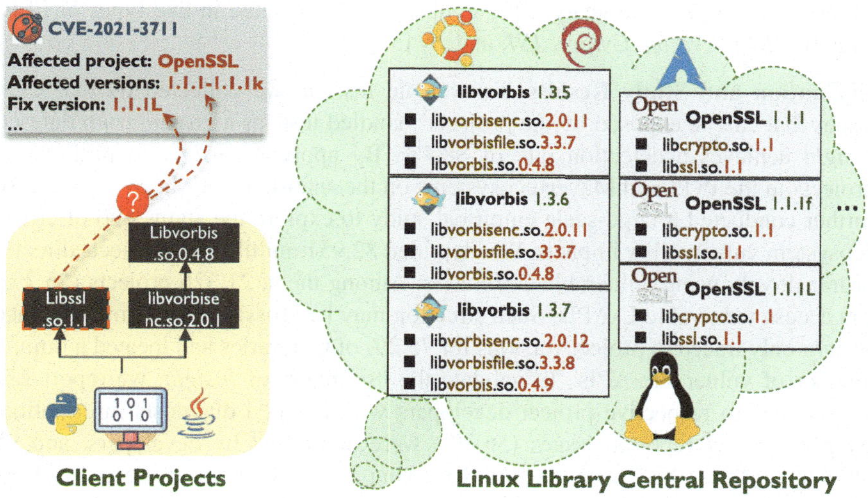

Fig. 7.1 Challenges of finding source code provenances of libraries

reliably identify their project version. As a result, it is challenging to determine if the `libssl.so.1.1` library used by a client project originates from a vulnerable OpenSSL version.

(2) Varieties of FFIs. FFIs with different syntax rules and mechanisms are supported in PyPI and Maven ecosystems for interfacing Java/Python code with the APIs in C libraries. For instance, three types of FFIs are commonly used for bridging between Python and C, including *CFFI* [1], *Cython* [6], and *Ctypes* [7]. Two types of FFIs, namely *JNI* [2] and *JNA* [8], are often adopted to bind Java and C code. There is no automated analysis technique to accurately extract the concerned APIs invoked by the various types of FFIs, which support different syntax rules and mechanisms.

Approach To address the above challenges, we develop an automated tool, *Insight*, which can continually monitor the impacts of vulnerable C libraries on their client projects in PyPI and Maven ecosystems and report CLV issues detected to the project developers. To determine if a C library can introduce vulnerabilities, *Insight* identifies the C project version where the library originates. The identification is achieved in two steps. First, *Insight* constructs a large-scale knowledge repository indexing the metadata of all C project versions with their known compiled libraries published in the mainstream Linux distributions. Second, *Insight* determines a C library's identity by matching the similarity of the library's feature against those in our knowledge repository. The similarity matching is performed by leveraging a state-of-the-art technique *LibRARIAN* [9]. If the C library is compiled from vulnerable C project versions identified by CVE reports, *Insight* further analyzes the accessibility of corresponding vulnerable APIs via parsing cross-language invocations and generates diagnosis info for the CLV issues. Various parsing patterns are proposed to analyze the C library APIs invoked in five types of FFIs, namely *CFFI*, *Cython*, *Cytpes*, *JNI*, and *JNA*.

Evaluation and Study Results To evaluate *Insight*, we collected 69 real CLV issues that can be exposed by the projects' bundled tests as a ground truth dataset. *Insight* achieves a detection rate of 88.4%. By applying *Insight* to millions of projects in the PyPI and Maven ecosystems on the snapshots on March 1, 2022, we further conducted a large-scale empirical study to explore the status quo of cross-ecosystem vulnerability impacts. We identified 82,951 multilingual projects directly or transitively using vulnerable C libraries. Among them, 21,326 projects (25.7%) can access vulnerable C-APIs. Such situation may be grossly underestimated since *Insight* only traced to project versions for 75.2% of C libraries and located a limited number of vulnerable APIs. To validate the usefulness of *Insight*, we report 226 CLV issues to respective project developers with detailed diagnosis information. Eventually, 127 reported issues (56.2%) were confirmed by developers, and 95 of them (74.8%) had been fixed/under fixing by well-known projects, such as `Mongodb` [10], `Libgit2` [11], and `Eclipse/Sumo` [12].

7.2 Background

7.2.1 C Library Releases and Their Naming Rules

Typically, a version of C project is compiled into multiple C libraries in the form of `*.so` files, and publish them to the Linux library central repository. As of March 1, 2022, three mainstream Linux distributions, including *Ubuntu* [13], *Debian* [14], and *Arch Linux* [15], host 485,021 versions of 165,347 C projects, involving 829,242 C libraries. With the access to such rich facilities, client projects in an ecosystem can leverage `*.so` files compiled from various C project versions as third-party libraries according to their requirements.

Linux community recommends a set of semantic versioning rules for C libraries (i.e., `*.so` files). Specifically, a fully qualified soname consists of a prefix "*lib*," a library name, and a phrase "*.so*," followed up by a version number. Official documentation [16] encourages C developers to adopt the form of "*Major.Minor.Patch*" to specify the unique version numbers for libraries, based on versioning rules.

However, our investigation in the library central repositories of three Linux distributions indicated that developers often violated the semantic versioning rules in C library releases. We find that among the 451,233 C libraries in *Ubuntu* distribution, 364,420 of them (80.8%) were published with nonstandard version numbers, in the form of "*Major*" or "*Major.Minor*." These libraries did not increment the version numbers for stating API changes or bug fixes during evolution. Similarly, in *Debian* and *Arch Linux* distributions, nearly 80.0% of C libraries are published with nonstandard version numbers (*Debian*: 511,825/636,132 = 80.5% and *Arch Linux*:

25,646/ 30,824 = 83.2%). As a result, such version numbers of `*.so` files cannot be taken as the identity of C libraries.

7.2.2 A Motivating Example

Existing build tools of PyPI and Maven fail to report the dependency on vulnerable C libraries. Developers in these ecosystems can easily miss CLV issues induced by such libraries. They need to diagnose the root causes when CLV issues are noted. Due to the different version naming schemes between C projects and their compiled libraries, such diagnosis is time-consuming. Figure 7.2 gives an illustrative example. Developers filed an issue report #14623 [17] in project `Incubator`, in which they expressed that the Python project introduced a critical vulnerability *CVE-2018-18557* [18] in a C library `libmxnet.so`. Since the *soname* ignores a version number, they figured out the project version (`Libtiff` 4.0.9) where this library originates, based on `Incubator`'s development documentations. `Incubator` is a deep learning framework designed for both efficiency and flexibility, achieving over 20,000 stars on GitHub and 329,000 monthly downloads. Due to its considerable impacts on the ecosystem, this issue attracts seven developers to participate in the discussions. To avoid such vulnerability issues from C libraries, they decided to keep an eye on the C projects' release notes in the future, since `Incubator` highly depends on 18 `*.so` files.

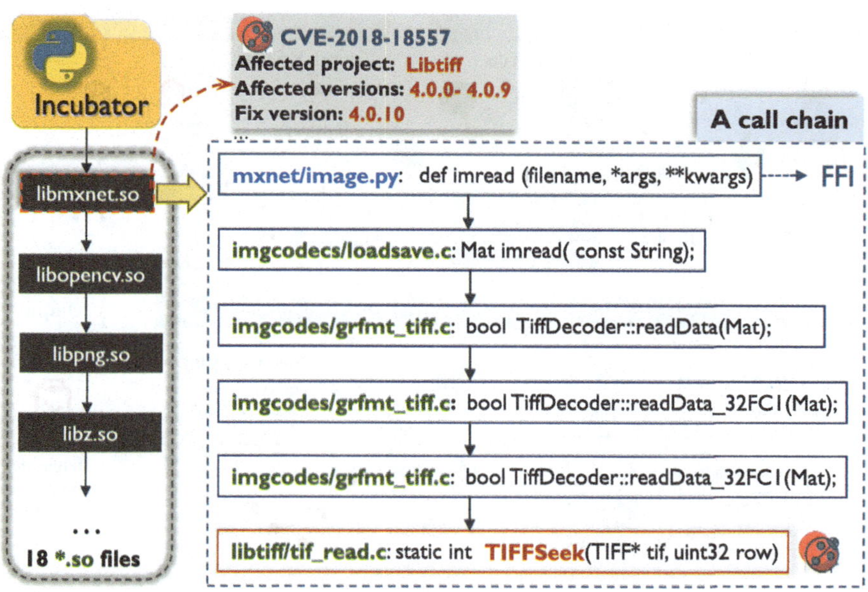

Fig. 7.2 An illustrative example of issue #14623 [17] in `Incubator`

Three years later, a downstream project using an old version of `Incubator` triggered this vulnerability *CVE-2018-18557* issue. The developer posted a call chain that can access to the vulnerable C-API `TIFFSeek()` in report #14623, to arouse other `Incubator` users' attentions to validate if they were affected by such a vulnerability.

Similar situations can be found in many issue reports. In the CLV issue report #167 [19] of Java project `Etlflow`, an experienced developer commented that "*An automated tool for detecting vulnerability affects from C dependencies is required to help us perform the exhaustive analyses.*" This motivates us to develop a mechanism to help developers combat CLV issues and conduct a study on the status quo of these issues in popular ecosystems.

7.3 Insight Approach

To locate the PyPI and Maven projects that are dependent on vulnerable C libraries, we developed a tool, *Insight*, to capture CLV issues from CVE reports. We deploy it at PyPI and Maven ecosystems to continually detect and diagnose CLV issues induced by libraries compiled from vulnerable C projects.

Figure 7.3 gives an overview of *Insight*. We refer to the PyPI and Maven projects that directly depend on C libraries as *client projects*. *Insight* comprises three stages: C library extraction, C project version tracing, and vulnerable C-API analysis.

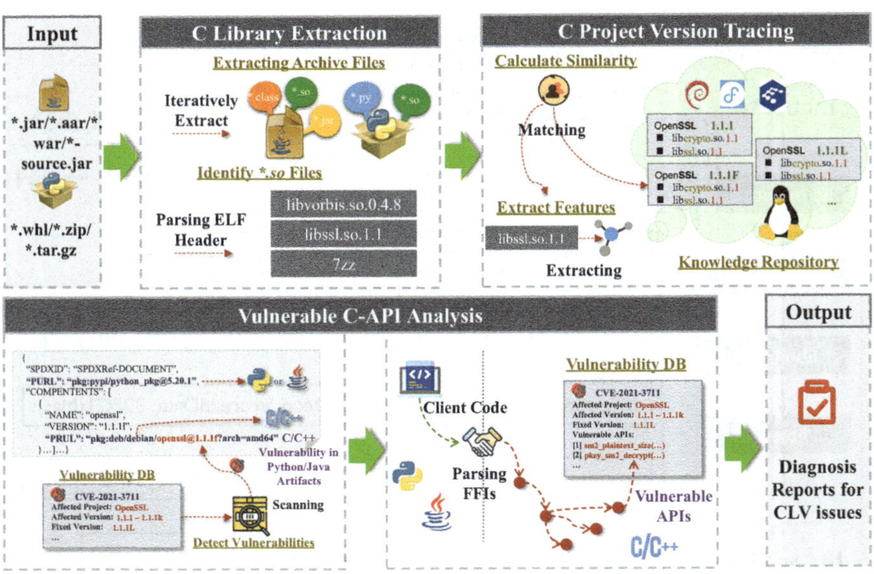

Fig. 7.3 The overall architecture of *Insight*

Insight identifies the C libraries used by a client project from its archive in the ecosystem. To trace an extracted C library to its originated C project version, *Insight* constructs a large-scale knowledge repository indexing the main features inherent to C library versions published in three mainstream Linux distributions. Leveraging a recent tool *LibRARAIN* [9], *Insight* determines the project version of a given C library, by iteratively comparing it with the known version instances in our knowledge repository based on similarity matching. To boost automation, *Insight* collects the metadata of vulnerability reports directly from the official security advisory websites to construct a large-scale vulnerability database. *Insight* checks for each extracted C library whether its parent C project version contains vulnerabilities. Finally, based on the parsing patterns that we design for various types of FFIs, *Insight* performs cross-language program analysis to determine if the client project code can access the concerned vulnerable C-APIs.

7.3.1 C Library Extraction

Project developers in PyPI and Maven ecosystems are required to publish project archives at central repositories. The archives include binaries, configuration files, and all necessary dependencies such as copies of the C libraries used. *Insight* can therefore determine if a client project depends on C libraries by extracting `*.so` files, which are copies of C libraries, from its published archive. The extraction works in two steps:

- ***Step 1: File exploration.*** *Insight* takes the archives (`*.whl` packages for PyPI and `*.Jar` or `*.aar` packages for Maven) of client projects as inputs and leverages tools *Wheel unpack* [20] and *Zipfile* [21] to explore the files in these archives. Since an archive may contain `*.Jar` and `*.aar` packages, *Insight* iteratively expands these packages for file exploration until no further packages can be found.
- ***Step 2: C library extraction.*** Based on the C library naming rules, *Insight* uses the regex "`lib.+.so(.[0-9]+){0,3}`" to extract C libraries (e.g., *libcrypto.so.1.1*) from the explored files.

7.3.2 C Project Version Tracing

To decide if an extracted `*.so` file can introduce vulnerabilities into its associated client project, *Insight* traces the C project version from which the file was compiled. To achieve that, *Insight* incorporates a state-of-the-art technique, *LibRARIAN* [9], which proposes to determine the parent project of a C library embedded in an Android APK by matching its features with those of the libraries compiled from the project. To adopt the technique for CLV issue detection in PyPI and Maven ecosystems, *Insight* constructs a large-scale knowledge repository by collecting the metadata of millions of C libraries with their known versions published in the mainstream Linux distributions. The construction of the knowledge repository took over 6 months. The repository is over 3.2 TB in size, indexing 485,021 C project versions and 829,242 C libraries as of March 1, 2022 (see statistics in Table 7.1). For a given `*.so` file, *Insight* decides its identity by matching its feature similarity with those in the knowledge repository. We explain the procedures taken to adopt *LibRARIAN* for tracing the parent project versions of extracted C libraries in *Insight* below.

- ***Extracting characterization features of C library versions.*** C libraries are packaged as *.so files of ELF (*E*xecutable and *L*ink-able *F*ormat) binaries. Each file contains a symbol table with externally visible identifiers such as function names, global symbols, local symbols, and imported symbols. Following *LibRARIAN*, *Insight* extracts five features from each *.so file to characterize its library version, by parsing ELF metadata: (a) *Exported Globals*: visible variables that can be accessed externally, (b) *Imported Globals*: variables from other libraries that are used in this library, (c) *Exported APIs*: visible APIs that can be called by other libraries, (d) *Imported APIs*: APIs from other libraries that are used in this library, and (e) *Dependencies*: library dependencies that are loaded by the ELF object. The five features represent the code elements of a library that would be expected to change based on a versioning scheme during evolution, which can distinguish different libraries and their versions. The five features are chosen because of their stability across platforms, regardless of the underlying architecture or compilation environments. Like *LibRARIAN* [9], we do not characterize C libraries using their code structure features (e.g., control flow features) as they can be volatile and subject to change between compilations and across architectures.
- ***Constructing knowledge repository for C libraries.*** *Insight* constructs a large-scale knowledge repository by collecting the metadata of all `*.so` library files compiled by C project versions published in three mainstream Linux distributions, including *Ubuntu*, *Debian*, and *Arch Linux*. By crawling the information of C projects in these distributions, *Insight* indexes collected C libraries to their corresponding project versions. Each C library version is characterized by a vector of the five aforementioned features. We represent the metadata of a C project version in a 3-tuple $<P, Lib, Src>$, where:
  - P denotes the project name with a version number.
  - Lib is a collection of C libraries compiled from the project version P. Each C library is a 2-tuple $<soname, FV>$, where $soname$ corresponds to the name of its `*.so` file, and FV denotes a vector recording the features extracted from `*.so` file.
  - Src denotes the source code of the project version P.

Insight monitors the evolution of Linux library central repositories and incrementally updates the knowledge repository when a new distribution version is published.

- ***Determining project version by feature similarity.*** The large-scale knowledge repository enables *Insight* to determine the project version where a C library originates, based on similarity matching. It works in two steps:
  - *Step 1: Reducing the number of C libraries for comparison.* For each `*.so` file extracted from a client project, *Insight* searches for the C libraries matched with its *soname* in the constructed knowledge repository, using the regex `soname([0-9]*)`. As discussed in Sect. 7.2, since the version number of a `*.so` file may remain unaltered after API changes or bug fixes, the search may return multiple `*.so` files. *Insight* considers the returned files as candidates for feature similarity comparison.
  - *Step 2: Similarity comparison. Insight* extracts the feature vector FV_1 from the `*.so` file under analysis and iteratively compares it with those of the returned libraries FV_2 in our knowledge repository. The comparison adopts the similarity score metric bin^2sim proposed by *LibRARIAN* [9]:

$$bin^2sim(FV_1, FV_2) = \frac{|FV_1 \cap FV_2|}{|FV_1 \cup FV_2|} \in [0, 1] \tag{7.1}$$

  bin^2sim allows *Insight* to account for addition or removal of features between different libraries and versions. The similarity score is a real number between 0 and 1, with a score of 1 indicating identical features, a score of 0 indicating no shared features between the two libraries, and a fractional value indicating a partial match. *Insight* considers the `*.so` file successfully matched a collected library version in the knowledge repository if the bin^2sim is above 0.85, which is the threshold adopted by *LibRARIAN*. *Insight* determines the matching project version based on the highest bin^2sim value, in the cases that more than one comparison achieves a similarity score above the threshold.

7.3.3 Vulnerable C-API Analysis

After tracing the C project version of an extracted `*.so` file, *Insight* can determine if it contains vulnerabilities based on the disclosed vulnerability reports. Furthermore, *Insight* reports whether the Python/Java client code can access the vulnerable APIs in C libraries by analyzing the cross-language invocations.

- ***Constructing Vulnerability Database.*** *Insight* constructs a large-scale vulnerability database by collecting the metadata of vulnerability reports from three official security advisory websites: *Ubuntu Security* [22], *Debian Security* [23], and *Arch Linux Security* [24]. For each CVE report, it identifies the vulnerability's *unique identifier*, *affected project*, *affected project versions*, *fix versions*, and *severity level*. In addition, *Insight* identifies the GitHub commits or GitLab commits provided in vulnerability reports for patching the corresponding CVEs. Like existing studies [25–27], it further identifies the revised APIs in relevant commits as the vulnerable APIs that induced the security issues. *Insight* continually monitors the security advisory websites and updates the vulnerability database.
- ***Analyzing Cross-Language Invocations.*** Based on the constructed vulnerability database, for each C library extracted from a client project, *Insight* checks whether its parent C project version contains a CVE. If so, *Insight* further analyzes whether the client code can access the concerned vulnerable APIs. *Insight* takes the source code of client project and C libraries as inputs and generates diagnosis reports for CLV issues. The reports point out the call chains from entry C-APIs to the concerned vulnerable functions from C libraries to facilitate developers' diagnosis.

  To perform the analysis, *Insight* parses the FFIs that support cross-language invocations to locate the entry APIs of C libraries used by client projects. However, each type of FFIs has its own syntax rules and mechanism to interface with the APIs in C libraries. To address the challenge, we design parsing patterns for five popular FFI types by studying its official FFI documentation. To allow the parsing scaling up to the large number of projects in an ecosystem, each pattern is so designed that it can be automated by scripts. Figure 7.4 shows the five FFI parsing patterns. Each parsing pattern identifies the concerned FFI configurations on the Python/Java side, according to the FFI syntax rules. For example, *Ctypes* uses function `cdll.LoadLibrary()` or `CDLL()` to create instance objects of C libraries in `*.py` file. Leveraging a C static analysis tool on program control flows, *CFlow* [28], *Insight* obtains the function call graphs within C libraries rooting at the entry C-APIs declared in FFIs. It reports a CLV issue with the diagnostic information of a function calling sequence in C libraries to reach the concerned vulnerable C-API.

7.4 Empirical Study and Evaluation

In this section, we present our empirical study and evaluation. Specifically, we aim to answer the following four research questions.

Programming Language	FFI Type	Parsing Pattern	Illustrative Example

Python-C	CFFI	(1) Identify the *.py file declared as a parameter assigned to the CFFI attribute cff_modules of function setup() in the script setup.py;
		(2) Locate the entry C-APIs declared in the function cdef() from the above identified *.py file
			# xmlstarlet/setup.py
			setup(...
			cffi_modules = ["xmlstarlet_build.py: FFIBUILDER"], ...)
			# xmlstarlet/xmlstarlet_build.py
			FFIBUILDER.cdef('''
			int selMain(int argc, char **argv);
			int trMain(int argc, char **argv);
			''')

	Cython	Identify the entry C-APIs and C header file *.h in the Cython configuration file *.pxd	# cython-hidapi/chid.pxd
			cdef extern from "hidapi.h":
			int hid_get_manufacturer_string(hid_device*, wchar_t *, size_t);
			int hid_get_product_string(hid_device*, wchar_t *, size_t);

	Ctypes	(1) Identify the instance objects of C libraries created by *Ctypes* function cdll.LoadLibrary() or CDLL() in the script *.py that imports *Ctypes* module; (2) Locate the entry C-APIs invoked through the above identified instance object	#PublicFiles/usb_device.py from ctypes import * USB2XXXLib = cdll.LoadLibrary("./lib/linux/ARMv7/libUSB2XXX.so") def DEV_GetDeviceInfo(DevHandle, pDevInfo, pFunctionStr): return USB2XXXLib.DEV_GetDeviceInfo(DevHandle, pDevInfo, pFunctionStr)

Java-C	JNI	(1) Identify the native methods in *.java file;
		(2) Locate the entry C-APIs wrapped by the JNI functions whose name containing the above native method name in the JNI implementation file *.c
			#zstd/Zstd.java
			public class Zstd{
			public static native long decompressUnsafe(long dst, long dstSize, long srcSize);}
			# native/jni_zstd.c
			JNIEXPORT jlong JNICALL Java_com_zstd_decompressUnsafe(JNIEnv *env) {
			return ZSTD_decompress((void *)(intptr_t) dst_buf_ptr, (size_t) dst_size); }

	JNA	(1) Identify an interface that extends the interface com.sun.jna.Library, in which a C library is loaded via the function Native.loadLibrary();
		(2) Locate the entry C-APIs declared in the above identified interface
			# gethostname4j/Hostname.java
			private interface UnixCLibrary extends Library {
			UnixCLibrary INSTANCE = Native.loadLibrary("c", UnixCLibrary.class);
			public int gethostname(byte[] hostname, int bufferSize);
			}

Fig. 7.4 *Insight*'s parsing patterns for various types of FFIs

- **RQ1 (Effectiveness of *Insight*)**: ***How effective is Insight in detecting CLV issues?*** To answer RQ1, we construct a benchmark dataset containing 69 real CLV issues for validating whether *Insight* can capture these issues in their corresponding buggy project versions.
- **RQ2 (Pervasiveness of Use of C Libraries)**: ***What is the scale of projects that depend on C libraries in the PyPI and Maven ecosystems?*** To answer RQ2, we gather the statistics of projects that directly or transitively depend on C libraries on recent snapshots of PyPI and Maven ecosystems.
- **RQ3 (Cross-Ecosystem Vulnerability Impacts)**: ***To what extent are vulnerable C libraries used by projects in the PyPI and Maven ecosystems?*** To answer RQ3, we apply *Insight* to real-world projects to explore the status quo of cross-ecosystem vulnerability impacts.
- **RQ4 (Usefulness of *Insight*)**: ***Is the diagnosis information provided by Insight useful to developers for dealing with CLV issues? To what extent do practitioners concern the CLV issues?*** To answer RQ4, we report the detected CLV issues together with diagnosis information to respective developers. We evaluate *Insight*'s usefulness based on developers' feedback.
- **RQ5 (Fixing Strategies and Challenges)**: ***What are common practices for fixing CLV issues? What are challenges of figuring out a fix?*** To answer RQ5, by digging into developers' feedback on our reported CLV issues, we distill their common fixing strategies and challenges to be addressed.

7.4.1 Data Collection

Insight's detection capability relies on its construction of *knowledge repository for C libraries* and *vulnerability database*. At the time of carrying out our experiments, we collected metadata from the snapshots of three mainstream Linux distributions: *Ubuntu* [13], *Debian* [14], and *Arch Linux* [15], on March 1, 2022.

7.4.1.1 *Insight*'s Knowledge Repository for C Libraries

Table 7.1 summarizes the statistics of *Insight*'s knowledge repository. It comprises 485,021 C project versions released in three Linux distributions, involving 829,242 C libraries. By collecting the metadata of C projects provided by respective maintainers, *Insight* maps the C libraries to their corresponding project versions. More importantly, for each C library, it constructs a unique feature vector as the identification of its precise version.

7.4.1.2 *Insight*'s Vulnerability Database

Table 7.2 depicts the statistics of *Insight*'s vulnerability database. Our vulnerability database consists of 45,473 vulnerability reports collected from three official security advisory websites: *Ubuntu Security* [22], *Debian Security* [23], and *Arch*

Table 7.1 Statistics of *Insight*'s knowledge repository for C libraries

Linux Distribution	*#C Project*	*#C Project Versions*	*#C Libraries*
Ubuntu	121,507	273,813	451,233
Debian	111,122	269,950	636,132
Arch Linux	12,264	12,297	30,824
Sum	165,347	485,021	829,242

Table 7.2 Statistics of *Insight*'s vulnerability database

	# CVE vulnerability reports					
Vulnerability DB	Critical	High	Medium	Low	Sum	# CVEs with vulnerable APIs
Ubuntu Security	2,530	12,917	16,317	1,830	33,594	16,750
Debian Security	553	2,130	2,523	255	5,461	2,255
Arch Linux Security	897	5,871	6,303	607	13,678	7,902
Sum[a]	3,119	18,536	21,291	2,527	45,473	21,384

[a]The duplicated vulnerabilities in three databases are filtered out.

Linux Security [24]. In total, we collected vulnerable APIs corresponding to 21,384 vulnerability reports.

The vulnerability metadata collection took 4 months for three Ph.D. students who have over 2 years vulnerability analysis experience to implement and test. We adopted an effective tool *Ctags* [29] to precisely extract the signatures of vulnerable APIs from code commits. More importantly, the three authors conducted daily manual validation for the vulnerability info.

7.4.2 RQ1: Effectiveness of Insight

Study Methodology To evaluate *Insight*'s capability in CLV issue detection, we constructed a high-quality benchmark consisting of real CLV issues because there is no related benchmark publicly available. Each CLV issue is a 5-tuple $clv = <P_b, Vul, Cp, vr, A>$, where P_b is the buggy version of a PyPI or Maven project; Vul denotes a CVE identifier disclosed in the vulnerable C project Cp, vr is the vulnerable version range of Cp affected by Vul, and A is a collection of the concerned vulnerable APIs in Cp. Note that the information of Cp, vr, and A can be identified in Vul's CVE report. We collected the benchmark dataset in two steps:

- First, we located a set of projects on GitHub that use Python or Java as primary language, and their commit log messages in code repositories described the CVE identifier of a C project (e.g., *CVE-2016-4658*). We found 341 such project versions. We manually checked these commits and only kept the project versions that satisfy (1) their commit log messages explicitly state that the revisions of build scripts aimed to remedy the concerned CVEs, (2) bundling test files (for triggering CLV issues), and (3) achieving more than 10 *Stars* (popularity). Finally, 232 project versions with CVE patching commits were retained. We considered these project versions before merging the commits as buggy versions potentially inducing CLV issues.
- Second, we executed the tests bundled with the buggy project versions to validate if they can actually invoke the relevant vulnerable APIs. To this end, we manually inserted log statements into each vulnerable API in C libraries and then checked the outcomes after running tests. Finally, we obtained 69 validated CLV issues where the concerned vulnerable C-APIs can be triggered by the tests bundled with the buggy project versions.

The benchmark construction took over 1 month for two authors to implement. Table 7.3 shows the statistics of our benchmark. The collected 69 real CLV issues cover 27 and 32 projects in PyPI and Maven ecosystems, respectively, involving 39 vulnerable C libraries. In the following, we run *Insight* on these buggy project versions to validate whether it can detect the CLV issues. Specifically, if one of the identified C project versions satisfies the vulnerable version range vr of Cp affected by vulnerability Vul, we consider *Insight* correctly determining the concerned C

Table 7.3 Statistics of 69 real CLV issues in our benchmark

PyPI	Maven	#Vulnerable Libraries
27 projects; **32** CLV issues	**32** projects; **37** CLV issues	**39**

†Some projects induce more than one CLV issue.

Table 7.4 Effectiveness of *Insight* on CLV issue detection

Types \ Stage	*Detection Rate*	***Stage 1***	***Stage 2***	***Stage 3***
CLV Issues in PyPI Projects	29/32 = 90.6%	32/32	30/32	29/30
CLV Issues in Maven Projects	32/37 = 86.5%	37/37	32/37	30/30
Detection Rate = 61/69 = 88.4%				

Stage 1: *C Library Extraction;* ***Stage 2:*** *C Project Version Tracing;* ***Stage 3:*** *Vulnerable C-API Analysis*

library's identity. For a CLV issue involving multiple vulnerable APIs, we consider *Insight* correctly capturing the issue if it reports one of them.

Results Table 7.4 shows our experiment results. *Insight* reports 61 CLV issues in the 59 benchmark projects. All the reported CLV issues are true positives, where the vulnerable libraries and APIs are correctly identified. In other words, *Insight* accurately reports 88.4% of the 69 CLV issues in the benchmark. We manually investigated the eight cases that were missed by *Insight* and divided them into two categories:

- *Insight failed to determine the identities of C libraries.* For seven of the missing cases, *Insight* obtained low similarity scores (bin^2sim value was below *LibRARIAN*' threshold 0.85) when matching the features of C libraries with those of known version instances in our knowledge repository. In the two missing cases of PyPI projects, *Insight* could not determine the identities of C libraries, because the corresponding C project maintainers only published the vulnerability fix versions to the Linux library repository. Since there is no metadata of the concerned vulnerable versions, our tool failed to determine the library identities via feature matching. For instance, vulnerability *CVE-2018-15686* [30] affects project version `systemd` 227 [31], while only `systemd` 229-249 can be found in *Unbuntu* library repository. In the PyPI project `Ble-driver` 0.16.2 [32] with *CVE-2018-15686*, *Insight* reported that library `libudev`.so was compiled from project `systemd` but failed to identify the project version.

  In the five missing cases of Maven projects, by checking the feature lists extracted from C libraries, we found that these client projects mixed their FFI declarations with the referenced C code and recompiled them into `*.so` files. Such recompilation affects our feature matching results, leading to low bin^2sim values. For instance, the Maven project `Emodb` 0.3.1 [33] with *CVE-2019-*

17543 [34] inserted their *JNI* code into the C library `liblz4.so`. We observed that the original exported functions in the feature list were replaced with the *JNI* functions after the recompilation. As a result, *Insight* obtained a bin^2sim of 0.46.

- *Insight failed to analyze the accessibility of vulnerable APIs based on parsing FFIs.* The remaining missing case concerns the PyPI project `Swiglpk` [35] that uses *SWIG* FFI [36]. Since the current implementation of *Insight* does not support the related parsing pattern, it fails to capture the vulnerable C-API accessed by the project. *Insight* is able to capture the vulnerable C-APIs in 68 out of 69 (98.6%) projects in our benchmark using the parsing patterns designed for *JNI*, *JNA*, *CFFI*, *Cython*, and *Ctypes*. This also demonstrates the effectiveness of our parsing patterns.

Answer to RQ1:
Insight accurately identifies 61 out of 69 (88.4%) CLV issues collected in our benchmark, achieving high detection rates for both PyPI and Maven projects.

7.4.3 RQ2: Pervasive Dependency on C Libraries

Study Methodology For a large-scale empirical study, we collected metadata for all projects in the PyPI and Maven ecosystems using the open-source discovery service *Libraries.io* [37] on its snapshot on March 1, 2022. Table 7.5 shows the statistics of our collected subjects. We deployed *Insight* to iteratively analyze 9,090,665 project versions in PyPI and Maven ecosystems, to investigate if their released archives (e.g., `*.Jar`, `*.aar`, and `*.whl`) bundled `*.so` files (i.e., directly depending on C libraries). More importantly, our metadata from *Libraries.io* also maps the dependency relationships between project versions, which enables us to explore whether C libraries are introduced into other projects via transitive dependencies.

Results Table 7.6 summarizes the statistics of our investigation results. With a longitudinal analysis of 774,134 projects, we identified 195,045 (46.7%) and 114,330 (32.1%) projects that directly or transitively depend on C libraries in the

Table 7.5 Statistics of subjects in the PyPI and Maven ecosystems

Ecosystem	*#Projects*	*#Project Versions*	*#Dependency Relationships*
PyPI	417,416	3,383,391	12,382,505
Maven	356,718	5,707,274	28,945,967

Table 7.6 Empirical results of RQ2

Results	PyPI	Maven
# Multilingual Projects	**195,045**/417,416 46.7%	**114,330**/356,718 32.1%
# Projects Directly Depending on C Libraries	**11,402**/195,045 5.8%	**10,227**/114,330 8.9%
# Projects Transitively Depending on C Libraries	**183,643**/195,045 94.2%	**104,103**/114,330 91.1%
# Multilingual Project Versions	**1,383,554**/3,383,391 40.9%	**2,037,098**/5,707,274 35.7%
# Project Versions Directly Depending on C Libraries	**96,505**/1,383,554 7.0%	**110,063**/2,037,098 5.4%
# Project Versions Transitively Depending on C Libraries	**1,287,049**/1,383,554 93.0%	**1,927,035**/2,037,098 94.6%

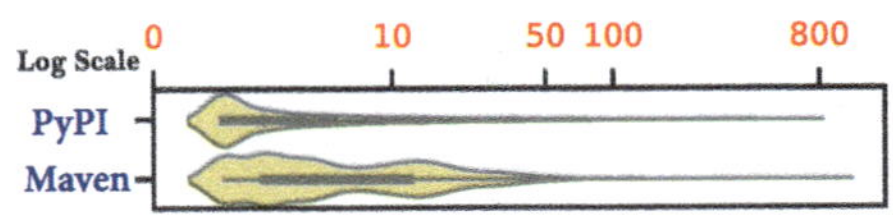

Fig. 7.5 Number of C libraries in each multilingual project version

PyPI and Maven ecosystems, respectively, involving 3,420,652 project versions. In fact, 93.0% of multilingual projects transitively use C libraries through a small fraction of pivotal projects that bundle `*.so` files. For example, we observed that a popular project `Pillow` [38] leverages C libraries to provide efficient image processing capabilities. Due to its powerful features, in PyPI, `Pillow` is depended by 46,268 downstream projects, achieving over 10 million of downloads per month. Similarly, project `RocksDB` [39] is developed by *Facebook Database Team* for storing data on flash drives based on C libraries. At present, in Maven, there are 16,649 downstream projects using `RocksDB` to implement Flash and RAM storage. Such pivotal projects introduce C libraries into a significant number of projects in the PyPI and Maven ecosystems via dependency chains, which should arouse practitioners' awareness.

By further inspecting the multilingual projects, we found that in total, there are 87,668 C libraries being introduced into these two ecosystems, as of March 1, 2022. The distribution plot in Fig. 7.5 presents the number of C libraries in each project version. Our results show that the number of dependent C libraries varies from 1 to 790 (i.e., 8.7±23.3). In both PyPI and Maven ecosystems, the projects of machine learning modeling and computer vision toolkits, etc. typically depend on many C libraries to enhance their performances. For example, a popular Python project `PyAV` 9.1.1 [40] bundles 93 `*.so` files. These C libraries originate from a leading multimedia framework `FFmpeg` [41] to help decode, encode, and transcode audios and videos. A Java project `Scalismo` 4.0.0 [42] used for statistical shape modeling depends on 203 C libraries, which originate from 41 C projects, including the high performance data management project `Hdf5` [43] and the image processing project `vtk` [44]. Such heavy use of C libraries can increase the projects' attack surface through cross-language invocations.

Answer to RQ2:
Based on a recent snapshot of PyPI and Maven ecosystems, 11,402 (5.8%) PyPI and 10,227 (8.9%) Maven projects directly depend on C libraries. The direct dependencies cause 183,643 (94.2.0%) and 104,103 (91.1%) projects transitively depending on C libraries, respectively, involving 3,420,652 project versions. Most projects tend to introduce multiple C libraries, increasing their attack surface through cross-language invocations.
Implication: *A small number of popular projects can introduce C libraries to a large number of PyPI and Maven projects through dependency chains.*

7.4.4 RQ3: Cross-Ecosystem Vulnerability Impacts

Study Methodology For the projects depending on C libraries identified in RQ2, we applied *Insight* to diagnosing if they (1) depend on vulnerable C libraries and (2) invoke vulnerable APIs from C libraries. To understand if developers were unaware of such CLV issues, we quantitatively analyzed the time taken by the developers to upgrade a vulnerable C library version in their projects after the fixing release of the library version.

Results *Insight* successfully traced the project versions for 65,949 out of 87,668 C libraries (75.2%) that were introduced into PyPI and Maven ecosystems. For 5,162 out of 9,352 identified vulnerable C libraries (55.2%), our vulnerability database collected the vulnerable APIs from their corresponding CVE reports. Based on the above captured vulnerable C libraries and APIs, we summarized the statistics of our investigation results in Table 7.7. In these two ecosystems, we observed that 33,254 project versions directly depend on vulnerable C libraries. In total, they were transitively used by 798,398 versions of their downstream projects. It is noteworthy that *Insight* identified 43 PyPI projects and 41 Maven projects (involving 1,532 project versions) that can directly invoke vulnerable APIs from C libraries. These project versions transitively affect 173,927 versions of downstream projects. The figures may underestimate the real situation since only a limited number of vulnerable APIs were explicitly identified from the CVE reports.

Figure 7.6a plots the distribution of vulnerability counts introduced in each project version. It is noticeable that the vast majority of projects contain more than one vulnerability. The number of vulnerabilities in these projects varies from 1 to 151 (i.e., 6.9 ± 11.0). For example, project `pdftopng` [45] depends on four vulnerable C libraries, involving four critical-level and nine high-level CVEs. By

Table 7.7 Empirical results of RQ3

Results	PyPI	Maven
Projects Directly Depending on Vunlerable C Libraries	**1,556**/11,402 13.6%	**1,305**/10,227 12.8%
Projects Transitively Depending on Vulnerable C Libraries	**59,118**/183,643 32.2%	**20,972**/104,103 20.1%
Projects Directly Invoke Vulnerable APIs from C Libraries	**43**/1,556 2.8%	**41**/1,305 3.1%
Projects Transitively Invoke Vulnerable APIs from C Libraries	**14,213**/59,118 24.0%	**7,029**/20,972 33.5%
Project Versions Directly Depending on Vulnerable C Libraries	**15,942**/96,505 16.5%	**17,312**/110,063 15.7%
Project Versions Transitively Depending on Vulnerable C libraries	**381,129**/1,287,049 29.6%	**417,269**/1,927,035 21.7%
Project Versions Directly Invoke Vulnerable APIs from C Libraries	**662**/15,942 4.2%	**870**/17,312 5.0%
Project Versions Transitively Invoke Vulnerable APIs from C Libraries	**72,814**/381,129 19.1%	**101,113**/417,269 24.2%

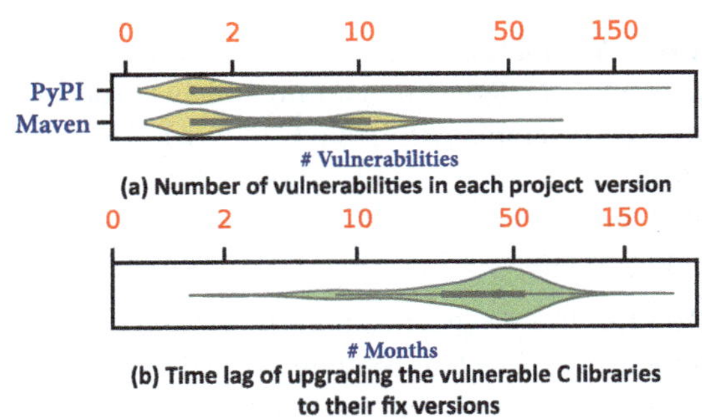

Fig. 7.6 Investigation results of RQ3 (log scale)

parsing the FFIs in `pdftopng`, *Insight* points out 15 call chains that can access 12 vulnerable APIs.

Among the 2,861 projects directly dependent on vulnerable C libraries, 2,603 of them (91.0%) have not yet remediated the vulnerabilities in their latest versions. We further inspected the 2,218 active projects disseminating new releases in the past year, to analyze the time lag in adopting the fixes of vulnerable C library versions. Figure 7.6b presents the above investigation results (only focusing on vulnerabilities with critical and high severity levels). We observed that 75.0% of C libraries have already remediated the vulnerabilities for more than 2 years. However, project developers in PyPI and Maven communities probably were unaware of these problems and still depend on the vulnerable C library versions.

Answer to RQ3:
In the PyPI and Java ecosystems, we identified 82,951 multilingual projects (26.8%) directly or transitively using vulnerable C libraries. Among them, 21,326 projects (involving 175,459 versions) can invoke vulnerable APIs from C libraries.
Implication: *The cross-ecosystem vulnerability impacts may be greatly underestimated since Insight identified project versions for 75.2% of C libraries and located a limited number of the involved CVE reports. Future research may focus on improving the effectiveness of security analyzers to help developers capture the CLV issues.*

7.4.5 RQ4: Usefulness of Insight

Study Methodology To further validate the usefulness of diagnosis information generated by *Insight* for CLV issues, we report them to respective developers. We focused on two types of CLV issues in the PyPI and Maven ecosystems: (1) *API-level CLV issues*: the projects whose latest versions could invoke vulnerable APIs from C libraries and (2) *library-level CLV issues*: the pivotal projects whose latest versions directly depend on vulnerable C libraries. Specifically, we considered the projects that are directly or transitively used by more than 500 downstream projects as the pivotal ones. We concern the library-level CLV issues in the condition that their corresponding vulnerable APIs cannot be explicitly identified in the CVE reports. In such cases, the pivotal projects using vulnerable C libraries can bring potential security risks to large amounts of downstream projects. We filtered out 178 CLV issues whose associated projects had no maintenance records in the last two years and submitted 226 reports to the active projects' issue trackers.

Ethical Considerations To avoid spamming the open-source community and developers, we only concerned the pivotal projects with CLV issues and thoroughly validated the diagnosis info generated by *Insight*. All the 226 issue reports were submitted in compliance with the projects' contributing guidelines and licenses.

Results Table 7.8 summarizes the statistics of our CLV issue reports. In total 127 reports (56.2%) were quickly confirmed by developers, and 95 confirmed reports (78.4%) have been fixed or are being fixed based on our suggestions. For the remaining 32 confirmed issues (25.2%), developers tried to upgrade vulnerable C libraries but encountered challenges during fixing process. Eleven library-level issue reports (4.9%) were rejected because the vulnerable functionalities in C libraries were not actually used by client code after developers' validation. The other reports are still pending likely due to the less active maintenance of the projects.

Table 7.8 Statistics of 226 CLV issues reported by *Insight*

♦ Fixed issues; ♣ Issues that were under fixing; ★ Confirmed issues but facing challenges during fixing process; ■ Rejected issues; ▲ Pending issues.
More detailed information of issue reports is provided on our homepage (**http://insight-clv-detection.com/**).

Types	*Issue Reports*
PyPI *API-level*	xmlstarlet#199♦; capstone-get#1864♦; chiavdf#108♦; depthai#543♦; digital-rf#40♦; electrumsv-secp256kl#5♦; mikecore#21♦; pdftopng#125♦; pyrsb#12♦; python-gdcm#13♦; healpy#758♦; psycopg-binary#262♦; triton#489♦; libsonata#189♦; ligo-skymap#12♣; mpegcoder#4♣; pyfast#155♣; pymssql#753♣; pyopencap#41♣; pytraj#1607♣; pyhdf#54★;
PyPI *Library-level*	hidapi#135♦; rasterio#81♦; opencv-python#646♦; python-casacore#229♦; python-mbedtls#59♦; eclipse-sumo#10456♦; healpy#758♣; python-gdcm#13♣; django-social#1♣; shape-detection#1♣; archi#15♦; Stratega#118♦; robobag#1♣; jdla#1♣; docbarcodes#38♣; ssh2-python#171♣; arbor#1874♣; zelos#140♣; crypto-msg-parser#1♣; fastjet#80★; klayout#1046★; skia-python#175★; smt-switch#299♣; sqlcipher3-binary#12♣; urh#973♣; kongalib#1♣; miller-rabin#1♣; pygit2#1136♣; mmedit#830♣; redlibssh2#1♣; regina#1♣; lpk#62♣; gudhi#599♣; regionmask#347♣; atlite#232★; geocube#100★; rioxarrary#503★; terracotta#261★; mapchete#455★; pytraffic#14183★; sourcery-cli#216★; kivy#7851★; lavavu#99★; medaka#364★; pymeshlab#205★; mip#263★; pysam#1097■; pro-gan-pth#65■; wbia-pyhesaff#9■; wbia-vtool#16■; gphoto2#139■; mixstream#35■; pysurvive#269▲; asmc-preparedecoding#11▲; carla#5289▲; curlyboi#5▲; cyvcf2#239▲; daisykit#12▲; disparity-interpolation#6▲; ecell4-base#495▲; extractcode-libarchive#21▲; imread#40▲; tuplex#90▲; wasmer-compiler-llvm#623▲; mpdaf#25▲; mvdtool#105▲; ndsi#77▲; pyapr#54▲; pybbi#21▲; pycreds#81▲; pygroupsig#92▲; pyinvariant#8▲; pylibtermkey#1▲; pysseract#17▲; pytoulbar2#18▲; pyuwsgi#2424▲; pywf#28▲; qif#4▲; quickfix-ssl#390▲; pyzswagcl#79▲; deep-learning-plus#1▲; vp-suite#33▲; object-detector#2▲; nd2#48▲; taxa-sdk#9▲; manga-scraper#4▲;
Maven *API-level*	JVips#120♦; idml#34♦; pipes#3♦; sparkey#52♦; yosegi#177♦; blacklite#24♦; terse#139♦; isarn#26♦; spark-utils#23♦; glow#508♦; rasterframes#583♦; servicecomb#753♦; bzffmpegcmd#4♦; pdf2htmlEX#59♦; coral#1♦; Indigo#719♣; apng#106♣; cognitive-services#1475♣; liberium#7♣; scalismo#6★;
Maven *Library-level*	libpag#298♦; OpenMLDB#1723♦; BigDL#4517♦; realm#803♦; zippelin#4354♦; finagle#927♣; laurelin#102♣; incubator#83♣; ignite#9974♣; mongo-java-driver#917♣; timeshape#94♣; APE#55♣; etlflow#167♣; smart#511♣; clickntap#14♣; JPPF#39♣; caoyx-rpc#13♣; enos#20♣; wasp#9♣; Orchid#413♣; LibRawFX#2♣; 180protocol#50■; pulsar#15124■; huaweicloud#73▲; incubator#82♣; alive-detect#2♣; hyperdriver#264★; netflow#82★; druid#12462♣; nebula#78♣; ffsampledsp#14★; FloorPlan#65★; azure-sdk#1090★; recommenders#1701★; jctp#3★; paparazzi#417★; trino#12082★; h5jan#11★; J2V8#581★; FastAsync WorldEdit#1701★; snowflake#426★; mongo-spark#68★; amazon-codeguru#1★; overwatch#352■; parquet4s#263■; djl#1561■; fun-io#21▲; logisland#605▲; embulk#84▲; thrift#16▲; gamioo#1▲; wasp#10▲; aiven#105▲; parquet#8▲; fm-common#41▲; armor#48▲; topleet#1▲; AndroidDocumentScanner#42▲; ebiznext#653▲; featran#619▲; rumble#1192▲; damavis#11▲; octavo#25▲; bitcoin#4263▲; nix-java#80▲; konduit#517▲; ssj#40▲; AudioMixer#8▲; libxmfunsdk#2▲; NIM#3▲; artcodes#4▲; Frankenstein#8▲; RxGalleryFinal#315▲; spectrum#1842▲; qtjambi#11▲; unidbg#423▲; kafka-connect#13▲; tessera#1446▲; Habanero#10▲; LTSample#1▲; MMVideoSDK#1▲; langx#35▲; MMSPlayer#1▲; ClassRoomSDK#1▲; ijkrtspdemo#5▲; oss-allegro#31▲; rovio#26▲; web3-event#36▲; Takin#121▲; hawkbit#78▲; chameleon#9▲; cordova#1▲; moip#144▲; iot#16▲; cf4j#22▲; FFmpegTools#1▲; opensrp#863▲; HeartSaVioR#38▲; fresco#2671▲;

Feedback on Reported CLV Issues The high confirmation rates in the two ecosystems suggest that developers are deeply concerned about the CLV issues induced in their projects and tend to timely resolve the issues. We discuss a few selected cases below:

- *API-Level CLV Issues. Insight* reported 41 issues to the projects whose latest versions could invoke the vulnerable C-APIs, achieving a 100% of confirmation rate. Of those 39 (95.1%) were fixed/under fixing by developers. It is noteworthy that, for all the API-level CLV issue reports, we received developers' quick confirmation within 2 days. The detailed diagnosis information generated by *Insight* indeed aroused their awareness of the call chains reaching to vulnerable C-APIs. For example, in #199 [46] of `Xmlstarlet`, we pointed out four call chains starting from the FFI declarations in Python client code to the vulnerable C-APIs disclosed in four CVE reports (i.e., *CVE-2019-11068* [47], *CVE-2017-5029* [48], *CVE-2016-2073* [49], and *CVE-2016-3627* [50]). Developers were previously unaware of the risk and commented "*Thanks for the thorough report! I will prepare a new release with a fix this week.*"
- *Library-Level CLV Issues. Insight* reported 185 issues to pivotal PyPI and Maven projects whose latest version depends on vulnerable C libraries. Since the involved CVE reports do not explicitly point out the vulnerable APIs, such vulnerabilities can lead to an uncertain attack surface in the ecosystems. 46.5% of these influential projects confirmed our CLV issue reports, and developers expressed that they should take actions to avoid bringing potential risks to large amounts of downstream projects in the ecosystems. For example, in #135 [51], the project `cython-hidapi` that implements *Cython* FFI for interfacing Python

with C quickly upgraded their C libraries to fix the CLV issues. Since they had over 70,000 downstream users, the developers took our report seriously and commented that "*This report makes sense. We should fix the issue and publish a new wheel package.*"

The responsive CLV issue reports cover many well-known projects, such as `Mongodb` [10], `Libgit2` [11], `Eclipse/Sumo` [12], etc. *Insight*'s generated reports arouse the awareness of 95 projects to remediate CLV issues. Their corresponding fix versions could be incorporated by 49,118 downstream projects, significantly reducing the attack surface in PyPI and Maven ecosystems.

Feedback on *Insight* Developers also showed great interest in the *Insight* tool. For example, we reported an issue `#171` [52] to `ParallelSSH`, which aroused project developers' attention. Since `ParallelSSH` provides C-APIs for Python clients to build SSH2 (*Secure Shell*) protocol, they take vulnerabilities seriously. One developer supported our suggestions and left a comment:

"*The diagnosis info is absolutely useful to us! How did you generate the call chains? I would be interested in automated notifications of vulnerabilities in the C libraries we use. Since Python build tools cannot figure out C dependencies for security checking, we rely on people to report any C vulnerabilities.* " Developers' feedback suggests that *Insight* is useful in warning developers against CLV issues.

Answer to RQ4:
The feedbacks indicate that detecting the vulnerability impacts across ecosystems is indeed important to and welcomed by real-world developers. The diagnosis information provided by Insight is also useful to help developers diagnose CLV issues in practice.
Implication: *Continuously monitoring the vulnerability impacts across ecosystems is of great values for building healthy open-source communities. Future research may focus on generalizing the technical framework of Insight to other pairwise software ecosystems to help capture CLV issues.*

7.4.6 RQ5: Fixing Strategies and Challenges

Study Methodology We performed an in-depth analysis on (1) the patches of 42 fixed CLV issues and (2) clear fixing plans and relevant discussions in the 38 confirmed CLV issues. We followed an open coding procedure [53], a widely used approach for qualitative research, to categorize the fixing strategies and challenges discussed in our reported issues. Two Ph.D. students, who have over 3 years of Java and Python development experience, independently analyzed the fixes and developers' discussions on the issue reports. In order to adjust the taxonomy, they gathered to compare and discuss their results. The conflicts of labeling were discussed during meetings and resolved by the third author.

Results We observed two fixing strategies from the issue reports.

Fixing Strategy 1 *Upgrading the C direct dependencies that directly or transitively introduce the vulnerabilities (55/80).* This strategy was adopted by 55 reports (68.8%) to resolve CLV issues. For example, in #118 [54] of `Stratega`, the client project directly depended on a vulnerable library `libfreetype.so`, which was originated from C project `Freetype` 2.6.1 containing four CVEs. Following our suggestions, developers incorporated the `libfreetype.so` from the CVE fix version `Freetype` 2.9.1.

Fixing Strategy 2 *Upgrading the target OS of client project (25/80).* We observed that 25 projects (31.3%) adopted this strategy to fix CLV issues, since their referenced vulnerable `*.so` files are automatically bundled by Linux OS during the building process. In such cases, project developers have to upgrade their target OS versions to introduce the vulnerability fix versions of C libraries. For example, in #15 [55] of `Archi`, the client project transitively used a vulnerable C library `liblz4.so` which was bundled by OS `Ubuntu` 16.04. Developers resolved this issue by upgrading its target OS to `Ubuntu` 18.04 to introduce the CVE fix version of `liblz4.so`.

Regarding the fixing challenges, we found clues in 43 CLV issue reports and summarized them as follows:

Challenge 1: Developers have to resolve the dependency conflict issues induced by upgrading dependencies/target OS (10/43). Upgrading libraries/target OS can fix CLV issues but may introduce new dependencies that violate the dependency constrains specified by other C libraries/the build environment. For example, in #6 [56], project `scalismo` bundled 203 C libraries, which made it quite difficult to deploy. Library `libjhdf5.so` originating from `Hdf5` 1.8.10 contains 14 CVEs whose vulnerable APIs can be accessed by the Java client code. Project developers tried to upgrade `libjhdf5.so`, but its CVE fix version introduced new dependencies whose specified version constraints were incompatible with the existing ones. `Scalismo` team opened a discussion for addressing the induced dependency conflicts.

Challenge 2: Developers cannot easily figure out which version of C direct dependency/target OS can transitively introduce the vulnerability fixes (20/43). For example, in #54 [57] of `Pyhdf`, the client project transitively depends on a vulnerable C library `libjpeg.so` through the direct dependency `libcpython.so`. Specifically, `libjpeg.so` was compiled from the C project `libjpeg-turbo` 1.3.0 containing two CVEs, whose vulnerable APIs can be invoked by the Python client code. To resolve this issue, developers tried out different versions of `libcpython.so` but could not figure out a patch that transitively introduced the CVE fix version of `libcpython.so`.

Challenge 3: Developers have to request the Linux community to remediate the vulnerabilities (13/43). In the cases that projects' compatible target OS versions have not bundled the CVE fix versions of C libraries, developers have to request the Linux distribution to remediate such vulnerable C libraries. For example, in #1046 [58] of `Klayout`, the project automatically introduced a vulnerable C library through its target OS `CentOS7` during building process. Developers failed to identify a compatible OS version having incorporated the vulnerability fixes. As a result, they forwarded our issue report to the Linux community (see report [59]), seeking for assistance to remediate the vulnerable libraries.

> ***Answer to RQ5:***
> *We observed that the vulnerable C libraries can be introduced as a client project's direct dependencies/transitive dependencies or even automatically bundled by the target OS during the building process. According to the different forms of introducing C libraries, project developers determine their fixing strategies accordingly.*
> ***Implication:*** *Future research may focus on addressing the three fixing challenges to design automated approaches for repairing CLV issues.*

7.5 Threats to Validity

Internal Validity The internal threat relates to the identification of C libraries. We leverage an existing technique *LibRATIAN* to extract main features inherent to C library versions for matching the similarity with those in our knowledge repository. However, these features may lead to misidentifications for consecutive versions. The consecutive versions with minor revisions may not change, add, or remove exported symbols. To mitigate these threats, we significantly reduced the similarity matching scope in our knowledge repository for post analysis to a few candidate versions.

Conclusion Validity In our study, we focus on the C libraries targeting Linux OS in the form of `*.so` files because the community provides centralized library repositories for mainstream Linux distributions and continuous services for collecting vulnerability reports of C libraries. The above metadata enables the implementation of our automated tool but poses threats to the conclusion validity. Future studies may improve our knowledge repository and feature extraction approaches for adapting to C libraries targeting Windows OS (in the form of `*.dll` files).

7.6 Related Work

Multilingual Program Analysis Khomh et al. [60, 61] defined a catalog of design smells related to multilingual projects and provide empirical evidence on their severity and impact on software quality. Tan et al. [62] empirically studied on a large collection of Python projects to understand the interaction inefficiencies between Python code and native libraries written in C/C++/Fortran. Bai et al. [63] proposed a bidirectional dynamic taint tracking method, *BridgeTaint*, to detect cross-language privacy leaks and code injection attacks in hybrid apps using JavaScript bridges. Lee et al. [64] proposed an approach to analyze the *JNI* invocations between Java and C, in order to extract semantic summaries from multilingual programs. Li et al. [65] developed a tool *NatiDroid*, to facilitate cross-language analysis on the Android system and extract the permission-API protection mappings from the native libraries on Android apps. The study most relevant to our work is done by Almanee et al. [9]. They propose a technique *LibRARIAN*, which leverages different features extracted from C libraries to determine their project versions. Our *Insight* incorporates *LibRARIAN* to trace to the identities of C libraries and provides a turn-key solution to diagnose CLV issues. To adopt the *LibRARIAN* for CLV issue detection in PyPI and Maven ecosystems, *Insight* constructs a large-scale knowledge repository by collecting the metadata of millions of C libraries with their known versions.

Software Ecosystems Decan et al. [66, 67] conducted a quantitative empirical analysis of the similarities and differences between the evolution of package dependency networks for seven software ecosystems, including *Cargo*, *CPAN*, etc. Approaches [68, 69] pointed out the fragility of software ecosystems and gave insights on the challenges software developers face. They examined the *Eclipse*, *CPAN*, and *npm* ecosystems, focusing on what practices cause API breakages. In work [70, 71], researchers conducted empirical investigations with millions of *npm* packages and suggested that *npm* developers should be careful about the selection of packages and how to keep them updated. Kula et al. [70, 72] suggested developers to be aware of how sensitive their third-party dependencies were to critical changes in the software ecosystem. Jafari et al. [73] conducted surveys with practitioners, to identify and quantify seven dependency smells with varying degrees of popularity and investigate why smells are introduced. Wittern et al. [74] investigated the evolution of *npm* using metrics such as dependencies between packages, download count, and usage count in JavaScript applications. Shariffdeen et al. [75] empirically studied the bug fix issues in the Linux ecosystem and proposed a patch backporting technique transferring patches from the mainline version of Linux into older stable versions. To the best of our knowledge, our work is the first attempt to study the vulnerability impacts across multiple software ecosystems.

Vulnerable Dependencies In approaches [76] and [77], researchers empirically studied the evolution and decay of vulnerabilities in source code and found that due to the code reuse and third-party libraries, most vulnerabilities are recurring. Cox et al. [78] introduced metrics to qualify the "dependency freshness" of software projects, to understand the relations between outdated dependencies and vulnerabilities based on an industry benchmark. Studies [79–82] investigated millions of *npm* packages to analyze how and when these vulnerabilities were discovered and fixed, and to what extent they affected other packages. Zimmermann [81] pointed out a small proportion of individual vulnerable packages could impact large parts of the entire ecosystem. Whereas approaches [83–91] studied the evolution and impacts of vulnerable packages in specific communities, including Firefox, and Docker Images, Android, etc. Recent studies [92–96] were proposed to address the overestimation problem for reporting the vulnerable dependencies. They provided fine-grained assessment approaches using static or dynamic analysis to determine whether the located vulnerable code would be reachable. In this chapter, we conducted a thorough study to investigate whether the Python or Java code can invoke vulnerable APIs in C libraries, by parsing diversified FFIs.

7.7 Conclusion and Future Work

In this chapter, we conducted a large-scale empirical study to understand the status quo of vulnerability impacts across ecosystems. The study also leads to the development of the first automated tool, *Insight*, which provides a turn-key solution to help practitioners capture the CLV issues. Our study arouses the awareness of vulnerable C libraries in popular ecosystems and presents related analysis results. In the future, we plan to generalize the technical framework of *Insight* to other software ecosystems and involve various programming languages into our empirical study.

References

1. CFFI. 2022. https://cffi.readthedocs.io/en/latest/. Accessed: 2022-03-01.
2. Java Native Interface(JNI). 2022. https://docs.oracle.com/en/java/javase/17/docs/specs/jni/index.html. Accessed: 2022-03-01.
3. Maven. 2022. https://maven.apache.org/. Accessed: 2022-03-01.
4. Pip. 2022. https://packaging.python.org/en/latest/key_projects/#pip. Accessed: 2022-03-01.
5. Dependabot. 2022. https://github.com/dependabot. Accessed: 2022-03-01.
6. Cython. 2022. https://cython.readthedocs.io/en/latest/src/tutorial/clibraries.html. Accessed: 2022-03-01.
7. Ctypes. 2022. https://docs.python.org/3/library/ctypes.html. Accessed: 2022-03-01.
8. Java Native Access(JNA). 2022. http://java-native-access.github.io/jna/5.10.0/javadoc/overview-summary.html. Accessed: 2022-03-01.
9. Almanee S, Ünal A, Payer M, Garcia J. Too Quiet in the Library: An Empirical Study of Security Updates in Android Apps Native Code. In: 2021 IEEE/ACM 43rd International Conference on Software Engineering (ICSE). 2021. New York: IEEE. p. 1347–1359.
10. Mongodb. 2022. https://www.mongodb.com/. Accessed: 2022-03-01.
11. Libgit2. 2022. https://libgit2.org/. Accessed: 2022-03-01.
12. Eclipse/Sumo. 2022. https://www.eclipse.org/sumo/. Accessed: 2022-03-01
13. Ubuntu. 2022. https://ubuntu.com/. Accessed: 2022-03-01.
14. Debian. 2022. https://www.debian.org/. Accessed: 2022-03-01.
15. Arch Linux. 2022. https://archlinux.org/. Accessed: 2022-03-01.
16. Guidelines for naming C libraries. 2022. https://tldp.org/HOWTO/Program-Library-HOWTO/shared-libraries.html#AEN46. Accessed: 2022-03-01.

17. Issue#14623 of Incubator. 2022. https://github.com/apache/incubator-mxnet/pull/14623. Accessed: 2022-03-01.
18. CVE-2018-18557. 2022. https://cve.mitre.org/cgi-bin/cvename.cgi?name=CVE-2018-18557. Accessed: 2022-03-01.
19. Issue#167 of Etlflow. 2022. https://github.com/tharwaninitin/etlflow/issues/167. Accessed: 2022-03-01.
20. Wheel unpack. 2022. https://wheel.readthedocs.io/en/stable/reference/wheel_unpack.html. Accessed: 2022-03-01.
21. Zipfile. 2022. https://docs.python.org/zh-cn/3/library/zipfile.html. Accessed: 2022-03-01.
22. Ubuntu Security. 2022. https://ubuntu.com/security/cve. Accessed: 2022-03-01.
23. Debian Security. 2022. https://lists.debian.org/debian-security-announce/. Accessed: 2022-03-01.
24. Arch Linux Security. 2022. https://security.archlinux.org/issues/all. Accessed: 2022-03-01.
25. Xu C, Chen B, Lu C, Huang K, Peng X, Liu Y. TRACER: Finding Patches for Open Source Software Vulnerabilities. 2021. arXiv preprint arXiv:2112.02240.
26. Jang J, Agrawal A, Brumley D. ReDeBug: finding unpatched code clones in entire OS distributions. In: 2012 IEEE Symposium on Security and Privacy. 2012. New York: IEEE. p. 48–62.
27. Kim S, Woo S, Lee H, Oh H. VUDDY: A scalable approach for vulnerable code clone discovery. In: 2017 IEEE Symposium on Security and Privacy (SP). 2017. New York: IEEE. p. 595–614.
28. CFlow, is part of the GNU project, which analyzes a collection of C source files and prints the call chains between functions. 2022. https://savannah.gnu.org/projects/cflow/. Accessed: 2022-03-01.
29. Ctags tool. 2022. http://ctags.sourceforge.net/. Accessed: 2022-03-01.
30. CVE-2018-15686. https://nvd.nist.gov/vuln/detail/CVE-2018-15686. 2022. Accessed: 2022-03-01.
31. Systemd. 2022. https://systemd.io/. Accessed: 2022-03-01.
32. Ble-driver. 2022. https://github.com/NordicSemiconductor/pc-ble-driver-py. Accessed: 2022-03-01.
33. Emodb. 2022. https://github.com/bazaarvoice/emodb. Accessed: 2022-03-01.
34. CVE-2019-17543. https://nvd.nist.gov/vuln/detail/CVE-2019-17543. 2022. Accessed: 2022-03-01.
35. Swiglpk. 2022. https://pypi.org/project/swiglpk/. Accessed: 2022-03-01.
36. SWIG. 2022. https://swig.org/. Accessed: 2022-03-01.
37. Libraries.io. 2022. https://libraries.io/. Accessed: 2022-03-01.
38. Pillow. 2022. https://github.com/python-pillow/Pillow. Accessed: 2022-03-01.
39. RocksDB. 2022. https://github.com/facebook/rocksdb. Accessed: 2022-03-01.
40. PyAV. 2022. https://github.com/PyAV-Org/PyAV/. Accessed: 2022-03-01.
41. FFmpeg. 2022. https://ffmpeg.org/. Accessed: 2022-03-01.
42. Scalismo. 2022. https://github.com/unibas-gravis/scalismo-native. Accessed: 2022-03-01.
43. Hdf5. 2022. https://www.hdfgroup.org/solutions/hdf5. Accessed: 2022-03-01.
44. Vtk. 2022. https://vtk.org/. Accessed: 2022-03-01.
45. Pdftopng. 2022. https://github.com/vinayak-mehta/pdftopng. Accessed: 2022-03-01.
46. Issue#199 of Xmlstarlet. 2022. https://github.com/dimitern/xmlstarlet/issues/199. Accessed: 2022-03-01.
47. CVE-2019-11068. 2022. https://nvd.nist.gov/vuln/detail/CVE-2019-11068. Accessed: 2022-03-01.
48. CVE-2017-5029. 2022. https://nvd.nist.gov/vuln/detail/CVE-2017-5029. Accessed: 2022-03-01.
49. CVE-2016-2073. 2022. https://nvd.nist.gov/vuln/detail/CVE-2016-2073, Accessed: 2022-03-01.
50. CVE-2016-3627. 2022. https://nvd.nist.gov/vuln/detail/CVE-2016-3627. Accessed: 2022-03-01.

51. Issue#135 of cython-hidapi. 2022. https://github.com/trezor/cython-hidapi/issues/135. Accessed: 2022-03-01.
52. Issue#171 of ParallelSSH. 2022. https://github.com/ParallelSSH/ssh2-python/issues/171. Accessed: 2022-03-01.
53. Lewis S. Qualitative inquiry and research design: Choosing among five approaches. Health Promot Pract 2015; 16(4):473–475.
54. Issue#118 of Stratega. 2022. https://github.com/GAIGResearch/Stratega/issues/118. Accessed: 2022-03-01.
55. Issue#15 of Archi. 2022. https://github.com/whtsky/archi/issues/15. Accessed: 2022-03-01.
56. Issue#6 of Scalismo. 2022. https://github.com/unibas-gravis/scalismo-native/issues/6. Accessed: 2022-03-01.
57. Issue#54 of Pyhdf. 2022. https://github.com/fhs/pyhdf/issues/54. Accessed: 2022-03-01.
58. Issue#1046 of KLayout. 2022. https://github.com/KLayout/klayout/issues/1046. Accessed: 2022-03-01.
59. The forwarded issue report in Linux community. 2022. https://github.com/pypa/manylinux/issues/1302. Accessed: 2022-03-01.
60. Abidi M, Openja M, Khomh F. Multi-language design smells: A backstage perspective. In: Proceedings of the 17th International Conference on Mining Software Repositories. 2020. p. 615–618.
61. Abidi M, Rahman MS, Openja M, Khomh F. Are multi-language design smells fault-prone? an empirical study. ACM Trans Softw Eng Methodol (TOSEM) 2021; 30(3):1–56.
62. Tan J, Chen Y, Liu Z, Ren B, Song SL, Shen X, Liu X. Toward efficient interactions between Python and native libraries. In: Proceedings of the 29th ACM Joint Meeting on European Software Engineering Conference and Symposium on the Foundations of Software Engineering. 2021. p. 1117–1128.
63. Bai J, Wang W, Qin Y, Zhang S, Wang J, Pan Y. BridgeTaint: A bi-directional dynamic taint tracking method for JavaScript bridges in android hybrid applications. IEEE Trans Inf Forensics Secur. 2018; 14(3):677–692.
64. Lee S, Lee H, Ryu S. Broadening horizons of multilingual static analysis: Semantic summary extraction from C code for JNI program analysis. In: Proceedings of the 35th IEEE/ACM International Conference on Automated Software Engineering. 2020. p. 127–137.
65. Li C, Chen X, Sun R, Xue J, Wen S, Ahmed ME, Camtepe S, Xiang Y. NatiDroid: Cross-Language Android Permission Specification. 2021. arXiv preprint arXiv:2111.08217.
66. Decan A, Mens T, Grosjean P. An empirical comparison of dependency network evolution in seven software packaging ecosystems. Empir Softw Eng. 2019;24 1:381–416.
67. Decan A, Mens T, Claes M. An empirical comparison of dependency issues in OSS packaging ecosystems. In: 2017 IEEE 24th international conference on software analysis, Evolution and Reengineering (SANER). New York: IEEE; 2017. p. 2–12.
68. Bogart C, Kästner C, Herbsleb J. When it breaks, it breaks: How ecosystem developers reason about the stability of dependencies. In 2015 30th IEEE/ACM International Conference on Automated Software Engineering Workshop (ASEW). New York: IEEE; 2015. p. 86–89.
69. Bogart C, Kästner C, Herbsleb J, Thung F. How to break an API: cost negotiation and community values in three software ecosystems. In Proceedings of the 2016 24th ACM SIGSOFT International Symposium on Foundations of Software Engineering. 2016. p. 109–120.
70. Kula RG, Ouni A, German DM, Inoue K. On the impact of micro-packages: An empirical study of the NPM JavaScript ecosystem. 2017. arXiv preprint arXiv:1709.04638.
71. Abdalkareem R, Nourry O, Wehaibi S, Mujahid S, Shihab E. Why do developers use trivial packages? an empirical case study on npm. In: Proceedings of the 2017 11th joint meeting on foundations of software engineering. 2017. p. 385–395.

72. Trockman A, Zhou S, Kästner C, Vasilescu B. Adding sparkle to social coding: An empirical study of repository badges in the npm ecosystem. In: Proceedings of the 40th International Conference on Software Engineering. 2018. p. 511–522.
73. Jafari AJ, Costa DE, Abdalkareem R, Shihab E, Tsantalis N. Dependency smells in JavaScript projects. IEEE Trans Softw Eng. 2021;48(10):3790–3807.
74. Wittern E, Suter P, Rajagopalan S. A look at the dynamics of the JavaScript package ecosystem. In Proceedings of the 13th International Conference on Mining Software Repositories. 2016. p. 351–361.
75. Shariffdeen R, Gao X, Duck JG, Tan SH, Lawall J, Roychoudhury A. Automated patch backporting in Linux (experience paper). In: Proceedings of the 30th ACM SIGSOFT International Symposium on Software Testing and Analysis. 2021. p. 633–645.
76. Di Penta M, Cerulo L, Aversano L. The life and death of statically detected vulnerabilities: An empirical study. Information and Software Technology. 2009;51(10):1469–1484.
77. Pham HN, Nguyen TT, Nguyen HA, Nguyen NT. Detection of recurring software vulnerabilities. In: Proceedings of the IEEE/ACM international conference on Automated software engineering. 2010. p. 447–456.
78. Cox J, Bouwers E, Van Eekelen M, Visser J. Measuring dependency freshness in software systems. In: 2015 IEEE/ACM 37th IEEE International Conference on Software Engineering, vol. 2. 2015. New York: IEEE. p. 109–118.
79. Decan A, Mens T, Constantinou E. On the impact of security vulnerabilities in the npm package dependency network. In: Proceedings of the 15th International Conference on Mining Software Repositories. 2018. p. 181–191.
80. Duan R, Bijlani A, Xu M, Kim T, Lee W. Identifying open-source license violation and 1-day security risk at large scale. In: Proceedings of the 2017 ACM SIGSAC Conference on computer and communications security. 2017. p. 2169–2185.
81. Zimmermann M, Staicu C-A, Tenny C, Pradel M. Small world with high risks: A study of security threats in the NPM ecosystem. In: 28th USENIX Security Symposium (USENIX Security 19). 2019. p. 995–1010.
82. Chinthanet B, Kula RG, McIntosh S, Ishio T, Ihara A, Matsumoto K. Lags in the release, adoption, and propagation of npm vulnerability fixes. Empir Softw Eng. 2021; 26(3):1–28.
83. Massacci F, Neuhaus S, Nguyen VH. After-life vulnerabilities: A study on Firefox evolution, its vulnerabilities, and fixes. In: International Symposium on Engineering Secure Software and Systems. Berlin: Springer. 2011. p. 195–208.
84. Zerouali A, Cosentino V, Mens T, Robles G, Gonzalez-Barahona JM. On the impact of outdated and vulnerable JavaScript packages in docker images. In: 2019 IEEE 26th International Conference on Software Analysis, Evolution and Reengineering (SANER). New York: IEEE. 2019. p. 619–623.
85. Piantadosi V, Scalabrino S, Oliveto R. Fixing of security vulnerabilities in open source projects: A case study of apache http server and apache tomcat. In: 2019 12th IEEE Conference on software testing, validation and verification (ICST). New York: IEEE. 2019. p. 68–78.
86. Cadariu M, Bouwers E, Visser J, van Deursen A. Tracking known security vulnerabilities in proprietary software systems. In: 2015 IEEE 22nd International Conference on Software Analysis, Evolution, and Reengineering (SANER). New York: IEEE. 2015. p. 516–519.
87. Mojica IJ, Nagappan M, Adams B, Berger T, Dienst S, Hassan AE. On Ad Library Updates in Android Apps. IEEE Softw. 2016; 33(2):74–80.
88. Linares-Vásquez M, Bavota G, Escobar-Velásquez C. An empirical study on android-related vulnerabilities. In: 2017 IEEE/ACM 14th International Conference on Mining Software Repositories (MSR). 2017. New York: IEEE. p. 2–13.
89. Gao J, Li L, Kong P, Bissyandé TF, Klein J. Understanding the evolution of android app vulnerabilities. IEEE Trans Reliab. 2019; 70(1):212–230.
90. Cheng X, Wang H, Hua J, Xu G, Sui Y. DeepWukong: Statically detecting software vulnerabilities using deep graph neural network. ACM Trans Softw Eng Methodol (TOSEM). 2021; 30(3):1–33.

91. Bagheri H, Wang J, Aerts J, Ghorbani N, Malek S. Flair: Efficient analysis of Android inter-component vulnerabilities in response to incremental changes. Empir Softw Eng. 2021 26(3):1–37.
92. Zapata RE, Kula RG, Chinthanet B, Ishio T, Matsumoto K, Ihara A. Towards smoother library migrations: A look at vulnerable dependency migrations at function level for NPM JavaScript packages. In: International Conference on Software Maintenance and Evolution (ICSME). 2018. p. 559–563.
93. Plate H, Ponta SE, Sabetta A. Impact assessment for vulnerabilities in open-source software libraries. In: 2015 IEEE International Conference on Software Maintenance and Evolution (ICSME). 2015. Berlin: IEEE. p. 411–420.
94. Ponta SE, Plate H, Sabetta A. Beyond metadata: Code-centric and usage-based analysis of known vulnerabilities in open-source software. In: 2018 IEEE International Conference on Software Maintenance and Evolution (ICSME). 2018. New York: IEEE. p. 449–460.
95. Pashchenko I, Plate H, Ponta SE, Sabetta A, Massacci F. Vulnerable open source dependencies: Counting those that matter. In: Proceedings of the 12th ACM/IEEE International Symposium on Empirical Software Engineering and Measurement. 2018. p. 1–10.
96. Pashchenko I, Plate H, Ponta SE, Sabetta A, Massacci F. Vuln4Real: A Methodology for Counting Actually Vulnerable Dependencies. IEEE Trans Softw Eng. 2020; 48(5):1592–609.

Chapter 8
Boosting the Propagation of Vulnerability Fixes in the *npm* Ecosystem

Abstract Vulnerabilities are known reported security threats that affect a large amount of packages in the *npm* ecosystem. To mitigate these security threats, the open-source community strongly suggests vulnerable packages to timely publish vulnerability fixes and recommends affected packages to update their dependencies. However, there are still serious lags in the propagation of vulnerability fixes in the ecosystem. In our preliminary study on the latest versions of 356,283 active *npm* packages, we found that 20.0% of them can still introduce vulnerabilities via direct or transitive dependencies although the involved vulnerable packages have already published fix versions for over a year. Prior study by Chinthanet et al. (Empir Softw Eng 26(3):1–28, 2021) lays the groundwork for research on how to mitigate propagation lags of vulnerability fixes in an ecosystem. They conducted an empirical investigation to identify lags that might occur between the vulnerable package release and its fixing release. They found that factors such as the branch upon which a fix landed and the severity of the vulnerability had a small effect on its propagation trajectory throughout the ecosystem. To ensure quick adoption and propagation of a release that contains the fix, they gave several actionable advices to developers and researchers. However, it is still an open question how to design an effective technique to accelerate the propagation of vulnerability fixes. Motivated by this problem, in this chapter, we conducted an empirical study to learn the scale of packages that block the propagation of vulnerability fixes in the ecosystem and investigate their evolution characteristics. Furthermore, we distilled the remediation strategies that have better effects on mitigating the fix propagation lags. Leveraging our empirical findings, we propose an ecosystem-level technique, *Plumber*, for deriving feasible remediation strategies to boost the propagation of vulnerability fixes.

8.1 Introduction

Context *npm* is the largest software registry for JavaScript programming language, which hosts over 1.8 million third-party packages as of January 2022. Unfortunately, *npm*'s fast growth comes with security risks. Vulnerabilities disclosed in third-

Y. Wang et al., *Managing Software Supply Chains*,
https://doi.org/10.1007/978-981-96-1797-5_8

party packages (i.e., *vulnerable packages*) are a growing concern for developers. An investigation of an npm snapshot from November 2, 2017, indicates that among 610,097 packages, 21.9% of them directly depend on vulnerable packages. Such vulnerability impact on the *npm* ecosystem can significantly increase if transitive dependencies are taken into account.

Vulnerabilities if adversely exploited can cause immense damages to the ecosystem [2, 3]. In fact, there are many examples of such incidents. A well-known example is the vulnerability *CVE-2021-28918* [4] in package `netmask`. It exposed private IP addresses and led to a variety of attacks such as malware delivery. Upon its disclosure, over 278,000 client projects were believed to be affected by the security vulnerability. To mitigate these security risks, the ecosystem strongly suggests vulnerable packages to timely publish vulnerability fixes and recommends affected packages to update their dependencies.

Problem and Motivation Our preliminary study on the 3,948 vulnerability reports for *npm* packages found that 60.6% of the involved packages had timely released fix versions after the vulnerabilities were discovered. To facilitate vulnerability fix adoption, the open-source community launched tools such as `npm audit` [5] and `Dependabot` [6] to alert the projects that directly or transitively depend on vulnerable package versions. However, there are still serious lags in the propagation of vulnerability fixes in the *npm* ecosystem. We investigated the latest versions of 356,283 active npm packages from the npm snapshot on August 1, 2021, and found that 20.0% of these packages can introduce vulnerabilities through their dependencies, although the involved vulnerable packages have published fixed versions for over a year (see descriptions in Sect. 8.4).

We made two observations on the lags in propagating vulnerability fixes:

- *Most packages remediated only the vulnerabilities in their highest major version trains, without transplanting the fixes to their earlier popular versions (i.e., backporting*[1]*). However, many downstream packages have difficulties in upgrading their dependencies to higher versions due to incompatibility issues or inactive transitive dependencies.* A recent study [7] on over a million *npm* packages indicated that only a small proportion (6.6%) of them have backporting practices. It implies that many affected downstream packages cannot timely benefit from the vulnerability fix versions.
- *Many packages did not realize that they were the cruxes of blocking fix propagation in the ecosystem, affecting a large amount of downstream packages.* Due to the lack of a full picture of the ecosystem-level dependency graph, package developers hardly realized that they were the pivotal factors preventing fixes from propagating too many of their downstream packages.

[1] Backporting refers to the process of applying a software update, typically a patch that fixes a bug or vulnerability to a lower version of the software [7]. Backporting enables users of lower releases to benefit from more recent vulnerability fixes.

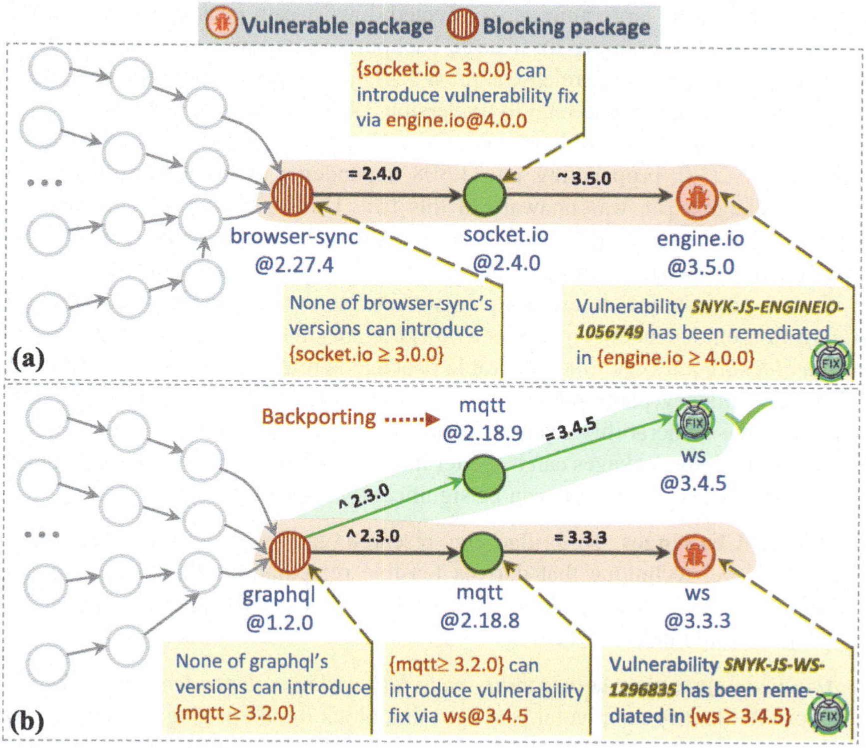

Fig. 8.1 Illustrative examples of blocking propagation of vulnerability fixes

Figure 8.1 gives two illustrative examples. As shown in Fig. 8.1a, the latest version of package `browser-sync` transitively depends on a vulnerable package `engine.io`@3.5.0. However, `browser-sync`'s developers did not realize that the vulnerability *SNYK-JS-ENGINEIO-1056749* had already been remediated by `engine.io` since version 4.0.0. Besides, `browser-sync`'s direct dependency `socket.io` can also introduce this vulnerability fix via `engine.io`@4.0.0 since version `socket.io`@3.0.0. As a popular package in the *npm* ecosystem, `browser-sync`@2.27.4 was a package used by 2,417 projects. Unfortunately, the propagation of the fix in `engine.io` to these projects was blocked by this pivotal package (i.e., `browser-sync`@2.27.4).

Another example is shown in Fig. 8.1b. A vulnerability *SNYK-JS-WS-1296835* was transitively introduced to 146 active *npm* projects transitively via 1,308 dependency paths. All these paths share a common dependency chain: `graphql`@1.2.0 $\rightarrow$ `mqtt`@2.18.8 $\rightarrow$ `ws`@3.3.3. We observed that package `ws` had published the vulnerability fix versions { $\geq$ 3.4.5}, and these fix versions could be resolved by {`mqtt` $\geq$ 3.2.0}. However, the fix propagation was blocked by `graphql`, since this package was inactively maintained by developers (the latest update was on January 2019).

Nevertheless, the large amount of affected downstream packages could quickly incorporate the vulnerability fix if `mqtt` backports to its lower version train 2.18.* (i.e., `mqtt` publishes a new release `mqtt`@2.18.*, in which it upgrades dependency `ws` from vulnerable version 3.3.3 to fix version 3.4.5). In this manner, `mqtt`@2.18.* with vulnerability fix would be automatically resolved by its specified version constraint ^ 2.3.0, propagating into 1,308 dependency paths. Unfortunately, the pivotal package `mqtt` was unaware of this fact. Until a backporting request was reported in `mqtt#1306` [8], developers transplanted such a vulnerability fix to `mqtt`@2.18.9, in order to mitigate the security threats to its downstream projects.

To ease presentation, in this chapter, we refer to the package that blocks the fix propagation on dependency paths as a *blocking package*. And the dependency path from a *blocking package* to a vulnerable package is referred to as a *blocking chain*. All the dependency paths passing through the same blocking chain would suffer from the same vulnerability issues. The above examples show that if the developers of pivotal blocking packages can be better informed of their impacts on vulnerability fix propagation, such situation can be significantly improved.

Goal and Challenges To bridge the research gap, we develop *Plumber*, an ecosystem-level technique that derives feasible remediation strategies for pivotal packages, boosting the propagation of vulnerability fixes. To achieve this goal, two challenges should be addressed:

- *Acquiring up-to-date vulnerability metadata and npm dependency metadata.* To precisely identify the pivotal packages that block the fix propagation, we should obtain the vulnerability metadata and ecosystem-level dependency metadata, continuously updating these two pieces of metadata with package evolution in *npm*.
- *Understanding the evolution characteristics of blocking chains and their impacts on the vulnerability fix propagation.* To mitigate the fix propagation lags, we need to derive effective remediation strategies from the evolution characteristics of blocking chains and their impacts on the vulnerability fix propagation.

Approach and Results To address the two challenges, we first conducted a large-scale empirical study on the recent snapshots of the *npm* ecosystem, to learn (RQ1) the scale of blocking packages and their impacts on other projects, (RQ2) the evolution characteristics of blocking chains on consecutive *npm* snapshots, and (RQ3) the remediation strategies that have better effects on propagating vulnerability fixes. Leveraging our empirical findings, we propose *Plumber*, a novel technique to (1) model the vulnerability and *npm* dependency metadata and incrementally update their evolution, (2) identify pivotal blocking chains that hinder the vulnerability fixes from propagating through dependency paths, and (3) analyze the features of packages on blocking chains and customize remediation schemes. In the remediation scheme, *Plumber* arouses package developers' awareness of the lags in fix version updates and explains the benefits of their dependency updates to the whole ecosystem.

To evaluate the remediation effectiveness of *Plumber*, we conducted an ecosystem-level study. We applied *Plumber* to generating 268 remediation reports for the top influential blocking chains. 47.4% of our remediation reports received positive feedback from many well-known *npm* projects, such as `Tensorflow/tfjs` [9], `Ethers.js` [10], and `GoogleChrome/workbox` [11]. These reports indeed aroused the pivotal packages' awareness to perform dependency upgrades/backporting/migrations in order to remediate vulnerabilities, benefiting the whole ecosystem. Encouragingly, *Plumber*'s generated reports boosted the propagation of vulnerability fixes into 16,403 active *npm* projects via 92,469 dependency paths. On average, each remediated package version received 72,678 downloads per week. The results indicate its wide remediation effectiveness and impact. It is thus necessary to deploy *Plumber* to continuously capture the pivotal blocking chains and suggest proper remediation strategies with impact analysis.

8.2 Background

8.2.1 Disclosed Vulnerabilities in the npm *Ecosystem*

A *vulnerability* is a security threat[2] that exposes some package versions in a software ecosystem to attacks. We refer to the packages where such vulnerabilities disclosed as *vulnerable packages* and their affected versions as *vulnerable package versions*.

Nowadays, several recognized vulnerability databases such as *GitHub Advisory DB* [12], *Snyk Vulnerability DB* [13], and *NPM Security Advisories* [14] provide the continuous security monitoring service, which collects vulnerability reports of third-party packages to warn project developers against such vulnerable package versions. As shown in Fig. 8.2, each vulnerability report contains information about (1) affected package, (2) affected package versions, (3) unique CVE identifier, (4) severity levels (e.g., critical, high, medium, and low based on CVSS score [15]), (5) dates when it is disclosed and published, and (6) remediated versions (if available).

We crawled the vulnerability reports for *npm* packages published before August 1, 2021 from three databases and listed the statistics in Table 8.1. On average, 60.6% of vulnerable packages have remediated the disclosed vulnerabilities. However, our investigation on the latest versions of 356,283 active *npm* projects revealed that 71,320 of them (20%) are still directly or transitively depending on vulnerable package versions, although the vulnerability fix versions of these packages have already been released for over a year (see detailed descriptions in Sect. 8.3). There are serious lags in the propagation of vulnerability fixes in the *npm* ecosystem.

[2] Security threats can allow unauthorized actions or access to be performed. These actions are typically used to break through the system and violate its security policies.

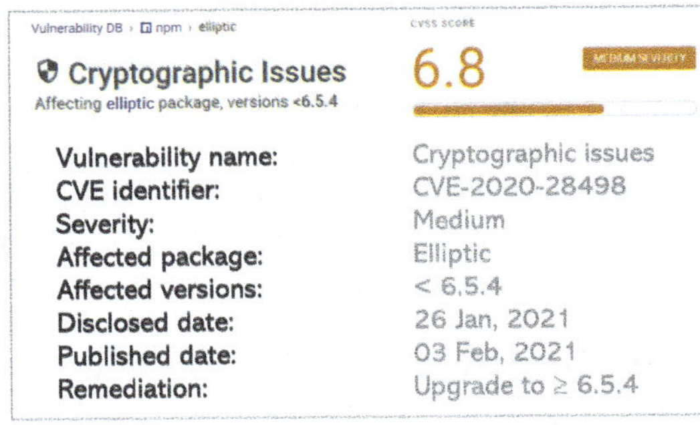

Fig. 8.2 An illustrative vulnerability report for npm package

Table 8.1 Statistics of exposed vulnerabilities in the *npm* ecosystem

Database	#Vulnerability reports	#Vulnerability reports with fixes	Fixing ratio
GitHub Advisory DB[1]	1,990	1,115	56.0%
Snyk Vulnerability DB[2]	3,119	2,225	69.9%
NPM Security Advisories[3]	1,614	1,166	71.3%
Union set	3,948	2,391	60.6%

1. https://github.com/advisories;
2. https://snyk.io/vuln;
3. https://www.npmjs.com/advisories.

†The three databases are maintained by different communities and contain overlapping reports.

8.2.2 *npm Package Version Constraints*

A version of package p_a can explicitly declare a dependency relationship to another package p_b with a specified version constraint. For example, constraint $< 2.1.0$ defines the version range [0.0.0, 2.1.0), signifying that any version below 2.1.0 of p_b is allowed to be installed. In fact, *the highest available version within this range* will be selected for installation by the package manager.

npm customizes *node-semver* [16], a semantic version parser for Node.js. It inherits the version operators from semantic versioning (i.e., $<, =, >$) and also introduces advanced range syntax (i.e., $*$, $^\wedge$, $\sim$), to allow flexible and backward compatible version control. For example, $2.1.* = \sim 2.1.0$, to allow the range [2.1.0, 2.2.0) of backward compatible package versions, while $2.*.0 = {}^\wedge\, 2.0.0$ denotes version range [2.0.0, 3.0.0). In this chapter, we refer to the version ranges specified with $*$, $^\wedge$, $\sim$ as *open version constraints*. Such range syntax allows flexibility, which enables projects to automatically deploy the new versions of their required packages that satisfy the specified version range (the highest available version installation rule). In other words, new package versions with the vulnerability fixes can be automatically propagated into the downstream projects if open constraints are assigned.

8.2.3 Terminology

This section introduces the following concepts used throughout this chapter. We let $p_i@v_m$ be a version of *npm* package (e.g., `electron`@12.0.0), where p_i denotes the unique package name released in *npm* and v_m denotes its version number. Since a package version $p_i@v_m$ usually directly and transitively depends on a collection of third-party packages, the referenced package versions and dependency relations among them form a package dependency graph $G_{i,m}$. We refer to $p_i@v_m$ as a *root project* in its corresponding package dependency graph $G_{i,m}$.

Definition 1 (Vulnerable Path) Suppose that $p_j@v_n$ is a vulnerable package version where vulnerability μ_t disclosed. In the package dependency graph $G_{i,m}$, we define a dependency path from root project $p_i@v_m$ to vulnerable package version $p_j@v_n$, $P_{\mu_t}(p_i@v_m, p_w@v_k, \cdots, p_j@v_n) = p_i@v_m \rightarrow p_w@v_k \rightarrow \cdots \rightarrow p_j@v_n$, as a *vulnerable path.* This dependency path is u_t-vulnerable if $p_i@v_m$ directly or transitively uses $p_j@v_n$, i.e., $p_i@v_m$ potentially invokes the vulnerable APIs defined in $p_j@v_n$. Note that there could be more than one vulnerable path from a root project to a vulnerable package version. Remediated vulnerable paths can reduce the potential for accessing the disclosed vulnerable code, which minimizes the risk of being attacked through the vulnerabilities.

Definition 2 (Safe Version Set) Suppose that vulnerable package p_j has remediated vulnerability μ_t in its versions $\{v_1, v_2, \cdots, v_u\}$, and then we consider $p_j.S_{\mu_t} = \{v_1, v_2, \cdots, v_u\}$ as p_j's *safe version set* for μ_t. For each package on a vulnerable path $P_{\mu_t}(p_i@v_m, p_w@v_k, \cdots, p_j@v_n)$, we consider its safe version set as the versions that can directly or transitively depend on a safe version $v \in p_j.S_{\mu_t}$ or the versions that deprecated package p_j.

Definition 3 (Blocking Package) On vulnerable path $P_{\mu_t}(p_i@v_m, \cdots, p_w@v_k, \cdots, p_j@v_n)$, if package p_w's safe version set $p_w.S_{\mu_t} = \emptyset$ and all the packages depended by p_w have already published safe versions for vulnerability μ_t, we define p_w as a *blocking package*. We consider p_w blocks the propagation of vulnerability μ_t's fix through path $P_{\mu_t}(p_i@v_m, \cdots, p_w@v_k, \cdots, p_j@v_n)$, causing the lags of vulnerable package updates.

Definition 4 (Blocking Chain) Let p_w be a blocking package on vulnerable path $P_{\mu_t}(p_i@v_m, \cdots, p_w@v_k, p_e@v_g, \cdots, p_j@v_n)$. We define the subpath from blocking package to vulnerable package $B_{\mu_t}(p_w@v_k, p_e@v_g, \cdots, p_j@v_n) = p_w@v_k \rightarrow p_e@v_g \cdots \rightarrow p_j@v_n$ as a blocking chain. All the vulnerable paths passing through the blocking chain $B_{\mu_t}(p_w@v_k, p_e@v_g, \cdots, p_j@v_n)$ suffer from the same vulnerability issues.

Consider a dependency graph as shown in Fig. 8.3a. Vulnerabilities μ_a and μ_b disclosed in packages `interface-adapter` @0.4.21 and `elliptic`@6.5.3, respectively. To diagnose how root project `truffle-upgrades`@1.5.0 introduces μ_a and μ_b, we identify two vulnerable paths P_{μ_a}(`truffle-upgrades`@1.5.0, `contract`@4.3.13, `interface -adapter`@0.4.21, `ethers`@4.0.48, `elliptic`@

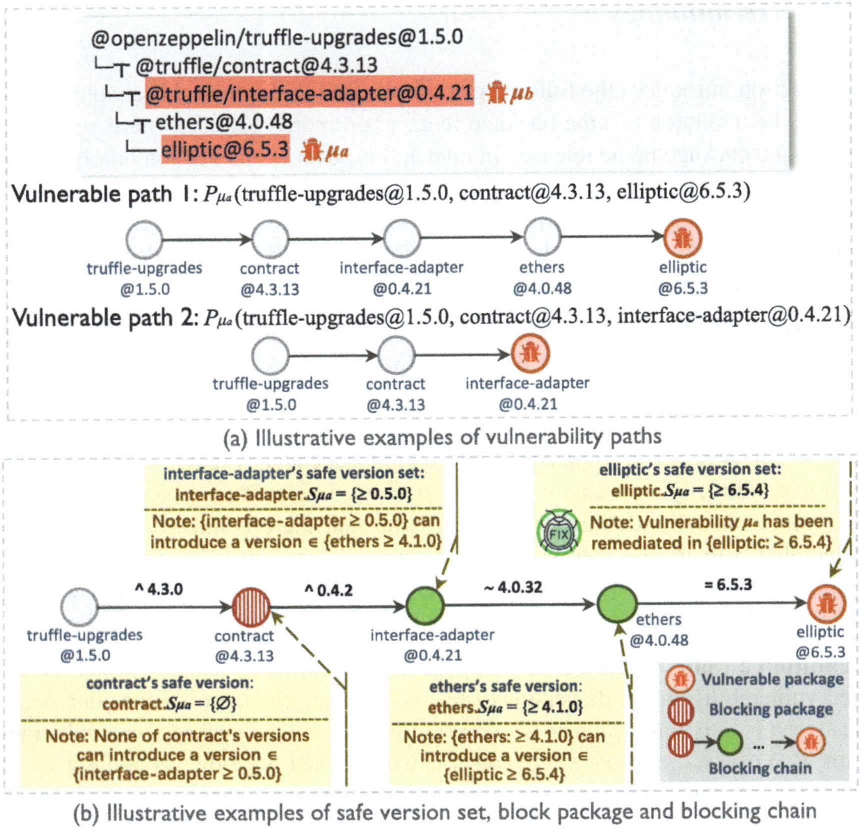

Fig. 8.3 Examples for illustrating the introduced concepts

6.5.3) and P_{μ_b}(`truffle-upgrades`@1.5.0, `contract`@4.3.13, `interface-adapter`@0.4.21). In Fig. 8.3b, we illustrate how to calculate the safe version set of each package on the former path. Because vulnerability μ_a only affects {`elliptic` $\leq$ 6.5.3}, `elliptic`'s safe version set is { $\geq$ 6.5.4}. However, although on the vulnerable path, `ethers`@4.0.48 depends on `elliptic`@6.5.3, since version 4.1.0, `ethers` upgraded `elliptic` to its safe version within { $\geq$ 6.5.4} to remediate vulnerability μ_a. Accordingly, `ethers`'s safe version set for μ_a is { $\geq$ 4.1.0}. As an analogy, the safe version sets of remaining packages on this vulnerable path can be obtained. Notably, none of `contract`'s versions can introduce μ_a's fix, while package `interface-adapter` referenced by `contract` has already resolved such a vulnerability issue in versions { $\geq$ 0.5.0}. We consider `contract` as a blocking package, which blocks the propagation of vulnerability μ_a's fix through path P_{μ_a}(`truffle-upgrades`@1.5.0, `contract`@4.3.13, `interface - adapter`@0.4.21, `ethers`@4.0.48, `elliptic`@6.5.3). In the *npm* ecosystem, all the vulnerable paths passing through the blocking chain B_{μ_a}(`contract`@4.3.13,

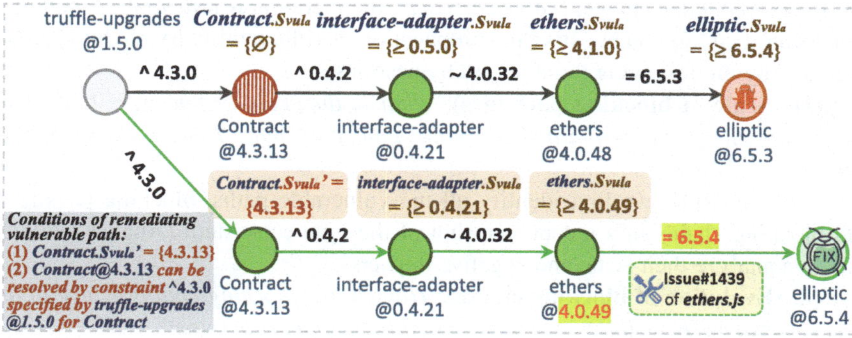

Fig. 8.4 A real example of unblocking the vulnerable path

`interface-adapter`@0.4.21, `ethers`@4.0.48, `elliptic`@6.5.3) suffer from the same vulnerability issues.

Definition 5 (Remediating Vulnerable Path) Suppose that p_w is a blocking package on vulnerable path $P_{\mu_t}(p_i@v_m, \cdots, p_e@v_g, p_w@v_k, \cdots, p_j@v_n)$, and package p_j has remediated vulnerability μ_t in versions $p_j.S_{\mu_t}$ ($v_n \notin p_j.S_{\mu_t}$). To remediate such a vulnerable path, allowing the vulnerability μ_t's fix to be propagated into root project $p_i@v_m$, two conditions must be satisfied: (1) p_w's safe version set $p_w.S_{\mu_t} \neq \emptyset$ (via updating version of package on the vulnerable path), and (2) one safe version $v \in p_w.S_{\mu_t}$ can be resolved by the version constraint c_w specified by package $p_e@v_g$ for p_w.

In Fig. 8.3, we can tell that `ethers`'s versions { $\geq$ 4.1.0} have remediated such a vulnerability by referencing `elliptic`'s safe versions { $\geq$ 6.5.4}. However, {`ethers` $\geq$ 4.1.0} cannot be resolved by constraint $\sim$ 4.0.32 (i.e., [4.0.32, 4.1.0)) that is specified by its inactively maintained precursor `interface-adapter`. To resolve this vulnerability issue, `truffle-upgrades`'s developer filed an issue report #1439 [17] to `ethers.js`. They requested `ethers.js` to backport to version 4.0.49, in which it upgraded `elliptic` to version 6.5.4 (vulnerability μ_a's fix version). As shown in Fig. 8.4, `elliptic`@4.0.49 can be transitively referenced by `constract` @4.3.13. Therefore, `constract` @4.3.13 turned out to be a safe version for μ_a. In this manner, such a vulnerability fix is propagated into root project `truffle-upgrades`@1.5.0, remediating the vulnerable path P_{μ_a}(`truffle-upgrades`@1.5.0, `contract`@4.3.13, `interface-adapter`@0.4.21, `ethers`@4.0.48, `elliptic`@6.5.3).

8.3 Empirical Study

In this section, we empirically investigate the scale of packages that block the propagation of vulnerability fixes in the *npm* ecosystem. By digging into evolution history of blocking chains, we characterize their common remediation patterns, which can shed light on boosting the propagation of vulnerability fixes. Our analysis is guided by the following three research questions:

***RQ1* (Scale of blocking packages)**: *What is the scale of packages that block the propagation of vulnerability fixes in the npm ecosystem? To what extent do they affect other projects?*

To answer RQ1, we first identify all the vulnerable paths, blocking packages, and blocking chains in a recent snapshot of the *npm* ecosystem (August 1, 2021) and then analyze their scale and negative impacts.

***RQ2* (Evolution of blocking chains)**: *How do the blocking chains evolve in the npm ecosystem? How long have they existed in the npm ecosystem?*

To answer RQ2, we investigate the evolution trends of blocking chains across consecutive *npm* snapshots over the past year (from August 1, 2020 to August 1, 2021).

***RQ3* (Remediation patterns)**: *How were the blocking chains removed from the vulnerable paths? Are there common remediation patterns that can be distilled to facilitate the propagation of vulnerability fixes?*

To answer RQ3, we select a collection of real instances of blocking chains that have better remediation effects as subjects. Via replaying the package evolution history of these collected instances, we observe their package updates that can remediate blocking chains, their preconditions of propagating the vulnerability fixes, and the corresponding remediation costs.

8.3.1 Vulnerability Propagation Model

To investigate our RQs, we construct a **V**ulnerability **P**ropagation (VP) model, which locates the vulnerable package versions in the ecosystem-level dependency graph to facilitate a holistic analysis of vulnerability affects. Figure 8.5 shows an overview of VP model construction. It first crawls a snapshot of *npm dependency metadata* and *vulnerability metadata*. By parsing the version constraints on package

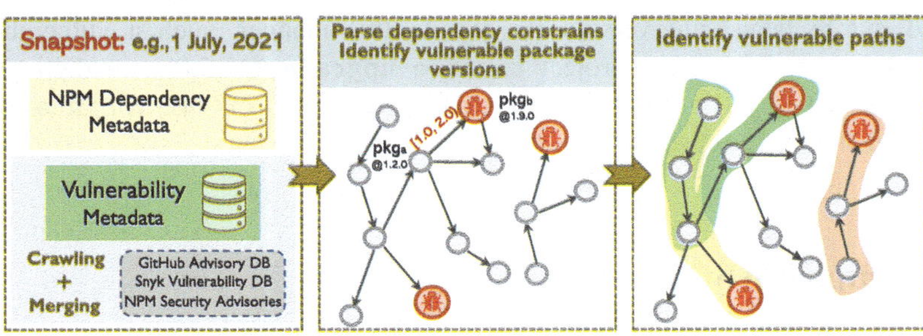

Fig. 8.5 An overview of VP model construction

dependency relations and identifying vulnerable package versions, all the vulnerable paths can be identified.

Collecting Vulnerability Metadata To collect more complete vulnerability metadata, we crawl vulnerability reports published before August 1, 2021, from three recognized vulnerability databases, i.e., *GitHub Advisory DB*, *Snyk Vulnerability DB*, and *NPM Security Advisories*. Since the vulnerability information is usually described in plain text, for each vulnerability report, VP model needs to filter programming languages and identify its *unique identifier*, *affected package*, *affected package versions*, *fix versions*, and *severity level*.

Collecting npm Dependency Metadata *npm* public registry [18] provides RESTful APIs to obtain the metadata of all packages published in *npm*. The metadata describes the complete info of all releases of a given package. With the aid of such APIs, we capture the dependency metadata of *npm* ecosystem and described it as a directed graph $G = (V, E, C)$, to retrieve packages and resolve their dependencies. It consists of a set of package versions V and a set of dependency relations $E = \{p_i@v_a \rightarrow p_j@v_b | p_i@v_a, p_j@v_b \in V\}$. Each relation $p_i@v_a \rightarrow p_j@v_b \in E$ is determined by its corresponding dependency constraint $c(p_i@v_a, p_j) \in C$, where $c(p_i@v_a, p_j)$ denotes a version constraint specified by $p_i@v_a$ for p_j, and v_b is the highest version of p_j that satisfies the constraint (*npm*'s dependency resolution rule).

In our study, we analyze the dependency metadata of the *npm* snapshot on August 1, 2021. To understand the status quo of vulnerability effects on the whole ecosystem, on such a *npm* snapshot, we filter out the legacy packages and only collect the latest versions of active packages and the package versions they directly or transitively depend on. Note that we consider a package is active if it published new versions in the past year, following the assumption given by approaches [7, 19, 20].

Identifying Vulnerable Paths By mapping the vulnerability metadata into *npm* dependency metadata $G = (V, E, C)$, in set V, we locate all the vulnerable package versions with detailed vulnerability info. We consider the latest versions of active packages in V as root nodes and vulnerable package versions in V as leaf nodes, to identify all the vulnerable paths via reachability analysis. However, a vulnerable package version may contain multiple vulnerabilities and each vulnerability corresponds to a safe version set. To precisely analyze the effects of each known vulnerability, when identifying vulnerable paths, a vulnerable package version with multiple vulnerabilities is distinguished as multiple leaf nodes. As such, a vulnerable path involves a unique vulnerability.

Statistics of VP Model Table 8.2 shows the statistics of metadata collected by VP model. To ease presentation, we denote ***root projects*** as the latest versions of active packages. Our vulnerability metadata includes 3,948 vulnerability reports; 2,391 of them (60.6%) have published vulnerability fix versions, especially for the ones with higher severity levels. For *npm* dependency metadata, VP model collected 521,413 latest versions of active packages which directly or transitively depend on 689,350

Table 8.2 Statistics of metadata collected by *Plumber*

Vulnerability metadata			
#Vulnerabilities **3,948**			
Critical: **473**	High: **1,910**	Medium: **1,374**	Low: **191**
#Vulnerabilities without fixes **1,557**			
Critical: **96**	High: **677**	Medium: **643**	Low: **141**
#Vulnerabilities with fixes **2,391**			
Critical: **140**	High: **1,021**	Medium: **1,078**	Low: **152**
#Vulnerable packages: **2,289**		*#Vulnerable package versions*: **38,166**	
#Vulnerabilities per package **1.7±2.9**			
npm dependency metadata			
#Root projects **356,283**			
#Package versions directly or transitively depended by root projects **689,350**			
#Dependency relations **2,542,753**			
#Vulnerable paths **1,245,694**			
#Vulnerable paths whose corresponding vulnerabilities have released fixes **1,065,723**			

Root projects denote the latest versions of active packages.

package versions. Among the 2,542,753 dependency relations among packages, it identified 1,065,723 vulnerable paths that are affected by the vulnerable packages having published fix versions. In our study, we considered the above 1,065,723 vulnerable paths that block the propagation of vulnerability fixes as subjects to study their characteristics.

Data Validation The VP model took 4 months for three Ph.D. students who had over 2 years of vulnerability analysis experience to implement and test. The two experienced authors conducted daily manual validation of vulnerability metadata independently. Disagreements were reconciled with the third author joining the discussions. Specifically, we carefully checked two cases during the data validation process: (1) *Case 1*: Multiple databases share the vulnerability reports with the same CVE identifier. We only kept a vulnerability with unique CVE identifier in our dataset and filter out the duplicated ones. (2) *Case 2*: A vulnerability with unique CVE identifier may be disclosed in multiple packages. We recorded all the affected packages and their corresponding versions. The *Cohen's kappa* for their data validation is 0.92, indicating a near perfect inter-rater agreement [21]. For the eight disagreement cases, the information of shared vulnerability reports (e.g., affected package versions) was different from multiple vulnerability databases. Eventually, the third author checked the release notes of vulnerable package and kept our records to be consistent with that originated from package publishers. The three authors reached a consensus on our final dataset.

8.3.2 RQ1: Scale of Blocking Packages

8.3.2.1 Methodology

To answer RQ1, we gather the statistics of vulnerable paths, blocking packages, and blocking chains, to analyze their scale and negative impacts on the *npm* ecosystem. To achieve this, for each vulnerability μ_t, we first identify the corresponding safe versions S_{μ_t} of a vulnerable package p_j where it is disclosed. For each vulnerable path $P_{\mu_t}(p_i@v_m, \cdots, p_k@v_g, p_w@v_h, \cdots, p_j@v_n)$, starting from the vulnerable package p_j, we iteratively find each package's safe versions for μ_t, until a blocking package p_k whose safe version set $p_k.S_{\mu_t} = \emptyset$ is located. Accordingly, a blocking chain $B_{\mu_t}(p_k@v_g, p_w@v_h, \cdots, p_j@v_n)$ from blocking package to vulnerable package on each vulnerable path can be identified. In particular, we count the number of vulnerable paths and root projects that are affected by blocking chains, to investigate their influence on impeding propagation of vulnerability fixes.

8.3.2.2 Results

Table 8.3 shows our investigation results of RQ1. In our study, we only focused on the 2,289 vulnerable packages that have published fix versions for their involved vulnerabilities. However, such vulnerability fix versions are not widely spread. 71,320

Table 8.3 Statistics of investigation results in RQ1

Vulnerable paths	Critical	High	Medium	Low
#Root projects affected by the vulnerabilities **71,320**	**690**	**34,548**	**59,918**	**16,160**
#Vulnerable paths referenced by each root project (Avg) **14.9±70.8**	**2.4±10.9**	**5.9±40.7**	**14.4±62.0**	**5.1±33.9**
#Vulnerabilities referenced by each root project (Avg) **4.4±7.5**	**1.1±0.3**	**3.0±5.3**	**3.0±3.4**	**1.9±1.7**
Blocking packages and blocking chains				
#Blocking packages	**45,148**			
#Blocking chains	**358,422**			
#Vulnerable paths affected by blocking packages	**983,336**			
#Root projects affected by blocking packages	**68,413**			
#Vulnerable paths affected by each blocking package (Avg)	**21.8±344.3**			
#Root projects affected by each blocking package (Avg)	**3.6±65.9**			
#Vulnerable paths affected by each blocking chain (Avg)	**2.7±77.2**			
#Root projects affected by each blocking chain (Avg)	**1.9±25.3**			

We only consider the vulnerable paths that are affected by the vulnerabilities with fixes out of 356,283 (20.0%) active root projects in the *npm* ecosystem still directly or transitively depend on these vulnerable packages via 1,065,723 vulnerable paths. On average, each root project is affected by 4.4±7.5 vulnerabilities. Even worse, 48.5% of the widespread vulnerabilities are rated as high/critical severity level issues.

We identified 45,148 blocking packages in the *npm* ecosystem, which involved 358,422 blocking chains. All the published versions of blocking packages could only reference the vulnerable package versions through 983,336 vulnerable paths, causing the lags in propagation of vulnerability fixes into 68,413 root projects. In addition, we observed that 82,387 out of 1,065,723 vulnerable paths (7.7%) did not pass through blocking packages, since their root projects have ever introduced the vulnerability fix versions but then rolled back to vulnerable versions due to incompatibility issues. For instance, on a vulnerable path, root project `zos`@2.4.3 introduces vulnerable package `lodash`@4.17.10 through a direct dependency `truffle`, whereas its previous version `zos`@2.4.2 has ever transitively referenced the fix version `lodash` @4.17.21 for vulnerability *CVE-2021-23337* but then rolled it back because version 4.17.21 induced an incompatibility issue#1147 [22] in `truffle`.

Interestingly, we observed a clear centrality on both blocking packages and blocking chains. Figure 8.6 shows the influence of blocking packages/blocking chains on the whole ecosystem. The y-axis denotes the percentage of vulnerable paths/root projects that pass through the corresponding blocking packages/blocking chains presented in x-axis. While x-axis indicates the blocking packages/blocking chains that are ranked by the number of vulnerable paths/root projects affected by them. We can tell that the top 20% influential blocking packages hinder the vulnerability fixes from propagating through 92.1% vulnerable paths, affecting 75.2% root projects. Similarly, a small proportion (20%) of influential blocking chains can affect the vast majority (75.6%/65.5%) of vulnerable paths/root projects.

Table 8.4 lists the statistics of top ten influential blocking packages and blocking chains in the *npm* ecosystem. Take the most influential blocking

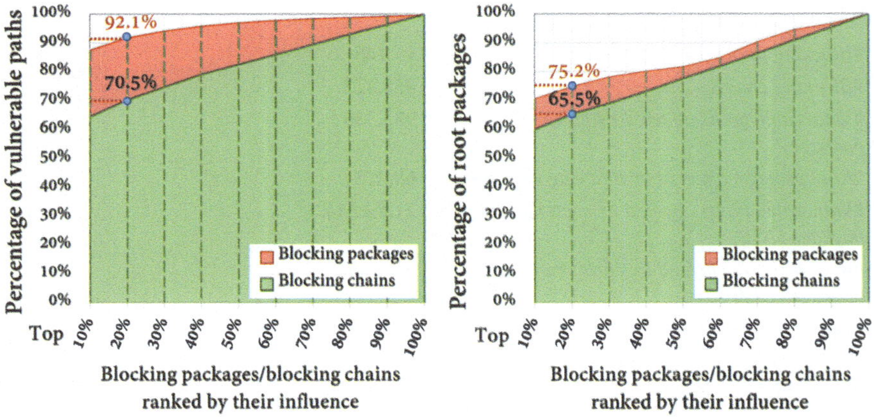

Fig. 8.6 The influence of blocking packages/blocking chains

Table 8.4 Statistics of top ten influential blocking packages and blocking chains

Top ten influential blocking packages

Rank	Blocking package	#Induced blocking chains	#Affected paths	#Affected root projects	Vulnerabilities
1	`swap-core`	291	41,278	395	CVE-2021-23358, CVE-2020-28498
2	`glob-base`	1	33,656	17,683	CVE-2020-28469
3	`embark-utils`	769	28,937	81	CVE-2020-28499, CVE-2021-23358
4	`watchpack-chokidar2`	1	15,608	10,340	CVE-2020-28469
5	`@0x/subproviders`	928	11,164	130	CVE-2020-28500, CVE-2021-23337
6	`react-scripts`	57	8,368	4,166	CVE-2021-33587, CVE-2020-28469
7	`tree-sync`	2	8,278	1,306	npm:underscore. string:20170908
8	`koa-ejs-remote`	2	7,431	150	CVE-2020-28168
9	`glob-stream`	2	6,849	3,117	CVE-2020-28469
10	`@svgr/plugin-svgo`	3	6,601	5,134	CVE-2021-33587

Top ten influential blocking chains

Rank	Blocking chain	#Affected paths	#Affected root projects	Vulnerabilities
1	`glob-base`@0.3.0 → `glob-parent`@2.0.0	33,656	17,683	CVE-2020-28469
2	`watchpack-chokidar2`@2.0.1 → `chokidar`@2.1.8 →`glob-parent`@3.1.0	15,608	10,340	CVE-2020-28469
3	`@evolab/coreutils`@4.2.0 → `url-parse`@1.4.7	6,276	76	CVE-2021-3664,CVE-2021-27515
4	`web3-eth-abi`@1.2.6 → `ethers`@4.0.0 →`elliptic`@6.3.3	6,087	856	CVE-2020-28498
5	`koa-ejs-remote`@1.1.6 → `axios`@0.18.1	4,830	150	CVE-2020-28168
6	`Bwrapper`@4.1.0 →`BVcheck`@4.0.0 → `Bversion`@3.1.0 →`Sregex`@2.0.0	4,312	1,533	SNYK-JS-SEMVERREGEX-1047770
7	`squeak`@1.3.0 →`lpad-align`@1.1.2 →`meow`@3.7.0 →`Tnewlines`@1.0.0	4,252	1,486	CVE-2021-33623
8	`glob-stream`@6.1.0 → `glob-parent`@3.1.0	4,210	2,255	CVE-2020-28469
9	`glob-watcher`@5.0.5 → `chokidar`@2.1.8 → `glob-parent`@3.1.0	3,870	1,535	CVE-2020-28469
10	`@S/plugin-svgo`@5.5.0 → `svgo`@1.3.2 → `css-select`@2.1.0 →`css-what`@3.4.2	3,394	2,843	CVE-2021-33587

package `swap-core` [23] as an example. It affects 41,278 vulnerable paths, transitively introducing two vulnerabilities into 395 root projects. In total, various versions of package `swap-core` induce 291 influential blocking chains. Among them, `swap-core@0.1.0` is the most popular version with 24,283 weekly downloads, which introduces a blocking chain `swap-core@0.1.0` → `hdwallet-provider@1.0.17` → `web3@1.2.1` → `web3-bzz@1.2.1` → `underscore@1.9.1` into 234 root projects via 6,503 vulnerable paths. Such influential blocking chains are the cruxes of impeding propagation of vulnerability fixes in the ecosystem. Accordingly, remediating the influential blocking chains can benefit the whole ecosystem, enabling the vulnerability fixes to be spread into a large amount of projects simultaneously.

Answer to RQ1: *In the recent snapshot of the npm ecosystem, there are 45,148 blocking packages and 358,422 blocking chains causing the lags in propagation of vulnerability fixes through 983,336 dependency paths. There is clear centrality on both influential blocking packages and blocking chains. 20% of blocking packages and blocking chains affect the vast majority of vulnerable paths.*
Implication: *Remediating the influential blocking chains enables the vulnerability fixes propagating into a large amount of root projects, which significantly benefits the whole ecosystem.*

8.3.3 RQ2: Evolution of Blocking Chains

8.3.3.1 Methodology

To answer RQ2, we construct a collection of consecutive snapshots of *npm* dependency metadata (denoted as s_1–s_7) over the past year (from August 1, 2020 to August 1, 2021), in order to investigate the evolution trends of blocking chains. The interval between two consecutive snapshots (s_{i-1} and s_i $(1 < i \leq 7)$) is taken as 2 months, since the *npm* projects in snapshot s_1 published new releases every 1.85 months on average. To observe the evolution of blocking chains ever since they appeared, for vulnerability metadata, we focus only on the vulnerabilities that were disclosed with fixes before the date of snapshot s_1.

The statistics of our mined vulnerabilities and seven *npm* snapshots are listed in Tables 8.5 and 8.6, respectively. On each snapshot, we consider the latest versions of active packages as root projects and collect all the package versions directly or transitively referenced by them. As previously presented, a root project is regarded as active if it published new versions in the past year (from the date of snapshot

Table 8.5 Statistics of vulnerabilities disclosed in July 2020

#Vulnerabilities with fixes: 61			
Critical: 1	High: 25	Medium: 30	Low: 5
#Vulnerable packages: 35		*#Vulnerable package versions*: 312	

Table 8.6 Statistics of *npm* snapshots

Snapshots	#Root projects	#Dependency relations
s_1: *August 1, 2020*	220,819	1,576,547
s_2: *October 1, 2020*	238,833	1,596,379
s_3: *December 1, 2020*	253,339	1,613,350
s_4: *February 1, 2021*	269,140	1,676,070
s_5: *April 1, 2021*	289,673	1,764,397
s_6: *June 1, 2021*	313,208	1,871,487
s_7: *August 1, 2021*	356,283	2,542,753

s_i). We identify all the blocking chains and vulnerable paths induced by the above vulnerabilities in snapshots s_1–s_7 and then investigate their evolutionary trends.

Specifically, we perform two tasks in the investigation: (a) By comparing the statistics of snapshot s_i $(1 < i \leq 7)$ with that of s_1, we investigated the scale of blocking chains, vulnerable paths, and affected root projects in s_1 that have been remediated by developers during a year of evolution. (b) By comparing the statistics of two consecutive snapshots s_{i-1} and s_i, we counted the number of remediated blocking chains, vulnerable paths, and affected root projects during every 2 months interval. Besides, we also concern whether s_i introduced new cases compared with s_{i-1}. We analyze the three cases as follows:

- *Remaining cases*: Since the package versions keep evolving across s_1-s_7, we consider two blocking chains/vulnerable paths in s_m and s_n $(m \leq n)$ as the equivalent ones, if they share the same packages in the same sequence, but s_n involves updated versions. Similarly, the root projects in s_m are regarded equivalent with their updated versions in s_n. Such equivalent cases in s_n are the remaining ones of s_m that have not been remediated yet.
- *Remediated/newly introduced cases*: Suppose BC_k, VP_k, and ARP_k are the sets of blocking chains, vulnerable paths, and affected root projects identified in snapshot s_k, respectively. We then consider $BC_m - BC_n$, $VP_m - VP_n$, and $ARP_m - ARP_n$ as the cases that have been remediated during the interval between snapshots s_m and s_n $(m \leq n)$, while $BC_n - BC_m$, $VP_n - VP_m$, and $ARP_n - ARP_m$ are regarded as the blocking chains, vulnerable paths, and affected root projects newly introduced into snapshot s_n, since the date of snapshot s_m.

8.3.3.2 Results

Figure 8.7 shows the scale of remediated/remaining blocking chains, vulnerable paths, and affected root projects in s_i $(1 < i \leq 7)$, comparing with the initial snapshot s_1. After a year of evolution, among the 13,914 blocking chains identified in s_1, 10,713 of them (77.0%) still exist in the *npm* ecosystem. Only 37.1% (11,689/31,509) of vulnerable paths have been remediated, and the number of root projects affected by these blocking chains falls by 17.3% (2,081/12,031). Figure 8.8 depicts the severity levels of vulnerabilities that affect the remaining cases in the latest snapshot s_7. It is worth noting that 76.7% of remaining vulnerable paths and 83.0% root projects still reference the high/critical severity level vulnerabilities. Such low remediation rates of vulnerable paths and affected root projects reveal that the pivotal blocking chains do not arouse developers' awareness or have challenges to be remediated.

Figure 8.9 shows the statistics of remediated/newly introduced blocking chains, vulnerable paths and affected root projects between two consecutive snapshots. As of the vulnerable packages are disclosed in July 2020, the number of new blocking chains (179 on average) emerge in each snapshot significantly lower than the remediated ones (581 on average). However, on average, each snapshot newly introduced

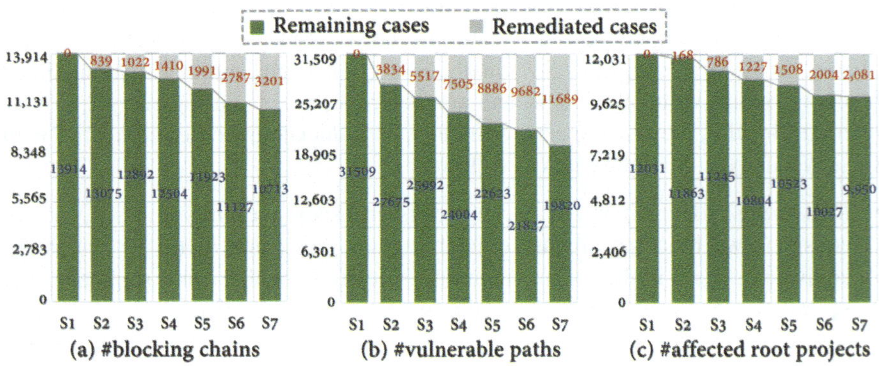

Fig. 8.7 Evolutionary trend analysis (comparing s_i with s_1)

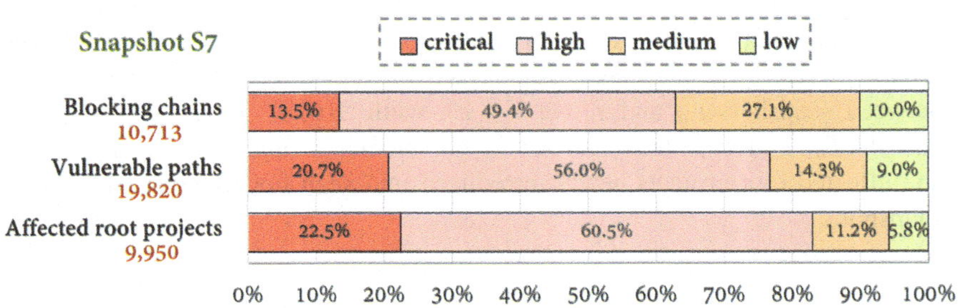

Fig. 8.8 Severity of vulnerabilities that affect the remaining cases

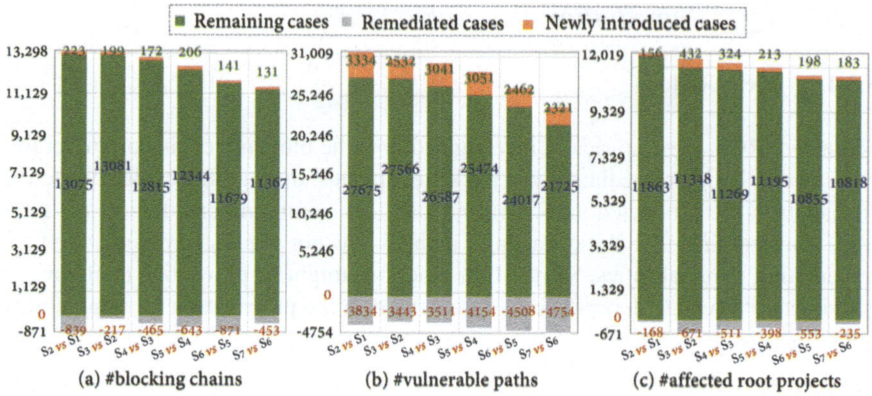

Fig. 8.9 Evolutionary trend analysis (comparing s_i with s_{i-1})

2,790 vulnerable paths and 251 affected root projects via referencing blocking packages as the projects evolve. The phenomenon occurs because some popular blocking packages (i.e., high downloads) can be easily adopted as dependencies during evolution, even if they would transitively introduce vulnerable packages into projects. For instance, `glob-base`@0.3.0 is influential in the ecosystem (4,755,881 weekly downloads), which depends on a vulnerable package `glob-parent`@ $\leq$ 5.1.2 (*CVE-2020-28469*). We consider `glob-base` as a blocking package since all its published versions cannot reference the vulnerability's fix versions (safe version set is ∅ for *CVE-2020-28469* on the vulnerable paths). Between the interval of snapshots s_1 and s_7, such a popular version `glob-base`@0.3.0 has been newly introduced into 143 root projects via 843 dependency paths. The results indicate that remediating pivotal blocking chains cannot only boost the propagation of vulnerability fixes into the existing vulnerable paths but also reduce the risk of introducing new vulnerable paths into root projects.

Answer to RQ2: *In the npm snapshot of August 1, 2020, 77.0% of identified blocking chains still exist after a year of evolution. During this period, the number of vulnerable paths and root projects affected by these blocking chains fall by 37.1% and 17.3%. 9,808 blocking chains bundled with higher level vulnerabilities are still referenced by 9,904 active root projects through 17,612 vulnerable paths.*

Implication: *The low remediation rates of vulnerable paths and affected root projects indicate that developers do not realize the influence of blocking chains or have challenges to remediate them.*

8.3.4 RQ3: Remediation Patterns

8.3.4.1 Methodology

To answer RQ3, we empirically investigated how the blocking chains or vulnerable paths were being remediated via package updates during the evolution across snapshots s_1-s_7 (collected in RQ2) and distilled common remediation patterns. It is worth noting that these package updates are not necessarily performed for remediating vulnerabilities. Some of the reactions might be preventive maintenance activities for package dependencies but resulted in the propagation of vulnerability fixes.

Subject Selection We focus on two types of blocking chains that have been remediated via package updates with significant effects of propagating vulnerability fixes:

- ***Type A.*** *The blocking chains existed in snapshots s_1-s_{i-1} ($1 < i \leq 7$), while were remediated in snapshot s_i.* Note that, as the remediation of these blocking chains, all the vulnerable paths passing through them can introduce the vulnerability fixes.
- ***Type B.*** *The blocking chains that existed in snapshots s_1-s_7, while the number of vulnerable paths affected by them significantly reduced during evolution.* On average, the blocking chains were passed through by 59.4±13.4 vulnerable paths in s_1 and had fallen by 46.9%±10.3% in s_7. In our study, we consider the blocking chains as *Type B* cases if the number of their involved vulnerable paths is more than 59.4 in s_1 (above average value) and has fallen by over 46.9% in s_7 (above average value).

The remediation patterns of these two types of blocking chains can help us understand how to facilitate the propagation of vulnerability fixes in the *npm* ecosystem. For each type of blocking chain, we only selected the instances involving high/critical severity level vulnerabilities, which are worthy of developers' attentions. Table 8.7 provides the demographic information of our selected blocking chain instances. As we can see, the selected 369 blocking chains involve diverse blocking packages and vulnerable packages. In total, they affect 887 root projects via 26,884 vulnerable paths. We distill common features in their vulnerability remediation and summarize their taxonomy of remediation patterns.

Table 8.7 Statistics of the selected blocking chain instances

126 Type A blocking chain instances			
#Blocking packages	#Vulnerable packages	#Root projects	#Vulnerable paths (Avg)
38	28	542	34.4±32.7
243 Type B blocking chain instances			
#Blocking packages	#Vulnerable packages	#Root projects	#Vulnerable paths (Avg)
62	22	604	92.8±12.5

Data Analysis Specifically, we performed three tasks to analyze the characteristics and remediation patterns of our selected blocking chain instances:

- *Task 1.* For each blocking chain instance, we investigate its three aspects of characteristics:
  (a) *Whether the packages on the blocking chain are active* (i.e., publishing new versions in the past year from the date of snapshot). *Characteristic a* helps us understand which packages can update their dependencies to remediate such a blocking chain.
  (b) *Whether the packages on the blocking chain are specified with open version constraints* (i.e., the range syntax, such as 2.1.∗, ~ 2.1.0, and ^ 2.1.0, enables new package versions that satisfy its specified constraints to be installed). With the aid of *Characteristic b*, we can observe how vulnerability fixes are propagated into blocking chains/vulnerable paths.
  (c) *Whether the packages need to upgrade/downgrade their direct dependencies' major versions, in order to introduce the concerned vulnerability fixes.* According to the semantic versioning strategy [24], developers are suggested to increase their projects' major version number, if they make incompatible API changes. As such, upgrading/downgrading dependencies' major versions would take project developers' more efforts on modifying or testing code. We can estimate the remediation costs of blocking chains/vulnerable paths via *Characteristic c*.
- *Task 2.* For each blocking chain of *Type A*, we first identified the snapshot s_i ($1 < i \leq 7$) in which it had been remediated. For each package on such a blocking chain, we collected all its versions publishing between the interval of snapshots s_1 and s_i. Based on the chronological order of these version releases, we iteratively replayed the version updates of each package on this blocking chain, to check which version update enabled the remediation of blocking chain (i.e., blocking package can use the vulnerability fix version). Finally, we recorded the duration (#days) from the date of the blocking chain being remediated to the date of snapshot s_1.
- *Task 3.* For each blocking chain of *Type B*, we collected the vulnerable paths passing through it on snapshot s_1 but were remediated on snapshot s_i ($1 < i \leq 7$). Furthermore, for each package on such remediated vulnerable paths, we collected all its versions publishing between the interval of snapshots s_1 and s_i. Based on the chronological order of these version releases, we iteratively replayed the version updates of each package on the selected vulnerable paths and checked which version update enabled the remediation of vulnerable paths (i.e., root project can use the vulnerability fix version). Finally, we recorded the duration (#days) from the date of the vulnerable path being remediated to the date of snapshot s_1.

Similar to many existing empirical studies [25, 26], we followed an open coding procedure [27] to inductively categorize the common remediation patterns in a bottom-up manner, which involves two labeling processes:

- *Labeling process 1:* Initially, two authors performed an in-depth analysis on the above characteristics of blocking chains and their involved vulnerable paths, to understand how they were remediated as the packages evolved. They first analyzed 50% of both *Types A* and *B* blocking chains independently and marked those unclear or insufficient categories. They then discussed and adjusted their category tags during meetings, with the help of a third author to resolve conflicts. In this way, we constructed the pilot taxonomy.
- *Labeling process 2:* Next, the first two authors continued to label remediation pattern of the remaining 50% of blocking chains and iteratively refined the results and the labeling strategy. Conflicts were reconciled with the third author joining the discussions. We adjusted the pilot taxonomy and obtained the final result.

Specifically, the number of conflicts in the two labeling processes is 31 and 26, respectively. Since the labeling involves much manual work, errors could be induced in any of the three tasks when analyzing block chain instances, causing labeling conflicts between the two authors. *Cohen's kappa* for our two labeling processes is 0.79 and 0.80, respectively, indicating a substantial inter-rater agreement [21].

8.3.4.2 Results

Via replaying the package evolution history of the collected blocking chain instances across snapshots s_1–s_7, we observed three common remediation patterns. Figure 8.10 summarizes the taxonomy of remediation patterns, their preconditions of propagating the vulnerability fixes, and the corresponding costs. In the following, we discuss each remediation pattern in detail. To ease presentation, we refer to the package in between the blocking and vulnerable packages on a blocking chain as an *intermediate package*.

Remediation Pattern A *The blocking package publishes a new release in its highest major version train, in which it upgrades the direct dependency to transitively introduce the vulnerability fix (46.1% of* Type B *blocking chain instances).* 46.1% of *Type B* blocking chain instances were remediated via *Pattern A*. Among the 243 *Type B* blocking chain instances, 112 of them are induced by active blocking packages. The lags in dependency updates of such blocking packages are the key causes of hindering root projects from introducing vulnerability fixes. As such, they finally remediated vulnerabilities in their highest available versions, by upgrading the direct dependencies to the safe versions.

In this scenario, for the vulnerable paths on which the blocking packages were specified with open version constraints (i.e., the remediated higher versions can be resolved by the constraints), vulnerability fixes could be automatically propagated into the root projects. Among the 112 instances that adopt remediation *Pattern A*, 34 of them needed to upgrade the major versions of dependencies with an average duration of 107.6 days, while the remaining 78 instances only took 33.5 days (Avg) for the remediation.

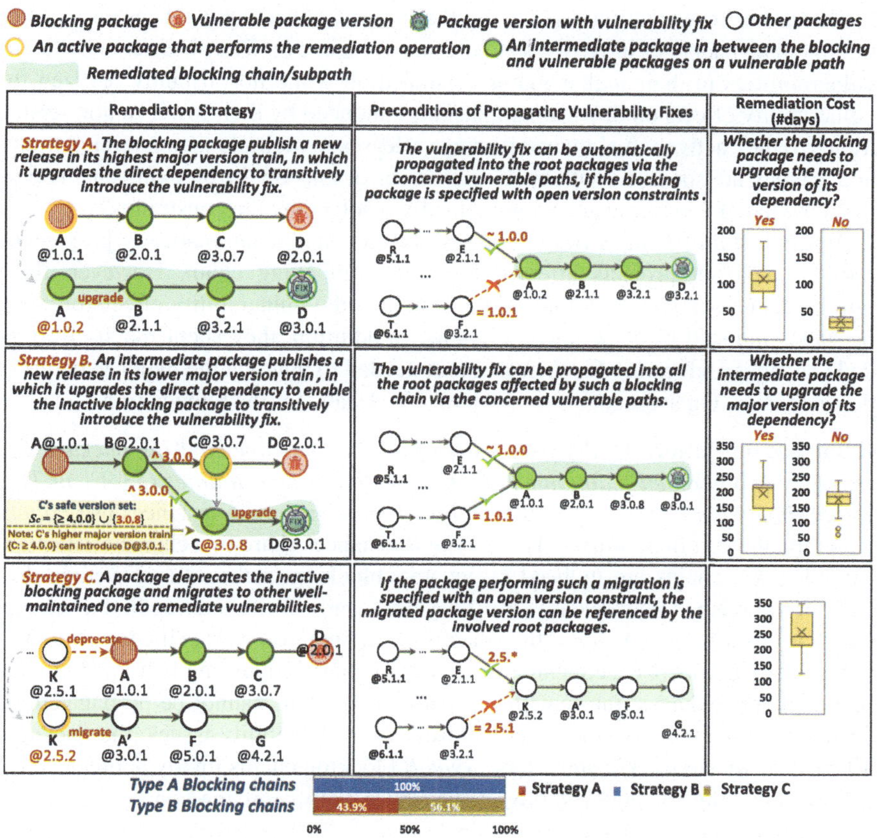

Fig. 8.10 Descriptions of remediation patterns

Remediation Pattern B *An intermediate package publishes a new release in its lower major version train, in which it upgrades the direct dependency to enable the inactive blocking package to transitively introduce a vulnerability fix (100% of* Type A *blocking chain instances).* 100% of *Type A* blocking chain instances are remediated via *Pattern B*. These instances share a common feature: The involved blocking packages are inactively maintained by developers (86.5% of them have not published new releases for over 3 years), which can hardly remediate the concerned vulnerabilities. To allow the inactive blocking package to transitively reference the vulnerability fix, an intermediate package published a new release in its lower major version train, in which it upgraded its direct dependency to safe versions. In studies [7, 28], the above process is referred to as *backporting*. Such backporting practices can bring the benefit of vulnerability fixes to the substantial number of downstream packages that have to depend on the lower major version train of intermediate packages due to incompatibility issues.

By further investigation, we can tell that in our collected *Type A* instances, such intermediate packages have two shared characteristics: (a) They had remediated the vulnerabilities in their higher major version train while not instantly realized the vulnerability effects on downstream packages induced by their lower major version train, (b) they actively maintained package releases in multiple major version trains, and (c) they are specified with open version constraints on the blocking chains (i.e., the remediated versions can be automatically resolved by the constraints).

With the aid of *Pattern B*, the vulnerability fix can be automatically propagated into all the root projects affected by such a blocking chain. However, these intermediate packages took more time to realize the vulnerability effects on other packages induced by their lower versions. In addition, they spent much effort on code changes and testing for the cases that needed to upgrade the major versions of dependencies. On average, *Pattern B* took 195.1 days for the remediation.

Remediation Pattern C *A package deprecates the inactive blocking package and migrates to other well-maintained one to remediate vulnerabilities (53.9% of Type B blocking chain instances).* 53.9% of *Type B* blocking chain instances use *Pattern C* to remediate vulnerabilities. These *Type B* instances share two characteristics: (a) The blocking chains are induced by inactive blocking packages (on average they have not published new releases for 2.6 years), and (b) the intermediate packages on such blocking chains are either inactively maintained or specified with locked version constraints. Consequently, even if the vulnerabilities can be remediated by intermediate packages, the remediated package versions cannot be propagated via such locked version constraints. To address the vulnerability issues, the packages affected by the above 131 intractable *Type B* blocking chains finally deprecated the inactive blocking package and migrated to other well-maintained ones.

If the packages that deprecate the blocking ones are popular in the *npm* ecosystem and specified with open version constraints, their remediated versions can be automatically propagated into many root projects. Generally, package migration needs more efforts than package upgrades. To achieve this, developers have to identify high-quality packages with similar functionalities to replace the inactive blocking ones and spend efforts to modify and test code as well. On average, *Pattern C* took 251.5 days for the remediation.

In general, remediation costs token by the three patterns follow: *Pattern A* < *Pattern B* < *Pattern C*. *Patterns B* and *C* bring more burden to package developers. Based on our empirical findings, for the blocking chains induced by active blocking packages, *Pattern A* is highly recommended to remediate vulnerabilities. For the blocking chains induced by inactive blocking packages, in the cases that the intermediate packages on vulnerable paths are specified with open version constraints, remediation *Pattern B* would be feasible if they can backport to the lower version trains. Otherwise, the packages affected by such blocking chains can adopt *Pattern C* to deprecate the inactive blocking packages.

To remediate vulnerabilities, many prior works have been proposed to suggest practitioners to timely upgrade vulnerable dependencies [19, 29–34], backport to lower versions [7] and migrate the outdated dependencies [19, 35]. By contrast, the three distilled remediation patterns in our study synthesize three factors: (1) the above three dependency update operations, (2) characteristics of blocking chains, and (3) preconditions of propagating the vulnerability fixes. Our empirical findings shed light on how to update pivotal packages' version constraints based on semantic versioning mechanism, for mitigating the lags in propagating vulnerability fixes in an ecosystem.

Answer to RQ3: *We distilled three common remediation patterns and their preconditions of propagating the vulnerability fixes. For the blocking chains induced by active blocking packages, such blocking packages can remediate vulnerabilities in their highest available version (Pattern A). For the blocking chains induced by inactive blocking packages, the intermediate packages can remediate vulnerabilities in their lower major version trains to enable the inactive blocking packages to transitively introduce vulnerability fixes (Pattern B). Besides, a package affected by a blocking chain can also deprecate the inactive blocking package and migrate to other well-maintained one to remediate vulnerabilities (Pattern C).*
Implication: *Combining the three common patterns to remediate pivotal blocking chains can significantly boost the propagation of vulnerability fixes in the npm ecosystem.*

8.4 The Plumber Approach

Inspired by our empirical findings, we propose *Plumber*, a novel technique to boost the propagation of vulnerability fixes in the *npm* ecosystem, via remediating pivotal blocking chains. Figure 8.11 gives the overall architecture of *Plumber*. Its core idea is to (1) model the vulnerability and *npm* dependency metadata and continuously monitor their evolution, (2) identify which pivotal blocking chains hinder the vulnerability fixes from propagating through vulnerable paths (based on findings in RQ1), and (3) analyze the features of pivotal blocking chains and derive their remediation schemes combining the three patterns learnt from our empirical findings in RQ3. In the remediation scheme, *Plumber* can provide detailed information for package developers to arouse their awareness of the lags in fix version updates and the vulnerability effects on the *npm* ecosystem (based on findings in RQ2).

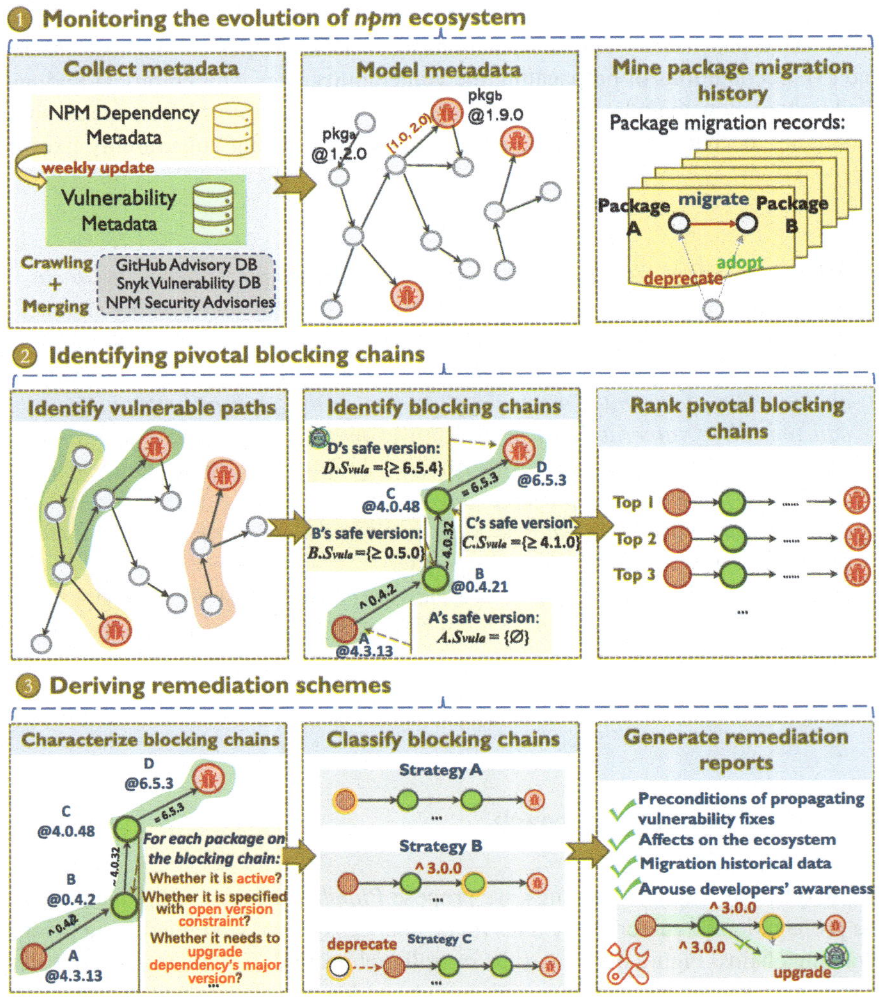

Fig. 8.11 Architecture of *Plumber*

8.4.1 Monitoring the Evolution of the npm Ecosystem

To precisely capture the propagation of vulnerability fixes in the whole ecosystem, *Plumber* continuously collects vulnerability metadata and dependency metadata among *npm* packages. By comparing two contiguous snapshots of *npm* dependency metadata, we can also mine the migration history of packages, in order to provide clues for deriving remediation strategies (as we will show later in Sect. 8.4.3.1).

8.4.1.1 Modeling and Collecting Metadata

Metadata Model We model the metadata of *npm* snapshot s_i as a 2-tuple $\mathcal{M}(s_i) = (dm_i, G_i)$:

- $dm_i = \{\mu_1, \mu_2, \cdots, \mu_n\}$ is a collection of disclosed vulnerabilities, where $\mu_k = (Id_k, sl_k, p_k, ver_k)$. Fields Id_k and sl_k denote unique identifier and severity level of μ_k. Fields p_k and $ver_k = \{v_1, v_2, \cdots, v_n\}$ represent the package name and its published versions affected by such a vulnerability.
- $G_i = (V_i, E_i, C_i)$ is a directed graph depicting the dependency metadata of *npm* snapshot s_i. V_i denotes a collection of package versions published on snapshot s_i. $E_i = \{p_k@v_a \rightarrow p_u@v_b | p_k@v_a, p_u@v_b \in V_i\}$ represents a set of dependency relations among the package versions in V_i. Each relation $p_k@v_a \rightarrow p_u@v_b \in E_i$ is determined by its corresponding dependency constraint $c(p_k@v_a, p_u) \in C_i$, where $c(p_k@v_a, p_u)$ denotes a version constraint specified by $p_k@v_a$ for p_u, and v_b is the highest version of p_u on snapshot s_i that satisfies the constraint (*npm*'s dependency resolution rule).

Metadata Collection As described in Sect. 8.3.1, *Plumber* crawls the above vulnerability metadata dm_i from three representative databases *GitHub Advisory DB*, *Snyk Vulnerability DB*, and *NPM Security Advisories*, while the dependency metadata G_i is crawled with the aid of RESTful APIs provided by *npm* public registry [18].

Plumber weekly updates the metadata model $\mathcal{M}(S_i)$ to continuously monitor the evolution of vulnerability and *npm* dependency metadata. To analyze the propagation of vulnerability fixes in the *npm* ecosystem, dm_i only records the vulnerabilities that have been remediated with fixes.

8.4.1.2 Mining Package Migration History

During evolution, *Plumber* compares the dependency graphs G on two contiguous *npm* snapshots s_i and s_{i+1} to identify package migration records, which can provide clues for deriving remediation *Strategy C*. We formally define a package migration record as follows.

Definition 6 (Package Migration Record) If a project deprecates package p_m and adopts p_n as a substitute, we define $p_m \Rightarrow p_n$ as a migration record, where p_m is the *source package*, while p_n is the *target one* in the migration.

Combining library migration mining approach [35] with our collected dependency metadata, *Plumber* collects a package migration record based on two criteria:

- If $p_k@v_a \rightarrow p_u@v_b \in E_i$ exists in snapshot s_i, while in snapshot s_{i+1}, $p_k@(v_a+1)$ deprecates package p_u and depends on a new package p_t, *Plumber* records $<p_u, p_t>$ as a dependency change pair. *Plumber* considers $p_u \Rightarrow p_t$ as possible migration record, iff such a dependency change pair appears over M times in different projects during evolution. *Plumber* takes the default value of $M = 5$, which can effectively reduce noise via our experiment validation (see discussions in Sect. 8.5.3). We leave its adaptive tuning to future work.

- For each possible migration record $p_u \Rightarrow p_t$, to guarantee its reliability, *Plumber* searches for its corresponding migration commits on GitHub using keywords "replace p_u" OR "deprecate p_u" OR "remove p_u" OR "switch p_u" OR "migrate p_u" OR "delete p_u." *Plumber* determines $p_u \Rightarrow p_t$ as a certain migration record, iff the newly added package p_t can be identified in the returned code commits.

It is worth noting that for a source package, *Plumber* could find multiple target packages in the migration records. When deriving remediation *Strategy C*, all possible suggestions can be provided for developers to migrate problematic packages.

8.4.2 *Identifying Pivotal Blocking Chains*

The metadata model $\mathcal{M}(s_i) = (dm_i, G_i)$ built by *Plumber* contains sufficient information for identifying vulnerable paths and blocking chains.

8.4.2.1 Identifying Vulnerable Paths

Let $vl \subset V_i$ be a set of vulnerable package versions affected by the vulnerabilities in dm_i and $vr \subset V_i$ be a set of latest versions of active packages (i.e., publishing versions in the past year). On dependency graph G_i, *Plumber* considers package versions $p_k@v_m \in vr$ as root nodes and vulnerable package versions $p_u@v_n \in vl$ as leaf nodes, to identify all the vulnerable paths $\mathcal{P} = \{P_{\mu_t}(p_k@v_m, p_w@v_r, \cdots, p_u@v_n) | \mu_t \in dm_i\}$ via reachability analysis. Note that *Plumber* only considers vulnerable paths whose root nodes are the latest versions of active packages, in order to analyze the status quo of vulnerability effects on the whole ecosystem.

However, a package version may contain multiple vulnerabilities, and each vulnerability corresponds to a specific safe version set. For example, `Dotty` 0.1.0 contains two vulnerabilities *CVE-2021-23624* [36] and *CVE-2021-25912* [37], while the safe versions of `Dotty` for these two vulnerabilities are $\{\geq 0.1.1\}$ and $\{\geq 0.1.2\}$, respectively. To precisely find the blocking packages, when identifying vulnerable paths, a package version containing multiple vulnerabilities is distinguished as multiple leaf nodes. In this manner, *Plumber* ensures that a vulnerable path $P_{\mu_t}(p_k@v_m, p_w@v_r, \cdots, p_u@v_n)$ involves a unique vulnerability μ_t.

8.4.2.2 Identifying Pivotal Blocking Chains

The detailed process of identifying blocking chains is described in Algorithm 1. For each vulnerable path $P_{\mu_t}(p_k@v_m, \cdots, p_w@v_r, p_e@v_f, \cdots, p_u@v_n) \in \mathcal{P}$,

Algorithm 1: Identifying blocking chains

Input: $P_{\mu_t}(p_k@v_m, p_w@v_r, \cdots, p_u@v_n)$, V_i and ver_t
Output: B_{μ_t}
1 $Queue \leftarrow ReverselyTraverse(P_{\mu_t})$;
2 $p_b \leftarrow Queue.pop()$;
3 $p_b.S_{\mu_t} \leftarrow PublishedV(V_i, p_b) - ver_t$;
4 **while** $p_b.S_{\mu_t} \neq \emptyset$ **do**
5 $\quad p_a \leftarrow Queue.pop()$;
6 $\quad p_a.S_{vul_t} \leftarrow ResolvedSV(PublishedV(V_i, p_a), p_b)$;
7 $\quad p_b \leftarrow p_a$;
8 **return** $B_{\mu_t}(p_b@v_r, \cdots, p_u@v_n)$;

starting from the vulnerable package p_u, *Plumber* iteratively calculates each package's safe versions for vulnerability μ_t, until a blocking package p_w whose safe version set $p_w.S_{\mu_t} = \emptyset$ is found. Then, *Plumber* considers $B_{\mu_t}(p_w@v_r, p_e@v_f, \cdots, p_u@v_n)$ as a blocking chain.

Specifically, the safe versions of each package are resolved as follows:

- For vulnerable package p_u, *Plumber* records its safe version set as $p_u.S_{\mu_t} = PublishedV(V_i, p_u) - ver_t$, where $PublishedV(V_i, p_u)$ denotes a collection of p_u's published versions in the *npm* snapshot s_i and ver_t records the p_u's vulnerable versions affected by μ_t (Lines 1–3).
- For other package p_a $(a \neq u)$ on the vulnerable path, *Plumber* uses function $ResolvedSV$ to calculate its safe version set. Suppose that p_b is the direct dependency of p_a on the vulnerable path. $ResolvedSV$ returns the p_a's versions that depend on a safe version $v \in p_b.S_{\mu_t}$ or p_a's versions that deprecate package p_b (Lines 5–7).

Finally, *Plumber* ranks the identified blocking chains based on the number of vulnerable paths passing through them. The top ranking blocking chains are considered as pivotal ones should be remediated to enable the propagation of vulnerability fixes into a large amount of packages.

8.4.3 Deriving Remediation Schemes

Leveraging our empirical findings, *Plumber* aims to derive remediation schemes for the top K pivotal blocking chains. By characterizing these blocking chains, it reports which packages should perform remediation operations and how should they update dependencies to boost the propagation of vulnerability fixes in the whole ecosystem.

8.4.3.1 Characterizing Blocking Chains

Our empirical findings reveal that the blocking chains remediated using the same strategy share common characteristics. To facilitate deriving remediation schemes, *Plumber* characterizes the top K pivotal blocking chains according to

(1) *whether the packages are active*, (2) *whether the packages are specified with open version constraints*, and (3) *whether the packages need to upgrade their direct dependencies' major versions to introduce the concerned vulnerability fixes*. The activity degree of packages determines which package on the blocking chain can update their dependencies. The open version constraints specified for packages can help automatically propagate vulnerability fixes. Since upgrading dependencies' major versions takes more efforts on changing and testing code, *Plumber* considers this factor when deriving remediation schemes to avoid bringing more burdens to package developers. Specifically, *Plumber* classifies the top pivotal blocking chains into three categories:

- ***Blocking chains to be remediated via Strategy A***: For a blocking chain $B_{\mu_t}(p_w@v_r, p_e@v_f, \cdots, p_u@v_n)$, if blocking package p_w is actively maintained, *Plumber* arouses p_w's awareness to upgrade its direct dependency p_e to a safe version $v \in p_e.S_{\mu_t}$, in order to introduce the vulnerability fix.
- ***Blocking chains to be remediated via Strategy B***: For a blocking chain $B_{\mu_t}(p_w@v_r, \cdots, p_g@v_h, p_e@v_f, p_c@v_d, \cdots, p_u@v_n)$, *Plumber* remediates it using *Strategy B*, if the blocking chain satisfies:

  - *a*. Blocking package p_w is inactively maintained.
  - *b*. There exists at least one intermediate package $p_e@v_f$ that is specified with open version constraint $c(p_g@v_h, p_e)$ ($p_e@v_f$ is in between the blocking package $p_w@v_r$ and vulnerable package $p_u@v_n$).
  - *c*. Upgrading intermediate package p_e's direct dependency p_c from version v_d to a safe version $v \in p_c.S_{\mu_t}$ need not to cross p_c's major version.

  In this case, *Plumber* suggests the intermediate package $p_e@v_f$ to release a new version that can be resolved by constraint $c(p_g@v_h, p_e)$, in which it upgrades package p_c to a safe version $v \in p_c.S_{\mu_t}$. As such, the vulnerability fix can be propagated into blocking package $p_w@v_r$, remediating the blocking chain.
- ***Blocking chains to be remediated via Strategy C***: For a blocking chain $B_{\mu_t}(p_w@v_r, \cdots, p_u@v_n)$, *Plumber* suggests developers to migrate the blocking package p_w, if the blocking chain satisfies:

  - *a*. Blocking package p_w is inactively maintained.
  - *b*. There are no intermediate packages that are specified with open version constraints.
  - *c*. Although there exist intermediate packages that are specified with open version constraints, upgrading their concerned direct dependencies to the safe versions has to cross major version train.

  Based on the collected package migration records (in Sect. 8.4.1.2), it generates remediation schemes. If there exists a record $p_w \Rightarrow p_m$ and package p_m does not introduce other vulnerabilities, *Plumber* suggests the packages depending on blocking package p_w to perform the migration to package p_m.

To summarize, our empirical findings indicate that remediation costs token by the three strategies typically follow: *Strategy A* < *Strategy B* < *Strategy C*. As such, for the blocking chains induced by actively maintained packages, *Plumber* highly suggests remediation *Strategy A*. For the blocking chains induced by inactive blocking packages, in the cases that the intermediate packages (i.e., packages in between the blocking and vulnerable packages) are specified with open version constraints, *Plumber* suggests remediation *Strategy B* if they can backport to their lower version trains. Otherwise, *Plumber* adopts remediation *Strategy C* to migrate the inactive blocking chains.

8.4.3.2 Generating Remediation Reports

Based on the characteristics of blocking chains, *Plumber* identifies which packages should perform the remediation operations and then customizes reports with applicable solutions. Figure 8.12 shows the templates of remediation reports generated by *Plumber*. Specifically, in each report, it provides the following customized information:

- To arouse developers' awareness, *Plumber* gives the issue description with potential vulnerability impact analysis on the *npm* ecosystem: (1) the number of affected vulnerable paths and (2) the scale of affected downstream projects.
- To boost the propagation of vulnerability fixes, *Plumber* explicitly points out how the packages update their dependencies: (1) suggesting the package version number to perform the remediation and (2) listing the safe versions of dependencies to be upgraded.
- To facilitate developers migrate the inactive blocking packages, *Plumber* suggests the possible target packages and provides the migration records (including the corresponding commit ID) performed by other projects as a reference.

8.5 Evaluation and an Ecosystem-Level Study

In the evaluation section, we conducted an ecosystem-level study to answer the following three research questions:

RQ4 (Effectiveness of Plumber): *Are the remedial strategies derived by Plumber consistent with those made by developers?*

RQ5 (Remediation challenges): *How challenging is remediating the blocking chains in the npm ecosystem?*

RQ6 (Usefulness of Plumber): *Can Plumber boost the propagation of vulnerability fixes in the npm ecosystem and provide useful remediation strategies to developers?*

To answer RQ4, we first identified a collection of package updates performed by developers that could remediate blocking chains with significant propagation effects of vulnerability fixes as a benchmark. We applied *Plumber* to analyzing the

Remediation Reports of *Strategy A*

Issue Description:

A vulnerability $\mu_t.Id_t$ is introduced in package p_a (affected versions: ver_t) via path $p_a@v_m \rightarrow p_g@v_h \rightarrow \ldots \rightarrow p_u@v_n$. Since $p_a@v_m$ (n_d downloads per week♠) is referenced by n_r downstream projects (e.g., $p_e@v_f$, $p_p@v_q$, *etc.*) through n_p paths, vulnerability $\mu_t.Id_t$ can be propagated into these projects and expose security threats to them.

Remediation Suggestions:

Upgrade dependency p_g from version v_h to $v \in p_g.S_{\mu_t}$ in p_a's highest major version train to decrease downstream users' pain.

Remediation Reports of *Strategy B*

Issue Description:

A vulnerability $\mu_t.Id_t$ is introduced in package p_a (affected versions: ver_t) via path $p_a@v_m \rightarrow p_g@v_h \rightarrow \ldots \rightarrow p_u@v_n$. Although such a vulnerability has been remediated in versions $pkg_a.S_{\mu_t}$, p_a's popular previous version $v \in ver_t$ (n_d downloads per week) is still transitively referenced by n_r downstream projects (e.g., $p_e@v_f$, $p_w@v_q$, *etc.*) through n_p paths. If p_a can backport to the widely used lower version train, such a vulnerability fix can be automatically propagated into a large amount of downstream projects.

Remediation Suggestions:

Upgrade dependency p_g from version v_h to $v \in p_g.S_{\mu_t}$ in p_a's lower version train $v \in ver_t$ to benefit the downstream projects.

Remediation Reports of *Strategy C*

Issue Description:

A vulnerability $\mu_t.Id_t$ is introduced in package p_a (affected versions: ver_t) via path $p_a@v_m \rightarrow p_g@v_h \rightarrow \ldots \rightarrow p_u@v_n$. However, p_g is not actively maintained by developers. If p_a can migrate p_g to other package, then n_p vulnerable paths can be remediated.

Remediation Suggestions:

Replace p_g with other package to remediate a large amount of vulnerable paths. As a reference, the migration records for p_g in other project repositories are listed below:
1. Project $p_s@v_c$ has migrated p_g to p_m via commit *commitID*.
...

♠The downloads info can be mined from https://www.npmjs.com/.
p_a is the package identified by **Plumber** to perform the remediation operations.
Customized information by **Plumber**

Fig. 8.12 Simplified templates of generated remediation reports

above blocking chains and then compare our derived remediation strategies with benchmark, in order to quantify the tool's effectiveness.

To answer RQ5, for the identified 358,422 blocking chains on the recent *npm* snapshot on August 1, 2021, we classified them into different difficulty levels of remediation. Furthermore, we observe their distribution and discuss the remediation challenges.

To answer RQ6, we applied *Plumber* to generating remediation reports for the top pivotal blocking chains and evaluate the remediation effectiveness based on developers' feedback. In our generated reports, we described the detected vulnerability issues together with remediation suggestions. More importantly, to arouse developers' awareness, we explained the vulnerability impacts on the *npm* ecosystem and the benefits of their dependency updates to the propagation of vulnerability fixes.

8.5.1 RQ4: Effectiveness of Plumber

Experimental Setup To evaluate the effectiveness of *Plumber*, we constructed a benchmark by collecting a set of package updates performed by developers. These package updates not only remediated blocking chains but also enabled significant propagation effects of vulnerability fixes. The benchmark construction process involves three steps:

- *Constructing npm snapshots:* Based on our VP model, we constructed a collection of consecutive snapshots (s_1'–s_7') of *npm* dependency metadata from July 1, 2019 to July 1, 2020, which were not used in our empirical study. Statistics of the *npm* snapshots are listed in Table 8.8. The seven snapshots only contain the active root projects and the package versions directly or transitively used by them. To precisely identify the blocking chains in snapshot s_1', we only considered the vulnerabilities that were disclosed with fixes before July 1, 2019.
- *Identifying the blocking chains that have been remediated with significant effects of propagating vulnerability fixes:* Similar as the subject selection strategy adopted in RQ3, we focused on two types of blocking chains: (1) ***Type A.*** The blocking chains existed in snapshots $s_1' - s_{i-1}'$ $(1 < i \leq 7)$, while were remediated in snapshot s_i'. All the vulnerable paths passing through *Type A* blocking chains can introduce the vulnerability fixes. (2) ***Type B.*** The blocking chains existed in snapshots s_1'-s_7', while the number of vulnerable paths affected by them significantly reduced during evolution. On average, the blocking chains

Table 8.8 Statistics of the *npm* snapshots

Snapshots	#Root projects	#Dependency relations
s_1': *July 1, 2019*	168,432	1,332,859
s_2': *September 1, 2019*	171,764	1,342,622
s_3': *November 1, 2019*	173,552	1,353,335
s_4': *January 1, 2020*	187,230	1,376,942
s_5': *March 1, 2020*	192,784	1,421,438
s_6': *May 1, 2020*	206,642	1,486,321
s_7': *July 1, 2020*	210,538	1,521,230

were passed through by 56.5±23.6 vulnerable paths in s'_1 and had fallen by 52.3%±9.2% in s'_7. In our study, we consider the blocking chains as *Type B* cases if the number of their involved vulnerable paths was more than 56.5 in s'_1 and had fallen by over 52.3% in s'_7.

- *Identifying the package updates that remediate the blocking chains of Types A and B:* We identified the package updates that remediated *Types A* and *B* blocking chains as our benchmark. Specifically, we performed two tasks below:
  - For each *Type A* blocking chain, we first identified the snapshot s'_i $(1 < i \leq 7)$ in which it had been remediated. Furthermore, for each package on such a blocking chain, we collected all its versions publishing between the interval of snapshots s'_1 and s'_i. Based on the chronological order of these version releases, we iteratively replayed the version updates of each package on this blocking chain, to check which version update enabled the remediation of blocking chain (i.e., blocking package can use the vulnerability fix version).
  - For each *Type B* blocking chain, we collected the vulnerable paths passing through it on snapshot s'_1 but were remediated on snapshot s'_i $(1 < i \leq 7)$. Furthermore, for each package on such remediated vulnerable paths, we collected all its versions publishing between the interval of snapshots s'_1 and s'_i. Based on the chronological order of these version releases, we iteratively replayed the version updates of each package on the selected vulnerable paths and checked which version update enabled the remediation of vulnerable paths (i.e., root project can use the vulnerability fix version).

Table 8.9 shows the statistics of our collected benchmark. The 362 package updates remediated 385 blocking chains, involving diverse blocking packages and vulnerable packages. They enabled the propagation of vulnerability fixes into 1,103 root projects via 12,926 vulnerable paths. Specifically, these package updates can be divided into three categories: (1) *dependency version updates by blocking packages*, (2) *backporting by intermediate packages*, and (3) *migration of inactive blocking packages*. Furthermore, we applied *Plumber* to deriving remediation strategies for

Table 8.9 Statistics of our benchmark

92 Type A blocking chain instances			
#Blocking packages	#Vulnerable packages	#Root projects	#Vulnerable paths(*Avg*)
32	25	630	38.4±24.5
293 Type B blocking chain instances			
#Blocking packages	#Vulnerable packages	#Root projects	#Vulnerable paths(*Avg*)
76	35	803	72.3±26.2
362 package updates			
Dependency updates by blocking packages	*Backporting by intermediate packages*	*Migration of inactive blocking packages*	
221	42	99	

Fifteen package updates remediate more than one blocking chains.

Table 8.10 Effectiveness of *Plumber* in deriving remediation strategies

	Consistent remediation strategies	Inconsistent remediation strategies			
		NU	*NB*	*NR*	*NP*
Benchmark	–	0	2	71	2,585
Plumber	79.8% (289/362)	41	32	0	4,679

NU: # Dependency updates by blocking packages (*Strategy A*)
NB: # Backporting by intermediate packages (*Strategy B*)
NR: # Migration of inactive blocking packages (*Strategy C*)
NP: # Vulnerable paths remediated by package updates

the 385 blocking chains. To quantify the effectiveness our tool, we validated if the derived remediation strategies were consistent with the real package updates in benchmark.

Results Table 8.10 presents our evaluation results. In total, 289 out of 362 remediation strategies (79.8%) derived by *Plumber* are consistent with those in benchmark. Among the 289 consistent remediation strategies, 221 of them (76.6%) suggest blocking packages to update dependencies, 40 of them (13.8%) suggest intermediate packages to backport to their lower versions, and 28 of them (9.7%) suggest the affected packages to migrate inactive blocking packages to other ones. Consequently, 10,341 vulnerable paths introduced vulnerability fixes via the effective package updates.

For the 73 blocking chains, *Plumber* derived inconsistent remediation strategies with those in benchmark. Via balancing the remediation costs and propagation effects of vulnerability fixes, *Plumber* suggested 41 of them to be remediated based on *Strategy A* and 32 of them to be resolved using *Strategy B*. However, since our derived 71 remediation strategies either need to upgrade dependencies crossing major version trains or raise awareness of backporting practices, developers decided to migrate the inactive blocking packages to other well-maintained ones in our benchmark. For example, when resolving vulnerability issues, package `Reaction`'s developers tried to upgrade the vulnerable package `Meteorite` from 0.7.2 to its safe version 0.9.0 but encountered incompatibility issues. As described in issue `Meteorite#299` [38], they decided to migrate `Meteorite` to other alternative packages with high quality. In another example, the intermediate package `React-reality` on a blocking chain refused to backport to its lower versions (see discussions in issue `React-reality#1` [39]), due to a series of technical challenges. As a result, the affected projects had to migrate inactive blocking package `Configtest` [40], in order to remediate vulnerability issues. In addition, for the remaining two blocking chains, *Plumber* suggested the active blocking packages to upgrade dependencies to their safe versions (i.e., *Strategy A* with less remediation efforts). However, in our benchmark, developers eventually performed backporting practices to bring the benefit of vulnerability fixes to their downstream projects (clues could be found in issues `Mapbox#7` [41] and `Opac#1034` [42]).

*The evaluation results indicate the effectiveness of our Plumber in deriving remediation strategies for blocking chains. 289 out of 362 remediation strategies (**79.8%**) derived by Plumber are consistent with those in our benchmark. For the 73 inconsistent remediation strategies, our tool generates the suggestions via balancing the remediation costs and propagation effects of vulnerability fixes. However, due to the incompatibility issues or technical challenges, the package updates in our benchmark resolved the vulnerability issues in alternative ways.*

8.5.2 RQ5: Remediation Challenges

Experimental Setup To understand how challenging is remediating the blocking chains in the *npm* ecosystem, we analyzed the identified 358,422 blocking chains on the recent *npm* snapshot on August 1, 2021 and classified them into different difficulty levels of remediation. Based on the packages' characteristics on each blocking chain, leveraging our empirical findings in RQ3, we identify the blocking chains that are difficult/less difficult to be remediated, according to the following criteria:

- ***Type A. Blocking chains are of high difficulty to remediate.***
  - *a. The blocking chains that are induced by inactive blocking packages, whose involved intermediate packages are all specified with locked version constraints (Strategy C).*
  - *b. The blocking chains that are induced by inactive blocking packages, whose involved intermediate packages are specified with open version constraints but need to upgrade dependencies' major versions to introduce vulnerability fixes (Strategy C).*
  - *c. The blocking chains that are induced by active blocking packages, but blocking packages have to upgrade dependencies' major versions in order to introduce vulnerability fixes (Strategy A).*

  For *Types A.a* and *A.b* blocking chains, developers cannot easily remediate them through upgrading dependencies. They are suggested to spend efforts to migrate the blocking packages. For *Type A.c* blocking chains, *Plumber* encourages the blocking packages to upgrade their dependencies, which requires more efforts to test the packages crossing their major versions.
- ***Type B. Blocking chains are of medium difficulty to remediate.***
  - *The blocking chains that are induced by inactive blocking packages, whose involved intermediate packages are specified with open version constraints but*

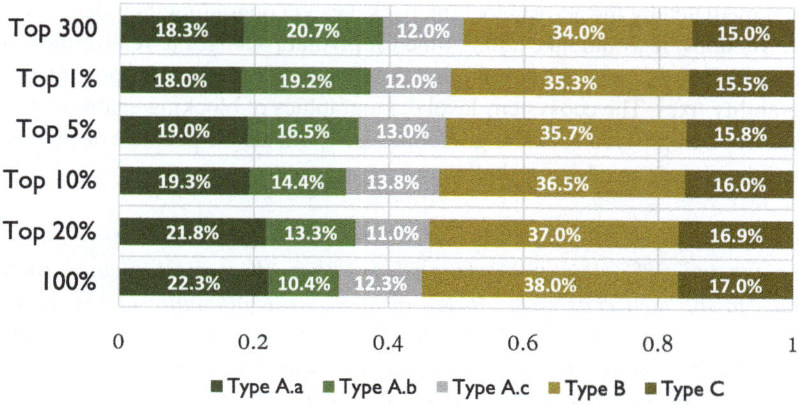

Fig. 8.13 Distribution of blocking chains with different remediation difficulty levels

need not to upgrade dependencies' major versions to introduce vulnerability fixes (Strategy B).

Type B blocking chains would be remediated if the involved intermediate packages can backport to their lower version trains. However, the backporting practices need package developers to spend efforts on supporting multiple version trains.

- ***Type C. Blocking chains are of low difficulty to remediate.***
  - *The blocking chains that are induced by active blocking packages, and the blocking packages need not to upgrade dependencies' major versions to introduce vulnerability fixes (Strategy A).*

  Type C blocking chains can be remediated by active blocking packages via upgrading dependencies with fewer compatibility issues, which are highly recommended by *Plumber*.

Results Figure 8.13 shows the distribution of blocking chains with different remediation difficulty levels. To see trends, we divided all blocking chains into six groups (overlapping) based on their influence ranking: top 300, 1%, 5%, 10%, 20%, and 100%. For the top 20% pivotal blocking chains that affect most of vulnerable paths in the *npm* ecosystem, 46.1% of them (*Types A.a*, *A.b*, and *A.c*) are challenging to remediate. In total 81,044 packages depending on *Types A.a* and *A.b* blocking chains should migrate the inactive blocking packages to avoid inducing vulnerability fixes, which bring heavy burden to developers. For the 11.0% *Types A.c* blocking chains, the blocking packages have to upgrade their dependencies' major versions to introduce vulnerability fixes, which need more testing efforts to avoid incompatibility issues.

Moreover, to remediate the 37.0% top pivotal blocking chains of *Type B*, 26,523 involved intermediate packages specified with open version constraints should backport to their lower version trains. Only 16.9% *Types C* blocking chains can be easily remediated by the active blocking packages via upgrading their dependencies to safe versions. It would take a long time for pivotal packages to realize the effects of their dependency upgrades/migrations/backporting practices on propagation of vulnerability fixes. The ecosystem-level demographics of blocking chains generated by *Plumber* can provide concrete guidelines and policies for package developers to address the above remediation challenges.

For the top 20% pivotal blocking chains that affect most of vulnerable paths in the npm ecosystem, ***46.1%*** *of them are challenging to remediate. They either need to migrate the inactive blocking packages or upgrade their dependencies' major versions to introduce vulnerability fixes, which need more code changing and testing efforts.* ***37.0%*** *top pivotal blocking chains can be remediated via backporting practices of the involved intermediate packages. Only* ***16.9%*** *top pivotal blocking chains can be easily remediated by active blocking packages via upgrading their dependencies to safe versions with fewer incompatibility issues.*

8.5.3 RQ6: Usefulness of Plumber

Experiment Setup For the top 300 pivotal blocking chains, we deployed *Plumber* to report remediation suggestions to corresponding package developers. As shown in Fig. 8.13, 27.0% (81 *Types A.c* and *C*) and 34.0% (102 *Type B*) blocking chains should be remediated using *Strategies A* and *B*, respectively. For the remaining 39.0% blocking chains (117 *Types A.a* and *A.b*), based on *Strategy C*, *Plumber* should warn developers to migrate the involved 56 inactive blocking packages.

As of September 1, 2021, *Plumber* located 48,325 dependency change pairs $<p_u, p_t>$ (i.e., a project deprecated dependency p_u and added a new dependency p_t across two consecutive *npm* snapshots). Figure 8.14 shows the occurrences of each dependency change pair M in different projects during evolution (on average $M = 2.15 \pm 3.50$). For 1,081 out of 48,325 (2.2%) dependency change pairs $<p_u, p_t>$, *Plumber* found migration keywords in the commit messages on GitHub (e.g., "replace p_u") and identified the addition of package p_t in the corresponding code commits as well. The 1,081 migration records appear at least five times in different projects during evolution ($M \geq 5$). *Plumber* considered such dependency change pairs as certain migration records. Among the 56 inactive blocking packages in the

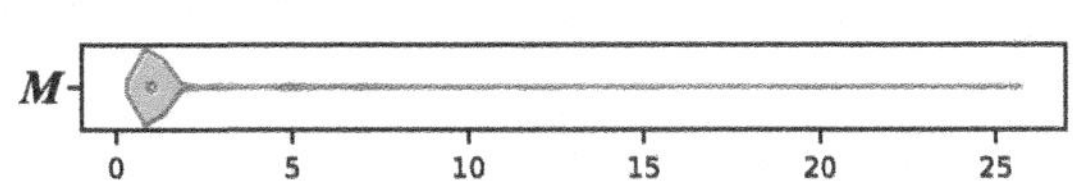

Fig. 8.14 Occurrences of each dependency change pair M in different projects during evolution

117 *Types A.a* and *A.b* pivotal blocking chains, 43 of them (76.8%) can be migrated according to our mined records.

It is worth noting that *Plumber* only concerned the blocking chains induced by vulnerabilities with critical, high, or medium levels and merged the remediation suggestions that should be performed by the same package into one report. In total, it submitted 268 remediation reports (73 reports using *Strategy A*, 98 reports using *Strategy B*, and 97 reports using *Strategy C*) to packages' issue trackers. To arouse developers' awareness, in the remediation reports, we explained the vulnerability impacts on the *npm* ecosystem and the benefits of dependency updates to the propagation of vulnerability fixes. We evaluate the usefulness of *Plumber* based on developers' feedback.

Ethical Considerations To avoid spamming the open-source community and developers, we only remediated the top 300 pivotal blocking packages and thoroughly validated the information of reports generated by *Plumber*. We guaranteed that there were no editing errors in our remediation reports and have checked the correctness of vulnerability information (e.g., unique CVE identifier, severity level, and affected versions of vulnerable package). More importantly, we manually validated if the affected downstream projects could introduce the concerned vulnerability fix, combining the *npm* dependency metadata with *node-semver* rules. All the 268 remediation reports were submitted in compliance with the projects' contributing guidelines and licenses.

Results Table 8.11 summarizes the statues of our remediation reports. In total 127 reports (47.4%) were quickly confirmed by developers, and 84 confirmed reports (66.1%) were later remediated or were under remediation using our strategies. And 22 reports (8.2%) had been rejected since the relevant vulnerabilities were considered as false positives or inaccurate records in vulnerability DB through developers' validation while in our 22 reported issues (8.2%) developers expressed that they did not care about vulnerabilities. The other reports were still pending, likely due to the less active maintenance of the projects.

Impacts on Boosting the Propagation of Vulnerability Fixes In Table 8.12, *#AVP'* and *#ARP'* denote the number of vulnerable paths and root projects that can introduce vulnerability fixes after the concerned blocking chains being remediated. *#RD* denotes the download count of package versions having been remediated based on our suggestions (recorded on https://www.npmjs.com/ as of December 23, 2021). We use these three metrics to estimate the impacts of our submitted remediation reports on propagation of vulnerability fixes.

After the 84 packages published their remediated versions according to our reports, in total, the involved vulnerability fixes can be propagated into 16,403 root projects via 92,469 vulnerable paths. It is worth noting that 15,719 vulnerable paths (17.0%) are remediated based on backporting practices, while 14,425 paths (15.6%) get rid of vulnerabilities by migrating inactive blocking packages. On average, each remediated package version is receiving 72,678 downloads per week by the time of this work. The results indicate the usefulness of *Plumber* in boosting the propagation

Table 8.11 Statistics of remediation reported by *Plumber*

Report Status	*Strategy A*	*Strategy B*	*Strategy C*
♠ *Vulnerabilities remediated using our strategies*	25	27	32
♣ *Vulnerabilities under remediation using our strategies*	7	5	4
★ *Remediation strategies confirmed, but inducing incompatibility issues*	9	18	0
• *Developers were unwilling to create backports*	0	7	0
♦ *False positive vulnerabilities checked by developers*	3	10	9
■ *Inaccurate info in the vulnerability DB*	1	1	0
▼ *Do not care about vulnerabilities*	7	12	3
▲ *Reports pending*	21	18	49
Confirmation rate = 47.4% (127/268)	**56.2%**(41/73)	**51.0%**(50/98)	**37.1%**(36/97)
Remediation rate = 66.1% (84/127)	**61.0%**(25/41)	**54.0%**(27/50)	**88.9%**(32/36)

More detailed info of reports is provided on http://plumber-npm.com/.

of vulnerability fixes in the ecosystem. It is thus necessary to deploy *Plumber* to continuously capture the pivotal blocking chains and suggest proper remediation strategies with impact analysis.

> *Plumber's generated remediation reports have boosted the propagation of vulnerability fixes into 16,403 root projects via 92,469 vulnerable paths. On average, each remediated package version received 72,678 downloads per week.*

Feedback on Remediation Reports Generated by *Plumber* Different remediation strategies achieved different confirmation rates (*Strategy A:* 56.2%, *Strategy B:* 51.0%, and *Strategy C:* 37.1%). Most submitted reports received developers' positive feedback. In 45 reports, developers were unwilling to remediate vulnerabilities because they encountered challenges (e.g., incompatibility issues) during the fixing process or did not care about security issues (see discussions in Sect. 8.5.4). We discuss the representative cases that reveal the usefulness of *Plumber* in five aspects:

- ***The responsive reports cover many well-known npm projects.*** Totally 25 (*Types A.c* and *C*) and 27 (*Type B*) pivotal blocking chains were remediated by developers using *Strategies A* and *B*, respectively. Thirty-two packages migrated the inactive blocking packages based on our remediation *Strategy C*. The responsive reports cover many well-known *npm* projects, such as

Table 8.12 The impacts of our remediated reports on propagating vulnerability fixes

ID	Issue reports	Strategy	#AVP'	#ARP'	#RD	ID	Issue reports	Strategy	#AVP'	#ARP'	#RD
1	glob-entries-plugin#19	C	576	565	1, 539	138	browser-extension#463	C	143	25	1, 148
2	storybook#15830	C	1, 759	327	523, 504	139	bst#677	C	97	61	1, 808
3	ethers.js#1782	B	12, 471	1, 792	100, 099	140	victory#1945	A	536	137	30, 353
7	just#555	C	320	13	6, 619	141	openVectorEditor#760	C	535	449	3, 230
8	workbox#2912	C	297	31	2, 425	143	amcharts4#3684	A	530	480	24, 796
9	off-main-thread#46	A	2, 922	2, 528	596, 269	147	fis3#1328	A	543	511	5, 314
10	actionhero#1907	C	51	34	1, 081	150	cross-fetch#112	B	1, 083	704	148, 135
11	assetgraph-builder#892	C	241	33	1, 141	152	react-components#265	C	515	431	6, 441
13	hads#65	C	37	11	1, 797	154	release-it#794	B	511	487	18, 580
14	node-windows#293	C	112	5	2, 974	156	ibm-security#1083	C	508	440	1, 383
18	swig-email-templates#50	C	71	53	2, 525	157	jsonld.js#457	B	642	453	37, 234
24	oc#1197	C	368	211	2, 364	158	plugin-i18n-json#44	C	174	35	31, 366
28	vue-cli#6632	C	163	71	2, 509	163	node-jose#322	B	1, 009	304	128, 959
34	MQTT.js#1306	B	1, 394	228	30, 998	165	node-console-stamp#54	A	504	492	9, 456
42	strider#1124	C	242	13	2, 434	166	rendition#1361	C	502	434	2, 837
44	universalviewer#808	C	234	11	2, 820	169	easy-peasy#684	B	501	432	2, 964
47	google-p12-pem#337	B	1, 265	683	205, 683	172	mammoth.js#290	A	543	334	10, 773
57	react-native#31987	A	10, 189	1, 016	77, 208	173	sequelize#13398	B	956	632	81, 364
65	vf-core#1644	C	103	74	2, 415	189	terminal-kit#182	B	482	442	7, 620
69	pdfkit#1273	A	909	498	136, 646	193	spectral#1755	B	475	455	2, 559
75	rsuite#1852	C	778	613	3, 969	194	auth0.js#1193	A	476	412	19, 988
79	imodeljs#2066	C	36	6	1, 111	195	powerapps-docs#2663	C	121	5	1, 289
82	http-server#707	B	799	557	13, 820	199	nodejs-storage#1538	B	783	398	72, 336
86	azure-storage-node#691	A	754	625	25, 460	204	apisauce#269	B	498	447	14, 732

(continued)

Table 8.12 (continued)

ID	Issue reports	Strategy	#AVP'	#ARP'	#RD	ID	Issue reports	Strategy	#AVP'	#ARP'	#RD
94	assetgraph#1187	C	15	13	1, 701	206	xml-crypto#231	B	464	443	42, 446
97	enact#2941	C	646	527	1, 409	209	gax-nodejs#1062	B	678	475	128, 095
102	js-libp2p-webrtc-star#374	A	741	332	1, 546	211	iot-device-sdk-js#376	A	474	355	33, 420
103	tedious#1297	B	606	553	51, 840	213	node-sqlite3#1493	A	485	459	263, 472
104	avatar-image-cropper#42	C	114	2	1, 008	214	fabric#98	A	454	354	13, 057
106	jupyterlab#10818	C	137	43	1, 154	219	js-peer-id#153	B	2, 788	290	6, 986
111	syntax-highlighter#417	B	2, 101	389	214, 515	220	nestjs-mailgun#21	C	125	9	2, 167
112	father#391	A	650	507	2, 234	224	importers#136	A	598	433	4, 730
116	spatial-navigation#104	C	571	490	1, 731	231	DefinitelyTyped#55072	B	471	329	2, 755
120	oas-kit#467	A	562	464	8, 310	232	engine.io-client#676	B	2, 452	668	53, 578
122	lint-staged#995	B	592	398	530, 750	234	z-schema#269	B	458	165	240, 864
123	commitlint#2687	B	563	517	48, 814	238	markdown-preview#101	B	440	313	5, 378
125	patternfly-react#6153	C	561	479	1, 459	239	ng2-rest#18	A	1, 113	105	12, 003
127	node-convict#396	B	613	540	19, 981	243	celo-monorepo#8521	A	3, 478	604	3, 273
128	bundle-stats#1578	C	552	470	1, 683	246	tfjs#5492	A	588	537	5, 875
132	json-rpc-middleware#99	B	551	389	3, 540	256	rollup-plugin-styles#188	A	420	420	15, 707
133	rollup-plugin-postcss#386	A	549	530	149, 887	260	node-xlsx#156	A	422	400	7, 565
135	git-up#27	A	542	370	1, 587, 296	262	parse-server#7491	A	457	283	4, 014

Tensorflow/tfjs#5492 [9] (*Strategy A*), Ethers.js#1782 [10] (*Strategy B*), Googleapi#337 [43] (*Strategy B*), Google-gax#1062 [44] (*Strategy B*), Google-cloud/storage#1538 [45] (*Strategy B*), GoogleChrome/workbox #2912 [11] (*Strategy C*), and Microsoft/just#555 [46] (*Strategy C*).

- ***Many remediation reports struck a chord with downstream packages.*** For example, Node-sqlite3 is a blocking package, which hinders the propagation of a vulnerability fix (*CVE-2021-32803* with high severity) along vulnerable paths. Our submitted remediation report Node-sqlite3#1493 [47] (*Strategy A*) attracted 17 developers' comments to request their dependency upgrades and was linked to 16 real vulnerability issues of the downstream projects. A downstream user of Node-sqlite3 commented that *"It is package developers'/maintainers' responsibilities to remove the vulnerabilities. Otherwise, such effects on other packages like a cancer in the ecosystem."*
- ***Our remediation reports indeed aroused the pivotal packages' awareness to backport to their lower version trains to benefit the whole ecosystem.*** For example, in report Peer-id#153 [48] (*Strategy B*), we suggested Peer-id to backport to version 0.12.5, in order to mitigate the effects of vulnerability *CVE-2020-7720* on 450 vulnerable paths. Encouragingly, this report was quickly confirmed by developers and left a comment: *"This vulnerability had already been resolved since Peer-id@0.14.3. We typically don't maintain versions far back, but make an exception for this case whose weekly download rate is rather high."*
  In approach [19], Chinthanet et al. concluded that practitioners should provide developers more awareness mechanisms to enable quicker planning of dependency updates. This point of view is echoed by the above developers' feedback in our study.
- ***Many projects were willing to migrate the inactive blocking packages to remediate vulnerabilities.*** For example, in report Image-cropper#42 [49] (*Strategy C*), we suggested Image-cropper to replace the inactive blocking package Babel-cli that introduces vulnerability *CVE-2020-28469* with a high-quality package Webpack. After checking the historical migration record Babel-cli $\Rightarrow$ Webpack (Commit#*8616b1* [50] in Learn-webpack) provided by *Plumber*, developers accepted our remediation suggestion.
  Similar findings can be found in study [19]. Among the 5,417 projects investigated by Chinthanet et al., 1,389 (25.64%) decided to remove vulnerable dependencies to mitigate the secure risks. Instead of waiting for the vulnerability fix, client projects might remove the vulnerable package if they were able to find a similar one as a replacement.
- ***Developers showed great interest in the Plumber tool.*** For example, one developer left a comment in report Xml-crypto#231 [51]: *"I noticed that you have raised similar issues in other code repositories. Are you using an automated tool? It seems that the tool can help the vulnerability patches propagate into our npm projects."* Besides, *Plumber*'s remediation report Meow#195 [52] struck a chord with the affected downstream packages. A developer supported our suggestions for Meow and commented that *"Based on the detailed issue reports, there exist*

more than 33,500 affected downstream projects. Would you be willing to slightly compromise your principles in exchange for making a lot of downstream users happy?"

Such feedback indicates that remediating pivotal blocking chains with proper strategies is indeed important to and welcomed by real-world *npm* developers. Encouraged by such comments, we are planning to release our tool for public use to help build a healthy *npm* ecosystem.

> *47.4% of our remediation reports received positive feedback from many well-known npm projects, such as* `Tensorflow/tfjs`*,* `Ethers.js`*,* `Googleapi`*,* `GoogleChrome/workbox`*, etc. These reports indeed aroused the pivotal packages' awareness to perform dependency upgrades/backporting/migrations in order to remediate vulnerabilities, benefiting the whole ecosystem. Besides, developers showed interest in the Plumber tool and recognized its usefulness in building a healthy npm ecosystem.*

8.5.4 Discussions

Lessons Learnt from Developers' Feedback Developers were unwilling to resolve our remediation reports mainly because of five cases: (1) *They had weak awareness of vulnerability affects and did not care about them*, (2) *dependency upgrades induced incompatibility issues*, (3) *they were unwilling to create backports to remediate vulnerabilities*, (4) *they only concerned the exploitable vulnerability code*, and (5) *vulnerability DB recorded inaccurate information*.

Based on developers' feedback, we can label the packages of *Cases (1), (2), and (3)* as improper ones to perform remediation. *Plumber* regards the improper packages as equivalent of inactive packages to derive more feasible remediation strategies for blocking chains. Regarding *Cases (4)* and *(5)*, the remediation ability of *Plumber* can be further improved, if *vulnerability info correction* and *vulnerability reachability analysis* techniques are integrated into its architecture. Several approaches have been proposed to correct vulnerability records [53] and identify the unexploitable vulnerabilities [54–56], which provide technical references for tool enhancement.

Backporting Practices *Plumber*'s remediation *Strategy B* is inspired by backporting practices. Backporting requires additional efforts from package developers, as it entails transplanting important bug and vulnerability fixes to earlier versions [7]. Downstream projects can directly benefit from backported fixes without having to upgrade their dependencies to higher major or minor versions. Thus, backporting practices of packages on the pivotal blocking chains can significantly boost the propagation of vulnerability fixes in the ecosystem.

In our study, we found an interesting phenomenon that many developers were willing to support their lower major releases for a period of time, after which they have no backporting plans to avoid giving downstream packages a false sense of security. Instead, they encourage downstream users to abandon the old versions and bump to higher ones. For example, in remediation report `Angular-cli#21608` [57], a developer expresses that *"`Angular-cli`'s versions prior to 10.0.0 (released two years ago) are no longer supported, since the backporting request goes against our maintenance policy: (a) 6 months of active support, during which regularly-scheduled updates and patches are released; (b) 12 months of long-term support, during which only critical fixes and security patches are released."* According to developers' feedback, *Plumber* gives higher priority to request package developers to backport to their lower versions that have been published within 1 year.

Similar empirical findings were given by Decan et al. in work [7]. Their investigation for backporting practices in open-source community indicated that continued support of lower major trains might have the adverse effect of delaying the migration of dependents to the highest major release. Since lower major releases are unlikely to be maintained forever even when they benefit from backports, package producers should devise and advertise a clear phaseout strategy of lower major trains.

Noteworthy Blocking Chain Cases Among the top 300 blocking chains remediated in our study, we noticed two types of interesting blocking chain cases:

- *Multiple blocking chains share the same packages but involve different vulnerabilities.* On such blocking chains, each package has different safe version sets corresponding to different vulnerabilities. When deriving remediation strategies, for each package, *Plumber* identifies the intersection of safe versions for all the involved vulnerabilities. Figure 8.15a shows three blocking chains passing through the same packages, but the package `sanitize-html` contains three vulnerabilities *CVE-2021-26539*, *CVE-2021-26540*, and *SNYK-JS-SANITIZE HTML-585892*. Since each vulnerability corresponds to a safe version set for `sanitize-html`, to remediate all of them, *Plumber* suggests `postman-collection` to publish version 3.4.*, in which it upgrades `sanitize-html` from version 2.2.1 to 3.5.3 (the lowest version satisfying the intersection of three safe versions). However, in report collection#1215 [58], the developers chose to upgrade sanitize-html from version 2.2.1 to 2.3.2 to fix two vulnerabilities (*CVE-2021-26539* and *CVE-2021-26540*) without moving to the major version 3.5.3, in order to avoid potential compatibility issues.
- *Multiple blocking chains intersect at an active package.* In the cases that multiple blocking chains intersect at an active package, *Plumber* suggests the intersection to perform remediation by upgrading multiple dependencies. Figure 8.15b shows an illustrative example. Three blocking chains intersect at `parse-server@2.19.1`, on which `parse-server` is all specified with the open version constraint ^ 2.19.1. In report `parse-server#7491` [59], *Plumber*

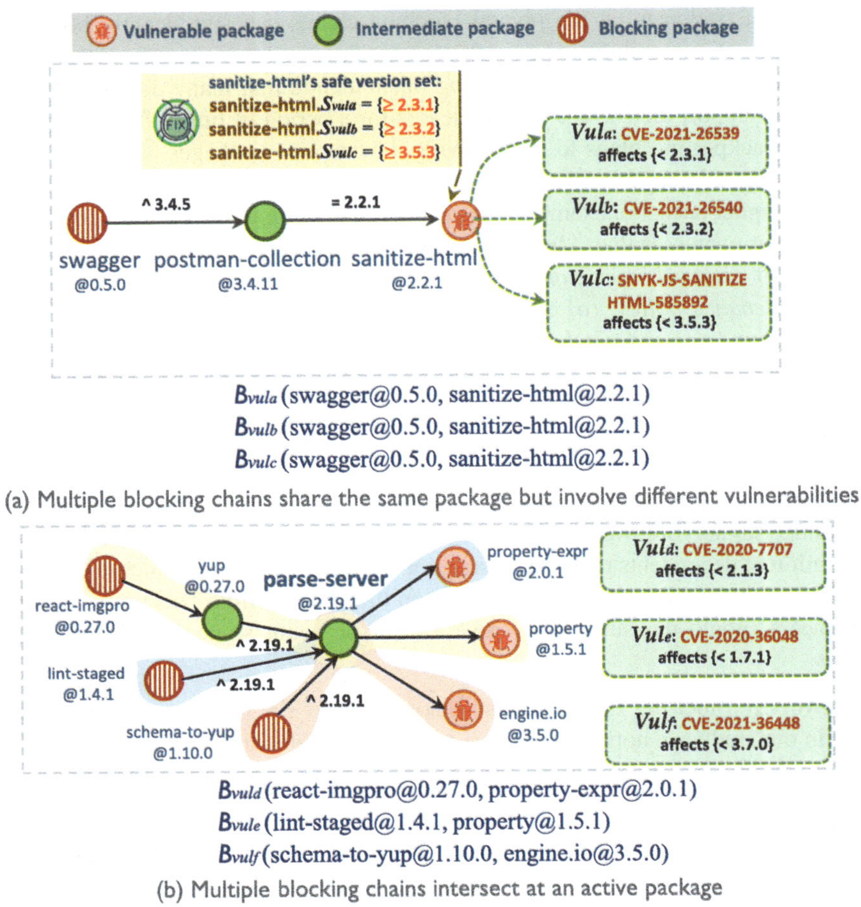

Fig. 8.15 Illustrative examples of noteworthy blocking chains

suggested `parse-server` to publish a version 2.19.* (2.19.* could be referenced by all the three blocking packages), in which it upgraded three dependencies `property-expr`, `property`, and `engine.io` to the corresponding safe versions. Encouragingly, `parse-server`'s backporting remediated the three blocking chains together, allowing three vulnerability fixes to be propagated into 283 root projects via 457 dependency paths.

Responsibility for Remediating Pivotal Blocking Chains After deriving remediation strategies for pivotal blocking chains, *Plumber* sends alert notifications to the issue trackers of certain packages that are feasible to update dependencies. The customized issue reports with applicable solutions can arouse developers' awareness of mitigating lags in vulnerability fix propagation. In our evaluation, package developers' feedback indicates the effectiveness of our notification mechanism. However, the remediation reports only reflect the authors' personal views rather than the organizational position. To build a long-term healthy ecosystem, *Plumber*'s vision is to continuously report the identified pivotal blocking chains together with remediation strategies to the large-scale reporting entities such as CERT (**C**omputer **E**mergency **R**esponse **T**eam).[3] According to our validated remediation reports, the entities can alert relevant organizations or package vendors to perform the dependency updates within a guaranteed time frame, on behalf of the open-source community. Achieving acknowledgement by the large-scale reporting entities is the direction for our future efforts.

***Plumber*'s Generality Beyond the npm Ecosystem** Our methodology can be generalized to other programming language ecosystems if two conditions below are satisfied:

- It is feasible to collect and model the metadata of package dependency relationships and vulnerabilities in the ecosystem, which enables *Plumber* to continuously monitor their evolution and identify blocking chains.
- The programming language ecosystem should resolve package dependencies using the similar semantic version syntax as *npm* (e.g., *PyPI* and *Cargo*). The version range syntax allows flexibility, which enables projects to automatically deploy the new versions of their required packages that satisfy the specified version range (the highest available version installation rule). In this manner, *Plumber* can boost the propagation of vulnerability fixes via open constraints if the new remediated package versions are released.

8.6 Threats to Validity

Following the structure provided by Wohlin et al. [60], we discuss the main threats to validity of our research.

Threats to External Validity The main external threat is the generality of our results to other ecosystems. In this study, we made all observations on *npm* packages. However, our analysis is applicable to other ecosystems that have similar package management systems, e.g., *PyPI* for Python and *NuGet* for the .NET. Additionally, as packages evolve over time, our experiment results are limited to the time period (August 1, 2020–August 1, 2021) when we conducted those experiments. Therefore, the findings may not generalize well to all the projects. In the future, we would like to include more projects and involve various programming languages into our empirical study, so that our findings would be more representative.

[3] A Computer Emergency Response Team (CERT) is a group of information security experts responsible for the protection against, detection, of and response to an organization's cybersecurity incidents.

Threats to Internal Validity Threats to internal validity concern the external factors not considered in our study. The vulnerability dataset used for our case study may not cover all known vulnerabilities. To reduce the threat, we crawl vulnerability reports from three recognized vulnerability databases, i.e., *GitHub Advisory DB*, *Snyk Vulnerability DB*, and *NPM Security Advisories*, and filtered out the duplicated ones. The dataset covers 3,948 vulnerabilities, involving 2,289 vulnerable packages and 38,166 vulnerable package versions. Hence, this threat has minimal influence on our analysis results.

The second internal threat is the correctness and completeness of the remediation strategy taxonomy constructed by our manual inspection in RQ3. Our study involved much manual work. We understand that such a manual process is subject to errors. To reduce the threat, we followed an open coding procedure to inductively categorize the common remediation strategies.

8.7 Related Work

The work most related to our study falls into three categories: studies on *vulnerable dependencies*, *software ecosystems*, and *library package updates*. This section covers a comprehensive portion of prior work on these topics and reflects on how the work compares with ours.

Vulnerable Dependencies Several studies [1, 29, 30, 61–66] in the literature investigated vulnerabilities that come from dependencies. In approaches [29] and [30], researchers empirically studied the evolution and decay of vulnerabilities in source code and found that due to the software code reuse and third-party libraries, most vulnerabilities are recurring. Cox et al. introduced metrics to qualify the "dependency freshness" of software projects, to understand the relations between outdated dependencies and vulnerabilities based on industry benchmark. Their investigation results show the projects using outdated dependencies four times as likely to have security issues as opposed to the projects that were up-to-date. Studies [1, 61, 62] investigated millions of *npm* packages to analyze how and when these vulnerabilities were discovered and fixed and to what extent they affected other packages. Zimmermann [62] pointed out that a small proportion of individual vulnerable packages could impact large parts of the entire Ecosystem, whereas approaches [63–66] studied the evolution and impacts of vulnerable packages in specific communities, including Firefox, Docker Images, Apache HTTP Server and Tomcat, and Proprietary Systems. They reported their findings and provided guidelines for software maintainers and tool developers to improve the process of dealing with security issues.

Recent studies [53–56] were proposed to reduce the false alarms for reporting vulnerable dependencies. Since CVE reports are used to share information about software vulnerabilities and provide a baseline for security measures, their correctness is crucial for detecting and patching software vulnerabilities. Woo et al. [53] proposed a precise mechanism *V0Finder* for discovering the correct origin of publicly reported software vulnerabilities, which can enhance the credibility of information provided by the CVEs. Pashchenko et al. [20, 67] presented precise methodologies for counting actually vulnerable dependencies, which combined the code-based analysis of patches with information on build, test, and update dates. Afterward, the evaluation on 25,767 Java libraries shows that the proposed methodology can reduce the number of false alerts for vulnerable dependencies. Zapata et al. [54] assessed the security risks of having vulnerabilities in dependent libraries by analyzing call graphs of the vulnerable functions. They manually validated 60 projects that depend on vulnerabilities and found that 73.3% of them were actually safe because they did not make use of the vulnerable functionality of their dependencies. In approaches [55, 56], Ponta et al. provided a fine-grained assessment approach using static and dynamic analysis to determine whether the located vulnerable code would be reachable.

Since vulnerabilities can easily be propagated through code clones, the vulnerable code clones are increasing in conjunction with the open-source software, potentially contaminating many projects [68, 69]. Approaches [70, 71] are proposed to efficiently and accurately detect vulnerable code clones in large software projects. Kim et al. [70] developed a scalable tool *Vuddy*, leveraging function-level granularity and a length-filtering technique to reduce the number of signature comparisons. Such an efficient design enables *Vuddy* to preprocess a billion lines of code in 14 hour and 17 minutes, after which it requires a few seconds to identify code clones. Besides, they also presented a security-aware abstraction technique, which extends the scope of *Vuddy* to identify variants of known vulnerabilities with high accuracy. The evaluation results demonstrated its effectiveness in detecting 0-day vulnerabilities in widely used software projects. Jiang et al. [71] proposed a scalable binary code clone detection framework *QuickBCC* for vulnerability scanning. The framework was built on the idea of extracting semantics from vulnerable binaries both before and after security patches and comparing them to target binaries. In order to improve performance, they created a signature based on the changes between the pre- and post-patched binaries and implemented a filtering process when comparing the signatures to the target binaries. *QuickBCC* outperformed other approaches in terms of performance when detecting well-known vulnerabilities with acceptable level of accuracy.

The study most relevant to our work is done by Chinthanet et al. [19]. The researchers conducted an empirical investigation to identify lags that may occur between client project-side fixing releases and package-side fixing releases. Through a preliminary study on 231 package-side fixing releases, they observed that nearly 85.72% of them bundled commits that were unrelated to a vulnerability fix. Even if the package-side fixing release was quick, the stale clients require additional efforts to introduce the fixes. This work lays the groundwork for mitigating propagation lags in an ecosystem. Compared with all the work mentioned above, our study is different in terms of the research scope and study method. In this chapter, we introduced the concepts of blocking packages and blocking chains and focused on how to remediate them for facilitating the propagation of vulnerability fixes. In addition to a thorough empirical study to characterize the blocking chains, we also propose a technique to automatically monitor and generate remediation strategies for pivotal packages.

Software Ecosystems Software ecosystem research has been rapidly growing in the past years. Several studies compared different ecosystems. Decan et al. [72, 73] conducted a quantitative empirical analysis of the similarities and differences between the evolution of package dependency networks for seven package ecosystems: *Cargo* for Rust, *CPAN* for Perl, *CRAN* for R, *npm* for JavaScript, *NuGet* for the .NET, *Packagist* for PHP, and *RubyGems* for Ruby. They introduced novel metrics to capture the growth, changeability, reusability, and fragility of these dependency networks and use these metrics to analyze and compare their evolution. Approaches [74–76] pointed out the fragility of software ecosystems and gave insights on the challenges software developers face. They examined the *Eclipse*, *CPAN*, and *npm* ecosystems, focusing on what practices cause API breakages. They found that developers in fact struggle with dependency updates, even if their projects were affected by vulnerable packages.

Approaches [77–81] specifically focused on the *npm* ecosystem. In work [77, 78], researchers conducted empirical investigations with millions of *npm* packages to understand (i) the widespread phenomena of micro-packages, (ii) the size of dependencies inherited by a micro-package, and (iii) the costs (i.e., fetch, install, and load times) of using a micro-package. Kula et al. [77] suggested developers to be aware of how sensitive their third-party dependencies were to critical changes in the software ecosystem. Abdalkareem et al. [78] suggested that *npm* developers should be careful about the selection of packages and how to keep them updated. Jafari et al. [79] defined a set of dependency management issues (i.e., dependency smells) in the *npm* ecosystem. They then conducted surveys with practitioners, to identify and quantify seven dependency smells with varying degrees of popularity and investigate why smells are introduced. Wittern et al. [80] investigated the evolution of *npm* using metrics such as dependencies between packages, download count, and usage count in JavaScript applications. Their findings helped understand the evolution of *npm*, design better package recommendation engines, and can help developers understand how their packages are being used. Liu et al. [81] proposed a knowledge graph-based dependency resolution, which resolved the inner dependency relations of dependency trees, and investigated the security threats from vulnerabilities in dependency trees at a large scale. To the best of our knowledge, our work is the first attempt to diagnose and monitor the lags in propagation of vulnerability fixes in the *npm* ecosystem.

8.8 Conclusion and Future Work

In this chapter, we empirically studied the scale of packages that block the propagation of vulnerability fixes in *npm* ecosystem. By digging into the evolution history of blocking chains, we characterize their common remediation patterns, which can shed light on mitigating fix propagation lags. We refined our empirical findings into a technique, to derive effective remediation strategies for pivotal packages. The evaluation demonstrated the effectiveness of our efforts as a tool implementation *Plumber* in boosting the propagation of vulnerability fixes in the ecosystem.

In the future, we plan to improve the performance of *Plumber* in four aspects: (1) *Identifying unexploitable vulnerabilities.* To effectively reduce the false alerts, *Plumber* should integrate more precise program analysis techniques in order to identify the vulnerable dependencies that could not be exploited. (2) *Compatibility analysis.* To avoid inducing incompatibility issues, *Plumber* should identify proper safe versions of packages without API breaking changes, when deriving remediation strategies. (3) *Correcting vulnerability information.* Since the vulnerability database may provide inexact information (e.g., affected versions of vulnerable package), *Plumber* should gather and model metadata from other ecosystems that resolve dependencies using a semantic versioning syntax similar to npm (such as PyPI and Cargo) to extend our technique to other programming language communities. (4) *Generalizing Plumber to other ecosystems. Plumber* should gather and model metadata from other ecosystems that resolve dependencies using a semantic versioning syntax similar to *npm* (such as *PyPI* and *Cargo*) to extend our technique to other programming language communities.

References

1. Decan A, Mens T, Constantinou E. On the impact of security vulnerabilities in the npm package dependency network. In: Proceedings of the 15th international conference on mining software repositories (MSR). 2018. p. 181–191.
2. Sun X, Zhou T, Wang R, Duan Y, Bo L, Chang J. Experience report: Investigating bug fixes in machine learning frameworks/libraries. Front Comp Sci. 2021; 15(6):1–16.
3. Hu J, Huang L, Sun T, Fan Y, Hu W, Zhong H. Proactive planning of bandwidth resource using simulation-based what-if predictions for web services in the cloud. Front Comp Sci. 2021; 15(1):1–28.
4. CVE-2021-28918. 2021. https://nvd.nist.gov/vuln/detail/CVE-2021-28918. Accessed: 2021-08-01.
5. npm Audit. 2021. https://docs.npmjs.com/cli/v6/commands/npmaudit. Accessed: 2021-08-0.
6. Dependabot. 2021. https://dependabot.com/. Accessed: 2021-08-01.
7. Decan A, Mens T, Zerouali A, De Roover C. Back to the past–analysing backporting practices in package dependency networks. IEEE Trans Softw Eng. 2021; 48(10):4087–99
8. Mqtt.js#1306. 2021. https://github.com/mqttjs/MQTT.js/issues/1306. Accessed: 2021-08-01.
9. Tensorflow/tfjs. 2021. https://github.com/tensorflow/tfjs. Accessed: 2021-08-01.
10. Ethers.js. 2021. https://github.com/ethers-io/ethers.js. Accessed: 2021-08-01
11. GoogleChrome/workbox. 2021. https://github.com/GoogleChrome/workbox. Accessed: 2021-08-01.
12. GitHub Advisory DB. 2021. https://github.com/advisories. Accessed: 2021-08-01.
13. Snyk Vulnerability DB. 2021. https://snyk.io/vuln/. Accessed: 2021-08-01.
14. Npm Security Advisories. 2021. https://github.com/npm/npm/security/advisories. Accessed: 2021-08-01.

15. CVSS Score. 2021. https://www.first.org/cvss/. Accessed: 2021-08-01.
16. node-semver. 2021. https://github.com/npm/node-semver. Accessed: 2021-08-01.
17. Ethers.js#1439. 2021. https://github.com/ethers-io/ethers.js/issues/1439. Accessed: 2021-08-01.
18. npm Public Registry. 2021. https://docs.npmjs.com/cli/v7/usingnpm/registry. Accessed: 2021-08-01.
19. Chinthanet B, Kula RG, McIntosh S, Ishio T, Ihara A, Matsumoto K. Lags in the release, adoption, and propagation of NPM vulnerability fixes. Empir Softw Eng. 2021; 26(3):1–28.
20. Pashchenko I, Plate H, Ponta E, Sabetta A, Massacci F. Vuln4real: A methodology for counting actually vulnerable dependencies. IEEE Trans Softw Eng. 2020; 48:1592–1609.
21. McHugh ML. Interrater reliability: The kappa statistic. Biochem Med. 2012; 22(3). p. 276–282.
22. Truffle#1147. 2021. https://github.com/trufflesuite/truffle/issues/1147. Accessed: 2021-08-01.
23. Swap-core. 2021. https://github.com/pancakeswap/pancake-swap-core. Accessed: 2021-08-01.
24. semver. 2021. https://github.com/advisories. Accessed: 2021-08-01.
25. Chen Z, Cao Y, Liu Y, Wang H, Xie T, Liu X. A Comprehensive study on challenges in deploying deep learning based software. In: Proceedings of the 28th ACM Joint Meeting on European software engineering conference and symposium on the foundations of software engineering (ESEC/FSE). 2020. p. 750–762.
26. Humbatova N, Jahangirova G, Bavota G, Riccio V, Stocco A, Tonella P. Taxonomy of real faults in deep learning systems. In: Proceedings of the ACM/IEEE 42nd international conference on software engineering (ICSE). 2020. p. 1110–1121.
27. Creswell JW, Qualitative inquiry and research design: Choosing among five approaches. 3rd ed. New York: SAGE Publications, Inc. 2013.
28. Bogart C, Kästner C, Herbsleb J, Thung F. When and how to make breaking changes: Policies and practices in 18 open source software ecosystems. ACM Trans Softw Eng Methodol (TOSEM). 2021; 30(4):1–56.
29. Di Penta M, Cerulo L, Aversano L. The life and death of statically detected vulnerabilities: An empirical study. Inf. Softw. Technol. 2009; 51(10):1469–1484.
30. Pham NH, Nguyen TT, Nguyen HA, Nguyen TN. Detection of recurring software vulnerabilities. In: Proceedings of the IEEE/ACM International Conference on Automated Software Engineering (ASE). 2010. p. 447–456.
31. Kula RG, German DM, Ouni A, Ishio T, Inoue K. Do developers update their library dependencies?. Empir Softw Eng. 2018; 23(1):384–417.
32. Mirhosseini S, Parnin C. Can automated pull requests encourage software developers to upgrade out-of-date dependencies?. In: 2017 32nd IEEE/ACM International Conference on Automated Software Engineering (ASE). 2017. New York: IEEE. p. 84–94
33. Dietrich J, Pearce D, Stringer J, Tahir A, Blincoe K. Dependency Versioning in the Wild. In: 2019 IEEE/ACM 16th International Conference on Mining Software Repositories (MSR). 2019. New York: IEEE. p. 349–359.
34. Raemaekers S, van Deursen A, Visser J. Semantic versioning and impact of breaking changes in the maven repository. J Syst Softw. 2017; 129:140–158.
35. He H, He R, Gu H, Zhou M. A large-scale empirical study on Java library migrations: Prevalence, Trends, and Rationales. In: Proceedings of the 29th ACM Joint Meeting on European Software Engineering Conference and Symposium on the Foundations of Software Engineering (ESEC/FSE). 2021. p. 478–490.
36. CVE-2021-23624. 2021. https://security.snyk.io/vuln/SNYK-JSDOTTY-1577292. Accessed: 2021-08-01.

37. CVE-2021-25912. 2021. https://security.snyk.io/vuln/SNYK-JSDOTTY-1069933. Accessed: 2021-08-01.
38. Meteorite#299. 2021. https://github.com/oortcloud/meteorite/issues/299. Accessed: 2021-08-01.
39. React-reality#1. 2021. https://github.com/rhdeck/react-reality/issues/1. Accessed: 2021-08-01.
40. Configtest. 2021. https://github.com/codeconsole/configtest. Accessed: 2021-08-01.
41. Mapbox#7. 2021. https://github.com/mapbox/github-release-tools/issues/7. Accessed: 2021-08-01.
42. Opac#1034. 2021. https://github.com/scieloorg/opac/issues/1034. Accessed: 2021-08-01.
43. Googleapis. 2021. https://github.com/googleapis/googleapis. Accessed: 2021-08-01.
44. Google-gax. 2021. https://github.com/googleapis/gax-nodejs. Accessed: 2021-08-01.
45. Google-cloud/storage. 2021. https://github.com/googleapis/nodejs-storage. Accessed: 2021-08-01.
46. Microsoft/just. 2021. https://github.com/microsoft/just. Accessed: 2021
47. Node-sqlite3#1493. 2021. https://github.com/mapbox/nodesqlite3/issues/1493. Accessed: 2021-08-01.
48. Peer-id#153. 2021. https://github.com/libp2p/js-peer-id/issues/153. Accessed: 2021-08-01.
49. Image-cropper#42. 2021. https://github.com/likeconan/reactavatar-image-cropper/issues/42.
50. Commit#8616b1 in learn-webpack. 2021. https://github.com/AlNuN/learn-webpack/commit/837c45edfadbac033fa7f1cb88eb420d098616b1. Accessed: 2021-08-01.
51. Xml-crypto#231. 2021. https://github.com/yaronn/xml-crypto/issues/231. Accessed: 2021-08-01.
52. Meow#195. 2021. https://github.com/sindresorhus/meow/issues/195. Accessed: 2021-08-01.
53. Woo S, Lee D, Park S, Lee H, Dietrich S. V0Finder: Discovering the correct origin of publicly reported software vulnerabilities. In: 30th USENIX Security Symposium (USENIX Security). 2021. p. 3041–3058.
54. Zapata RE, Kula RG, Chinthanet B, Ishio T, Matsumoto K, Ihara A. Towards smoother library migrations: A look at vulnerable dependency migrations at function level for npm JavaScript Packages. In: International Conference on Software Maintenance and Evolution (ICSME). 2018. p. 559–563.
55. Plate H, Ponta SE, Sabetta A. Impact Assessment for Vulnerabilities in Open-source Software Libraries. In: 2015 IEEE International Conference on Software Maintenance and Evolution (ICSME). 2015. New York: IEEE. p. 411–420.
56. Ponta SE, Plate H, Sabetta A. Beyond Metadata: Codecentric and Usage-based Analysis of Known Vulnerabilities in Open-source Software. In: 2018 IEEE International Conference on Software Maintenance and Evolution (ICSME). 2018. New York: IEEE. p. 449–460.
57. Angular-cli#21608. 2021. https://github.com/angular/angular-cli/issues/21608. Accessed: 2021-08-01.
58. Xml-crypto#1215. 2021. https://github.com/postmanlabs/postmancollection/issues/1215. Accessed: 2021
59. Cssnano#7491. 2021. https://github.com/parse-community/parseserver/issues/7491. Accessed: 2021-08-01.
60. Basili VR, Selby RW, Hutchens DH. Experimentation in Software Engineering. IEEE Trans Softw Eng. 1986; 7:733–743.
61. Duan R, Bijlani A, Xu M, Kim T, Lee W. Identifying Open-source License Violation and 1-day Security Risk at Large Scale. In: Proceedings of the 2017 ACM SIGSAC Conference on Computer and Communications Security. 2017. p. 2169–2185.
62. Zimmermann M, Staicu C-A, Tenny C, Pradel M. Small world with high risks: A Study of Security Threats in the npm Ecosystem. In: 28th USENIX Security Symposium (USENIX Security). 2019. p. 995–1010.
63. Massacci F, Neuhaus S, Nguyen VH. After-life Vulnerabilities: A study on firefox evolution, its vulnerabilities, and fixes. In: International Symposium on Engineering Secure Software and Systems. 2011. Berlin: Springer. p. 195–208.

64. Zerouali A, Cosentino V, Mens T, Robles G, GonzalezBarahona JM. On the impact of outdated and vulnerable JavaScript Packages in Docker Images. In: 2019 IEEE 26th International Conference on Software Analysis, Evolution and Reengineering (SANER). 2019. New York: IEEE. p. 619–623.
65. Piantadosi V, Scalabrino S, Oliveto R. Fixing of security vulnerabilities in open source projects: A Case Study of Apache Http Server and Spache Tomcat. In: 2019 12th IEEE Conference on software testing, validation and verification (ICST). 2019. New York: IEEE. p. 68–78.
66. Cadariu M, Bouwers E, Visser J, van Deursen A. Tracking known security vulnerabilities in proprietary software systems. In: 2015 IEEE 22nd International Conference on Software Analysis, Evolution, and Reengineering (SANER). 2015. New York: IEEE. p. 516–519.
67. Pashchenko I, Plate H, Ponta SE, Sabetta A, Massacci F. Vulnerable open source dependencies: Counting those that matter. In: Proceedings of the 12th ACM/IEEE International Symposium on Empirical Software Engineering and Measurement (ESEM). 2018. p. 1–10.
68. Cai W, He F, Lv X, Cheng Y. A semi-transparent selective undo algorithm for multi-user collaborative editors. Front Comp Sci. 2021; 15(5):1–17.
69. Khoshnevis S. A search-based identification of variable microservices for enterprise SaaS. Front Comp Sci. 2023; 17(3):1–16.
70. Kim S, Woo S, Lee H, Vuddy OH. A scalable approach for vulnerable code clone discovery. In: 2017 IEEE Symposium on Security and Privacy (S&P). 2017. New York: IEEE. p. 595–614.
71. Jang H, Yang K, Lee G, Na Y, Seideman JD, Luo S, Lee H, Dietrich S. QuickBCC: Quick and scalable binary vulnerable code clone detection. In: IFIP international conference on ICT systems security and privacy protection. 2021. Berlin: Springer, p. 66–82.
72. Decan A, Mens T, Grosjean P. An Empirical Comparison of Dependency Network Evolution in Seven Software Packaging Ecosystems. Empir Softw Eng. 2019; 24(1):381–416.
73. Decan A, Mens T, Claes M. An empirical comparison of dependency issues in OSS Packaging Ecosystems. In: 2017 IEEE 24th International Conference on Software Analysis, Evolution and Reengineering (SANER). 2017. New York: IEEE. p. 2–12.
74. Bogart C, Kästner C, Herbsleb J. When it breaks, it breaks: How ecosystem developers reason about the stability of dependencies. In: 2015 30th IEEE/ACM International Conference on Automated Software Engineering Workshop (ASEW). 2015. New York: IEEE. p. 86–89.
75. Bogart C, Kästner C, Herbsleb J, Thung F. How to Break an API: Cost negotiation and community values in three software ecosystems. In: Proceedings of the 2016 24th ACM SIGSOFT International Symposium on Foundations of Software Engineering. 2016. p. 109–120.
76. Xu C, Qin Y, Yu P, Cao C, Lv J. Theories and techniques for growing software: Paradigm and beyond. SCIENTIA SINICA Inform. 2020. 50:1595–1611.
77. Kula RG, Ouni A, German DM, Inoue K. On the impact of micro-packages: An empirical study of the npm JavaScript Ecosystem. 2017. arXiv preprint arXiv:1709.04638.
78. Abdalkareem R, Nourry O, Wehaibi S, Mujahid S, Shihab E. Why Do Developers Use Trivial Packages? An Empirical Case Study on npm. In: Proceedings of the 2017 11th joint meeting on Foundations of Software Engineering. 2017. p. 385–395.
79. Jafari AJ, Costa DE, Abdalkareem R, Shihab E, Tsantalis N. Dependency Smells in JavaScript Projects. IEEE Trans Softw Eng. 2021; 48(10):3790–3807.
80. Wittern E, Suter P, Rajagopalan S. A look at the dynamics of the JavaScript Package Ecosystem. In: Proceedings of the 13th International Conference on Mining Software Repositories (MSR). 2016. p. 351–361.
81. Liu C, Chen S, Fan L, Chen B, Liu Y, Peng X. Demystifying the vulnerability propagation and its evolution via dependency trees in the NPM ecosystem. In: 44th International Conference on Software Engineering (ICSE). 2022.

Part V
Tools and Datasets

Chapter 9
"League of Legends" Toolkit

Abstract In this chapter, we provide a toolkit named "***League of Legends***" including five available tools to combat dependency issues in multiple ecosystems: *Piecer* (for machine learning pipelines/libraries), *NuFix* (for .NET), *Slimming* (for Java), *Insight* (across Java/Python to C/C++ ecosystems), and *Plumber* (for Node.js). We also provide datasets of library dependency metadata and vulnerability metadata to facilitate future research.

9.1 *Piecer*: Detecting Compatibility Issues for Machine Learning Libraries

9.1.1 Tool Description

A **M**achine **L**earning (ML) pipeline configures the workflow of a learning task using the APIs provided by ML libraries. However, a pipeline's performance can vary significantly across different configurations of ML library versions. Compatibility issues of ML libraries can cause significantly inconsistent performance upon changes in the versions of its configured libraries or the combination of these libraries. As a result, pipelines exhibit inferior performance, such as inefficient *executions*, *numeric errors*, and even *crashes*. To expose compatibility issues of ML libraries, we develop *Piecer* (***https://piecer-plc.github.io/***), an infrastructure that automatically generates a set of pipeline variants by varying different version combinations of ML libraries and detects their performance inconsistencies. Its main features are (1) constructing a ML library version pool for a given ML pipeline, (2) generating pipeline variants with different library version combinations, (3) analyzing performance changes among different library version combinations, and (4) constructing a repository of defective APIs, which can help capture the compatibility issues in real-world ML pipelines and ML libraries.

Y. Wang et al., *Managing Software Supply Chains*,
https://doi.org/10.1007/978-981-96-1797-5_9

9.1.2 How Does Piecer Work?

Piecer can scale up the impact analysis of possible ML library version combinations on pipelines' performances. It takes the ML pipelines as inputs and outputs the defective library version combinations with concerned APIs. In addition, with the aid of a repository of defective APIs, *Piecer* can help practitioners detect the compatibility issues in real-world ML pipelines and ML libraries.

Figure 9.1 gives the overall architecture of *Piecer*. It mainly includes three components:

Component 1: Constructing ML Library Version Pool For a given ML pipeline, *Piecer* constructs a dependency pool $Dp = \{V_{Lib_1}, V_{Lib_2}, \cdots, V_{Lib_n}\}$ to collect all the installable version candidates $V_{Lib_i} = \{v_1, v_2, \cdots, v_m\}$ of referenced ML libraries Lib_i. To achieve this, it first parses the pipeline's dependency management script (*Requirement.txt*, *Setup.py*, or *METADATA*) to identify all the versions of direct dependencies that satisfy the specified version constraints. For each version of direct dependency, it iteratively collects the version constraints of the required transitive dependencies. If a library Lib_i corresponds to multiple version constraints, *Piecer* considers their intersection as installable version candidates V_{Lib_i}. In the cases where a library Lib_i is specified with incompatible version constraints, we remove the versions of direct dependencies that induce such dependency conflicts (DCs) from Dp.

Component 2: Generating Pipeline Variants with Different ML Library Version Combinations To explore the impacts of library versions on a pipeline's performance, *Piecer* generates a set of pipeline variants with different version combinations of ML libraries selected from our dependency pool Dp. For a given ML pipeline, it considers the newest versions of referenced ML libraries as ***a version combination baseline.*** By defining a series of comparison rules, *Piecer* generates a set of ML library version combinations by varying the versions of concerned libraries and keeping the remaining library versions be consistent with the baseline.

According to the dependency resolution rules of Python build tool *pip*, it installs the newest library versions from PyPI central repository that satisfies the corresponding version constraint. To enable the installation of an expected version combination of ML libraries, *Piecer* customizes the dependency resolution rules of *pip* to select our specified library version candidates (satisfying the corresponding version constraints) from our dependency pool Dp.

Component 3: Analyzing Performance Inconsistencies For each ML pipeline, *Piecer* runs the baseline and all the variants to check their performance inconsistencies across various library version combinations. It focuses on three aspects of performance inconsistencies: *execution time*, *memory usage*, and *evaluation metrics* (e.g., *Precision* and *Recall*). Let a 3-tuple $D =< A, LV, P >$ be a defective API (combination) whose invocation(s) potentially trigger PLC issues, where A denotes the signature(s) of API (combination), LV denotes the defective

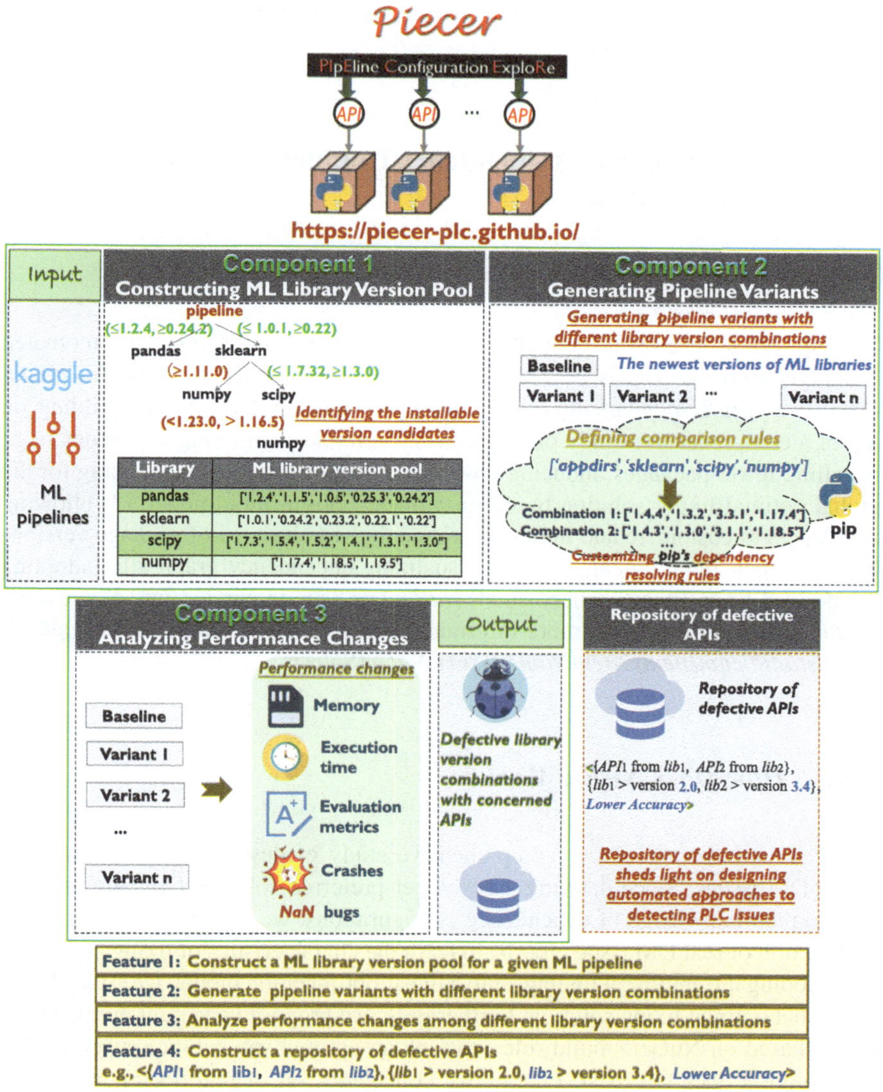

Fig. 9.1 Architecture of *Piecer*

library version range, and P denotes the aspects of performance changes (e.g., execution time, memory usage, and *Precision*). For example, $<$ {**Nltk**.$stem.porter.PorterStemmer()$, **Catboost**.$CatBoostClassifier()$}, {**Catboost** $=$ 1.0.3, **Nltk** $=$ 3.5}, $Executiontime$ $>$ denotes an API combination of **Nltk**.$stem.porter.PorterStemmer()$ and **Catboost**.$CatBoostClassifier()$ in libraries *Catboost* 1.0.3 and *Nltk* 3.5, respectively, which achieves worse performance in execution time. Leveraging the defective API repository, *Piecer* can capture the potential compatibility issues in real-world ML pipelines and ML libraries.

A video demo is available at ***https://youtu.be/cmt8_Jz0FJk***, which better illustrates how to use our *Piecer*.

9.2 *NuFix*: Repairing Dependency Conflict Issues in the .NET Ecosystem

9.2.1 Tool Description

To help .NET developers combat DC issues, we develop *NuFix*, an automated technique to repair DC issues. *NuFix* is implemented as a Visual Studio plugin (***http://www.nufix-dependency-maze.com/***). Its main features are (1) building on top of a comprehensive study of developers' preferences in fixing DC issues (e.g., installing fewer packages, inducing fewer risky build warnings), (2) seeking for the global optimal fixing solution based on a linear optimization model, (3) allowing developers to customize and iteratively refine the search scope of package versions based on their requirements, and (4) visualizing dependency graph after adopting the derived fixes. Since January 2024, *NuFix* has been integrated into Microsoft's *Visual Studio* platform. For more information, please refer to ***https://marketplace.visualstudio.com/items?itemName=vsext.NuGetSolver***.

9.2.2 How Does NuFix Work?

NuFix is built on top of our comprehensive study of developers' preferences in fixing DM issues. Since deriving a developer preferred solution typically requires rich domain knowledge of dependency configurations, we first empirically studied a collection of real DM issue reports, to learn the characteristics of fixing strategies. By encoding the empirical findings into a linear optimization model, *NuFix* seeks for the global optimal fixing solution. Furthermore, we proposed a variant optimization model based on NuGet's build rules, to seek an optimal sub-solution when a fully safe solution does not exist. Finally, we collected a set of real documented fixes of DM issues by .NET developers as a training dataset to learn the role played by each preference in determining a solution The core idea of *NuFix* is to formulate this task as a binary integer linear programming model, and our key insights include (1) building the model upon our comprehensive study of developers' preferences in fixing DM issues and (2) learning from real documented fixes to tune model hyperparameters rigorously.

Figure 9.2 gives the overall architecture of *NuFix*. It takes three inputs and automatically outputs fixing patches for DC issues:

- ***Problematic dependency configuration file (i.e., *.csproj).*** It configures the client project's direct dependencies and the specified version constraints on them.

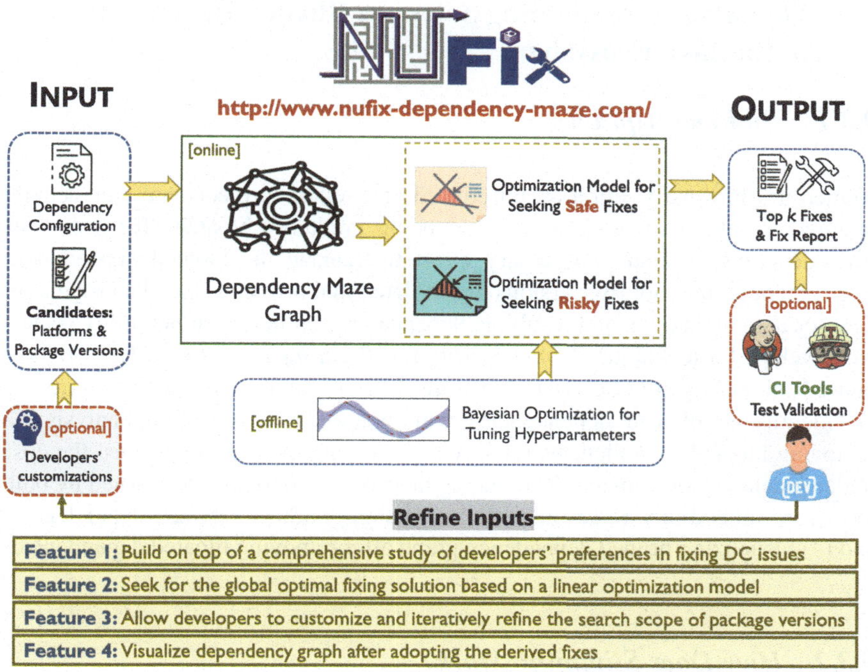

Fig. 9.2 Architecture of *NuFix*

- ***Candidate target .NET platforms.*** It is an ordered list of acceptable platforms, since one of our fixing strategies is to upgrade/migrate client project's target platform.
- ***Candidate range of direct dependencies' versions (developers' requirements) (optional).*** NuFix allows developers to customize their package upgrade requirements or the search scope of package versions to avoid inducing undesired program behaviors. For example, developers may want to specify the version of Lucene.Net to be limited within [3.0.3, 4.0.0), if they are already aware of the incompatible versions ($\geq$4.0.0) through experience. One alternative design is to only consider the package versions without introducing API breaking changes, but this is too strict: It is a common practice that developers may be willing to resolve the DC issues at an acceptable cost of adapting the API changes.

A video demo is available at ***https://youtu.be/52N4IPuOnxA***, which better illustrates how to use our *NuFix*.

9.3 *Slimming*: Streamlining Software Bloated Dependencies in the Java Ecosystem

9.3.1 Tool Description

Numerous third-party libraries introduced into client projects are not actually required, resulting in modern software being gradually bloated. To avoid software developers spend unnecessary effort to manage the bloated dependencies (e.g., keeping the library versions up-to-date, making sure that heterogeneous licenses are compatible, and resolving dependency conflict or vulnerability issues), we developed a technique, *Slimming* (***https://slimming-fat.github.io/***), to remove unused third-party libraries from software projects reliably. Its main features are (1) identifying bloated dependencies with precise Java reflection analysis, (2) removing bloated dependencies reliably by weighing the benefits against the costs of dependency management, (3) reducing the frequent false alarms warned by build tools for vulnerability issues and license/version conflicts between dependencies, and (4) visualizing pruned dependency graph after removing bloated dependencies.

9.3.2 How Does Slimming Work?

Figure 9.3 gives the overall architecture of *Slimming*. It takes the binary files of a Maven projects as inputs and generates the debloating solutions. It mainly includes two components:

Component 1: Static Reflection Analysis *Slimming* is empowered by effective static reflection analyses, which can precisely resolve (1) the reflections that are synthesized by dependency injections, annotations, and configurations in popular Java frameworks (e.g., *Java EE Servlets*, *Java Beans*, *Apache Struts*, *Spring*, *Spring Boot*, and *Tomcat*) and (2) nonconstant arguments of reflection APIs that are undergone a series of complex string manipulations. Leveraging static reflection analyses, *Slimming* captures all the bloated dependencies not actually used by the client projects.

Component 2: Bloated Dependency Analysis *Slimming* derives debloating solutions by making a trade-off between the benefits (e.g., removal of bloated dependencies can also resolve the issues of vulnerabilities/dependency conflicts/incompatible licenses/outdated dependencies) and the costs (e.g., potentially inducing more maintenance effort) of dependency management. According to the syntax rules of Maven dependency configurations, if the bloated dependencies are inherited from the parent module, *Slimming* removes them with the aid of *<provided>* tag of `POM.xml` file. Otherwise, *Slimming* performs debloating solutions using *<exclusion>* tag. *Slimming* triggers projects' bundled tests to validate whether the debloating solution will cause program errors. Our tool finally reports a collection

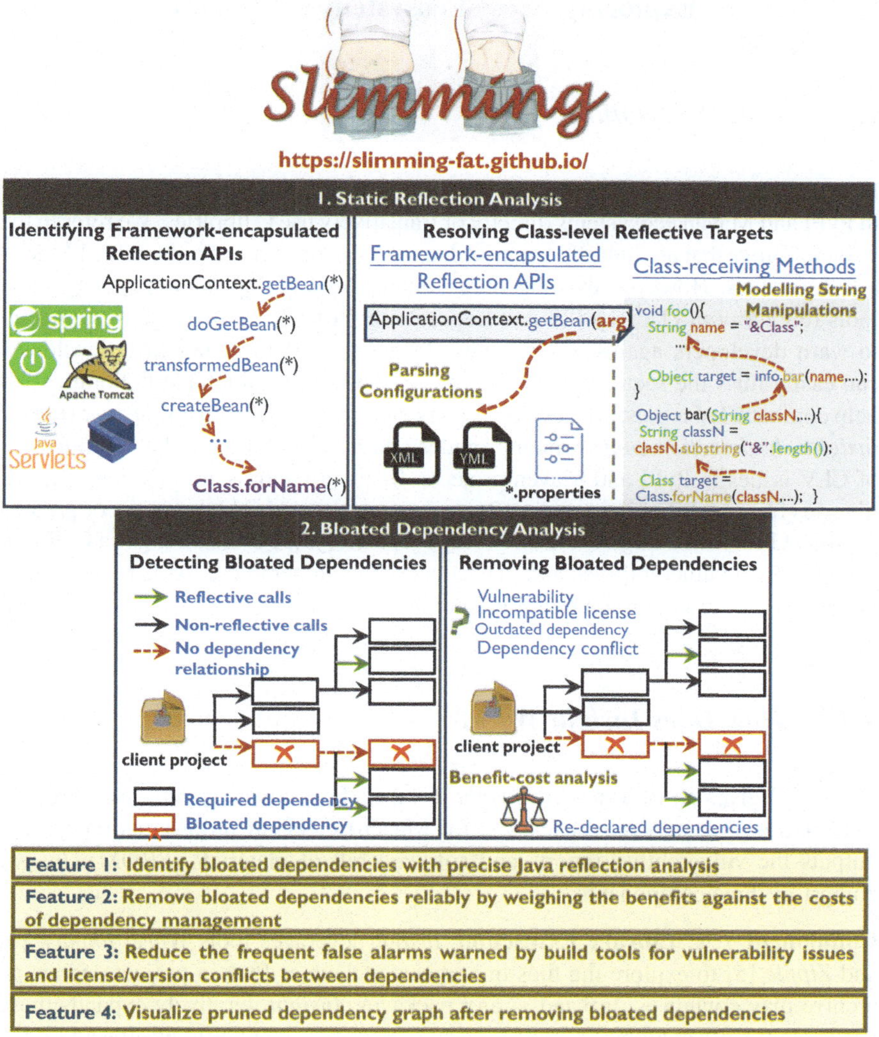

Fig. 9.3 Architecture of *Slimming*

of bloated dependencies and the corresponding debloating solution if all the tests are passed.

A video demo is available at ***https://youtu.be/wB6-f0dfaDY***, which better illustrates how to use our *Slimming*.

9.4 *Insight*: Exploring Cross Ecosystem Vulnerability Impacts

9.4.1 *Tool Description*

Previous investigation shows that, as of March 1, 2022, 46.7% and 32.1% of projects in PyPI and Maven ecosystems directly or transitively use C libraries. We refer to the vulnerabilities that are induced by cross-language invocations of vulnerable libraries as CLV issues. However, existing library managers and dependency management tools (e.g., `Maven` [1], `Pip` [2], and `DependencyBot` [3]) in these ecosystems fail to warn developers against CLV issues. As a result, Python and Java developers can easily miss the security risks induced by the use of vulnerable C libraries. To help combat CLV issues, we develop the first automated mechanism, *Insight* (***http://insight-clv-detection.com***), which provides a turn-key solution to the identification of CLV issues in PyPI and Maven projects. Its main features are (1) identifying C libraries from multilingual project, (2) tracing an extracted C library to its originated C project based on a large-scale knowledge repository, (3) determining if a C library can introduce vulnerabilities, and (4) deducing the vulnerable C-APIs by analyzing the usage of various foreign function interface.

9.4.2 *How Does Insight Work?*

Figure 7.3 gives an overview of *Insight*. It takes the archives (`*.whl` packages for PyPI and `*.Jar` or `*.aar` packages for Maven) of client projects as inputs and outputs the vulnerability reports and software bill of materials (SBOM). *Insight* comprises three components:

Component 1: C Library Extraction *Insight* leverages tools *Wheel unpack* [4] and *Zipfile* [5] to explore the files in archives of Java or Python projects. Since an archive may contain `*.Jar` and `*.aar` packages, *Insight* iteratively expands these packages for file exploration until no further packages can be found. Based on the C library naming rules, *Insight* uses the regex "`lib.+.so(.[0-9]+){0,3}`" to extract C libraries (e.g., *libcrypto.so.1.1*) from the explored files (Fig. 9.4).

Component 2: C Project Version Tracing To trace an extracted C library to its originated C project version, *Insight* constructs a large-scale knowledge repository indexing the main features inherent to C library versions published in three mainstream Linux distributions. Leveraging a recent tool *LibRARAIN* [6], *Insight* determines the project version of a given C library, by iteratively comparing it with the known version instances in our knowledge repository based on similarity matching.

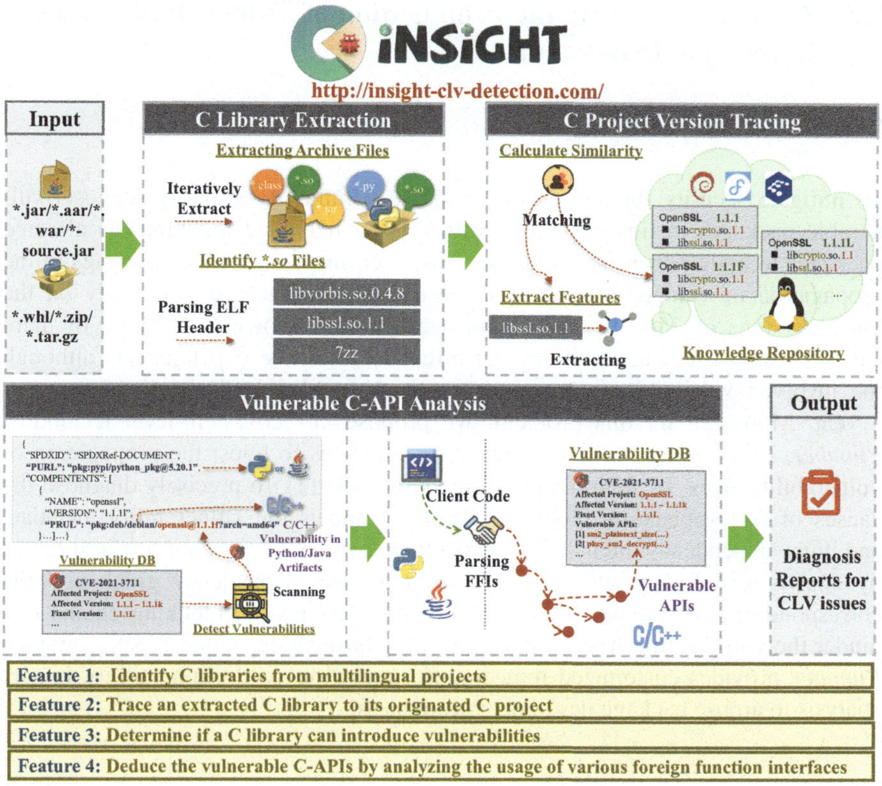

Fig. 9.4 Architecture of *Insight*

Component 3: Vulnerable C-API Analysis To boost automation, *Insight* collects the metadata of vulnerability reports directly from the official security advisory websites to construct a large-scale vulnerability database. *Insight* checks for each extracted C library whether its parent C project version contains vulnerabilities. Finally, based on the parsing patterns that we design for various types of FFIs, *Insight* performs cross-language program analysis to determine if the client project code can access the concerned vulnerable C-APIs.

A video demo is available at ***https://www.youtube.com/watch?v=CZfpa27QME0***, which better illustrates how to use our *Insight*.

9.5 *Plumber*: Boosting the Propagation of Vulnerability Fixes in the *npm* Ecosystem

9.5.1 Tool Description

To mitigate security threats, the open-source community strongly suggests vulnerable packages to timely publish vulnerability fixes and recommends affected packages to update their dependencies. However, there are still serious lags in the propagation of vulnerability fixes in the ecosystem. The previous study on the latest versions of 356,283 active *npm* packages has shown that 20.0% of them can still introduce vulnerabilities via direct or transitive dependencies although the involved vulnerable packages have already published fix versions for over a year. Motivated by this problem, we propose an ecosystem-level technique, *Plumber*, for deriving feasible remediation strategies to boost the propagation of vulnerability fixes. Its main features are as follows: (1) To precisely diagnose the causes of fix propagation blocking, *Plumber* models the vulnerability metadata and *npm* dependency metadata and continuously monitors their evolution, (2) by analyzing a full picture of the ecosystem-level dependency graph and the corresponding fix propagation statuses, it identifies pivotal blocking chains that hinder the vulnerability fixes from propagating through dependency paths, and (3) *Plumber* provides customized remediation suggestions with vulnerability impact analysis to arouse package developers' awareness.

9.5.2 How Does Plumber Work?

Figure 9.5 gives the overall architecture of *Plumber*. It takes the evolutionary information of *npm* ecosystem as input and generates remediation reports. *Plumber* comprises three components:

Component 1: Monitoring the Evolution of *npm* Ecosystem To precisely capture the propagation of vulnerability fixes in the whole ecosystem, *Plumber* continuously collects vulnerability metadata and dependency metadata among *npm* packages. By comparing two contiguous snapshots of *npm* dependency metadata, we can also mine the migration history of packages, in order to provide clues for deriving remediation strategies. *Plumber* weekly updates the metadata model to monitor the evolution of vulnerability and *npm* dependency metadata.

Component 2: Identifying Pivotal Blocking Chains. Based on the ecosystem-level dependency graph and the corresponding fix propagation statuses, *Plumber* identifies blocking chains that hinder the propagation of vulnerability fixes. *Plumber* ranks the identified blocking chains based on the number of vulnerable paths passing through them. The top ranking blocking chains are considered as pivotal ones should

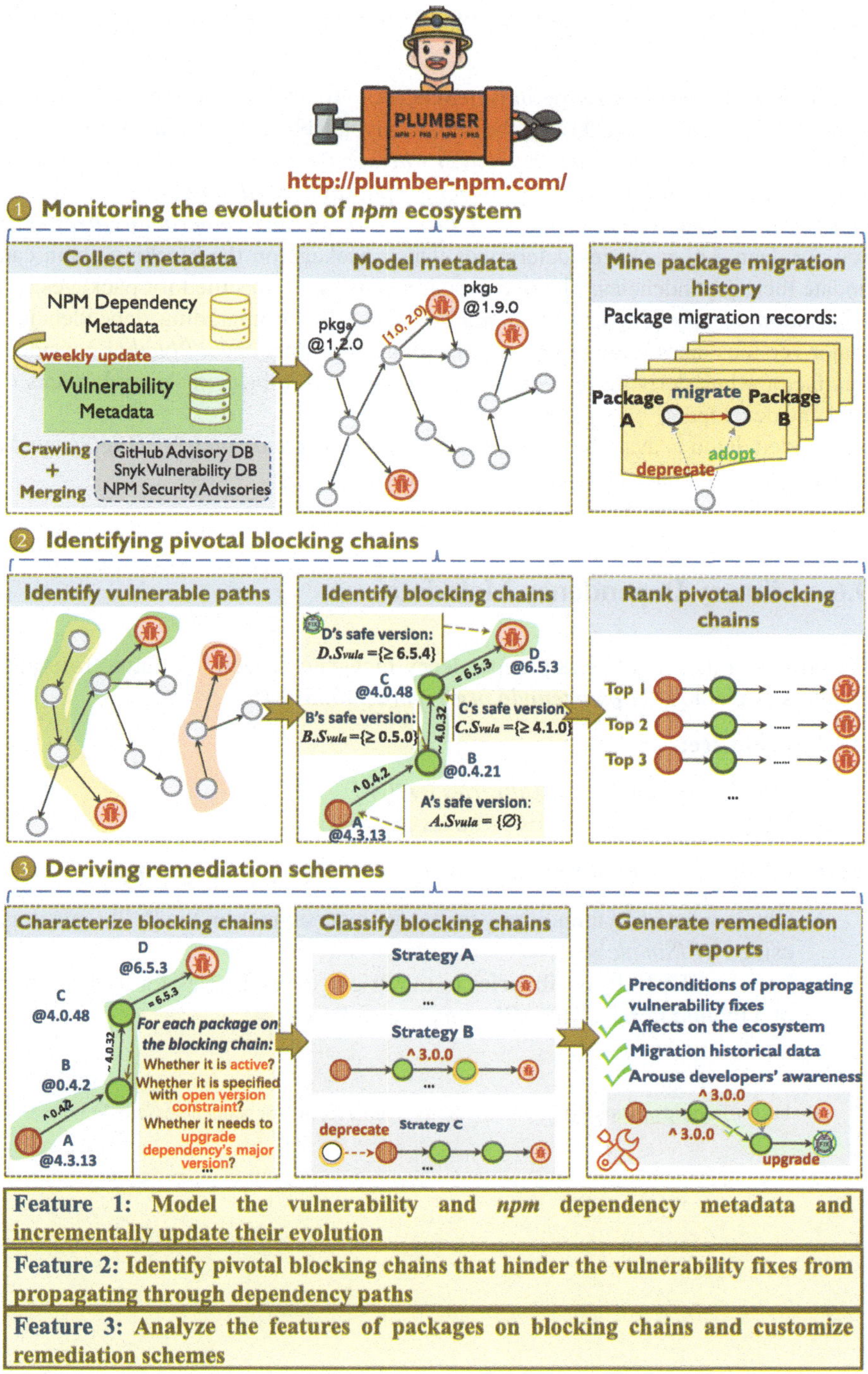

Fig. 9.5 Architecture of *Plumber*

be remediated to enable the propagation of vulnerability fixes into a large amount of packages.

Component 3: Deriving Remediation Schemes To facilitate deriving remediation schemes, *Plumber* characterizes the top K pivotal blocking chains according to (1) *whether the packages are active*, (2) *whether the packages are specified with open version constraints*, and (3) *whether the packages need to upgrade their direct dependencies' major versions to introduce the concerned vulnerability fixes*. The activity degree of packages determines which package on the blocking chain can update their dependencies. The open version constraints specified for packages can help automatically propagate vulnerability fixes. Since upgrading dependencies' major versions takes more efforts on changing and testing code, *Plumber* considers this factor when deriving remediation schemes to avoid bringing more burdens to package developers.

A video demo is available at ***https://www.youtube.com/watch?v=f19gi3wwjnA***, which better illustrates how to use our *Plumber*.

9.6 Library Dependency Metadata

We provide a dataset of library dependency metadata to facilitate future research, which is available at ***https://zenodo.org/records/13357741***.

(1) Data Source:

- PyPI Ecosystem: *https://libraries.io/PyPI*
- Maven Ecosystem: *https://libraries.io/Maven*

(2) Collection Method of Python Library Dependency Relationships:

- Obtain a list of Python library names with versions from the PyPI repository using *PyPISimple*[1] tool.
- Use the RESTAPI of **libraries.io** to retrieve dependencies for each version of a Python library. The API query is as follows:

```
https://libraries.io/api/Pypi/python_library_name/version/dependencies?api_key=***
```

[1] https://pypi.org/project/pypi-simple/

Table 9.1 Statistics of library dependency metadata

Ecosystem	# library	# library version	# dependency relationships
PyPI	417,416	3,383,391	12,382,505
Maven	356,718	5,707,274	28,945,967

(3) Collection Method of Maven Library Dependency Relationships:

- Obtain all the library GAVs[2] in the Maven central repository, by parsing the index file `nexus-maven-repository-index.gz`[3] using *Maven-Indexer*[4] tool.
- Use the RESTAPI of **libraries.io** to retrieve dependencies for each Maven library. The API query is as follows:

```
https://libraries.io/api/Maven/group_id:artifact_id/version/dependencies?api_key=***
```

(4) Storage Format of Dependencies:

- Store all dependencies in a *MySQL* database, where each record represents a library dependency relationship: `library1_name_version` → `library2_name_version`.
- Each dependency relationship consists of two fields: *Field 1* stores the `library1_name_version`, and *Field 2* stores its directly dependent `library2_name_version`.

(5) Statistics: We offer mirrors for the Python and Maven ecosystems as of June 2024 (statistics of library dependency metadata is shown in Table 9.1), with ongoing updates and maintenance of the library dependency metadata.

9.7 Vulnerability Metadata

We provide a dataset of vulnerability metadata to facilitate future research, which is available at ***https://zenodo.org/records/13354650***.

[2] GAV in Maven refers to the identifier structure consisting of Group ID, Artifact ID, and Version used to uniquely identify a software component.

[3] https://repo1.maven.org/maven2/.index/nexus-maven-repository-index.gz

[4] https://maven.apache.org/maven-indexer/index.html#about-maven-indexer

Table 9.2 Statistics of vulnerability metadata

Ecosystem	Severity levels Critical	High	Medium	Low	SUM	#Vulnerabilities with identified patches
C/C++	3,450	18,984	22,643	2,270	47,347	22,831
Java	822	1,956	2,740	143	5,661	2,740
Python	436	1,015	1,201	75	2,727	2,728
Rust	147	243	121	2	513	188
Go	456	1,336	1,460	77	3,329	1,595
JavaScript	610	1,069	802	9	2,490	2,378
SUM	5,921	24,603	28,967	2,576	62,067	32,460

(1) **Data Source:**

- The National Vulnerability Database (NVD) in the United States: *https://nvd.nist.gov/*.
- Snyk Security Vulnerability Database: *https://security.snyk.io/*.
- GitHub Advisory Security Vulnerability Database: *https://github.com/advisories*.
- Veracode Security Vulnerability Database: *https://sca.analysiscenter.veracode.com/vulnerability-database/search*.
- Ubuntu Security: *https://ubuntu.com/security/cves*.
- Debian Security: *https://security-tracker.debian.org/tracker/*.
- Arch Security: *https://security.archlinux.org/issues/all*.

(2) **Collection Method:**

Using Web scraping script or the RESTAPI provided by the CVE database[5] to retrieve CVE identifiers and all associated metadata.

(3) **Storage Format of Vulnerability:**

- The stored CVE metadata includes (1) *affected package*, (2) *affected package versions*, (3) *unique CVE identifier*, (4) *severity levels (e.g., critical, high, medium, and low based on CVSS score)*, (5) *dates when it is disclosed and published*, (6) *remediated versions (if available)*, and (7) *vulnerability patch URL (if available)*.

(4) **Statistics:** We offer mirrors of vulnerability databases as of June 2024 (statistics of vulnerability metadata is shown in Table 9.2), with ongoing updates and maintenance of the vulnerability metadata.

[5] https://www.cve.org/

References

1. Apache Maven is a software project management and comprehension tool, https://maven.apache.org/
2. 2022. Pip. https://packaging.python.org/en/latest/key_projects/#pip (2022). Accessed: 01 Mar 2022.
3. 2022. Dependabot. https://github.com/dependabot (2022). Accessed: 01 Mar 2022.
4. 2022. Wheel unpack. https://wheel.readthedocs.io/en/stable/reference/wheel_unpack.html (2022). Accessed: 01 Mar 2022.
5. 2022. Zipfile. https://docs.python.org/zh-cn/3/library/zipfile.html (2022). Accessed: 01 Mar 2022.
6. Almanee S, Ünal A, Payer M, Garcia J. Too quiet in the library: an empirical study of security updates in android apps native code. In: 2021 IEEE/ACM 43rd International Conference on Software Engineering (ICSE). IEEE, Piscataway; 2021. p. 1347–1359.

Chapter 10
Epilogue

10.1 Lessons Learned

In the realm of software industry security, managing open-source software artifacts and establishing/maintaining trustworthy, sustainable software library ecosystems are critical imperatives in the digital economy era. Examining the current research landscape, it is evident that the ecological governance of open-source software supply chains continues to grapple with six key technical challenges:

- **The progressively intricate software components across multiple programming languages pose challenges in identification.** Modern software's diverse resource dependencies introduce a plethora of third-party components from various origins, languages, diverse structures, and intricate configurations, presenting a heterogeneous sourcing paradigm. Consequently, software component clarity diminishes, leading to blurred system architecture boundaries.
- **Diagnosing component dependency conflicts within software dependency graphs proves challenging.** As software components evolve asynchronously during their development cycles, projects easily introduce different versions of the same component through direct and transitive dependencies. The build tools' component version arbitration mechanism results in the loading of a single version by the operating environment, overshadowing others and leading to dependency conflict issues. The prevalence and diversity of these conflicts complicate the diagnosis of their causes and consequences, posing risks to software dependency management.
- **Asynchronous evolution of software libraries in the software supply chain poses challenges for ensuring compatibility.** In the intricate software supply chain dependency network, differentiated dependency configuration patterns, version constraints, and diverse build mechanisms collectively lead to frequent compatibility issues between client projects and third-party components. With

Y. Wang et al., *Managing Software Supply Chains*,
https://doi.org/10.1007/978-981-96-1797-5_10

the arrival of compatibility issues, the evolution and maintenance of software library ecosystems become increasingly challenging.

- **Redundant dependency resources are challenging to remove in complex software with bloated dependency structures.** As software projects evolve through version iterations, the scale of modern software projects is increasing, and redundant dependency resources introduced through transitive dependencies are gradually accumulating. Software supply chains in various programming language ecosystems have become bloated due to redundant dependencies. The excessive size of software not only complicates project builds but also increases the complexity of testing and modifications during maintenance.
- **Evaluating the impact of defects and security vulnerabilities spreading within the software supply chain is challenging.** Central repositories hosting extensive software libraries often lack robust quality review and oversight mechanisms, enabling vulnerabilities to propagate unchecked along software library dependency chains. This issue is particularly pronounced in complex software dependency chains where the composition of software components is ambiguous, making it challenging to diagnose the spread of vulnerabilities across programming languages and assess associated risks effectively.
- **Unclogging the "propagation blockages" of defects and security vulnerability patches in the software supply chain is challenging.** Empirical investigations reveal that nearly 66% of security vulnerabilities have corresponding patch versions released by developers shortly after exposure. However, due to delayed library updates, mutual constraints imposed by versioning mechanisms between third-party libraries, and semantic versioning control rules, vulnerability patches are highly susceptible to encountering propagation blockages within software dependency chains. It is precisely due to these reasons that the majority of vulnerabilities in open-source ecosystems cannot be effectively remediated, significantly impacting the trustworthiness of the software supply chain.

10.2 Landscape of Software Supply Chains in the LLM Era

As described in Fig. 10.1, we present the landscape of software supply chains in the LLM era in three aspects: Diverse Forms of Software Supply Chain in the LLM Era, Dependency Relationships Between Models and Dataset, *and* Diverse Types of Security Risks.

Diverse Forms of Software Supply Chain in the LLM Era With the advent of the era of large language models (LLMs), the form of the software supply chain has undergone a disruptive change. In the software development process, there is not only a large amount of reuse of third-party software libraries, but developers also reuse code snippets generated by LLM, frameworks for developing applications powered by LLM, and pretrained models/cloud-based AI model service interfaces to improve development efficiency.

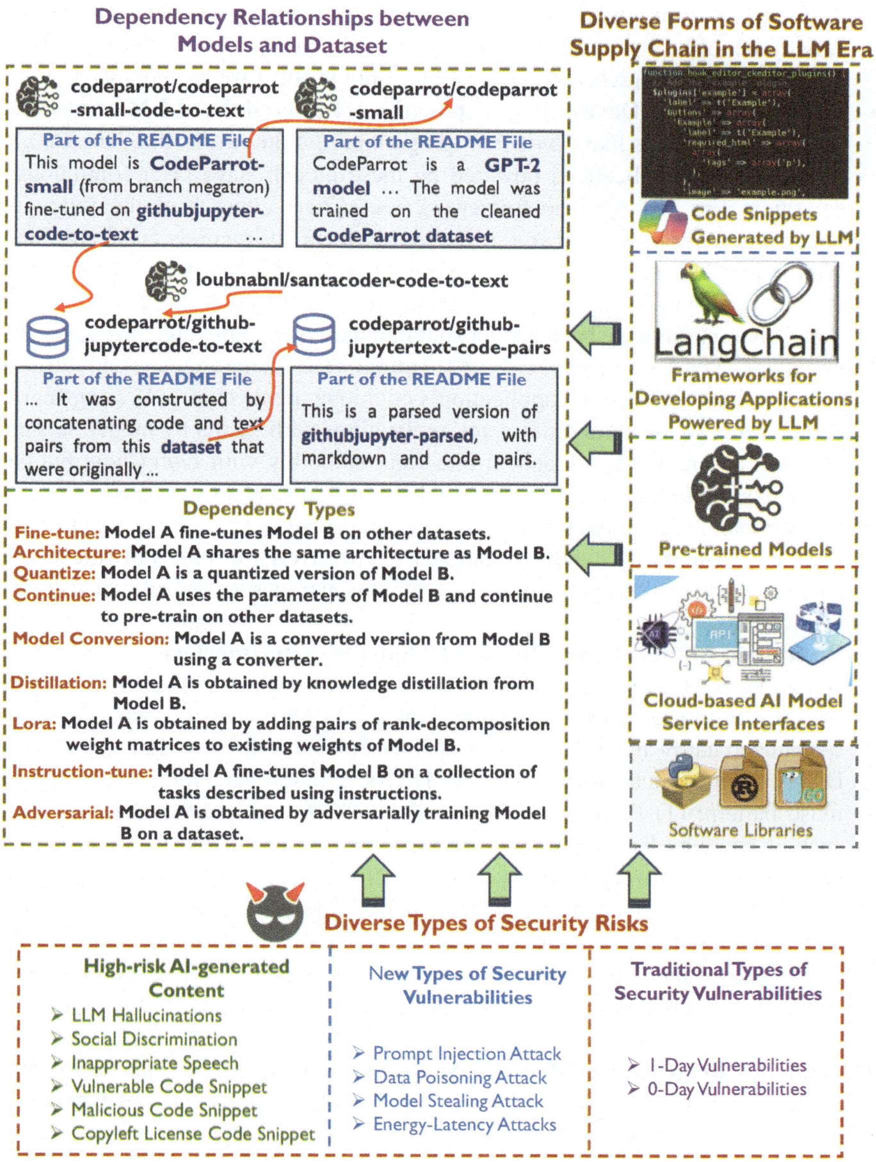

Fig. 10.1 Landscape of software supply chains in the LLM era

- **Code Snippets Generated by LLM:** Developers frequently use AI programming assistants like *Copilot*[1] to complete development tasks. AI programming assistants are powered by large datasets of open-source code artifacts, trained to

[1] https://marketplace.visualstudio.com/items?itemName=GitHub.copilot.

generate code through big models. Therefore, open-source software serves as the "raw material" for these large language models, and code generation by large language models represents a new supply chain in software development.

- **Frameworks for Developing Applications Powered by LLM:** Since the emergence of LLMs like *ChatGPT*,[2] programming frameworks like *LangChain*[3] for developing applications powered by these models have been continuously emerging. For instance, the framework *LangChain* consists of the following open-source libraries: (1) `langchain-core`: Base abstractions and LangChain Expression Language. (2) `langchain-community`: Third-party integrations. Partner packages (e.g., `langchain-openai`, `langchain-anthropic`, etc.): Some integrations have been further split into their own lightweight packages that only depend on `langchain-core`. (3) `langchain`: Chains, agents, and retrieval strategies that make up an application's cognitive architecture. (4) `LangGraph`: Build robust and stateful multi-actor applications with LLMs by modeling steps as edges and nodes in a graph. It integrates smoothly with *LangChain* but can be used without it. (5) `LangServe`: Deploy LangChain chains as REST APIs. (6) `LangSmith`: A developer platform that lets you debug, test, evaluate, and monitor LLM applications. The above components collectively form the software supply chain of LLM-based applications, determining the quality and risk of software applications.
- **Pretrained Models/Cloud-Based AI Model Service Interfaces:** Deep Neural Networks (DNNs) have become a common component in software systems over the past decade. Developing and training DNN models is costly, requiring specialized hardware and large datasets. While some software engineers develop DNNs from scratch, others integrate DNNs into software following a typical reuse pattern: (1) Pretrained DNN models (PTMs) are published to registries such as Hugging Face (analogous to traditional package registries such as *npm*) and (2) other software depends on these PTMs, accessed by library or cloud-based AI model service interfaces. Despite the widespread adoption of PTMs, our understanding of the software engineering practices and challenges surrounding PTM reuse remains limited. This understanding is critical for developing more sophisticated tools, mitigating risks, and guiding best practices.

Dependency Relationships Between Models and Dataset In recent study, Zhou et al.[4] present nine types of model reuse, which indicate dependency relationships between models and dataset:

- **Fine-tune:** Model *A* fine-tunes Model *B* on other datasets.
- **Architecture:** Model *A* shares the same architecture as Model *B*.
- **Quantize:** Model *A* is a quantized version of Model *B*.

---

[2] https://openai.com/chatgpt/.

[3] https://python.langchain.com/.

[4] Yang Z, Shi J, Lo D. *Ecosystem of Large Language Models for Code.* arXiv preprint arXiv:2405.16746, 2024.

- **Continue:** Model *A* uses the parameters of Model *B* and continue to pretrain on other datasets.
- **Model Conversion:** Model *A* is a converted version from Model *B* using a converter.
- **Distillation:** Model *A* is obtained by knowledge distillation from Model *B*.
- **Lora:** Model *A* is obtained by adding pairs of rank-decomposition weight matrices to existing weights of Model *B*.
- **Instruction tune:** Model *A* fine-tunes Model *B* on a collection of tasks described using instructions.
- **Adversarial:** Model *A* is obtained by adversarially training Model *B* on a dataset.

The above dependency relationships can help developers analyze the open-source license or security risks introduced by referencing PMT.

Diverse Types of Security Risks With the emergence of diverse forms of software supply chain in the LLM era, referencing them may bring diverse types of security risks to client software:

- **High-Risk AI-Generated Content:** Code or comments generated by LLMs may contain issues such as hallucinations, social discrimination, inappropriate speech, vulnerable code snippets, malicious code snippets, copyleft license code snippets, and more. Reusing AI-generated content can introduce potential security risks.
- **New Types of Security Vulnerabilities:** When incorporating PTMs as AI components, client project may be susceptible to security risks like *Prompt Injection Attack*,[5] *Data Poisoning Attack*,[6] *Model Stealing Attack*,[7] and *Energy-Latency Attack*.[8]
- **Traditional Types of Security Vulnerabilities:** Incorporating third-party libraries can introduce 0-day or 1-day vulnerabilities, thereby introducing unpredictable risks to client projects.

10.3 Future Research

Leveraging nearly two decades of research and practical experience, the governance technology of open-source software supply chain ecosystems has made remarkable progress. Nevertheless, to ensure the trustworthiness and sustainable evolution

[5] *Prompt Injection Attack*: In prompt injection attacks, hackers manipulate generative AI systems by feeding them malicious inputs disguised as legitimate user prompts.

[6] *Data Poisoning Attack*: Data poisoning is a type of cyberattack in which an adversary intentionally compromises a training dataset used by an AI model to influence or manipulate the operation of that model.

[7] *Model Stealing Attack*: It works by querying the target model with samples and using the model responses to forge a replicated model.

[8] *Energy-Latency Attack:* It is a form of attack targeting mobile or low-power devices that exploit energy consumption and latency characteristics during computational tasks to compromise security and privacy.

of open-source software libraries, researchers are required to further explore the following four key areas:

- **(1) Enhancing modeling and analysis capabilities for the open-source software supply chain.** The modern software dependency structure is intricately complex, with unclear component compositions. Therefore, modeling and analysis techniques should consider the following factors:
  - **Analyzing the diversified dependencies of third-party components thoroughly.** The invocation patterns of third-party components in modern software are diverse and complex, potentially utilizing *cross-language program interfaces*, *dynamic* and *static linking*, *process calls*, *service interfaces*, *plugin-based calls*, and more to reference third-party libraries. **They may also interact with a variety of cloud-based AI model service interfaces or directly load different forms of pretrained models using model loaders.** To dissect and identify the composition of modern software components, researchers need to distill commonalities and differences in component invocation mechanisms and propose a paradigm for analyzing third-party dependencies.
  - **Updating software library dependencies dynamically.** Incrementally updating the dependency topology of open-source software library ecosystems across multiple programming language communities is a primary challenge that needs to be addressed in open-source ecosystem governance.
  - **Interlinking software library dependency relationships with publicly available security vulnerabilities/critical defect datasets.** Building upon timely updates of dependency relationships and evolutionary behaviors in open-source software library ecosystems, integrating public security vulnerability datasets and critical defect datasets is essential for effective diagnosis of dependency issues. Moreover, it enables a balanced assessment of the pros and cons in governance decisions from an open-source ecosystem perspective.
- **(2) In-depth exploration of dependency issues in open-source software supply chain.** Researchers still need to make efforts and attempts in the following key technologies to address five common dependency issues, including software compatibility, open-source license violations, software library dependency conflicts, bloated dependencies, and the propagation of security vulnerabilities:
  - **Enhancing the program analysis capability.** Fine-grained and efficient program analysis can identify various levels of dependency relationships, such as call paths, control flow, and data flow, between client code and third-party components. This information is crucial for assessing whether *"compatibility issues with software library versions will lead to unexpected program behavior," "which combinations of software library versions are incompatible," "whether security vulnerabilities will pose a real threat to the software,"* and *"which code will directly or indirectly access AI components,"* thereby evaluating the risks introduced by third-party components. Precise program analysis capability is equally essential for diagnosing issues related

to software component analysis, bloated dependencies, dependency conflicts, and more, to avoid false alarms regarding dependency issues.

- **Modeling the disparities and commonalities in dependency management mechanisms across different programming languages.** Different programming language communities exhibit variations in *(a) dependency configuration patterns, (b) constraints on software library versions, (c) rules for resolving dependency conflicts, (d) characteristics of updating and maintaining library central repositories,* and *e. manifestations of dependency issues.* Modeling the disparities and commonalities in these areas aids in breaking down barriers between diverse programming language ecosystems, fostering a unified diagnostic approach for dependency issues.
- **Balancing pros and cons from an ecosystem perspective.** In the open-source software library ecosystem, diverse version combinations often lead to compatibility issues. Considering the propagative nature of defects within the open-source software supply chain, governance strategies for software projects should be derived from a comprehensive perspective of the ecosystem, incorporating multidimensional trade-offs to minimize mutual impact between software projects and promote governance strategies beneficial to the software ecosystem.

- **(3) Exploring new software supply chain management challenges in the era of large language models.** In software incorporating AI components, it is vital to understand the dependency issues that arise when utilizing third-party AI model service interfaces, pretrained models and frameworks like *LangChain*. It is worth noting that open-source licenses for AI models have added special clauses in the areas of source code, parameter weights, and datasets. The assessment of the contagiousness and copyright risks of client software by open-source licenses for AI models is an open question worth exploring. Researchers should persist in exploring and uncovering dependency management challenges within the open-source software supply chains, continuously advancing the development of governance technologies in this domain.
- **(4) Building open-source software supply chains for specific domains/platforms.** Existing governance technologies for open-source software library ecosystems can be generalized to the construction and maintenance of software supply chains tailored to specific domains; for example, the construction of software supply chains tailored to the HarmonyOS operating system/RISC-V instruction set architecture. With the emergence of the HarmonyOS operating system or RISC-V instruction set architecture, software library ecosystems originally developed for Android/iOS operating systems or X86/ARM instruction set architectures need to be migrated and adapted to the new platform. Software library migration requires addressing a multitude of compatibility/vulnerability issues between software and hardware, presenting a valuable research direction for exploration.

The manufacturer's authorised representative in the EU is Springer Nature Customer Service Centre GmbH, Europaplatz 3, 69115 Heidelberg, Germany. If you have any concerns regarding our products, please contact ProductSafety@springernature.com

Printed and bound by CPI Group (UK) Ltd, Croydon, CR0 4YY
30/09/2026
02225300-0009